# ESSENTIALS OF QUALITY

## WITH CASES AND EXPERIENTIAL EXERCISES

### Victor E. Sower
*Sam Houston State University*

**WILEY**

**JOHN WILEY & SONS, INC.**

| EDITOR: | LISE JOHNSON |
|---|---|
| ASSISTANT EDITOR: | CARISSA DOSHI |
| EDITORIAL ASSISTANT: | SARAH VERNON |
| MARKETING MANAGER: | DIANE MARS |
| DESIGNER: | JAMES O'SHEA |
| PRODUCTION MANAGER: | JANIS SOO |
| SENIOR PRODUCTION EDITOR: | JOYCE POH |

This book was set in 10/12 Times Roman by Laserwords Private Limited and printed and bound by Courier Westford. The cover was printed by Courier Westford.

This book is printed on acid free paper.

Evaluation copies are provided to qualified academics and professionals for review purposes only, for use in their courses during the next academic year. These copies are licensed and may not be sold or transferred to a third party. Upon completion of the review period, please return the evaluation copy to Wiley. Return instructions and a free of charge return shipping label are available at www.wiley.com/go/returnlabel. Outside of the United States, please contact your local representative.

*Library of Congress Cataloging-in-Publication Data*

Sower, Victor E.
   Essentials of quality with cases and experiential exercises/Victor E. Sower.
      p. cm.
   Includes bibliographical references and index.
   ISBN 978-0-470-50959-3 (pbk.)
   1. Total quality management. 2. Total quality control. I. Title.
   HD62.15.S6445 2009
   658.4′013–dc22

                                                              2009035910

Printed in the United States of America

10 9 8 7 6 5 4 3 2 1

# CONTENTS

## SECTION IV   CONTROL AND IMPROVEMENT OF QUALITY 177

# PREFACE

Teaching undergraduate students about quality is inherently difficult. In most cases these students have little experience in business. Their only thoughts about quality revolve around the products and services that they purchase. A further difficulty is that the quality discipline has a quantitative as well as a qualitative side and many undergraduate students are intimidated by quantitative materials. The same is true to a lesser extent for many graduate students.

I have taught quality management to undergraduate and graduate students for 15 years. My broad objectives in these course have been twofold: (1) to provide the students with a good grounding in the principles of quality—the history, background, theory of quality; (2) to provide the students with tangible, value-adding skills that they can put to work in their professional lives after graduation—be that in business or in graduate school. The first of these objectives could be addressed using traditional instructional methods—reading, lecture, homework. The second of these is best addressed using hands-on learning techniques—experiential exercises and cases. Over the years my teaching style has evolved more and more away from traditional methods toward experiential methods. This is not to say that I abandoned reading, lecture, and homework. What I have done is augment these traditional approaches with experiential approaches. The feedback that I receive from students and former students is that this approach has enhanced learning.

During the course of evolving from a traditional to experiential teaching style, I tried several texts but never found one that really suited this approach to teaching. So, I wrote my own, and I tested it for three years in my classes. I solicited student feedback about what they found to be helpful and what they found to be confusing. I listened and rewrote portions of the text many times. I asked several colleagues to test the text in their classes. I solicited their feedback and rewrote again. The result is the text you have before you, one that has been intensively classroom tested.

I also consult in the quality-management area. Many of the cases and exercises in the text have their genesis in my consulting work. I am fortunate that many of my clients have permitted me to include material from our work in sidebars, examples, and cases. Some of the exercises were designed or adapted from exercises I used in professional training activities. Some were adapted from other sources that I have credited. All have been tested.

Many of the texts that I have tried over the years are excellent reference resources, but my students reported that they were difficult to read or just boring. In developing this text I tried to write in a "nonacademic" but still rigorous style to make this text more readable and engaging. You will find explanations stated in ways that you won't find elsewhere. In Chapter 10, I write, "The sigma used to calculate the process capability is not the same as the sigma used to calculate the 3 sigma control limits on the x-bar chart." I wrote it that way because I have fielded the question about which sigma is which many times over the years. This is stated in a way that makes intuitive sense to the student. After that I define the difference in rigorous terms.

Part of my philosophy of teaching is that I want to "turn the students on" to the subject matter. Students do not need to be entertained—they need to be engaged. The exercises and cases do that. Look at the photograph of my students in the sidebar on page 163. How many times have you seen students smiling while learning experimental design? These students are engaged! When we finish the chapter and the catapult design of experiments (DOE) exercise, the students receive balsa wood glider kits. They design their own experiments to optimize the length of glide of the planes. The "final exam" for this portion of the course takes place in a glider competition in the hallway. Not surprisingly, the variation in design and flight length is relatively small. That tells me they mastered the material.

The text certainly can be used with traditional instructional methods. Each instructor has his or her own personality and way of teaching. If yours tends toward the traditional, this text will support that approach well. However, I encourage you to try out one or more of the experiential exercises and cases. Evaluate the results and take the actions that the results indicate. This is the continuous-improvement process that we teach. Why shouldn't we practice what we teach?

## ORGANIZATION OF THE BOOK

The sequencing of topics in the book has been the subject of much experimentation during the testing phase. Chapter 1 covers background information, including a brief history of the quality discipline and a discussion of its major contributors. This is followed by a discussion of the definition of quality. The rationale for this discussion is to introduce the idea that it is difficult to measure something that you cannot define. Therefore carefully defining what one means by the word *quality* is an important first step in all other quality-related activities.

In Chapter 2, the discussion centers around the idea that quality must be integrated into the strategic management process in order to be effective. Then, building on the discussion in Chapter 1, the chapter guides the reader through the process of obtaining and using customer input to operationalize a definition of quality into measures and metrics.

Chapters 3 and 4 deal with quality of design—how to design quality into products, services, and processes. Chapter 3 contains the first quantitative topic—reliability. A key aspect of creating a competitive advantage through quality is by creating an environment within the organization that encourages creativity and innovation—the subject of Chapter 4.

Chapter 5 addresses quality systems and the auditing of those systems. Included in quality systems are procedures for product, process, and materials control that is the subject of Chapter 6, which completes the introductory sequence of chapters. It is suggested that the first six chapters are best covered in their proper sequence. The order in which the subsequent eight chapters are covered is of much less importance and can be tailored by the instructor to fit the needs of the course.

Chapters 7 through 12 comprise the analytical portion of the book. Topics include experimental design (Chapter 7), problem solving and the tools of quality (Chapter 8),

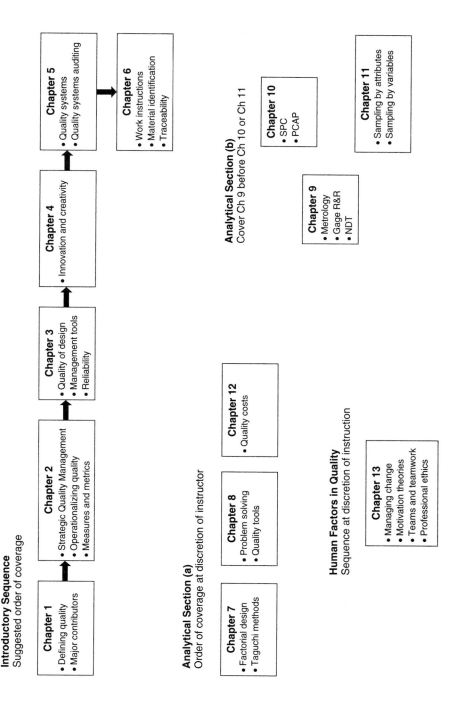

**Introductory Sequence**
Suggested order of coverage

**Chapter 1**
• Defining quality
• Major contributors

**Chapter 2**
• Strategic Quality Management
• Operationalizing quality
• Measures and metrics

**Chapter 3**
• Quality of design
• Management tools
• Reliability

**Chapter 4**
• Innovation and creativity

**Chapter 5**
• Quality systems
• Quality systems auditing

**Chapter 6**
• Work instructions
• Material identification
• Traceability

**Analytical Section (a)**
Order of coverage at discretion of instructor

**Chapter 7**
• Factorial design
• Taguchi methods

**Chapter 8**
• Problem solving
• Quality tools

**Chapter 12**
• Quality costs

**Analytical Section (b)**
Cover Ch 9 before Ch 10 or Ch 11

**Chapter 9**
• Metrology
• Gage R&R
• NDT

**Chapter 10**
• SPC
• PCAP

**Chapter 11**
• Sampling by attributes
• Sampling by variables

**Human Factors in Quality**
Sequence at discretion of instruction

**Chapter 13**
• Managing change
• Motivation theories
• Teams and teamwork
• Professional ethics

metrology (Chapter 9), statistical process control (Chapter 10), acceptance sampling (Chapter 11), and quality costs (Chapter 12). It is suggested that Chapter 9 be covered prior to Chapters 10 and 11, because it is important that the accuracy and precision of a measurement system be assessed before using it to collect data for statistical process control (SPC) or acceptance sampling.

Chapter 13 covers human factors in quality, including managing teams. Some might believe that this chapter is last because it is least important. However, this is far from true. Human resources and their management are by far the most critical elements in any quality system. This chapter may be appropriately covered at any point in the course at the instructor's discretion.

Although it is possible to cover all of the topics in the text in one semester, instructors will, however, have to make their own decisions about which topics to emphasize or deemphasize in order to do that. In addition to the "standard topics," you will find topics not generally included in quality-management texts. Chapter 4, for example, is devoted to innovation and creativity in quality. Chapter 2 devotes a number of pages to operationalizing the dimensions of quality for products and services so that they may be measured. Instructors may decide for themselves whether to include these topics in their courses.

I use a combination of *NWA Quality Analyst* and *Minitab* software packages in the course. I use this combination because several of the largest employers of my students that are Six-Sigma companies use this software. Students report that they find these packages to be easy to learn and use. Although I use the output from these software packages as illustrations in the text, the text is not otherwise tied to these packages, and any suitable statistical analysis package that can do control charts, ANOVA, and regression analysis may be used.

# ACKNOWLEDGMENTS

I am grateful to many colleagues, friends, research collaborators, and students for their assistance in putting this text together. Their insight and comments have made this a better book. In particular, I would like to thank Dr. Charles Bimmerle, consultant to management, for his review and comments on several chapters. Dr. Jo Ann Duffy, professor of management at Sam Houston State University, helped me develop the section on strategic quality management. Dr. Gerald Kohers, professor of MIS at Sam Houston State University, created the gauge R & R template and several illustrations. Dr. Frank Fair, professor of philosophy at Sam Houston State University, for his insight into creativity and Plato's ideas and how they apply to quality. Dr. Hank Maddux, assistant professor of management at Howard Payne University, for his input on making the book more student-friendly. Dr. Ross Quarles, professor and chair of accounting at Sam Houston State University, for his insight on cost of quality, ABC, and ERP. Dr. Joe Kavanaugh, associate professor of management at Sam Houston State University, for his insight into teams and team charters. Mr. Enrique Topete Martin, Ph.D. student at Universitat Politecnica de Catalunya, for his comments on acceptance sampling. Dr. R. Dean Lewis, dean of the College of Business Administration, Sam Houston State University, for allowing me to document SHSU's emergent strategy example in Chapter 2. Thanks to three of my graduate students—Mr. Richard Dalton, Ms. Melissa Loy, and Ms. Erin Patterson—for their contributions to the instructor's manual. Special thanks go to Dr. Pam Zelbst, assistant professor of management, Sam Houston State University, for her comments on several chapters and for her taking responsibility for the writing of the ancillary materials. Thanks to my consulting clients and research subjects who allowed me to use material from our work together to illustrate the book. I would also like to extend special thanks to my wife, Judy, for her patience with my late nights working on the book and for her encouragement throughout the process of putting this book together.

I especially acknowledge the following organizations for their assistance with this project:

The American Society for Quality for granting me permission to use material from their standards and other publications to illustrate the text.

Northwest Analytical—Output screens from *Quality Analyst*™ used to illustrate this book are printed with the permission of Northwest Analytical.

Minitab, Inc.—Portions of the input and output contained in this book are printed with the permission of Minitab, Inc.

Portions of this text were previously published in Sower, V., M. Savoie, and S. Renick, *An Introduction to Quality Management and Engineering*. Upper Saddle River, NJ: Prentice Hall, 1999.

Special thanks go to the following students for being the "guinea pigs" for the draft version of this book and for their many questions, suggestions, and comments that improved the quality of the book.

Michael Anzaldua
Jamie Buntin
Timothy Cobb
Rich Dalton
Mikael Dandy
Tony Davilla
Jamie Dockery
Malcolm Evans

Branson Fowle
Jason Frederick
Chris Galyen
Harry Golden
Jim Gregory
Mamie Hall
JJ Hawthorne
Hadyn Hughes

Erin Patterson
Amanda Pierce
Lawrence Powell
Joshua Ragsdale
Ned Robinson IV
Julie Siebers
Kent Vest
James Young

Ishme Allah
Leah Baucum
Amy Burrell
Alisha Fowler
Kevin Grimm
Edward Jackson
Katherine Johnson
Bryan Karasek

Robin Krzesienski
Crystal Lakey
Melissa Loy
Ryan Mader
Hollie Martin
Sharon Matchett
Matthew Munsell
Andrew Owens

Courtney Pickens
David Riggs
David Rodriguez
Martin Scott
Natalie Tobias
Laura Whatley
Ryan Wilcox

Darryl Adams
David Barnes
Byron Basker
Aimee Beridon
Mario Brown
Isela Cervantes
Harold DeWalt

Jennifer Henderson
Daniel Hirsch
Danna Long
Arica Loving
Pamela Mallory
Amanda Martin
Scott McJunkin

Elizabeth Ozaine
Josh Snow
Tiffany Suess
Brandon Trube
Emilie Zabel

Matt Adkisson
Karen Arce
Ruben Barrios
Monica Brown
Jennifer Dozier
Curtis Hale

Jessica Hanier
Melissa Hanier
Clifton Heuszel
William Mock
Eldric Moore
Linh Nguyen

Stacy Nobles
Katie Oday
Lloyd Oghogho
Jamaal Payne
Meagan Pratt

I would like to thank the reviewers of the proposal for this book for their insightful and encouraging comments. The reviewers are Verna Fitzsimmons, Kent State University; David Lewis, University of Massachusetts-Lowell; Dr. Jaideep Motwani, Grand Valley State University; Dr. Victor R. Prybutok, University of North Texas; Dr. Stanley C. Ross, Bridgewater State University; Willian H. Trappen, P.E., California State University Dominguez Hills; Michael H. Whitt, Ph.D., M.B.A., Purdue University; and Martha Wilson, California State University, Sacramento.

Finally, I appreciate the guidance and encouragement from Lise Johnson, Carissa Doshi, Sarah Vernon, Laura Finley, and Joyce Poh, and the entire staff at Wiley for taking this book from manuscript to completed text. I especially appreciate the encouragement from my Wiley publisher's representative and good friend Steve Gideon, for our discussions of this project over coffee and donuts, and for his encouragement to publish this text with Wiley.

Victor E. Sower is a consultant in the operations, innovation, and quality management fields. He is a distinguished professor emeritus of operations management at Sam Houston State University where he taught from 1990 to 2008. Prior to that, he worked for 18 years in industry in engineering, R&D management, and general management positions. He also served two years as an active duty officer in the U.S. Army Chemical Corps. He has a BS degree in chemistry from Virginia Polytechnic Institute and State University, an MBA from Auburn University, and a Ph.D. in Operations Management from the University of North Texas.

He has received a number of awards for his teaching, including the Sam Houston State University's 1996 Excellence in Teaching Award; the 1994 Innovative Achievement Award in Recognition of Outstanding Achievement in Curriculum Innovation from the Southwest Business Deans' Association; the 2002 Alpha Iota Delta Innovative Education Paper Award from the Southwest Decision Sciences Institute; and he was named a 2005 Piper Professor by the Minnie Stevens Piper Foundation of Texas. He has also received the Sam Houston State University's 2001 Excellence in Research Award and 2008 Excellence in Service Award. He is one of only three faculty members to have received the excellence awards in all three areas from Sam Houston State University.

Vic is a senior member of the American Society for Quality and is certified as a quality engineer (CQE) by that organization. He is also a senior member of the American Institute of Chemical Engineers, and a member of the Academy of Management, the Decision Sciences Institute, APICS, ISM, and the American Chemical Society. He is an honorary member of Golden Key International Honour Society and a member of Beta Gamma Sigma. He is a member of the editorial review boards for the *Journal of Operations Management, Health Care Management Review*, and the *Journal of Business Strategies*.

Vic has coauthored three previous books: Sower, V., J. Duffy, & G. Kohers, *Benchmarking in Hospitals: Achieving Best-in-Class Performance without Having to Reinvent the Wheel* (ASQ Quality Press, 2008); Sower, V., M. Savoie, & S. Renick, *An Introduction to Quality Management and Engineering* (Prentice Hall, 1999); and Sower, V., J. Motwani, & M. Savoie, *Classic Readings in Operations Management* (Dryden Press, 1995).

He has published more than 50 articles in refereed journals (including *Quality Management Journal, Quality Progress, International Journal of Quality and Reliability Management*, and *Benchmarking for Quality Management & Technology*) and refereed proceedings (including five American Society for Quality Annual Quality Congresses, The Israel Society for Quality, and International DSI Conferences) and has contributed case studies and exercises to leading texts in operations management. His current research interests are in the quality, innovation, and technology management areas. He is an active consultant to both service and manufacturing organizations.

# SECTION I

# QUALITY BASICS

## CHAPTER ONE

# *Introduction to Quality*

## CHAPTER OBJECTIVES

After completing this chapter, the reader should be able to:

- discuss the development of quality as a discipline;
- discuss the complexity of defining quality;
- compare and contrast the leading approaches to defining quality;
- discuss the differences between defining quality for manufactured goods and for services;
- discuss the major contributors to the quality profession; and
- define key quality management terms.

This book is about quality. Quality is a very important part of life today. It is important to effectively compete in business—both manufacturing and service. It plays an important role in assuring the safety of consumers. Quality of life is an increasingly used term that brings the concepts of quality into our personal lives.

But quality is also a frequently misunderstood and misapplied concept. Some believe that quality is still the responsibility of the quality department rather than of everyone in the organization. Some believe that quality is simply avoiding doing things that will dissatisfy customers. Others believe that quality is a manufacturing concept with limited applicability to services. Still others view quality as a sort of "magic bullet," as if nominally implementing some quality program or another will magically improve performance without changing the culture of the organization.

From a theoretical perspective, this book is designed to further the understanding of quality and its relationship to management systems. From a practical perspective, this book will help the reader understand the basic fundamentals and tools of quality, the interrelationship between quality and other functions in the organization, and how to use this knowledge to materially improve quality and impact the performance of the organization.

## WHY STUDY QUALITY?

In larger organizations such as Dow Chemical, General Electric, Motorola, Bank of America, MBNA, and Mayo Clinics, it is difficult to find a job that does not require knowledge of quality principles. Many smaller organizations such as Huntsville Memorial Hospital, El Chico, and Gallery Furniture also have made quality a central component of their strategic plans and management systems. Mrs. Fields' Cookies was founded on the basis of quality as the source of competitive advantage. Xerox used quality as the major building block in restructuring and revitalizing their company. Many governmental, charitable, and religious (Boggs, 2004) organizations have also embraced quality. In order to prepare for employment in the current environment and to prepare for increasing responsibilities within modern business, governmental, and service organizations, knowledge of quality principles is becoming increasingly important.

## HISTORY OF QUALITY

Quality is not a new concept. The very survival of early humanoids depended upon the quality of the tools that they fabricated from stone and bone, and later bronze and iron. Quality was fully integrated into the manufacturing processes that were passed along from one generation to the next. As civilization evolved, specialization of labor began to develop. The earliest recorded civilizations had experts in weaving, ceramics, metal working, and other crafts, who developed their techniques within various sorts of organizations such as guilds, masters-apprenticeships, and unions. To this point in history, quality was the responsibility of the craftsperson creating the product or rendering the service.

Beginning in the late eighteenth century, progressing through the Industrial Revolution and into the early twentieth century, industry moved from the craft concept to the concepts of specialization of labor, scientific management, and mass production. The invention of interchangeable parts that began in the 1700s made adherence to specifications vital. No longer were individual craftspeople free to adapt designs as they saw fit to create unique products and services for their customers. Each worker had to be sure that the parts he or she created were as identical as possible to those created by other workers in the organization. With many workers producing parts that had to fit together to form the final product, management had a need for systems to define material quality, work methods, and specifications and to control the processes that produced the parts. This led to the formalization of quality as a discipline.

## THE DEFINITION OF QUALITY

What is quality? This is a much more complex question than it first appears. Yet how do we go about studying quality, measuring quality, and designing quality into products and services, or improving quality if we do not know what it is? *Quality* is a much more complicated term than it appears. A historian of ideas suggests Plato should be credited with inventing the term *quality*.

> The more common a word is and the simpler its meaning, the bolder very likely is the original thought which it contains and the more intense the intellectual or poetic effort which went into its making. Thus, the word *quality* is used by most educated people every day of their lives, yet in order that we should have this simple word Plato had to make the tremendous effort (it is perhaps the greatest effort known to man) of turning a vague feeling into a clear thought. He invented a new word "poiotes," "what-ness," as we might say, or "of-what-kind-ness," and Cicero translated it by the Latin "qualitas," from "qualis." (Barfield, 1988)

Early debates over the definition of quality are dramatized by Plato in a number of his dialogues—for example, the one between Socrates and the sophist Hippias in *Greater Hippias*. In this dialogue, Socrates, after criticizing parts of an exhibition speech by Hippias as not being fine, asks the question, "What the fine is itself?" Cooper (1997), the editor of a translation of Plato, translates the Greek word *kalon* as "fine." This word is widely applicable as a term "of highly favorable evaluation, covering our 'beautiful,' 'noble,' 'admirable,' 'excellent,' and the like." What Socrates is seeking "is a general explanation of what feature any object, or action, or person, or accomplishment of any kind, has to have in order correctly to be characterized as highly valued or worth valuing in this broad way (i.e. as being fine)."

The philosophical development of the idea of quality can be traced beyond Plato (circa 400 BC) through Augustine (circa 600 AD), Smith (circa 1700), and Mill (circa 1800) to the modern quality movement beginning with Shewhart (circa 1930). Among the definitions of quality of things in *The Oxford English Dictionary* (1989), definition 9c most expresses the concept of quality in modern use by quality professionals: "Peculiar excellence or superiority." But dictionary definitions are usually inadequate in helping a quality professional understand the concept. Quality must be defined in ways that can be assessed and measured. Measurement of "excellence" and "superiority" is difficult because these terms are subject to differences in perceptions among individuals.

## Modern Definitions of Quality

The quality movement began in a systematic way in the United States during the late 1920s with the work of Walter Shewhart. The first modern quality revolution occurred in the United States during the World War II years, after which it declined in this country until the early 1970s. The second quality revolution occurred in Japan in the 1950s with the work of W. Edwards Deming, Joseph Juran, and Armand Feigenbaum, and it resulted in Japan's emergence as an economic power. The third quality revolution began in the United States during the early 1970s when the work of Deming, Juran, Feigenbaum, and Phillip Crosby was finally recognized and put into practice in this country.

During each of these revolutions, attention was paid to defining just what this "quality" was. The first modern definition of quality was offered by Shewhart during the first quality revolution. Most modern formal definitions trace back to the second quality revolution—primarily to the work of Juran and Feigenbaum. During the third quality revolution, David Garvin weighed in with a comprehensive analysis of the meaning of quality. The American Society for Quality has published its definition of quality. But as we have seen, these efforts to define quality are by no means the first.

ASQ defines quality as "a subjective term for which each person has his or her own definition. In technical usage, quality can have two meanings: (1) the characteristics of a product or service that bear on its ability to satisfy stated or implied needs and (2) a product or service free of deficiencies."

(Quality Glossary, 2002, p. 56)

Walter Shewhart (1931) was the first modern era quality expert to wrestle with the definition of quality. Shewhart suggested that quality has two aspects. The objective aspect refers to quality of a thing as "an objective reality independent of the existence of man." The subjective aspect refers to quality as "what we think, feel, or sense as a result of the objective reality." According to Shewart, although it is the objective aspect of quality that we usually attempt to measure, it is the subjective aspect that is of commercial interest. Deming (1933), in his last book, *The New Economics for Industry, Government, Education*, agreed that quality is subjective and must have commercial value. "What is quality? A product or service possesses quality if it helps somebody and enjoys a good and sustainable market. Trade depends on quality."

Building on Shewhart's work, Juran (1970) defined quality as "fitness for use" and Feigenbaum (1951) defined it as "best for certain customer conditions." These definitions form the basis for the modern definition of quality.

Parasuraram and others define quality as meeting or exceeding customer expectations. But in Deming's (1993, 30) words, "Just to have the customer satisfied is not enough . . . You have to do better than that." To operationalize the customer-focused definition, one must define who the customer is. *External customers* usually come to mind first. These are the people outside our organization who receive our goods and services. But even here there is some confusion. If we sell our products to a wholesaler, is he our only customer? How about the retailer and the ultimate consumer? *Internal customers* are often forgotten or taken for granted. These are the people inside our organization who receive our work services. In an assembly-line operation, the next station downstream from ours is an internal customer for our work. The Purchasing Department which receives a control report from the Accounting Department is the latter's internal customer. Every process has a customer.

Once the customer has been defined, ways must be found to meet or exceed customer expectations. Meeting customer expectations results in a satisfied customer. But where is the competitive advantage in that? Have you eaten in a restaurant in the past month? If so, did you select a restaurant that you expected would dissatisfy you? Probably not. You selected from a list of restaurants that you expected would. So satisfying customers merely keeps you in the game. Delighting customers (exceeding customer expectations) is where competitive advantage can be found. Restaurants that deliver larger-than-expected portions or lower-than-expected prices or better-than-expected service or better-than-expected ambiance have a competitive advantage over restaurants that simply satisfy customers.

## Product Quality

There is widespread agreement that quality is a multidimensional construct. A number of scholars in the quality field have developed lists of dimensions that define quality for a product and/or a service. David Garvin (1984) developed a list of eight dimensions of product quality, shown in Table 1.1, that are widely accepted as being applicable to most products albeit with varying levels of importance on particular dimensions. These dimensions were proposed to facilitate strategic quality analysis by breaking "down the word quality into manageable parts" so that management "can define the quality niches in which to compete."

The relative importance of each of these eight dimensions varies considerably. In fact, Garvin proposed that product design often cannot simultaneously maximize each of these eight dimensions. There are always tradeoffs to be considered. For example, compromises might have to be made in aesthetics in order to improve access to a computer CPU case to increase serviceability. Garvin suggests that it is the role of strategic quality management to select the dimensions on which to compete and to manage the tradeoffs.

**TABLE 1.1.   Garvin's (1987) Eight Dimensions of Product Quality**

| Dimension | Description | Example for Personal Computer |
|---|---|---|
| Performance | A product's primary operating characteristics | Clock speed; RAM; hard drive size |
| Features | Characteristics that supplement basic functioning | Wireless mouse; flat-screen monitor; DVD-RW |
| Reliability | Probability of a product malfunctioning within a specific time period | Mean time between failures |
| Conformance | The degree to which a product's design and operating characteristics meet established standards | Underwriter Laboratories labeled; mouse, monitor, keyboard included with CPU |
| Durability | Expected product life | Time to technical obsolescence; rated life of monitor |
| Serviceability | Speed, courtesy, competence, and ease of repair | Warranty conditions; availability of customer service and replacement parts |
| Aesthetics | How a product looks, feels, sounds, tastes, or smells | Computer housing color scheme; keyboard "touch" |
| Perceived Quality | Reputation and other indirect measures of quality | Brand name; advertising |

## Service Quality

Defining the dimensions of service quality is a more daunting task. A number of scholars have developed lists of service quality dimensions. These consist of five to ten dimensions and are general lists that serve as good starting points. But current research indicates that in terms of service quality, the dimensions and the relative emphases on each are different for different industries. So dimensions developed in one or a group of service industries may not be directly applicable to another group of service industries.

The SERVQUAL (Parasuraman, et al., 1988) instrument is often used to assess customer satisfaction in service industries. It measures quality by comparing customer perceptions of the quality of a service experience to customer expectations for that experience. The instrument is based on ten overlapping dimensions of service quality that is eventually distilled down to five dimensions shown in Table 1.2. The instrument was developed in four different service industries: banking, credit card, repair and maintenance, and long distance telephone.

Although SERVQUAL has been criticized and its applicability to other service industries questioned (Babacus & Boller, 1992; Cronin & Taylor, 1992), it provides a basis for understanding service quality and its dimensions. It would be dangerous, however, to utilize SERVQUAL or any other instrument without first validating that it is applicable in a particular industry.

Developing a list of quality dimensions for a specific service industry requires determining what is important to customers in that industry. Methodologies that are appropriate for this would include focus groups and surveys. The quality dimensions for hospitals (KQCAH Scale), shown in Table 1.3, were developed using focus groups conducted with recently discharged patients and their families, and with hospital personnel (Sower, et al., 2001). Knowledge of these dimensions facilitates the measurement of patient satisfaction by hospitals. Hospitals know that they are

**TABLE 1.2. SERVQUAL Dimensions of Service Quality (Parasuraman, et al., 1988)**

| Dimension | Description | Example for Bank |
|---|---|---|
| Tangibles | Physical facilities, equipment, and appearance of personnel | ATM access; lobby layout; tellers dressed professionally |
| Reliability | Ability to perform the promised service dependably and accurately | Promised deadlines met; reassuring problem resolution |
| Responsiveness | Willingness to help customers and provide prompt service | Respond quickly to customer requests; willingness to help customers |
| Assurance | Knowledge and courtesy of employees and their ability to inspire trust and confidence | Trustworthiness; safe environment around ATMs; polite tellers |
| Empathy | Caring, individualized attention the firm provides its customers | Personal attention to customers; convenient hours |

**TABLE 1.3. Eight Dimensions of Hospital Service Quality (Sower, et al., 2001)**

| Dimension | Description | Example for Hospital |
|---|---|---|
| Respect & Caring | The way in which hospital staff interacts with the patient | Staff paid attention to patient and was reassuring; privacy was protected; staff was friendly |
| Effectiveness & Continuity | Transition from unit to unit or hospital to home handling | Preparations for discharge; provision of necessary home care. |
| Appropriateness | Physical facilities and staff professionalism | Comfort and cleanliness of facilities; lighting; staff dress and behavior |
| Information | Keeping patient and family members informed | Quick provision of information about condition; availability of doctors; availability of counselors |
| Efficiency | Billing | Understandability of bill; availability of staff to explain bill; complaint handling |
| Meals | Quality and efficiency of meal service | Taste; timeliness; temperature |
| First Impression | First contact with hospital | Admission experience; hospital entrance |
| Staff Diversity | Staff composition generally reflective of community composition | Racial, gender diversity; availability of multilingual personnel |

measuring dimensions that are important to patients. But these dimensions are unlikely to define quality for other service industries such as restaurants, automobile repair shops, or banks.

The foregoing discussion could lead to the following definition of quality: Quality is a multidimensional construct, the dimensions of which must be uniquely established for each category of product or service being evaluated. Even though this definition might be philosophically unsatisfying, it does provide the basis for operationalizing quality in measurable ways.

## Different Approaches to Defining Quality

Another concept that developed during the 1990s is the strategic concept of order qualifiers and order winners (Hill, 2000). Order qualifiers are minimum characteristics that a product or service must have in order to be considered to be of acceptable quality. A flashlight that does not provide light would not be considered a quality item under this definition. One might make the argument that a product or service not meeting order qualifier standards would have no quality. In this context order qualifiers are those dimensions necessary to produce customer satisfaction. Order winners are those enhancements that exceed the minimum characteristics. Order winners could include enhanced battery life, custom fit to the hand, or enhanced beam focus in the case of a flashlight. One could conceive of order winners providing the basis for differentiating various levels of quality in a product or service and therefore leading to customer delight.

## Five Approaches to Defining Quality

David Garvin (1984) identified five major approaches to defining quality:

1. **The Transcendent Approach.** In this view "quality is synonymous with 'innate excellence'" and is "absolute and universally recognizable." This is the approach that most closely aligns with Socrates' question "What is the fine?" from *Greater Hippias* (Cooper, 1997). This approach implies that there is a construct called quality that is universally applicable. This approach is the basis for philosophical debate—but some say it is of little practical utility. Others argue that the transcendent approach is "the fundamentally most important approach to thinking about quality—particularly in the quality of design of breakthrough products and services" (Sower & Fair, 2005).

2. **The Product-based Approach.** In this view quality is "a precise and measurable variable" that is a composite of all the attributes that describe the degree of excellence of a product. This approach is illustrated by a draft of the ISO 8402 standard (1990) which stated that "quality . . . is the degree to which a . . . product possesses a specified set of attributes necessary to fulfill a stated purpose."

3. **The User-based Approach.** In this view quality is in the eye of the beholder—the customer. This approach has spawned tools such as quality function deployment (QFD). QFD is a structured approach to assure that the customer's voice is heard during product design. Although this approach has proven to be of practical value in the design of products based on incremental innovations, it is of limited value in designing products based on radical innovations. Products based on radical innovation enter a market that may not exist and where customers may not be able to articulate their needs. In the case of radical innovation, the transcendent approach may be of more than just philosophical interest.

"If we were to go back in time 100 years and ask a farmer what he'd like if he could have anything, he'd probably tell us he wanted a horse that was twice as strong and ate half as many oats. He would not tell us he wanted a tractor. Technology changes things so fast that many people aren't sure what the best solutions to their problems might be."

(Quigley, 2000)

4. The Manufacturing-based Approach. In this view quality is "conformance to (engineering and manufacturing) requirements." W. Edwards Deming (Walton, 1986) criticizes this approach as "the absurdity of meeting specifications... Specifications don't tell you what you need... Just to meet specifications—what you think the customer requires—no. That won't keep you in business" (Walton, 1986). Taguchi argued that the manufacturing-based approach was fundamentally flawed. He argued that simply meeting specifications is not good enough. He developed the quadratic loss function which shows that losses increase exponentially as a parameter deviates from its target value even if it still meets specifications. Others argue that conformance to specifications is a practical approach to defining quality if and only if the specifications derive from customer requirements (user-based approach). Philip Crosby (1979) goes so far as to say that "we must define quality as 'conformance to requirements' if we are to manage it. Instead of thinking of quality in terms of goodness or desirability (transcendent approach) we are looking at it as a means of meeting requirements... Quality means conformance. Nonquality is nonconformance."

5. The Value-based Approach. In this approach, quality is defined "in terms of costs and prices... A quality product is one that provides performance at an acceptable price or conformance at an acceptable cost." (Garvin, 1984) Philip Crosby (1979) also endorses this approach: "Quality is precisely measured by the cost of quality which... is the expense of nonconformance (to requirements)." This blends the value-based approach with the manufacturing-based approach.

It seems that every quality expert defines quality in a somewhat different way. There is a variety of perspectives that can be taken in defining quality (e.g., customer's perspective, specification-based perspective). Are there commonalities among these definitions? Is any one definition "more correct" than the other? Is one quality expert "right" and the other "wrong"? Quality professionals constantly debate these questions. More than 2,400 years after Plato's time we find ourselves still asking the question "What is quality?"

## MAJOR CONTRIBUTORS TO OUR UNDERSTANDING OF QUALITY

*Walter Shewhart* is considered by many to be the founder of the modern quality movement and an innovator in the application of statistics to quality. His seminal contributions were based on his work at Bell Telephone Laboratories and were published in two books: *Economic Control of Quality of Manufactured Product* in 1931 and *Statistical Method from the Viewpoint of Quality Control* in 1939. Interestingly, W. Edwards Deming authored the foreward in the 1939 book. Shewhart wrestled with the definition of quality and proposed that quality has both an objective and a subjective side. While acknowledging that the subjective side is of great commercial interest, he focused his attention on the objective side of quality. He stressed the need for operational definitions that are easily communicable.

Walter Shewhart. (Photo courtesy American Society for Quality www.asq.org. No further distribution allowed without permission.)

W. Edwards Deming. (Photo courtesy American Society for Quality www.asq.org. No further distribution allowed without permission.)

Besides contributing his thoughts on the definition of quality, Shewhart provided great insight into the collection, analysis, and presentation of data in the quality discipline. He recognized that processes are subject to variation from two sources: chance causes that are inherent in the system, and assignable or special causes that are signs of trouble in the system. He developed control charts that provide a statistical basis for separating these two types of variation. He defined the state of statistical control as a state of predictability that exists when there are is no assignable or special cause variation in a process.

He was an advocate of a systems approach to quality control. Shewhart recognized that the focus on the consumer was central and that all parts of the production process from raw materials, to methods, to inspection practices were crucial to producing quality products. He was also an advocate of continual improvement. He developed the Shewhart cycle for continual improvement: plan—do—check—act (PDCA). "The application of statistical methods in mass production makes possible the most efficient use of raw materials and manufacturing processes, and makes possible the highest economic standards of quality for the manufactured goods used by all of us" (Shewhart, 1939).

*W. Edwards Deming* invited Walter Shewhart to present a series of lectures before the Graduate School of the Department of Agriculture, lectures that eventually developed into Shewhart's 1939 book. Deming is best known for helping to lead the Japanese manufacturing sector out of the ruins of World War II to become a major presence in the world market. The highest quality award in Japan, The Deming Prize, is named in his honor. He is also known for his 14 points (a new philosophy for competing on the basis of quality), for the Deming chain reaction,

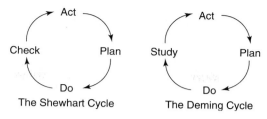

**Figure 1.1.** PDCA and PDSA

and for the theory of profound knowledge. (For an excellent summary of the theory of profound knowledge, go to http://www.maaw.info/DemingExhibit.htm). He also slightly modified the Shewhart cycle (plan, do, check, act), as shown in Figure 1.1, to what is now referred to as the Deming cycle (plan, do, study, act–PDSA).

Deming advocated improving the system rather than criticizing the workers. He believed that workers were already doing their best with the systems that management provided to them. But doing one's best without direction results in poor results. It is the responsibility of management to provide the direction that workers need, and this cannot be done by the use of management by objectives (which Deming referred to as management by fear) or annual performance reviews (which he condemned). The plan he proposed for management is embodied in his 14 points, shown in Figure 1.2, that must be implemented in their entirety in order to be effective. To skip one point will inhibit the effectiveness of the other 13 according to Deming.

1. Create constancy of purpose for improvement of product & service.
2. Adopt the new philosophy.
3. Cease dependency on mass inspection.
4. End the practice of awarding business on price tag alone.
5. Improve constantly and forever the system of production & service.
6. Institute training.
7. Institute leadership.
8. Drive out fear.
9. Break down barriers between staff areas.
10. Eliminate slogans, exhortations, and targets for the workforce.
11. Eliminate numerical quotas.
12. Remove barriers to pride of workmanship.
13. Institute a vigorous program of education & retraining.
14. Take action to accomplish the transformation.

**Figure 1.2.** Deming's (1981–1982) 14 Points for Management

## Mattress Mack, Gallery Furniture, and W. Edwards Deming

One advocate of the Deming approach to management is Jim "Mattress Mack" McIngvale, owner of Gallery Furniture in Houston, Texas—the biggest single retail store in America. Gallery thrived during the early 1980s, but began to feel the effect of the decline in the local economy in the late 1980s. After attending a Philip Crosby quality seminar, Mack was convinced that he should reinvent Gallery around quality. One thing bothered Mack about the Crosby approach—the idea of zero defects. That didn't seem reasonable in the retail environment. After hearing of W. Edwards Deming and attending two Deming seminars, Mack took what he referred to as a "hop of faith" and implemented some of Deming's points. It wasn't until he attended additional Deming seminars that he decided to take the leap of faith of implementing all 14 points.

Prior to implementing the Deming philosophy, Gallery operated on the traditional furniture retail model. Salespersons were on commission and ranked each month using an appraisal system that Mack characterizes as an "adult report card." Early on, Mack decided to fire the salesperson who had the lowest sales each month. In this environment customers sometimes felt as if they were walking into a flock of vultures when they entered Gallery Furniture. Each salesperson competed with all the others for each customer. The incentive was to sell the customer the highest-priced merchandise in order to maximize sales. Mack would rant and yell at employees who brought him bad news, creating an environment of fear.

After taking his leap of faith, Mack did away with commissions and the appraisal system. He found that managing by walking around—talking, listening, and watching employees and customers—was more effective. Rather than reacting negatively to bad news, Mack learned to thrive on it. He recognized that employees who are properly trained and empowered can bring problems to light early and assist in using bad news to fix and adjust the system. The result was a Gallery Furniture that was focused on customer delight, not on rating employees. Gallery Furniture's single-site store sells more furniture per square foot than any other store in the world. It is the most productive furniture store in the world.

(McIngvale, 2002, and various public speeches made by Mattress Mack)

The Deming chain reaction, shown in Figure 1.3, was first presented in 1950—early in Deming's time in Japan after World War II. It illustrated Shewhart's concept that productivity improves as variation is reduced and quality is improved. According to Deming, this became a way of life in Japanese industry.

Deming's theory of profound knowledge says that a production system is composed of many interacting subsystems. Management's job is to set the purpose for the system and to optimize the system. Variation is an inherent part of any system. Common causes of variation account for 80–90 percent of the total variation;

The Deming Chain Reaction

**Figure 1.3.** Adapted from Deming 1982

assignable causes account for the rest; and only management can address common causes of variation. Knowledge is not possible without theory. Experience alone does not establish a theory. Copying an example of someone else's success without understanding it with theory can lead to disaster.

Beginning in the early 1980s Deming finally came to prominence in the United States and played a major role in quality becoming a major competitive issue in American industry. His book, *Out of the Crisis* (1982), is considered a quality classic. Read more about Dr. Deming and his philosophy at the W. Edwards Deming Institute Home Page (http://www.deming.org/).

*Joseph Juran* also assisted the Japanese in their reconstruction after World War II. Juran first became well known in the quality field in the United States as the editor of the *Quality Control Handbook* (1951) and later for his paper introducing the quality trilogy: quality planning, quality control, and quality improvement (see Table 1.4). Quality planning provides a system that is capable of meeting quality standards. Quality control is used to determine when corrective action is required. Quality improvement seeks better ways of doing things. Questioning which of the quality trilogy is most important is similar to asking which leg of a stool is most important. Without all three, the stool (and the quality system) cannot function effectively as shown in Figure 1.4.

Joseph Juran. (Photo courtesy American Society for Quality www.asq.org. No further distribution allowed without permission.)

**TABLE 1.4.  Juran's (1986) Basic Quality Processes**

**Quality Planning**

Identify internal and external customers.

Determine customer needs.

Develop product and service features that respond to customer needs.

Establish quality goals that meet the needs of customers and suppliers at a minimum combined cost.

Develop a process that can produce the needed product/service features.

Prove process capability—that the process can meet the quality goals under operating conditions.

**Quality Control**

Choose what to control.

Choose units of measurement.

Establish measurement.

Establish standards for performance.

Measure actual performance.

Interpret the difference between actual and standard.

Take action on the difference.

**Quality Improvement**

Prove the need for improvement.

Identify specific projects for improvement.

Organize for discovery of causes.

Diagnose to find the causes.

Provide remedies.

Prove that the remedies are effective under operating conditions.

Provide for control to hold the gains.

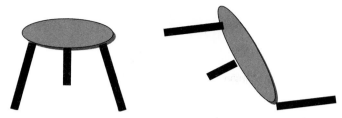

**Figure 1.4.** Juran's Quality Trilogy

Although Deming's approach is revolutionary (i.e., throw out your old system and adopt the new philosophy of his 14 points), Juran's approach is more evolutionary (i.e., we can work to improve your current system). Deming refers to statistics as the language of business while Juran says that money is the language of business and quality efforts must be communicated to management in their language. Juran agrees with Deming that more than 80 percent of defects are caused by the system rather than the workers, and he listed motivation of workers as a nonsolution to quality problems. Read more about Dr. Juran and his philosophy at the Juran Institute Web site (http://www.juran.com/).

*Armand Feigenbaum* is credited with creating the idea of total quality control in his 1951 book, *Quality Control—Principles, Practice, and Administration,* and in his 1956 article, "Total Quality Control." The Japanese version of this concept is called company-wide quality control, while it is called total quality management (TQM) in the United States and elsewhere. He was also the first to classify quality costs into costs of prevention, appraisal, and internal and external failure.

Armand Feigenbaum. (Photo courtesy American Society for Quality www.asq.org. No further distribution allowed without permission.)

*Philip Crosby* came to national prominence with the publication of his book *Quality is Free* (1979). He established the absolutes of quality management that includes "the only performance standard (that makes any sense) is Zero Defects," and the basic elements of improvement.

Philip Crosby. (Photo courtesy American Society for Quality
www.asq.org. No further distribution allowed without permission.)

Although Crosby, like Deming and Juran, stresses the importance of management commitment and error-cause removal, some aspects of Crosby's approach to quality are quite different from Deming's. Zero Defects, central to Crosby's philosophy, was criticized by Deming as being directed at the wrong people (workers) and generating worker frustration and resentment. Goal setting, central to Crosby, leads to negative accomplishment according to Deming. The reality is that Deming was probably reacting to the inappropriate uses of slogans and goals. Deming may not have condemned them were they always used properly within the Crosby system. Read more about Philip Crosby at the Phillip Crosby Associates II Web site (http://www.philipcrosby.com/).

*Kaoru Ishikawa* is credited with developing the idea of company-wide quality control in Japan. He pioneered the use of quality circles and championed the use of quality tools to understand the root causes of problems. He developed one of those tools, the cause and effect diagram, shown in Figure 1.5, which is also referred to as the Ishikawa diagram or the fishbone diagram.

Kaoru Ishikawa. (Photo courtesy American Society for Quality
www.asq.org. No further distribution allowed without permission.)

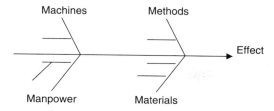

**Figure 1.5.** Ishikawa Diagram

*Genichi Taguchi* developed approaches to assess the outside influences (which he referred to as noise) on processes that he used to establish the signal-to-noise ratio as a measure of the quality of a process. He devised a quadratic function, referred to as the Taguchi loss function, which quantified the loss to society of the variation in processes that result in products not being produced exactly at the target values. He developed Taguchi Methods, an approach using orthogonal arrays and linear graphs, to understand and to optimize the performance of processes. He also developed the idea of robustness, which is the ability of a process or product to perform even in the face of uncontrollable outside influences (noise).

Genichi Taguchi. (Photo courtesy American Society for Quality www.asq.org. No further distribution allowed without permission.)

## SUMMARY

Quality is a difficult term to define. There is no single, simple definition that will suffice for all products, services, and situations. Perhaps the best modern definition that comes closest to universality is, quality is meeting or exceeding customer expectations. Customer expectations are often represented as dimensions of quality. The dimensions that matter most for specific products and services vary. This makes more difficult the process of defining quality in a way that facilitates assessment and improvement.

Many individuals have contributed to the body of knowledge that we characterize as quality management. Among the most prominent are Shewhart, Deming, Juran, Crosby, Feigenbaum, Ishikawa, and Taguchi. Although each of these "gurus" has made distinct contributions to the body of knowledge, there are many consistencies in their contributions and ideas. The fingerprints of each of these "gurus" may be found throughout this book.

## Quality Definitions

Different terms are used to describe approaches to quality. Often these terms are misunderstood and used incorrectly. It is important in an introductory chapter of a quality book to define some of the key terms used in modern quality control.

Strategic quality management (SQM) is a "systematic approach for setting and meeting quality goals throughout the company ... with upper management participation in managing for quality to an unprecedented degree" (Juran, 1988); SQM involves the complete integration of quality into the strategic management process.

Total quality management (TQM) is "a management approach to long-term success through customer satisfaction. It is based on the participation of all members of an organization in improving processes, products, services, and the culture they work in" (Quality Glossary, 2002).

Quality management is the totality of functions involved in the determination and achievement of quality (includes quality assurance and quality control) (ASQ Statistics Division, 1983).

Quality assurance (QA) is a broad concept that focuses on the entire quality system, including suppliers and ultimate consumers of the product or service. It includes all activities designed to produce products and services of appropriate quality. According to ASQ, quality assurance includes all those planned or systematic actions necessary to provide adequate confidence that a product or service will satisfy given needs (ASQ Statistics Division, 1983).

Quality control (QC) has a narrower focus than quality assurance. Quality control focuses on the process of producing the product or service with the intent of eliminating problems that might result in defects. According to ASQ, QC includes the operational techniques and the activities that sustain a quality of product or service that will satisfy given needs as well as the use of such techniques and activities (ASQ Statistics Division, 1983).

## DISCUSSION QUESTIONS

1. Briefly discuss why it is important to study quality.

2. Why might a dictionary definition of quality be inadequate for a quality professional? Which of the definitions discussed in this chapter do you feel is best? Why?

3. Explain the difference between internal and external customers.

4. List Garvin's 8 dimensions of product quality. Would these dimensions be equally applicable to services? Explain.

5. List SERVQUAL's 5 dimensions of service quality.

6. Discuss which of Garvin's 5 approaches to defining quality makes the most sense to you.

7. What might be some of the dangers of relying solely on customer input when designing or improving a product or service? What other inputs should be taken into account?

8. Compare and contrast Deming's, Juran's, and Crosby's philosophies about quality.

9. Discuss potential sources of resistance to the implementation of Deming's 14 points for management.

10. What is the difference between quality control and quality assurance?

## CASE STUDY 1.1: *The Battle of the Gurus*

©2006 Victor E. Sower, Ph.D., C.Q.E.

The voices from the conference room were loud and animated. Everyone on the first floor could tell that a heated debate was underway. Knowing that Bill Reyes and George Hales were in there, no one was surprised. They were like oil and water. If one claimed the sky is blue, the other would hotly debate the claim.

The debate concerned the direction that the company's quality system would take. Bill, the operations manager, had just read *The Deming Management Method* and was convinced that Deming's way was the only way. George had recently read *Quality is Free* and felt equally strongly that Crosby's was the right path.

Finally, the division VP had heard enough. She turns to you and says, "Obviously we need a neutral party to sort this out. You learn all you can about the Deming and Crosby systems and tell me which is best. I want your report next week. Next agenda item!"

1. Prepare a report summarizing the two quality systems and showing where they are similar and where they differ.

2. Is there a "best" system for all organizations? Discuss.

3. What types of organizational cultures would favor each of the two approaches?

## EXERCISES AND ACTIVITIES

1. Propose your own definition of quality. Compare and contrast your definition with other definitions of quality discussed in this chapter. Purchase three brands of low cost, disposable, medium point, black ink ball point pens. Use your definition of quality to determine which of these three pens is of the highest quality. Summarize your findings in a short paper.

2. Determine who are the customers for the following and classify the customers as internal or external:

   a. Manufactured goods that are sold to a wholesaler.
   b. Higher education.
   c. Financial statements prepared by the Accounting Department for use by company management.
   d. Applications for student housing filled out in the University Admissions Office and sent to Resident Life.
   e. Orders taken in a restaurant by a server and which are transmitted to the kitchen staff for preparation.

3. Consider your purchase of a hamburger at a fast food restaurant. What combination of Garvin's dimensions of product quality and the SERVQUAL dimensions of service quality would be applicable in assessing the quality of your experience?

4. Select two participants to play the roles of workers in two different departments. Have them sit at opposite ends of a table. Place a barrier in the center of the table that prevents the workers from seeing what the other is doing.

   Worker #1: Provide the first worker with a black marker and a ruler and instruct the worker to draw two 1-inch squares on a 3"× 5" card. When the worker completes the task, drop the card over the barrier.

   Worker #2: Provide the second worker with a bottle of White-Out® and a red marker. Instruct the second worker to use the White-Out® to cover the black line forming the right side of the squares and to replace the black lines with red lines.

   Allow the work to proceed for several minutes. Then inform each worker individually that you are instituting a process of continuous improvement and that you want them to think of ways they can increase their productivity. Implement their ideas and tally the results of their improvement efforts. An example of an idea for Worker #1 would be replacing the ruler with a square template to enable drawing the squares faster and more accurately (higher quality).

   Then remove the barrier and allow the workers to interact and to see what the other is doing. Inform them that they are to work as a team to improve their processes. Implement their ideas and tally the results. An example of an idea here would be to have Worker #1 omit the black right-hand line so that Worker #2 does not have to use the White-Out® to cover it before drawing the red line.

   Debrief the exercise using Deming's Point Number 9 as a basis.

# SUPPLEMENTARY READINGS

Crosby, P. (1979). *Quality is Free*. New York: McGraw-Hill.

Deming, W. (1982). *Out of the Crisis*. Cambridge, MA: MIT Center for Advanced Engineering Study.

Deming, W. (1981–1982). "Improvement of Quality and Productivity through Action by Management." *National Productivity Review* 1(1), 12–22. Reprinted in Sower, V. E., J. Motwani, & M. J. Savoie. (1995). *Classic Readings in Operations Management*. Ft. Worth, TX: Dryden, 231–247.

Feigenbaum, A. V. (1956). "Total Quality Control." *Harvard Business Review* 34(6), 93–101. Reprinted in Sower, V. E., J. Motwani, & M. J. Savoie. (1995). *Classic Readings in Operations Management*. Ft. Worth, TX: Dryden, 307–321.

Garvin, D. G. (1987). "Competing on the Eight Dimensions of Quality." *Harvard Business Review* 65(6), 101–109. Reprinted in Sower, V. E., J. Motwani, & M. J. Savoie. (1995). *Classic Readings in Operations Management*, Ft. Worth, TX: Dryden, 323–339.

Juran, J. M. (1986). "The Quality Trilogy." *Quality Progress* 9(8), 19–24. Reprinted in Sower, V. E., J. Motwani, & M. J. Savoie. (1995). *Classic Readings in Operations Management*. Ft. Worth, TX: Dryden, 277–287.

Parasuraman, A., V. Zeithaml, & L. Berry. (1988). "SERVQUAL: A Multiple-Item Scale for Measuring Consumer Perceptions of Service Quality." *Journal of Retailing* 61(1), 12–40.

Quality Glossary. (2002). *Quality Progress* 35(7), 43–61.

Shewhart, W. (1931). *Economic Control of Manufactured Product*. New York: D. Van Nostrand Co., Inc. Republished in 1980 as a 50th Anniversary Commemorative Reissue by ASQ Quality Press, Milwaukee, WI.

Shewhart, W. (1939). *Statistical Method from the Standpoint of Quality Control*. Washington, D.C.: Graduate School of the Department of Agriculture. Republished in 1980 by General Publishing Company, Toronto, Canada.

Sower, V. E., J. Motwani, & M. J. Savoie. (1995). *Classic Readings in Operations Management*, Ft. Worth, TX: Dryden.

Sower, V., J. Duffy, W. Kilbourne, G. Kohers, & P. Jones. (2001). "The Dimensions of Service Quality for Hospitals: Development of the KQCAH Scale." *Health Care Management Review* 26(2), 47–59.

Sower, V., & F. Fair. (2005). "There is More to Quality than Continuous Improvement: Listening to Plato." *Quality Management Journal* 12(1), 8–20.

Taguchi, G., & Y. Wu. (1980). *Introduction to Off-Line Quality Control*. Nagoya: Central Japan Quality Control Association.

# REFERENCES

ASQ Statistics Division. (1983). *Glossary & Tables for Statistical Quality Control*.

Babacus, E., & G. Boller. (1992). "An Empirical Assessment of the SERVQUAL Scale." *Journal of Business Research* 24, 253–268.

Barfield, O. (1988) *History in English Words*. Great Barrington, MA: Inner Traditions/ Lindisfarne Press. Reprint of original 1953 edition. London: Faber & Faber.

Boggs, W. (2004). "TQM and Organizational Culture: A Case Study." *Quality Management Journal* 11(2), 42–52.

Cooper, J. (ed.). (1997). *Plato: Complete Works*. Indianapolis, IN: Hackett Publishing Co., Inc., 898–921.

Cronin, J., & S. Taylor. (1992). "Measuring Service Quality: A Reexamination and Extension." *Journal of Marketing* 56(3), 55–68.

Crosby, P. (1979). *Quality is Free*. New York: McGraw-Hill.

Deming, W. (1981–1982). "Improvement of Quality and Productivity Through Action by Management." *National Productivity Review* 1(1), 12–22.

Deming, W. (1982). *Out of the Crisis*. Cambridge, MA: MIT Center for Advanced Engineering Study.

Deming, W. (1993). *The New Economics for Industry, Government, Education*. Cambridge, MA: MIT Center for Advanced Engineering Study.

Feigenbaum, A. (1951). *Quality Control—Principles, Practice, and Administration*. New York: McGraw-Hill. Reprinted in *Classic Readings in Operations Management (1995)*, V. Sower, J. Motwani, and M. Savoie. Ft. Worth, Texas: The Dryden Press, 289–306.

Garvin, D. (1984). "What Does Product Quality Really Mean?" *Sloan Management Review* 26(1), 25–43.

Garvin, D. (1987). "Competing on the Eight Dimensions of Quality." *Harvard Business Review* 65(6), 101–109.

Hill, T. (2000). *Manufacturing Strategy: Text and Cases*. Burr Ridge, IL: Irwin/McGraw-Hill.

ISO 8402. (1990). *International Standard ISO/CD 8402-1, Quality Concepts and Terminology—Part 1: Generic Terms and Definitions*. Geneva, Switzerland: International Organization for Standardization.

Juran, J. (1988). *Juran on Planning for Quality*. New York: The Free Press, 176–179.

Juran, J. (1986). "The Quality Trilogy." *Quality Progress* 9(8), 19–24.

Juran, J. (1970). "Consumerism and Product Quality." *Quality Progress* 3(7), 18. Reprinted in *Classic Readings in Operations Management* (1995), V. Sower, J. Motwani, and M. Savoie. Ft. Worth, Texas: The Dryden Press, 249–275.

McIngvale, J. (2002). *Always Think Big*. Chicago, IL: Dearborn Trade Publishing.

*Oxford English Dictionary*, 2nd edition. (1989). Available online at oed.com.

Parasuraman, A., V. Zeithaml, & L. Berry. (1988). "SERVQUAL: A Multiple-Item Scale for Measuring Consumer Perceptions of Service Quality." *Journal of Retailing* 61(1), 12–40.

Quality Glossary. (2002). *Quality Progress* 35(7), July, 43–61.

Quigley, P. (2000). *Readers' Digest*.

Shewhart, W. (1939). *Statistical Method from the Standpoint of Quality Control*. Washington, D.C.: Graduate School of the Department of Agriculture.

Sower, V., J. Duffy, W. Kilbourne, G. Kohers, & P. Jones. (2001). "The Dimensions of Service Quality for Hospitals: Development and Use of the KQCAH Scale." *Health Care Management Review* 26(2), 47–59.

Sower, V., & F. Fair. (2005). "There is More to Quality than Continuous Improvement: Listening to Plato." *Quality Management Journal* 12(1), 8–20.

Walton, M. (1986). *The Deming Management Method*. New York: Perigee Books.

## CHAPTER TWO

# Strategic Quality Management and Operationalizing Quality

## CHAPTER OBJECTIVES

After completing this chapter, the reader should be able to:

- define strategic quality management;
- discuss the strategic management process of strategic planning, strategic deployment, and strategic evaluation and control;
- operationalize the dimensions of quality into measurable characteristics;
- discuss ways to develop quality measures and metrics; and
- discuss ways in which customer input may be obtained through the use of focus groups and surveys.

In this chapter we will discuss the strategic importance of quality. In order to be competitive in today's world, organizations must explicitly include quality in their strategic planning processes. Measures and metrics are the means by which an organization determines progress made toward achieving strategic goals and strategies.

In Chapter 1 we discussed one definition of quality as a multidimensional construct, the dimensions of which must be uniquely established for each category of product or service being evaluated. In this chapter we will discuss ways of establishing the appropriate dimensions for various products and services and developing measures and metrics for those dimensions. Appropriate measures allow us to evaluate quality and compare quality to similar products and services. We refer to the process of developing measures and metrics as *operationalizing the dimensions of quality*. Metrics provide feedback to the strategic quality management process as well to continuous quality improvement programs.

## STRATEGIC QUALITY MANAGEMENT

Strategic quality management (SQM) is a term and concept that is credited to Garvin (1988), but Garvin himself says that the beginnings of SQM "cannot be dated precisely." Juran (1988) defined SQM as a "systematic approach for setting and meeting quality goals throughout the company...with upper management participation in managing for quality to an unprecedented degree." Others (Madu & Kuei, 1993) use the term strategic total quality management (STQM), which they define as an extension of TQM that "views quality as the driving force to the survivability and competitiveness of a firm." In this sense quality moves beyond the "quality of products and services" to the quality of everything that a firm does. The STQM process is compared to traditional quality management and TQM in Table 2.1.

Porter (1980) defined strategy as the application of resources to pursue the aims of policy. Strategy contains two critical elements: strategic thinking and conversion of the vision into plans to achieve realization of the vision. SQM involves incorporating quality and continuous improvement as strategic objectives of the firm and transforming the organization so that these strategic objectives become an integral part of the way the firm conducts business. Too often TQM is treated as an add-on to the organization's culture and way of doing business. In SQM, TQM is fully integrated into the strategy and operation of the business.

The strategic management process consists of three phases: strategic planning, strategic deployment, and evaluation and control. In SQM, quality is fully integrated into each phase of the process.

**TABLE 2.1.   QA versus TQM versus SQM**

| Principles of Quality | Traditional Quality Assurance (TQA) | Total Quality Management (TQM) | Strategic Total Quality Management (STQM) |
|---|---|---|---|
| Definition | Product driven | Customer driven | Customer and environment driven |
| Priorities | Emphasis is on cost and output | Emphasis is on outcome and quality is the means | Organizational focus and vision is driven by overall quality |
| Decisions | Short-term goals are emphasized | Short-term and long-term goals are emphasized | Short-term and long-term goals that are environmentally sound and sensitive are emphasized |
| Objective | Detect errors | Prevent errors | Prevent errors in products and services and maintain socially responsible decisions that are environmentally sound and sensitive |

*(continued overleaf)*

**TABLE 2.1.** *(continued)*

| Principles of Quality | Traditional Quality Assurance (TQA) | Total Quality Management (TQM) | Strategic Total Quality Management (STQM) |
|---|---|---|---|
| Costs | Quality increases costs | Quality reduces costs and improves productivity | Quality reduces costs, improves productivity and corporate image |
| Errors are due to | Special causes which result from workers' mistakes and inefficiency | Common causes which result from the failure of top management to manage effectively | Special and common causes as well as irresponsible management decisions and lack of commitment to social and environmental issues |
| Responsibility for quality | Inspection centres and quality control departments | Involves every member of the organization | Involves every member of the organization but requires top management to take the lead to ensure that socially responsible decisions are made and effectively implemented |
| Organization culture | Numerical targets are used and employees can be singled out for their mistakes | Continuous improvement is emphasized and team work is the approach | Never-ending philosophy of continuous improvement is emphasized. Employees are provided the necessary tools and skills to improve their performance and productivity |
| Organizational structure and information flow | Top-down and bottom-up approach, bureaucratic and restricts information flow, rigid | Horizontal approach, provides real time information, flexible | Horizontal/vertical approach, allows active participation of important stakeholder groups in making quality decisions |
| Decision making | Top-down approach | Team approach is used with team members comprising of employees | Team approach with team members comprising of employees and important stakeholder groups |

This table was published in *Long Range Planning* 26(6), Madu, C. & C. Kuei, "Introducing Strategic Quality Management," 121–131. © Elsevier 1993. Used with permission.

## The Strategic Planning Process

The overarching themes that guide the strategic planning process and are interactive with it are the organization's mission and vision. The mission is a statement of who we are while the vision is a statement of who we wish to be. Mission and vision are the domains of top management but require continuous input from all constituents. They must not be static but capable of evolving with changes in the organizations' internal and external environments.

The strategic planning process begins with the organization's mission and vision as shown in Figure 2.1. Then the organization scans its internal environment to identify strengths and weaknesses and its external environment to identify opportunities and threats. This is often referred to as a SWOT analysis. Strengths are internal factors that provide a source of sustainable competitive advantage to the firm. Weaknesses are internal factors that require attention to bring them up to acceptable standards. They are sources of competitive disadvantage. Opportunities are factors in the external environment that the firm may seek to exploit. Threats are factors in the external environment that pose a potential risk to the firm's competitive success.

In the strategic planning process, external factors are considered in relation to internal factors in an attempt to determine appropriate revisions to the mission and vision and to determine the most appropriate and feasible strategic goals the firm should include in its strategic plan. These goals are directed toward taking advantage of opportunities and strengths and appropriately addressing threats and weaknesses. Strategies are developed to enable the firm to achieve its goals. Deliberate strategies result in realization of intentions that existed previously. Emergent strategies result in realization of unplanned results. Recognition of the role of emergent strategies and their incorporation into the strategic planning process enable the organization to deal with strategic issues and opportunities that arise but are not included in the strategic plan. Although not planned for, these emergent strategies should be consistent with the mission and vision of the organization.

## Emergent Strategy

During the late 1990s Sam Houston State University (SHSU) learned of a plan by a local community college district to develop a multi-institutional teaching center (MITC) in the heart of the area from which the majority of SHSU students are recruited. All of the four-year universities within a 100-mile radius were invited to participate in the MITC. The main purpose of the MITC was to provide the graduates of the community college the opportunity to continue their education on the same campus in a new building dedicated exclusively to the MITC. The secondary purpose of the MITC was to provide other students in the area with the opportunity to earn undergraduate and graduate degrees from the participating universities without having to travel to the main campuses for classes. The four-year universities would be invited to offer particular noncompeting degree programs. A particular university would be selected for each degree program that

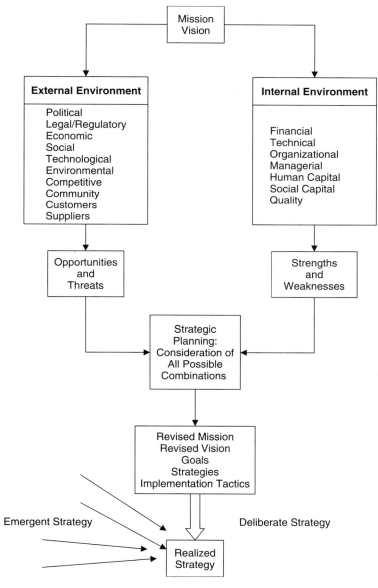

**Figure 2.1.** The Strategic Planning Process. Inspired by Mintzberg, et al. (2003). (Thanks to Dr. JoAnn Duffy and Dr. Joe Kavanaugh for their assistance in developing this figure).

they would have exclusive rights to offer at the MITC. SHSU became one of six senior universities selected to deliver undergraduate and graduate programs at the MITC.

The MITC was viewed as a potential threat to the growth objective of SHSU. If another university offered degree programs at the MITC that were in the areas targeted for growth at SHSU, recruiting efforts would be impacted. SHSU decided to initiate a defensive strategy of bidding on a number of degree programs at the MITC in order to protect its position in its target market. This was an emergent strategy. Although SHSU had established a strategic objective to increase its enrollment each year over the strategic planning horizon, participation in a MITC or establishment of a branch campus was not planned to be a part of its strategic plan to achieve this objective.

After winning the right to offer a number of degree programs at the MITC, SHSU examined how it was going to service those programs. The SHSU mission statement was clear about quality issues. Teaching was to be the top priority for faculty with research being a close second priority. SHSU built its competitive advantage in quality through low student/teacher ratios and high levels of student-faculty interaction. One approach to servicing the courses at the MITC, which was taken by some other universities, was to use distance learning as the primary delivery mode. This was rejected by SHSU as being inconsistent with the strategic plan. SHSU also elected to staff a full-time office at the MITC to assist students and to insure that the best interests of SHSU were represented on-site.

Despite some initial faculty reluctance to travel the 40 miles from the main campus to the MITC, SHSU elected to service its courses largely via technologically enhanced classroom instruction using the same faculty who taught those courses on the main campus. SHSU went to great effort to provide the same access to library, computing, academic advisement, and other essential services for the MITC students as were available on the main campus.

What started out as an emergent, defensive strategy in response to a threat has now turned into an integral part of SHSU's growth plans. Over the past two years SHSU has grown faster than it ever has in its history. It has used quality as a competitive advantage and has consistently serviced over 75% of the student credit hours produced at the MITC. MITC student enrollment is largely responsible for the phenomenal growth rate in key programs such as the SHSU MBA program. What was initially an emergent defensive strategy has now become a deliberate offensive strategy fully integrated into the strategic planning of the university that may lead to SHSU having its own building within the MITC.

Quality is often given little consideration in the traditional approach to strategic planning. Total quality management (TQM), although widely applied, is often not effective because it is not integrated into day-to-day business practices. One reason for this is that TQM is often not perceived to be part of the strategic plan but rather the responsibility of the quality department. In SQM, quality is fully integrated into the process at all levels. Quality is an integral part of the way the business is run and that is fully reflected in the every aspect of the organization including the strategic planning process.

## Strategic Deployment

Many organizations do an adequate job of strategic planning. Far fewer organizations do an adequate job of strategic deployment. In this step the strategic plan is shared with all members of the organization with the intent of creating consensus. Projects and actionable items are created throughout the organization and are directed toward achievement of the strategic goals. Responsibilities for these projects are assigned, resources are allocated, and key milestones and due dates are established. A commitment to quality in the mission statement is translated into, for example, projects to reduce total costs of quality, redesign products to increase reliability and manufacturability, redesign processes to reduce variability, empower employees to address problems with the systems, and develop more reliable suppliers. Responsibilities for these projects do not rest exclusively with the quality department but rather with engineering, operations, finance, human resources, and marketing—in short, all parts of the organization are involved. This is the step where the transformation of the organization from its present state to the state embodied in the vision statement occurs. Without strategic deployment, the strategic plan is an empty document.

Figure 2.2 shows how Bronson Methodist Hospital (BMH), which won the 2005 Malcolm Baldrige National Quality Award (MBNQA), integrated quality into its strategic management processes. Their Plan for Excellence is mission driven and focused on attaining the vision. Once the plan was developed and approved by the hospital board, it was deployed, starting with the Bronson Leadership System (Figure 2.3), by developing performance requirements, allocating resources, and developing short-term plans, goals, and priorities from top to bottom within the organization.

## Evaluation and Control

A feedback system is integral to the strategic management process. Systematic assessment systems must be in place to gather, process, and analyze data, and to disseminate information obtained in order to assess the effectiveness of the execution of the strategic plan. Measures and metrics are the fundamental building blocks of assessment systems. Selection of metrics must be approached carefully. The metrics must first achieve three major functions (Melnyk & Christensen, 2002):

1. They must deal with what is important to the organization and how the firm creates value.
2. They must provide effective feedback to the organization so that it can see how it is doing.
3. They must focus attention on those areas where gaps exist between the current level of performance and the desired level of performance.

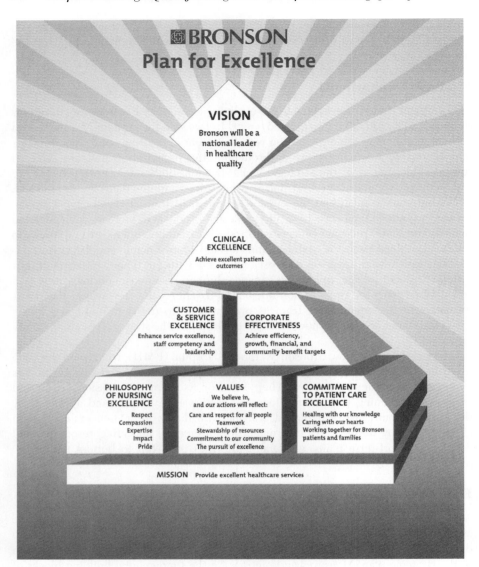

**Figure 2.2.** Bronson Plan for Excellence. (*Source*: Bronson Methodist Hospital. Used with permission.)

Figure 2.3 shows how Bronson Methodist Hospital uses its patient-focused Bronson Leadership System to deploy the strategic plan by developing performance requirements, identifying and providing necessary resources, and integrates outcome measures and metrics that are shown on the outer rim of the figure. These measures and metrics tie directly to the hospital's strategic plan for excellence (Figure 2.2).

Another important aspect of the evaluation and control stage is constant monitoring of the internal and external environments. The objective of this monitoring

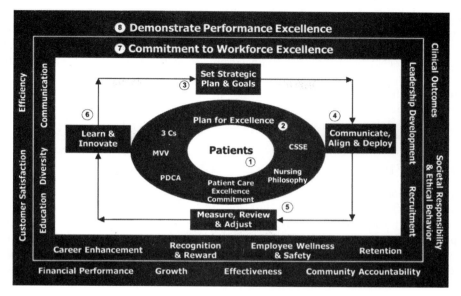

**Figure 2.3.** Bronson Leadership System. (*Source*: Bronson Methodist Hospital. Used with permission.)

is to detect changes in the environment that might render aspects of the strategic quality plan obsolete. Being alert to changes in the environment can prevent an organization from blindly following a strategic plan that has become obsolete. For example, makers of analog cellular telephones who developed their strategic quality plan prior to the availability of digital cellular technology would undoubtedly need to revise their plans based on the introduction of this new technology.

## Approaches to Monitoring Progress toward Strategic Goals

Two approaches that are often used in combination to assess progress toward the achievement of strategic goals are cost of quality (COQ), which is sometimes referred to as the cost of poor quality (COPQ), and the balanced scorecard.

*Cost of quality* will be discussed in detail in Chapter 12. According to Philip Crosby (1979, 15) the only measure of quality that makes any sense is the cost of quality. Cost of quality is a measure of the cost of those activities undertaken to prevent errors, to detect errors, and the costs incurred both internally and externally when errors do occur. A decline in the cost of quality can be a good indicator that overall quality of products, services, and processes is improving—thus providing a global measure of the effectiveness of the deployment of the strategic quality plan.

*The balanced scorecard* is a comprehensive management control system that balances traditional financial measures with operational measures relating to a company's critical success factors (Kaplan & Norton, 1992). The balanced scorecard provides a comprehensive control system that enables managers to focus on the critical success factors for the organization. The balanced scorecard is focused on the mission, strategy, and goals of the organization, and it assesses progress made by the firm from four interrelated perspectives: the financial perspective, the customers' perspective, the organization's learning and growth perspective, and the internal business process perspective. A main advantage of the balanced scorecard is its ability to transform large amounts of data into information that provides feedback on factors that are integral to the success of the organization and that are easy to communicate.

## DIMENSIONS, MEASURES, AND METRICS

In this section we will discuss transforming quality dimensions into quality metrics. Garvin's eight dimensions of product quality have gained wide acceptance as a framework for describing the multidimensional nature of product quality and are applicable to most products. These were originally proposed by Garvin (1987) as a way to broaden management's perspective about quality. They provide a framework for enabling a firm to explore the opportunities to distinguish its products from those offered by competitors and to establish strategic plans to do so. Garvin suggests that it is the role of strategic quality management to select the dimensions on which to compete and to manage the tradeoffs. Other dimensions have been developed for use in services (e.g., SERVQUAL) in general, and still other dimensions have been developed for specific service industries, such as the key quality characteristics for the assessment of hospitals (KQCAH) scale for hospitals as shown in Table 2.2.

To actually use the dimensions to measure the quality of a particular product or service, the dimensions must be operationalized—that is measurable characteristics (metrics) must be defined, characteristics which enable an assessment of the

**TABLE 2.2. Dimensions of Quality**

| Garvin's 8 Dimensions of Product Quality | SERVQUAL Dimensions of Service Quality | KQCAH Dimensions of Hospital Quality |
|---|---|---|
| Performance | Tangibles | Respect & Caring |
| Features | Reliability | Effectiveness & Continuity |
| Reliability | Responsiveness | Appropriateness |
| Conformance | Assurance | Information |
| Durability | Empathy | Efficiency |
| Serviceability | | Meals |
| Aesthetics | | First Impression |
| Perceived Quality | | Staff Diversity |

dimension they represent. For example, you cannot measure the *performance* of an automobile directly. You have to develop metrics for performance. One possible metric might be the time it takes to go from 0 to 60mph. This can be measured. Another metric might be fuel efficiency. By combining the metrics for a given dimension, a dimension score can be obtained. Two products can be compared by comparing their dimension scores.

A **measure** is "the criteria, metric or means to which a comparison is made with output."
A **metric** is a "standard for measurement."

"Quality Glossary." *Quality Progress* 35(7), July 2002, 53.

Measure and metric are often used interchangeably and sometimes a measure is also a metric. Consider the following example:

**Dimension** ⟶ **Measure** ⟶ **Metric**
Features            Does it come with a mouse?   Is a mouse present?

Sometimes a measure is not specific enough to measure directly. In this case a specific measurable metric must be defined.

| **Dimension** ⟶ | **Measure** ⟶ | **Metric** |
|---|---|---|
| Durability | Expected life | MTTF |
| Reliability | Frequency of repair | MTBF |
| Service to customers | Customer satisfaction | SERVQUAL Score |

In these cases the measures state how durability, reliability, and service to customers are operationalized while the metrics define exactly what is to be measured.

It is vital to include customer input—the voice of the customer—when operationalizing quality dimensions. Without input from the customer, quality professionals can never be certain that they have operationalized the dimensions in a way that accurately reflects customer concerns and priorities. If quality function deployment (discussed in Chapter 3) was used when designing the product or service, the voice of the customer matrix might provide the information needed to assure that appropriate metrics are defined. However, if significant time has elapsed since this matrix was created, care must be taken to assure that the metrics are still valid.

Product engineers in a division of the DuPont Company that made ink for the printing industry once decided to improve the quality of their inks. They realized that the inks contained "impurities"—particles not contributing to the function performed by the ink. Without consulting with customers, they initiated a program to filter out the "impurities." After deployment of the additional filtration process, customer complaints increased. The inks did not flow properly. Further analysis determined that the "impurities" did add to the fluidity properties that gave DuPont inks a competitive advantage in the marketplace. The engineers had to reverse the "improvement."

(Dr. Charles F. Bimmerle, Ph.D.)

It is important to assure that input is obtained from customers in the organization's target market. Information from society in general is often confusing and conflicting. Consider the case of an automobile. A teenager, a young family with children, and a retired couple will probably define performance and features in quite different ways. The correct way for the organization depends upon how the target market is defined. A "muscle car" with a custom sound system might best conform to the teenager's metrics, while a mini-van and a luxury sedan might best conform to the young family's and retired couple's metrics, respectively. Less confusing would be input from the particular demographic that constitutes the organization's target market rather than the market in general.

A number of researchers have shown that although service quality is also multidimensional, it is harder to find one set of quality dimensions that apply equally well to many types of services. It is often necessary to develop appropriate service quality dimensions on an industry-by-industry basis. Operationalizing the dimensions of service quality is frequently more challenging than operationalizing the dimensions of product quality. Operationalizing the JCAHO hospital service quality dimension of *respect and caring* could result in metrics such as *degree of personal interaction with staff, orientation to surroundings, degree of two-way understanding between patient and caregiver*, and *level of patient participation in decision making*. As you can see, these metrics are still more qualitative than quantitative. Other service quality dimensions are more easily operationalized. Timeliness could be operationalized as the hours of operation, and time as the total time for a transaction to be completed. These metrics can be objectively measured.

Another issue that must be addressed when operationalizing the dimensions of quality is the relative importance of each dimension. For example, performance might be twice as important as aesthetics for some products, or assurance might be more important than empathy for some services. The weighting of the dimensions should reflect the input obtained from customers about the relative importance of each dimension.

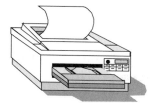

Consider the case of a laser printer for use with a personal computer. Garvin's eight dimensions of product quality might be operationalized as follows.

Performance:

Pages per minute

Print density

Features:

Multiple paper trays

Color capability

Reliability:

Mean time between failures (MTBF)

Conformance:

UL rated

Crispness of print relative to competitors

Durability:

Estimated time to obsolescence

Expected life of major components

Serviceability:

Availability of authorized repair centers

Number of copies per print cartridge

Aesthetics:

Control button layout

Case style

Perceived Quality:

Brand name recognition

Rating in *Consumer Reports*

Rating in *Byte* magazine

The relative importance of each dimension could be established by assigning each dimension a weight between 0 and 1 with the total weights = 1 as in Table 2.3. The assignment of weights should be based on customer input.

Each printer to be evaluated would be tested using the measures or metrics established for each dimension. Based on the test results, a metric score between 0 and 10 could be assigned, where 10 indicates perfection and 0 indicates total absence of that metric. The dimension score is a composite of the individual metric scores that measure the dimension. One approach to developing a dimension score for serviceability is shown in Figure 2.4.

Dimension scores for two different brands of printer are shown in Table 2.4.

**TABLE 2.3.  Dimensions and Weights**

| Dimension | Weight |
|---|---|
| Performance | 0.30 |
| Features | 0.05 |
| Reliability | 0.15 |
| Conformance | 0.10 |
| Durability | 0.15 |
| Serviceability | 0.10 |
| Aesthetics | 0.05 |
| Perceived Quality | 0.10 |
| **Total** | **1.00** |

| Dimension | Measure | Metric | Raw Value of Metric | Metric Score |
|---|---|---|---|---|
| Serviceability | Availability of repair centers (RC) | No. of RC within 50 mi. | 2 | 7 |
| | Life of cartridge | Rated no. of copies/cart. | 2,000 | 5 |

Dimension Score $= \dfrac{7+5}{2} = 6$ (assumes equal importance for metrics)

**Figure 2.4.**  Compositing Metrics into a Raw Dimension Score

**TABLE 2.4.  Raw Scores**

| Dimension | Weight | Brand X Score | Brand Y Score |
|---|---|---|---|
| Performance | 0.30 | 8 | 7 |
| Features | 0.05 | 6 | 2 |
| Reliability | 0.15 | 5 | 6 |
| Conformance | 0.10 | 8 | 7 |
| Durability | 0.15 | 9 | 8 |
| Serviceability | 0.10 | 6 | 9 |
| Aesthetics | 0.05 | 7 | 9 |
| Perceived Quality | 0.10 | 9 | 6 |
| **Total** | **100.00** | | |

**TABLE 2.5. Weighted Scores**

| Dimension | Weight | Brand X | | Brand Y | |
|---|---|---|---|---|---|
| | | Raw Score | Wtd. Score | Raw Score | Wtd. Score |
| Performance | 0.30 | 8 | 2.40 | 7 | 2.10 |
| Features | 0.05 | 6 | 0.30 | 2 | 0.10 |
| Reliability | 0.15 | 5 | 0.75 | 6 | 0.90 |
| Conformance | 0.10 | 8 | 0.80 | 7 | 0.70 |
| Durability | 0.15 | 9 | 1.35 | 8 | 1.20 |
| Serviceability | 0.10 | 6 | 0.60 | 9 | 0.90 |
| Aesthetics | 0.05 | 7 | 0.35 | 9 | 0.45 |
| Perceived Quality | 0.10 | 9 | 0.90 | 6 | 0.65 |
| **Total** | **100.00** | | **7.45** | | **6.95** |

Weight x Raw Score = Weighted Score

0.10  x 9          = 0.90

Multiplying the dimension score by the dimension weight yields a weighted dimension score. Summing these weighted scores over the eight dimensions yields an overall relative quality rating for each copier. This process can be easily done using a spreadsheet such as Excel™.

As Table 2.5 shows, in this case, Brand X is determined to be superior overall to Brand Y as Brand X's total weighted score is higher than Brand Y's.

The above analysis approach is an application of matrix diagrams that will be discussed more fully in Chapter 3.

## METHODS OF OBTAINING INPUT FROM CUSTOMERS

In Chapter 1 we discussed quality as a multidimensional construct, the dimensions of which must be uniquely established for each category of product or service being evaluated. What is the source of the dimensions? The answer is customers—both external and internal.

There are a number of approaches to obtaining input from customers. Each has its strengths and weaknesses, and the quality of the information obtained from each is subject to the skill with which the assessment methodology is applied. For this reason, the assistance of someone skilled in the art and science of the particular methodology is essential to obtaining beneficial information. Larger organizations often have such experts on staff, and there are many consultants who provide services in this area.

Two concerns that must be addressed in collecting input from customers are validity and reliability. Validity is the degree to which the method used to collect the data actually measures what it is intended to measure. Reliability is the consistency of the method. Discussion of how to measure validity and reliability are beyond the scope of this book. The reader is directed to Sower, Duffy, Kilbourne, Kohers, &

Jones (2001) in the reference section of this chapter for an example of how to assess the validity and reliability of a questionnaire. There are many instances of methods with unknown validity and reliability being used to collect data to guide the strategic planning and decision-making processes. The result can be GIGO—garbage in; garbage out. Decisions made using invalid or unreliable data are suspect at best and often may be detrimental.

Among the approaches to identifying key quality characteristics that are important to customers and turning them into dimensions, measures, and weights are focus groups and surveys.

## Focus Groups

A focus group is an unstructured interview conducted by a trained moderator in a relaxed, informal atmosphere with a small homogeneous group of respondents (Malhorta, 1993). Focus groups provide much richer information from customers than surveys, but analysis of the data obtained can be more challenging than with surveys because the information from focus groups is qualitative while the information from surveys is generally quantitative.

Focus groups are typically recorded on video or audio recordings. The skill of the moderator is vital in ensuring that the discussion remains open and lively, on-topic, and free of any implicit or explicit coercion. Focus questions are designed to address the objectives of the focus group. These questions are presented by the moderator to the group for discussion. The moderator may take notes during the discussion.

The recordings of the focus groups are usually subjected to content analysis by multiple, independent analysts. Content analysis is a qualitative technique for making replicable and valid inferences from focus group interviews (Krippendorff, 2004). Full use is made not only of what the focus group participants say, but also what they do not say, as well as their expressions and body language. The independent analyses are examined in total to determine areas of agreement and disagreement. The areas of disagreement are resolved by repeated viewing of the video recordings and discussion of the results. This process minimizes the potential for bias that could result from the use of a single analyst.

The content analysis of a focus group designed to determine the key quality characteristics important to consumers can often incorporate the use of affinity diagrams. Affinity diagrams, which will be discussed more fully in Chapter 3, are designed to help organize ideas and facts relating to a broad concept into categories. As the analysts view the video tapes of the focus groups, they may use affinity diagrams to categorize the comments, expressions, and body language into categories (see Example 2.1). These categories may be predetermined (e.g., Garvin's 8 dimensions of product quality) or they may emerge from the focus group data during the content analysis. The goal of this process is to identify those characteristics that are important to the customer in determining the quality of a product or service. From these characteristics come measures for assessing customer satisfaction.

## EXAMPLE 2.1

A local restaurant manager, with the assistance of an experienced focus group moderator, conducted a series of focus groups with potential customers in the service area to determine what a customer considers when judging the quality of a restaurant. Three experienced analysts conducted content analysis of the video tapes from the focus groups and identified the following key quality characteristics:

- Food temperature
- Server efficiency
- Food presentation
- Décor
- Cleanliness
- Courtesy
- Value
- Food taste
- Ability to substitute
- Affordability
- Ambiance
- Availability of children's menu

Using an affinity diagram, the key quality characteristics (KQC) were grouped into dimensions:

| Food | Service | Facilities | Cost |
|------|---------|------------|------|
| Temperature | Efficiency | Décor | Value |
| Presentation | Courtesy | Cleanliness | Affordability |
| Taste | Ability to substitute | Ambiance | Children's menu |

Measures and metrics were developed to assess each KQC. For example, the owner established minimum and maximum temperatures for hot foods and established a policy for how quickly the prepared food is delivered to the customer. Efficiency and courtesy were periodically assessed using surveys of recent customers. The aggregate dimension scores for each of the four dimensions were used as measures of how effectively the restaurant was meeting the quality expectations of its customers.

## Surveys

The survey methodology is a form of descriptive research that uses "questionnaires given to a sample of a population and are designed to elicit specific information from respondents" (Malhorta, 1993). The questionnaires are typically structured, meaning that the questions are presented in a prearranged order and require respondents to select from a predetermined set of responses. Among the concerns when using questionnaires are question design, question presentation order, response scale, nonresponse bias, and data analysis. The assistance of someone skilled in the art and science of questionnaire design, administration, and analysis is essential to obtaining useful information.

Surveys may be conducted in a variety of ways: mail, telephone, e-mail, and, increasingly common, Web-based. Regardless of the way in which they are conducted, surveys can be a relatively inexpensive way to obtain data in a relatively easy to analyze format. But survey methodology is not simple. There are a number of issues that must be appropriately addressed for the data obtained to be useful. For this reason, individuals experienced in survey methodology should be used to conduct the surveys. Important issues to address are:

- Target population—Who comprises the subjects of interest and, equally important, who is outside the target population?
- Sampling plan—Rarely is it beneficial or necessary to survey the entire target population. Usually surveys are conducted using a random sample of the population. How will this sample be selected?
- Survey instrument—Assessing the validity and reliability of the survey instrument is vital. Validity is the degree to which the instrument measures what it purports to measure. Reliability refers to the instrument's ability to provide consistent results. Assessing validity and reliability requires training and skill.

How would you respond to the following question from a survey if you liked the product but did not intend to purchase it again?

Did you like our product and will you purchase it again?    Yes    No

Compound questions like this compromise the value of the information obtained from the survey.

- Response rate—In today's world, people are bombarded with surveys. This has resulted in customer reluctance to take the time to complete another survey. Low response rates raise the question of whether the results obtained are biased. For example, if the target population and sample consist equally of men and women, but the response rate is low and the respondents are predominantly women, there is a real question about how well the data represent the target population. This is referred to as nonresponse bias.

- Data analysis—Although some survey data might be appropriately analyzed using simple statistical techniques such as frequencies, means, medians, and standard deviations, often more complex multivariate statistical techniques are required. These techniques require the analyst to have a higher level of statistical expertise.

## Focus Groups and Surveys in Combination

Often focus groups and surveys are used in combination. Focus groups can be used to determine the key quality characteristics in the eyes of the customer. This information is used to design survey questionnaires that are then used to assess customer satisfaction with products and services. This combination approach has been successfully employed in many sectors including retail (Babakus, et al., 2004) and health care (Sower, et al., 2001), and it helps assure that the survey questions address issues that are important to customers.

Quality function deployment (QFD) is a structured approach to ensuring that information obtained from customers using focus groups and/or surveys is explicitly integrated into the design process for products and services. QFD will be discussed in Chapter 3.

## SUMMARY

For quality to be fully used as a source of competitive advantage, it must be included in the strategic management process of the organization. When it is included, what was formerly known as total quality management becomes strategic quality management. But if the strategy process stops with planning, little happens within the organization. Strategic plans must be deployed and managed for the organization to achieve the strategic objectives. In the strategic deployment phase, operational plans are formulated to address the strategic objectives and resources are allocated. In the evaluation and control phase, measures and metrics are developed to evaluate how well the organization is moving toward the achievement of its strategic goals.

Input from multiple constituencies (especially customers) is vital throughout the strategic management process. This input can be obtained in a variety of ways, including focus groups and surveys. Regardless of the approach taken, attention must be paid to the validity and reliability of the data collected. Cost of quality and the balanced scorecard can be used as comprehensive measures of the effectiveness of the deployment of the strategic quality plan.

## DISCUSSION QUESTIONS

1. Discuss the differences between a strategic goal and a strategic objective.
2. What is a SWOT analysis and how does it fit into the strategic planning process?
3. What is the difference between SQM and TQM?

4. Discuss the differences between a dimension and a metric? How are they related? How do they differ?

5. Why is it important to assign weights to dimensions? What do the weights indicate?

6. How does a weighted dimension score differ from a raw dimension score?

7. What is nonresponse bias and how might it affect the quality of the results from a survey?

8. What is the difference between the validity and reliability of a survey questionnaire?

9. How might an affinity diagram assist in content analysis?

10. Discuss the role of the moderator of a focus group.

11. Why are focus groups often video recorded?

12. Why do you think it is important to have multiple analysts independently conduct content analysis of focus group video recordings?

13. What is the difference between an emergent strategy and a deliberate strategy? What might you infer about the quality of an organization's strategic planning process if most of their strategies are emergent?

14. Would "excellent product quality" be a strength for your firm if it your actual product quality was *equivalent* to that of competing products in the same market? Why or why not?

15. Why is the deployment phase of the strategic quality management process crucial to the achievement of an organization's vision?

16. What are the roles of feedback in the strategic quality management process?

17. Compare the strategic quality management (SQM) process to Juran's quality trilogy.

## PROBLEMS

1. Based upon consumer focus group analysis, a quality engineer has decided upon three metrics to operationalize the product dimension of *performance* for a computer: processor speed, amount of RAM, and amount of dedicated video card memory. She has assigned weights of 0.40, 0.40, and 0.20, respectively, to these metrics. She has rated one model as follows on a scale of 1 to 10 (10 is best): processor speed, 9; amount of RAM, 7; amount of

dedicated video card memory, 10. Calculate the dimension score for this computer.

2. The Admissions Office at State University has decided to begin measuring student perceptions of the quality of the services their office provides. They have collected data from high school seniors who have visited State U and two other universities in the area. Students were asked to rate on a scale of 1 to 5 (5 is best) the three universities on a number of metrics comprising the SERVQUAL dimensions. The director of admissions has tabulated the data as follows:

| Dimension | Weight | State U | University X | University Y |
|---|---|---|---|---|
| Tangibles | 0.10 | 5 | 4 | 4 |
| Reliability | 0.15 | 3 | 4 | 3 |
| Responsiveness | 0.30 | 4 | 3 | 3 |
| Assurance | 0.25 | 4 | 3 | 3 |
| Empathy | 0.20 | 5 | 4 | 2 |

Calculate the weighted dimension scores. How does State U compare to its competitors?

3. A quality engineer has used Garvin's eight dimensions of product quality to evaluate three different brands of automobile. His dimension weights and raw scores are shown below. Which of the brands is best?

| Dimension | Weight | Raw Score Brand A | Raw Score Brand B | Raw Score Brand C |
|---|---|---|---|---|
| Performance | 0.25 | 8 | 10 | 6 |
| Features | 0.10 | 7 | 9 | 1 |
| Reliability | 0.15 | 5 | 4 | 9 |
| Conformance | 0.10 | 6 | 7 | 8 |
| Durability | 0.20 | 9 | 4 | 8 |
| Serviceability | 0.10 | 6 | 4 | 8 |
| Aesthetics | 0.05 | 7 | 9 | 3 |
| Perceived Quality | 0.05 | 9 | 9 | 4 |
| **Total** | **1.00** | | | |

4. The following key quality characteristics were developed from a series of focus groups. The focus object was to determine how customers judged the quality of a high-quality ballpoint pen. Use an affinity diagram to assign these KQCs into Garvin's eight dimensions of product quality.

| | | |
|---|---|---|
| Barrel finish | Hand feel | Appearance |
| Writing smoothness | Pocket clip | Ease of refill replacement |
| Resistance to breakage | Warranty | Durability of finish |
| Wide range of color refills | Cost | Available of gold finish |
| No "warm up" needed | Refill life | Absence of ink "blobs" |

5. The quality director of a hospital management group has used the KQCAH dimensions of service quality for hospitals to evaluate the quality of three hospitals in her group. Her dimension weights and raw scores are shown below. What can you conclude about the quality of the three hospitals?

| Dimension | Weight | Hospital A | Hospital B | Hospital C |
|---|---|---|---|---|
| Respect & Caring | 0.20 | 8 | 9 | 7 |
| Effectiveness & Continuity | 0.25 | 7 | 9 | 6 |
| Appropriateness | 0.10 | 5 | 5 | 8 |
| Information | 0.15 | 8 | 7 | 6 |
| Efficiency | 0.15 | 9 | 7 | 8 |
| Meals | 0.05 | 6 | 4 | 8 |
| First Impression | 0.05 | 7 | 9 | 3 |
| Staff Diversity | 0.05 | 9 | 9 | 4 |
| **Total** | **1.00** | | | |

6. The quality director of County Hospital has conducted a series of focus groups with former patients to determine the key quality characteristics (KQC) for patient satisfaction with her hospital. Use an affinity diagram to assign these KQCs to the KQCAH eight dimensions of hospital service quality.

| | | |
|---|---|---|
| Reassurance from staff | Protection of privacy | Appearance of hospital |
| Information provided at discharge | They effectively treated my condition | Availability of advanced imaging services |
| Quiet | Grab bars in bathroom | Information from doctors |
| Staff listened to me | Meal quality | Check-in procedures |
| Pain control | Respect for family | Availability of nurse |

## Case Study 2.1: *Second National Bank*

©2004 Victor E. Sower, Ph.D., C.Q.E.

The management staff of Second National Bank is holding their third annual strategic planning retreat at the Water's Edge Country Club. Because of your low handicap, you have been invited to fill out the second foursome for the afternoon golf match. As a recent graduate, you look forward to the opportunity to listen to the discussions in the morning planning meeting.

"I'm disappointed that more progress has not been made," begins President and CEO Richard Miller. "At last year's strategic planning retreat we developed an extensive strategic plan. But today, I don't see that we are much different than we were before we developed the plan."

"What were some of the things we included in the plan?" asks VP Sharon Rock. "I remember our meeting and I'm sure that I got a copy of the plan, but I don't remember any of the specifics. Let me call my secretary and have her bring my copy here. I think it is on my bookcase. This won't take more than 15 minutes. Can we defer our discussion of the strategic plan until then?"

"Let's take our mid-morning break now to give your secretary time to get here with the plan. Does anyone else need her to bring your copies?" Several hands go up, a list is made, and everyone moves to the break area for coffee and donuts.

After the break, when everyone has their copies of last year's strategic plan, Miller begins a point-by-point review of the plan. "We agreed last year that we were going to be known as the friendliest bank in our area. What have we done about that?" After an embarrassing pause, Bob Wilson, the VP of operations begins, "Well, right after that meeting, I met with our tellers and clerks and reminded them to smile more when dealing with our customers." "Remember, we added the slogan 'Exxor County's Friendliest Bank' to our weekly advertisement in the county newspaper," adds Stone. "Yes, but how effective have these actions been? Are we friendlier now than last year?" Miller was frustrated that no one could provide any definitive evidence one way or the other.

The review continued item by item in much the same way. Then the meeting turned to creating the strategic plan for this year. After much discussion, it is agreed that, with a few minor modifications, last year's plan will work well for this year. With that business out of the way, it is time for lunch and golf.

1. What do you think of the idea of having an annual off-site retreat for top management to develop the strategic plan for the organization?

2. Critique the planning process for the Second National Bank.

3. CEO Miller is obviously disappointed in the progress that the bank has made during the past year. If you were invited to play golf in his foursome and he asked your opinion, what would you say to him?

## EXERCISES AND ACTIVITIES

1. Operationalize Garvin's eight dimensions of product quality for the three pens you purchased for Exercise 1 in Chapter 1. Prepare a brief report showing how you operationalized each dimension, the weighted score for each pen for each dimension, and the overall weighted score for each pen. Determine which is the highest-quality pen. Discuss how this process differs from the one you used when you first rated the pens. Did you select the same pen as being the best in both exercises?

2. Select a service operation with which you are familiar. Examples could include ordering a meal in a restaurant, getting a haircut or manicure, or renewing a drivers' license. Operationalize the SERVQUAL dimensions from Chapter 1 for the service you select. Use the metrics you develop to rate the quality of the service at your next opportunity.

3. Think about the fast food industry. It generally is classified as a service operation, but produces tangible products (hamburgers, fries, etc.). The concept of "the hamburger experience" encompasses both the product and service aspects of the business. Apply the SERVQUAL dimensions to the service aspect and Garvin's eight dimensions of product quality to the product aspect of the burger experience. Operationalize these dimensions for the hamburger experience.

    (Critical issue: do all dimensions apply in this case?)

    Order the same combination of comparable products (e.g., basic burger, small fries, and small soft drink) in the same way (e.g., drive-through) at about the same time of day (e.g., peak load or off peak load) from three different fast food restaurants. Determine which restaurant provides the best hamburger experience.

4. Obtain mission and vision statements of several business organizations. These are often published in annual reports or promotional materials used by the organization. Examine these mission and vision statements for evidence that quality is fully integrated into the way these organizations conduct their business.

5. Work with the local Small Business Development Center or Chamber of Commerce to locate a small business in need of assistance in developing a strategic plan. As a class project, assist the business in determining what is important to its customers. In conjunction with your instructor, determine the appropriate methodology to use to collect data and appropriate ways to analyze the data. Prepare a report for the business and a separate report for the instructor analyzing what you learned from the project.

# SUPPLEMENTARY READINGS

Garvin, D. (1987). "Competing on the Eight Dimensions of Quality." *Harvard Business Review* 65: 6, 101–109. Reprinted in Sower, V., J. Motwani, & M. Savoie. (1995). *Classic Readings in Operations Management*, Ft. Worth, TX: Dryden, 323–339.

Huberman, A., & M. Miles. (1994). "Data Management and Analysis Methods." In *Handbook of Qualitative Research*, edited by N. Denizin & Y. Lincoln. Thousand Oaks, CA: Sage.

Kaplan, R., & D. Norton. (1992). "The Balanced Scorecard: Measures that Drive Performance." *Harvard Business Review* 74(1), 71–79.

Miles, M., & A. Huberman. (1998). *Qualitative Data Analysis: An Expanded Sourcebook*, 2nd ed. Newbury Park, CA: Sage.

Parasuraman, A., V. Zeithaml, & L. Berry. (1988). "SERVQUAL: A Multiple-Item Scale for Measuring Consumer Perceptions of Service Quality." *Journal of Retailing* 61(1), 12–40.

Pryor, M., J. White, & L. Toombs. (1998). *Strategic Quality Management*. Houston, TX: Dame.

Sower, V., J. Duffy, & G. Kohers. (2008). *Benchmarking for Hospitals: Achieving Best-in-Class Performance Without Having to Reinvent the Wheel*. Milwaukee, WI: ASQ Quality Press.

# REFERENCES

Babakus, E., C. Bienstock, & J. Van Scotter. (2004). "Linking Perceived Quality and Customer Satisfaction to Store Traffic and Revenue Growth." *Decision Sciences* 35(4), 713–737.

Bronson Methodist Hospital. (2005). *2005 Malcolm Baldrige National Quality Award Application Summary*.

Crosby, P. (1979). *Quality is Free*. New York: McGraw-Hill.

Garvin, D. (1988). *Managing Quality, The Strategic and Competitive Edge*. New York: The Free Press.

Garvin, D. (1987). "Competing on the Eight Dimensions of Quality." *Harvard Business Review* 65(6), 101–109. Reprinted in Sower, V., J. Motwani, & M. Savoie. (1995). *Classic Readings in Operations Management*, Ft. Worth, TX: Dryden, 323–339.

Juran, J. (1988). *Juran on Planning for Quality*. New York: The Free Press, 176–179.

Kaplan, R., & D. Norton. (1992). "The Balanced Scorecard: Measures that Drive Performance." *Harvard Business Review* 74(1), 71–79.

Krippendorff, K. (2004). *Content Analysis: An Introduction to Its Methodology*. Thousand Oaks, CA: Sage.

Madu, C., & C. Kuei. (1993). "Introducing Strategic Quality Management." *Long Range Planning* 26(6), 121–131.

Malhortra, N. (1993). *Marketing Research*. Englewood Cliffs, CA: Prentice Hall, 188.

Melnyk, S., & R. Christensen. (2002). "Deconstructing the Metric." *APICS—The Performance Advantage* 12(9), 20.

Mintzberg, H., J. Lampel, J. Quinn, & S. Ghoshal. (2003). *The Strategy Process*. Upper Saddle River, NJ: Prentice Hall.

Porter, M. (1980). *Corporate Strategy*. Boston: The Free Press.

Sower, V., J. Duffy, W. Kilbourne, G. Kohers, & P. Jones. (2001). "The Dimensions of Service Quality for Hospitals: Development of the KQCAH Scale." *Health Care Management Review* 26(2), 47–59.

# SECTION II

# QUALITY OF DESIGN

## CHAPTER THREE

# Designing Quality into Products and Services

## CHAPTER OBJECTIVES

After completing this chapter, the reader should be able to:

- use the management tools to organize and communicate information;
- discuss Quality Function Deployment (QFD) and its role in product and service design;
- discuss Design for Six Sigma (DFSS);
- discuss Taguchi robustness concepts;
- calculate reliability for a system;
- discuss ways in which system reliability can be improved; and
- use the risk assessment tools of fault tree analysis (FTA) and failure mode and effects analysis (FMEA).

In this chapter we will address quality of design for products and services. Quality of design is not only necessary to achieve customer satisfaction, it is also important for safety and liability reasons. Poorly designed products and services can result in actionable losses, including injury and death. In order to ensure customer safety and minimize the organization's exposure to potentially costly liability lawsuits, products and services must be well designed and highly reliable.

As has been discussed in the previous chapters, products and services must be designed to satisfy and delight customers. Therefore product and service design must begin with input from the customer. In Chapter 2 we discussed ways to obtain that input. In this chapter we will discuss ways to incorporate that input into the design process. The seven management tools and quality function deployment (QFD) are two approaches to incorporating customer wants and needs into the design process.

Design for Six Sigma (DSS) and Taguchi's robustness concepts are frequently applied to the process of product and service design. These approaches address cost, reliability, and quality of products and services.

Reliability is a key issue when designing products. Reliability and safety are often linked. In this chapter we will discuss how to measure and improve reliability and how to identify root causes of potential product and service failures through fault tree analysis (FTA) and failure mode and effect analysis (FMEA).

## THE SEVEN MANAGEMENT TOOLS

The seven management tools are designed to assist in the organization and communication of information. They are particularly useful in the analysis of qualitative information to make it more useful in management planning. They can be useful in taking raw, largely qualitative, data and converting it to information that management can use in the design and redesign of products and services. The tools are:

Affinity Diagram

Tree Diagram

Process Decision Program Chart (PDPC)

Matrix Diagram

Interrelationship Digraph

Prioritization Matrix

Activity Network Diagram

*Affinity diagrams* are similar in function to cause-and-effect diagrams in that they are designed to help in the organization of ideas and facts relating to a broad concept into categories. Ideas that have affinities for each other are placed under the same category. For example, ideas generated in a brainstorming session or a focus group provide more information for planning purposes when they are organized into categories using an affinity diagram.

Figure 3.1 shows an affinity diagram developed by the owner of a pizza delivery service who was brainstorming ways that he could differentiate his pizza and delivery service from the competition.

*Tree diagrams* allow managers to plan the actions necessary to implement the ideas and objectives shown on the affinity diagram. Figure 3.2 shows a partial tree diagram for Roger's Pizza.

| Product | Service | Cost | Features |
|---------|---------|------|----------|
| Extra Value<br>Variety<br>Delivered Hot | 30 Min. Max. Wait<br>Friendly Drivers<br>Courteous Order Takers | Low Price<br>No Delivery Charge | More Topping<br>More Crust Variety<br>Coupons with Order |

**Figure 3.1.** Affinity Diagram for Roger's Take-Out Pizza

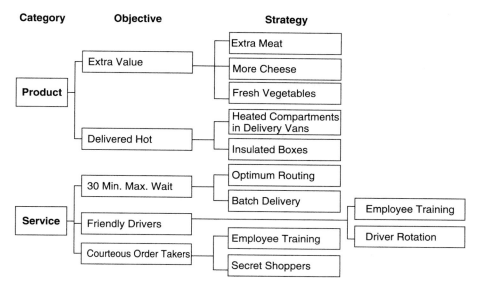

**Figure 3.2.** Partial Tree Diagram for Roger's Take-Out Pizza

A proactive approach to planning considers the possibility that plans will not work out as expected. The *process decision program chart (PDPC)* provides a framework for developing contingency plans for preventing the unexpected or dealing with it if it does occur. The PDPC begins with the tree diagram. Possible negative outcomes are considered for each branch of the tree diagram and contingency plans are listed for each as shown in Figure 3.3.

*Matrix diagrams* enable planners to graphically depict relationships between concepts. Figure 3.4 depicts a portion of a matrix diagram for Roger's Pizza. It shows the relationship between the desired objectives and possible actions that could be taken. The strength of the relationship is indicated by the shading of the dot. An

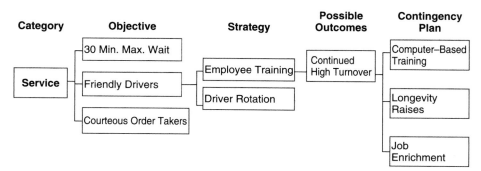

**Figure 3.3.** Partial Process Decision Program Chart for Roger's Take-Out Pizza

| Action / Objective | Improved Employee Training | Improved Kitchen Process | Improved Delivery Process | Improved Controls |
|---|---|---|---|---|
| 30 Min. Max. Wait | ● | ● | ● | ◉ |
| Friendly Drivers | ● | ○ | ◉ | ● |
| Courteous Order Takers | ● | | | ● |

**Key:**  ● Strong relationship
◉ Moderate relationship
○ Weak relationship

**Figure 3.4.** Partial Matrix Program Chart for Roger's Take-Out Pizza

objective not having a relationship with at least one action indicates that the action plan is incomplete.

The *interrelationship digraph* graphically depicts causal relationships among the categories from an affinity diagram. Figure 3.5 depicts the interrelationship digraph produced from the affinity diagram in Figure 3.1. Arrows indicate which categories affect which other categories, that is, which factors are drivers of other categories. From this digraph it is evident that *features* has the greatest effect on the factors that Roger's Take-Out Pizza believes are most important to differentiating themselves from the competition. *Features* has the most out-facing arrows. It is a driver of *cost, product*, and *service*—that is, any change in *features* will impact all the other categories. No other category drives as many other categories. As a result of this analysis, Roger's may decide to focus first on *features*.

The *prioritization matrix* allows the comparison of both quantitative and qualitative data in the same analysis. Figure 3.6 shows how a prioritization matrix is used to compare Roger's Take-Out Pizza to its leading competitor, X-O's Pizza. The dimensions used in the comparison are the categories from the affinity diagram (Figure 3.1). In developing the matrix, and prior to rating the two companies, Roger's decided on an importance weight for each category. These weights must add up to 1.0. The higher the weight, the more important is the category. Then each company is rated on each category using a scale of 1–10 (with 10 being the best). Roger's higher total weighted score indicates that overall, Roger's provides a better "pizza experience" than X-O's, the leading competitor. The positive difference weighted

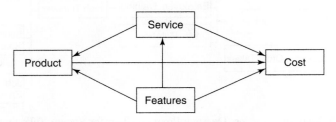

**Figure 3.5.** Interrelationship Digraph for Roger's Take-Out Pizza

| Category | Weight | Roger's Raw Score | Roger's Wtd. Score | X-O's Raw Score | X-O's Wtd. Score | Difference Wtd. Score |
|---|---|---|---|---|---|---|
| Product | 0.30 | 7 | 2.10 | 8 | 2.40 | +0.30 |
| Service | 0.25 | 6 | 1.50 | 7 | 1.75 | +0.25 |
| Cost | 0.25 | 8 | 2.00 | 6 | 1.50 | −0.50 |
| Features | 0.20 | 9 | 1.80 | 7 | 1.40 | −0.40 |
| **Total** | **1.00** | | 7.40 | | 7.05 | −0.35 |

**Figure 3.6.** Prioritization Matrix for Roger's Take-Out Pizza

scores for product and service indicate categories where X-O's has a competitive advantage and thus might be fruitful areas for Roger's to examine for improvement.

The seventh management tool is the *activity network diagram*, which is also known as PERT (program evaluation and review technique) or CPM (critical path method). Figure 3.7 is the activity network diagram for the evaluation of installing heated compartments on Roger's Take-Out Pizza's delivery vans.

The activity network diagram is both a project-planning and a project-control tool. As a project-planning tool, it requires that the entire project be broken down into its component activities, that the duration of each activity be forecast, and that the precedence relationship among the activities be defined. The estimated project duration can be determined by the length of the longest path through the network. This is called the critical path because a delay in any activity on this path will delay the entire project.

The estimated project duration for the evaluation of a prototype installation of a heated compartment on a Roger's Pizza delivery van is 15 weeks—the length of the longest path (1–2–3–5–6–7) in the diagram. Any delays in the completion of the activities on this path will delay the project. Because the length of the noncritical path is 12 weeks, a delay of up to three weeks in the 2–4 or 4–5 activities can be tolerated without delaying completion of the project.

## QUALITY FUNCTION DEPLOYMENT

Quality function deployment (QFD) was developed in Japan by Professor Yoji Akao. QFD is defined as "a structured method in which customer requirements

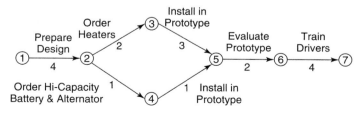

**Figure 3.7.** Activity Network for Evaluation of Heated Compartments in Delivery Vans of Roger's Take-Out Pizza

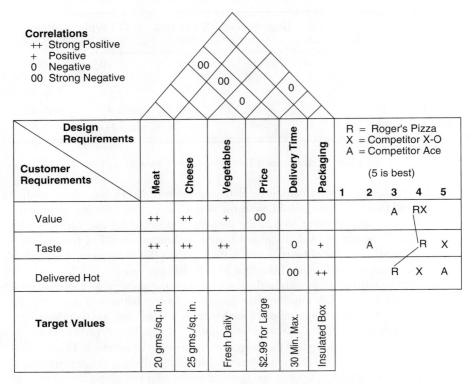

**Figure 3.8.** House of Quality for Roger's Pizza

are translated into appropriate technical requirements for each stage of product development and production. The QFD process is often referred to as listening to the voice of the customer" (Quality Glossary, 2002). A basic premise of QFD is that quality is defined by the customer. Information about what is important to the customer can be lost in transit from the marketing department, which usually gathers that information from the customer, to the product/service design team. QFD is a systematic way to ensure that the customer's definition of quality is considered during the product/service design process (the first QFD matrix is referred to as the house of quality) and throughout the production process (the subsequent QFD matrices).

QFD is a series of matrices as shown in Figure 3.8 that begins in the "west wing" of the first stage house of quality with customer requirements. The "second floor" of the house of quality is a translation of the customer requirements into design requirements. The "main floor" of the house is a matrix showing the correlation of the design requirements with the customer requirements. Each customer requirement should have a correlated design requirement. The "attic" is a matrix that shows the interrelationship of the design requirements. This matrix is useful in analyzing trade-offs among the design requirements. The "basement" contains the target values

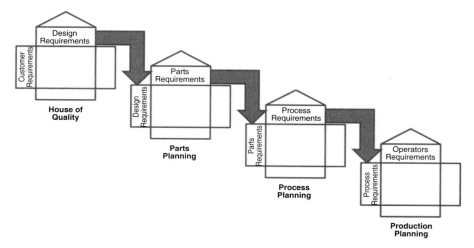

**Figure 3.9.** Four-Phase QFD Model

or specifications for the design requirements. The "east wing" shows a comparison of the product or service under design with its leading competitors.

Although the house of quality can be used as a stand-alone tool for product/service design, approaches have been developed to use it in conjunction with additional matrices. One of these approaches is the four-phase model (Hauser & Clausing, 1988). The model is illustrated in Figure 3.9. It uses a series of stages to translate customer requirements into parts characteristics, key process operations, and finally production equipment settings.

## DESIGN FOR SIX SIGMA

Design for Six Sigma (DFSS) was developed at General Electric in 1997 as an extension of the standard Six Sigma methodology (Snee & Hoerl, 2003). DFSS is defined as "a data driven quality strategy for designing products and processes (that) is an integral part of a Six Sigma quality initiative." It is an enhancement tool for new product development, not a replacement for current design processes (Mader, 2003). DFSS may be characterized as being proactive because it seeks to design products and processes capable of meeting the Six Sigma goal of fewer than 3.4 defects per million opportunities (DPMO). Six Sigma, on the other hand, may be characterized as being reactive in the sense that it seeks to improve existing processes by finding and fixing existing problems.

There is no standard approach to DFSS (Mader, 2003). As developed by General Electric, DFSS consists of five interconnected phases: define, measure, analyze, design, and verify (DMADV) (Quality Glossary, 2002), which build on the standard Six Sigma DMAIC process. DMADV seeks to create product/service designs that are robust, resource efficient, capable of reaching very high yields, and are highly linked to customer demands by focusing on critical-to-quality (CTQ) characteristics (Harry & Schroeder, 2000).

---

Critical-to-quality (CTQ) characteristics "are the items essential for customer satisfaction in a product or service."

(Breyfogle, et al., 2001, 95)

---

## TAGUCHI ROBUSTNESS CONCEPTS

Taguchi advocated designing products and systems that are robust. Robustness is defined as "the condition of a product or process design that remains relatively stable, with a minimum of variation, even though factors that influence operations or usage, such as environment and wear, are constantly changing" (Quality Glossary, 2002). Taguchi referred to these factors as "noise." Within a broader range of activities designed to improve company-wide quality and productivity, Taguchi advocated three steps to achieve robustness that start in product design and continue through production engineering and production operation (Taguchi, Elsayed, & Hsiang, 1989). These steps are:

1. System Design—This step includes development of a prototype design, selection of materials, parts, components, and production system that results in minimum deviation from target performance values.

2. Parameter Design—This step involves determining "the optimal levels for the parameters of each element in the system so that the functional deviations of the product are minimized" (Taguchi, Elsayed, & Hsiang, 1989). Designed experiments are often used in this step.

3. Tolerance Design—This step involves determining the quality loss and cost tradeoffs associated with each parameter. It is designed to "minimize the product cost for a given tolerable deviation from target values" (Taguchi, Elsayed, & Hsiang, 1989).

The result of taking this approach to product design is a more reliable product that can be produced economically.

## RELIABILITY

Increasing the reliability of a product or service is a key part of the design process. Reliability is defined as "the probability of a product performing without failure a specified function under given conditions for a specified period of time"

**TABLE 3.1. Dimensions of Reliability**

1. As a Probability:
   - frequency of successful uses out of certain number of attempts,
   - likelihood of an item lasting a given amount of time.
2. Definition of Failure:
   - a situation in which an item does not perform as intended.
3. Prescribed Operating Conditions:
   - how the product should be used,
   - "normal operating conditions".

(Quality Glossary, 2002). Note that in this definition, probability is used to quantify reliability.

There are three dimensions of reliability: as a probability, as a definition of failure, and as prescribed operating conditions (Stevenson, 2005). These three dimensions are shown in Table 3.1.

*Reliability as a probability* can be defined in two ways. The first is the probability that a system will perform on a given trial. Another way to state this is the frequency of successful performances of a system in a given number of attempts. An example of this definition would be the probability that a fire extinguisher would perform on a given attempt to use it. This probability could be determined through repeated trials to determine the frequency of successful uses as a percentage of attempts.

The second definition of probability as a reliability is the probability that an item will last for a given length of time in use. This can be illustrated by the example of a light bulb. Most bulbs are rated for a given life. This can be determined by life testing to failure a large number of bulbs and determining the average useful life. These data can be used to determine the probability the light bulb will last for a specified number of hours.

*Definition of a failure* may seem to be straightforward. In the case of the light bulb, it is—the bulb fails when it no longer produces light. This definition, however, is not so clear in other systems. Consider an automobile tire. Short of catastrophic failure (e.g., blowout), at what point is the tread considered to be depleted—that is, at what point is the tire considered to have failed or used up its useful life?

*Prescribed operating conditions* must be specified. Only light bulbs specially designed for outdoor use can achieve equivalent useful lives exposed to the weather as indoor bulbs in a more sheltered operating environment. Therefore, when discussing reliability of a system, the standard operating conditions for which the system was designed must be specified.

## Types of Reliability Systems

A serial system is one which consists of multiple parts or subassemblies, each of which must function in order for the system to function. System reliability is usually defined

## Putting it All Together

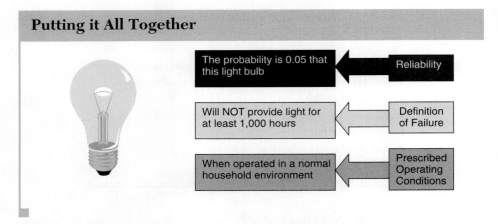

as the product of the individual reliabilities of the n parts or subsystems within a system.

$$P_s = P_1 \times P_2 \times P_3 \times \ldots \times P_n \qquad (3.1)$$

$P_s$ is the probability of the system working when called upon, and $P_n$ is the probability of component n working when called upon.

---

### EXAMPLE 3.1a

A manufacturing system consists of 1 subsystem with the following reliability:

$$P_1 = 0.970 \qquad \boxed{P_1}$$

What is the overall reliability of the system?

As the system has only one subsystem or component, the reliability of the subsystem is the reliability of the system = 0.970. This means that the probability of the system performing when called upon is 0.970.

### EXAMPLE 3.1b

A manufacturing system consists of four subsystems with the following reliabilities:

$P_1 = 0.970$
$P_2 = 0.997$
$P_3 = 0.985$
$P_4 = 0.990$

$$\boxed{P_1} - \boxed{P_2} - \boxed{P_3} - \boxed{P_4}$$

What is the overall reliability of the system?

Recognizing that system reliability is the product of the individual reliabilities of the subsystems, we use Equation 3.1 as follows:

$$P_s = P_1 \times P_2 \times P_3 \times P_4$$
$$P_s = 0.970 \times 0.997 \times 0.985 \times 0.990$$
$$P_s = 0.943$$

Although the assumption of system reliability equaling the product of the reliabilities of the subsystems is only true for serial systems, the formula serves two basic purposes. First, it highlights the effect of increased serial system complexity on overall system reliability. As the number of parts or subsystems increases in a serial system, system reliability decreases dramatically. Second, the formula is often a convenient approximation that can be refined as information becomes available on the interrelationships of parts.

Note that in Example 3.1b the reliability of the system is much lower than the reliabilities of individual components. This is because the components are in *series*, thus requiring that all components work if the system is to work. One way to increase the reliability of serial systems is to increase the reliability of each component.

## EXAMPLE 3.2

As the number of components increases, the reliability of the system decreases, all other things being equal. For critical systems, cost is of little concern when it comes to selecting the most reliable components. Consider a military jet consisting of 1,000,000 critical components. The manufacturer spares no expense to procure components that are 0.999999 reliable (that is, one failure in one million opportunities). What is the reliability of the jet manufactured using these components?

Using Equation 3.1, the reliability of the jet may be calculated as:

0.999999 × 0.999999 × 0.999999 × . . . one million times.

This may also be calculated as:

$$0.999999^{1,000,000} = 0.368$$

Who would want to go into combat with a jet that will fail almost two thirds of the time?

As Example 3.2 shows, for systems with many components, each of which must function in order for the system to function, there is a limit to how much system reliability can be increased by increasing component reliability alone. To further increase the reliability of the system, we can use *redundancy*. "Redundancy is the existence of more than one element for accomplishing a given task, where all elements must fail before there is an overall failure to the system" (Juran & Gryna, 1980). Parallel redundancy means that we add additional backup components or an additional backup system to the existing system. The extra components or system increase the overall reliability because if the primary system or component fails, the backup or redundant component or system can take over and the overall system will not fail. Redundancy, in addition to the use of extremely reliable components, is the key to making the jet fighter in Example 3.2 sufficiently reliable for use.

When parallel redundancy is used, the overall reliability of a component system consisting of one main component and a backup component is calculated using the following equation:

$$P_C = P_m + P_b(1 - P_m) \tag{3.2}$$

where

$$P_c = \text{reliability of the component system}$$
$$P_m = \text{reliability of the main component}$$
$$P_b = \text{reliability of the backup component}$$
$$(1 - P_m) = \text{probability that main component will fail}$$

---

**EXAMPLE 3.3**

Management desires to increase the overall reliability of the system in Example 3.1b.

**a.** Add a parallel *backup component* to each main component of the system with the backup having the same reliability as the *main component*. What does that do to the overall reliability of the system?

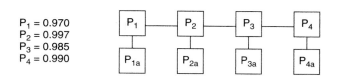

$$P_1 = 0.970$$
$$P_2 = 0.997$$
$$P_3 = 0.985$$
$$P_4 = 0.990$$

Use Equation 3.2 for each component $P_c = P_m + P_b(1 - P_m)$

$$P_{system} = [0.970 + 0.970(1 - 0.970)] \times [0.997 + 0.997(1 - 0.997)]$$
$$\times [0.985 + 0.985(1 - 0.985)] \times [0.990 + 0.990(1 - 0.990)]$$

$$P_{system} = 0.9991 \times 0.9999 \times 0.9998 \times 0.9999 = 0.9987$$

**b.** Add an identical *parallel system* to the *existing system*. What does that do to the overall reliability of the system?

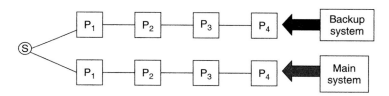

$$P_{existing\ system} = P_1 \times P_2 \times P_3 \times P_4$$
$$P_s = 0.970 \times 0.997 \times 0.985 \times 0.990 = 0.943$$
$$P_{backup\ system} = P_1 \times P_2 \times P_3 \times P_4$$
$$P_b = 0.970 \times 0.997 \times 0.985 \times 0.990 = 0.943$$
$$P_{system} = P_{existing\ system} + P_{backup\ system} (1 - P_{existing\ system})$$
$$P_{system} = 0.943 + 0.943(1 - 0.943) = 0.9968$$

When redundant components are incorporated into a system, a switch must be provided to activate the backup component when the primary component fails. Note that in Example 3.3, we assumed the reliability of the switch was 1. In the real world, however, switches can and do fail to work when called upon. In such a case, the redundant component does not have an opportunity to function when the main component fails—therefore the system fails. If we assign a probability to the switch, the reliability of the component with backup component and switch is calculated as follows:

$$P_{component} = P_{main\ component} + [P_{backup\ component} \times (1 - P_{main\ component})] \times P_{switch}$$

$$(3.3)$$

---

## EXAMPLE 3.4

Using the same reliabilities in Example 3.3-b, calculate the reliability of the system with a switch reliability of 0.99 (99 percent).

$$P_{system} = P_{main\ system} + [P_{backup\ system} \times (1 - P_{main\ system})] \times P_{switch}$$
$$P_{system} = 0.943 + [0.943 \times (1 - 0.943)] \times 0.99 = 0.9962$$

---

In many cases more than one parallel backup component is used. In the case of the Apollo moon missions, there were several backups in place for critical components such as the guidance computer. The reliability of a component with multiple backups may be calculated as

$$P_{system} = 1 - [(1 - P_{primary}) \times (1 - P_{first\ backup}) \times \ldots (1 - P_{nth\ backup}) \qquad (3.4)$$

If the backup components are identical to the primary, this reduces to

$$P_{system} = 1 - (1 - P_{components})^n \qquad (3.5)$$

where n is the number of components in the system.

---

## EXAMPLE 3.5

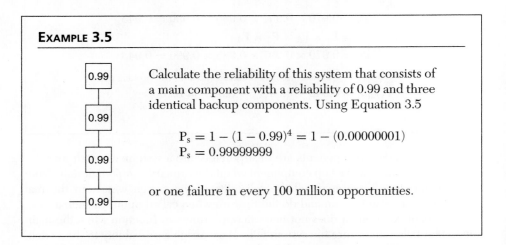

Calculate the reliability of this system that consists of a main component with a reliability of 0.99 and three identical backup components. Using Equation 3.5

$$P_s = 1 - (1 - 0.99)^4 = 1 - (0.00000001)$$
$$P_s = 0.99999999$$

or one failure in every 100 million opportunities.

---

## Reliability is Also Important in Services

"The Post Office Cancels Business With Two Airlines" blared the headline in the February 21, 2005 edition of *The New York Times*. After many months of unreliable service, the U.S. Postal Service announced it was ceasing to use American Airlines and US Airways for first-class mail delivery. Both airlines are working to improve their on-time performance. In order to win back the mail business, they must develop plans to increase reliability that are acceptable to the Post Office. In an already difficult financial environment for airlines, reliability problems that result in lost business can threaten the very existence of an airline.

## Reliability Life Characteristic Concepts (e.g., Bathtub Curve)

If we were to run a piece of equipment to failure, repair it, and repeat the process over and over again, recording the failure time for each run, we would have a set of data that would indicate the failure rate for that piece of equipment. Failure rate is defined as the number of failures per set unit of time. When we plot failure rate against time, we often see a pattern of failure known as a bathtub curve.

---

### EXAMPLE 3.6

The data in the table below were collected for a telephone switch. Plot the failure rate versus time for the switch.

| Time of Failure (weeks) | | | |
|---|---|---|---|
| 0.1 | 1.1 | 4.0 | 8.2 |
| 0.2 | 1.2 | 4.1 | 8.4 |
| 0.2 | 1.4 | 4.2 | 8.5 |
| 0.3 | 1.6 | 4.6 | 8.7 |
| 0.4 | 2.0 | 5.5 | 8.8 |
| 0.5 | 2.2 | 5.9 | 9.0 |
| 0.6 | 2.4 | 5.9 | 9.1 |
| 0.6 | 2.6 | 6.0 | 9.2 |
| 0.7 | 2.8 | 6.1 | 9.2 |
| 0.8 | 2.8 | 6.2 | 9.3 |
| 0.8 | 2.9 | 6.5 | 9.5 |
| 0.8 | 3.1 | 7.2 | 9.7 |
| 0.9 | 3.1 | 7.5 | 9.8 |
| 0.9 | 3.1 | 7.7 | 9.8 |
| 0.9 | 3.1 | 7.9 | 9.9 |
| 1.0 | 3.2 | 8.0 | 9.9 |

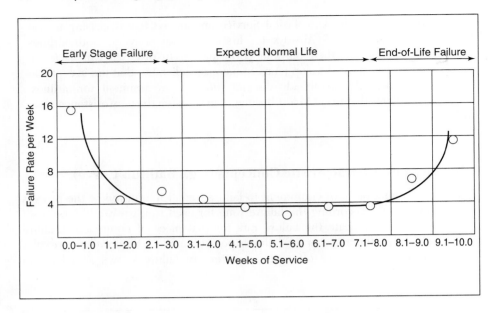

As you can see from Example 3.6, the curve that results resembles a bathtub. There are three distinct patterns in the curve:

1. *Early-Stage Failure*. This phase is characterized by high failure rates early in the life cycle of the switch. These failures are usually the result of design, manufacture, or use errors and are usually correctable given a good quality program. In order to minimize the incidence of early-stage failures, manufacturers of products such as computers incorporate a "burn-in" phase at the end of the manufacturing process. During burn-in, products are run for a specified number of hours. Only products that have successfully completed the burn-in are released for packaging and shipment to customers.

2. *Expected Normal Life of the Product*. At this stage, we see a pattern of constant and relatively low failure rate. Failures in this stage usually result from design limitations, changes in the environment, and damage caused by day-to-day use or maintenance. Training in the proper use and maintenance of the equipment can minimize accidents. To reduce the failure rate in this stage, however, would generally require a redesign of the product.

3. *End-of-Life Failure*. These are failures that occur when the product exceeds its intended normal life expectancy. Most products are designed for a set operating life. However, just as variations in manufacture cause some units to fail early, these same variations will allow some units to operate beyond their rated life expectancy. Failures at this stage are mostly the result of the daily wear and stress on equipment. Examples are metal fatigue, worn gears, and brittle or broken parts, etc. Many companies believe in running equipment *to failure*.

However, they fail to recognize the different degrees of failure. By continuing to operate equipment with worn or damaged parts, the organization runs the risk of producing an out-of-specification product as well as the danger of a catastrophic failure. Developing a preventative maintenance program will allow controlled replacement of old or worn equipment before a catastrophic failure can occur.

## Mean Time between Failures

Mean time between failures (MTBF) is defined as "the average time interval between failures for a repairable product for a defined unit of measure; for example operating hours, cycles and miles." (Quality Glossary, 2002) In analyzing failure rate data, it often turns out that the MTBF for both product and equipment can be modeled by a negative exponential distribution (see Figure 3.10). When the failure rate distribution matches the pattern in Figure 3.10, the exponential distribution can be used to determine various probabilities of interest:

> The probability of failure before some specified time, T, is equal to the area under the curve between the time the product was put into service (usually 0) and T.
>
> Reliability has been defined as the probability that a product will last at least until time T. Reliability is equal to the area under the curve beyond T.

Note that as the specified length of service increases, the area under the curve to the right of that point decreases. In other words, as the length of service increases, reliability decreases. When we perform this calculation of failure time for nonrepairable products—a light bulb, for example—we usually refer to mean time to failure (MTTF), as additional failures are not possible.

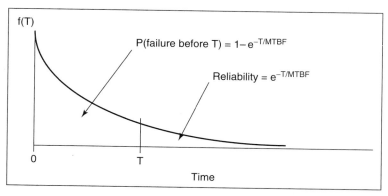

$$P(\text{failure before } T) = 1 - e^{-T/MTBF}$$

$$\text{Reliability} = e^{-T/MTBF}$$

**Figure 3.10.** Negative Exponential Distribution

There are frequently outliers that last far longer than expected. Note that the exponential distribution extends theoretically to infinity.

> "The world's longest lit light bulb, a 4-W job with a carbon filament, has been burning as a nightlight in a firehouse in Livermore, Calif. for 105 years."

("Department of Obscure Information," *Chemical & Engineering News*, 13 Feb. 2006)

To determine the value for the area under the curve to the right of a given point, T, we can use a table of exponential values (see Table 3.2). The table provides values of $e^{-T/MTBF}$ for known values of T and MTBF.

The exponential distribution is completely described by the distribution mean, which is the mean time between failures. If we allow T to represent the time in service, we can then determine the probability that failure will not occur before time T using the following equation:

$$P(\text{no failure before T}) = e^{-T/MTBF} \qquad (3.6)$$

where

$$e = \text{natural logarithm, } 2.7183\ldots.$$
$$T = \text{time in service before failure}$$
$$MTBF = \text{mean time between failures}$$

Because the total area under the curve is 1, the probability that there will be failure before time T is:

$$P(\text{failure before T}) = 1 - P(\text{no failure before T}) = 1 - e^{-T/MTBF} \qquad (3.7)$$

**TABLE 3.2.   Values of $e^{-T/MTBF}$**

| T/MTBF | $e^{-T/MTBF}$ | T/MTBF | $e^{-T/MTBF}$ |
|--------|---------------|--------|---------------|
| 0.10 | 0.9048 | 3.50 | 0.0302 |
| 0.50 | 0.6065 | 4.00 | 0.0183 |
| 1.00 | 0.3679 | 4.50 | 0.0111 |
| 1.50 | 0.2231 | 5.00 | 0.0067 |
| 2.00 | 0.1353 | 5.50 | 0.0041 |
| 2.50 | 0.0821 | 6.00 | 0.0025 |
| 3.00 | 0.0498 | 6.50 | 0.0015 |

---

## EXAMPLE 3.7

A computer power supply has a MTBF of 10,000 hours. What is the probability that there will be no failure in this power supply before 15,000 hours?

**a.** Using Table 1:

$$T/MTBF = 15,000/10,000 = 1.5$$

Finding the value of T/MTBF = 1.5 in Table 3.1, we read the probability of no failure before 15,000 hours = 0.2231.

**b.** Using Equation 3.6:

$$P(\text{no failure before T}) = e^{-T/MTBF} = e^{-15,000/10,000} = 0.2231$$

---

## Modeling Product Life with Normal Distribution

A process that is in statistical control and uses basic items such as ball bearings will rarely experience the early failure trends shown in the exponential distribution. Rather, failures will cluster around a "failure point." In cases such as this, the central limit theorem applies, and the normal distribution can be used to calculate the expected product life.

Using the standard normal distribution table, we can calculate the area under the curve from negative infinity to some point, z. z is a standardized value computed using the following equation:

$$z = T - \text{Mean wear-out time/Standard deviation of wear-out time} \qquad (3.8)$$

In order to work with the normal distribution, you need to know the mean of the distribution and its standard deviation. To obtain a probability that the service life will not exceed some time, T, use T to compute a z-value and then use the table in Appendix B to calculate the area under the curve to the left of z. To determine the probability that service life will exceed some time T, compute the z-value, find the area under the curve from the table, then subtract that value from 1.

The time value, T, for a given probability can also be determined. Find the probability of interest in the table in Appendix B. If the exact probability is not in the table, find the nearest probability to the left in the table, that is, the closest smaller value. Use the corresponding z-value in the above formula and solve for T.

## EXAMPLE 3.8

The mean life of a circuit array under normal use conditions can be modeled using a normal distribution with a mean of six months and a standard deviation of one month.

Determine each of the following:

1. The probability that a circuit array will wear out before seven months of service.
2. The probability that an array will wear out after seven months of service.
3. The service life that will provide a wear-out probability of 10 percent.

1. Compute z and use it to obtain the probability directly from the table in Appendix B.

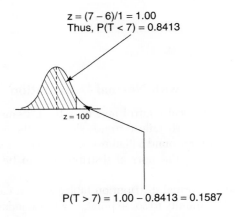

$$z = (7 - 6)/1 = 1.00$$
$$\text{Thus, } P(T < 7) = 0.8413$$

z = 100

$$P(T > 7) = 1.00 - 0.8413 = 0.1587$$

2. Subtract the probability, $P(T < 7)$ determined above, from 1.
3. Turn to the normal table and find the value of z that corresponds to an area under the curve of 0.10.

$$z = -1.28 = (T - 6)/1$$

Solving for T, we find T = 4.72 months.

## RISK ASSESSMENT TOOLS AND RISK PREVENTION

Tools are available to assist quality professionals assess potential risks and to assist designers produce more reliable and safer product and service designs. These tools may also be applied to analyze and improve existing products and processes. Two frequently used risk assessment tools are failure mode and effects analysis and fault tree analysis.

## Failure Mode and Effects Analysis

Failure mode and effect analysis (FMEA) is used to examine a product at the system and/or subsystem levels for all possible ways in which a failure may occur. For each potential failure, an estimate is made of its effect on the total system. The seriousness of the effect is also analyzed. A review is made of the corrective action being planned to minimize the probability and effect of any future failure. The failure "mode" is the symptom of the failure, which is distinct from the cause of failure. FMEA can be expanded to include such matters as safety, effect on downtime, access, repair planning, and design changes.

There are five basic steps to constructing a FMEA table:

1. Determine how the component can fail.
2. Determine possible cause(s) of failure.
3. Determine the effect on the product or system within which it operates (i.e., safety, downtime, repair requirements, tools required, etc.).
4. Determine the corrective action required.
5. Note any additional comments.

Figure 3.11 shows a partial design FMEA for a personal computer monitor.

FMEA can also be used for processes. Figure 3.12 shows a FMEA form used by hospitals to analyze processes.

The steps used for this application of FMEA are (Terninko, 2003):

1. Define the FMEA project.
2. List all of the tasks required for the project.
3. Identify potential failure modes.
4. Identify the potential effects of each failure mode. Assign a 5- or 10-point severity code for each effect. A typical 10-point system may use a code of 1 for None to 10 for Catastrophic.
5. Identify potential causes for the failures. Assign a 10-point occurrence rating for each potential cause. A typical 10-point system may use a code of 1 for Almost Never, to 10 for Almost Certain.
6. Identify design controls that are in place to control potential causes. Assign a detection probability rating for each potential cause. A typical 10-point system may use a code of 1 for Almost Certain, to 10 for Almost Impossible.
7. Calculate the risk priority measure (RPM) as the product: severity code × occurrence rating × detection probability. The RPM is used as the basis for determining which potential cause should be addressed first.
8. Determine actions necessary to address the potential causes.
9. Assign responsibility for the projects and the projected completion date.
10. List actions taken to address the potential causes.
11. Calculate a new REM for the improved process.

| Component Name | Failure Mode | Cause of Failure | Effect of Failure on System | Correction of Problem | Comments |
|---|---|---|---|---|---|
| Electrical Plug Part no. EP-1 | Loose wiring | Use, vibration, handling | Will not conduct current—system failure | Molded plug and wire | Uncorrected, could cause fire |
|  | Damaged contacts | User bends/breaks prongs when plugging or unplugging | Will not conduct current. May conduct current but fail to ground resulting in fire hazard, severe shock or death | Heavy duty prongs and protective molding | Clear warning on packaging to use three-prong grounded outlet |
| Monitor | Bad pixels | Excessive heat, dropping, bumping, shipping | Degrades picture | Improve shipping packaging to prevent damage | Depending on severity, may not be noticeable to user |
|  | Cracked | Excessive heat, bumping, dropping, shipping | No picture | Ensure material quality. Improve shipping packaging to prevent damage |  |
| Cabling to CPU | Broken, frayed | Fatigue, heat, carelessness, | Will not conduct signal. May cause shock or damage CPU. | Use wiring suitable for long life in anticipated environment | Dangerous warning included in instructions |
|  | Internal short circuit | Heat, brittle insulation | May cause electrical shock, damage CPU or Monitor | Use wiring suitable for long life in anticipated environment |  |

**Failure Mode and Effects Analysis**

| System: | ① Design Responsibility: | FMEA Number |
| Subsystem | Key Date: | Page |
| Event | | Prepared by: |
| Model: | | FMEA Date |

| Item-Part / Function | Potential Failure Mode | Potential Effect(s) of Failure | Sever | Class | Potential Cause(s) / Mechanism(s) of Failure | Occur | Current Design Controls | Detect | R P M | Recommend Action(s) | Responsibility & Target Completion Date | Action Results | | | | |
|---|---|---|---|---|---|---|---|---|---|---|---|---|---|---|---|---|
| | | | | | | | | | | | | Actions Taken | Sever | Occur | Detect | R P M |
| Enter a system function using verb/noun format ② | Failure mode = loss of function or negative of function ③ | Consequences on other systems, parts, or people ④ | | | From block diagram, determine if/how each element can cause system failure ⑤ | | Method, test or technique used to detect cause of failure ⑥ | | ⑦ | Design actions to reduce severity, occurrence and detection ratings. ⑧ | System design department and date ⑨ | Actions and actual completion date ⑩ | | | | ⑪ |

**Figure 3.12.** FMEA for a Process. (*Source:* Terninko, 2003. Reprinted with permission from ASQ. © 2003 American Society for Quality. No further distribution without permission.)

## Fault Tree Analysis (FTA)

Fault tree analysis (FTA) is a tool used to identify possible causes for potential operating hazards or undesired events. The starting point in FTA is a list of potential hazards or undesired events generated from historical data of accidents and/or near misses. Each hazard on the list becomes a failure mode requiring analysis. The possible direct causes of the hazard or event are then analyzed and the origins of these causes determined. Finally, methods or actions for avoiding these causes are formulated and analyzed. There are four basic steps to constructing a fault tree:

1. Define the flaws giving rise to the functional defects.
2. Identify the possible root causes and their direct and indirect effects.
3. Quantify, as best you can, the event's probability.
4. Determine which fault of a particular kind is most likely to occur and when (time dependency).

An example of FTA is given in Figure 3.13. The tree is composed of branches connected to two different types of nodes:

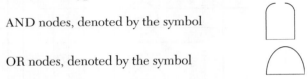

AND nodes, denoted by the symbol

OR nodes, denoted by the symbol

An AND node is used when all events must occur in order for the event above the node to occur. An OR node is used when at least one of the events must occur in order for the event above the node to occur.

The tools discussed in this chapter are seldom applied individually. The design of products, services, and processes is a complex endeavor. The methodologies discussed in this chapter can provide frameworks and resources for designers to ensure that the final design will delight the customer and can be produced efficiently.

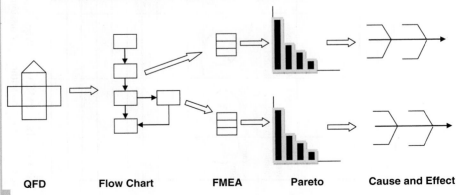

| QFD | Flow Chart | FMEA | Pareto | Cause and Effect |

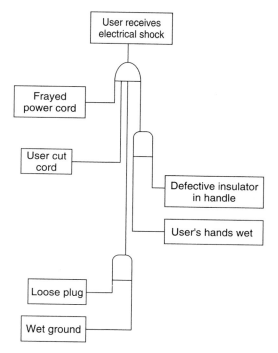

**Figure 3.13.** Simplified FTA for an Electric Trimmer

# ERROR PROOFING

An effective way to address potential problems identified by FMEA or FTA is error proofing. The Japanese term for error proofing is *poka-yoke*. Error proofing is built into U.S. electrical plugs. A 110v plug that requires grounding will not fit into an ungrounded outlet because there is no hole for the grounding prong in an ungrounded outlet. A 110v plug will not fit into a 220v outlet because the plugs are designed with completely different configurations.

Error proofing can also be incorporated into services. In order to prevent errors in recording customer orders in a restaurant, waiters may be trained to repeat the order to the customer before leaving the table to place the order in the kitchen. A standard procedure for bank tellers is that they count money twice—once to themselves, then again when they give the money to the customer.

*Poka-yoke* is defined as a "Japanese term that means mistake-proofing. A *poka-yoke* device is one that prevents incorrect parts from being made or assembled and easily identifies a flaw or error."

(Quality Glossary, 2002, 55)

## SUMMARY

Quality products and services cannot be manufactured or delivered unless quality has been incorporated into the design. Poor quality designs will result in poor quality products and services. The first step to designing quality into products and services is to be sure to focus on the customer. The seven management tools and quality function deployment are tools that can assist designers in ensuring that customer input is incorporated into the design process. Design for Six Sigma builds on traditional Six Sigma methodology to ensure that new products and services are designed to meet the Six Sigma goal of 3.4 defects per million opportunities.

Robust designs produce products and services that are capable of meeting customer needs even in the face of uncontrollable environmental factors. Robustness and reliability are related concepts. Reliability can be improved by increasing the reliability of individual components and also by building redundancy into the design. Potential failure modes for products and services can be addressed using tools such as failure mode and effects analysis and fault tree analysis. The result will be more reliable products that are robust to environmental uncertainty and that will better satisfy customers by providing them with products and services that meet their needs and are safe to use.

## DISCUSSION QUESTIONS

1. List the seven management tools and discuss how they might be used in developing a new product.
2. Discuss the relationship between an affinity diagram and a tree diagram.
3. How does the use of quality function deployment assure that the voice of the customer is heard during the design process?
4. What are the objectives of Design for Six Sigma?
5. Discuss what is meant by the term *robust*.
6. Discuss the two approaches to using probability to define the reliability of a product.
7. Discuss the importance of specifying standard operating conditions.
8. Discuss approaches to defining the failure of road-striping paint that is exposed to heavy traffic.
9. Is it always more effective to provide backups for all components than to provide a parallel system?
10. What is the effect of switch reliability on a system?
11. Explain what is meant by the bathtub curve.
12. What is the difference between MTBF and MTTF?
13. When might a normal distribution be a better model for failure rates than an exponential distribution?
14. Discuss the use of FMEA in product design.
15. Discuss the use of FTA in product design.

# PROBLEMS

1. An assembly line consists of four subsystems with the following reliabilities:

$P_1 = 0.998$
$P_2 = 0.997$
$P_3 = 0.988$
$P_4 = 0.990$

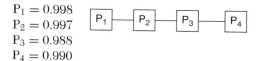

What is the overall reliability of the system?

2. An electronic device consists of five subsystems. The first two subsystems have reliabilities of 0.999. The last three subsystems have reliabilities of 0.997. What is the overall reliability of the system?

3. A system consists of just one component which has a reliability of 0.96. The primary component has a backup component which has a reliability of 0.95 as shown below. If either the primary or backup component functions, the system works.

What is the reliability of this system?

4. If an identical backup is added to just the first component of the system in Problem 1, what would be the reliability of the new system? Assume a switch reliability of 1.00.

5. What would be the reliability of the system in Problem 3 if the switch reliability is 0.995?

6. A smoke detector consists of three components with reliabilities of 0.995, 0.994, and 0.996.

   a. What is the reliability of the system?
   b. If identical backups are provided for each component, what is the reliability of the new system? Assume switch reliabilities of 1.0.
   c. What is the reliability of the system in part b if the switch reliability is 0.998?

7. A chemical company has determined that there will be an extreme hazard if a particular pump in their process were to fail. They buy the most reliable pump available, but its reliability is only 0.990. They have decided that it is necessary to provide redundancy to this pump in order to protect themselves from a failure. How many backups would be necessary in order to achieve a reliability of at least 0.999996? Assume a switch reliability of 1.0.

8. In order to increase the safety of its fleet, Safety-First Airlines (SFA) wants to install a redundant system to ensure against instrument malfunction. The original system consists of five components in series, with reliabilities of 0.995, 0.995, 0.999, 0.998, and 0.980. The airline has the choice of adding an identical backup to each component that will activate automatically if that component fails, or a completely separate backup system that is identical to the primary system. This separate system is activated via an automatic switch with a reliability of 0.995. Which option would you recommend SFA install in its planes?

9. A component has a reliability that fits the exponential distribution. The MTBF for the component is 2,500 cycles.

   a. What is the probability that the component will not fail before 5,000 cycles?
   b. What is the probability that the component will fail before 5,000 cycles?

10. Never-Fail Nightlights wants parents to be assured of the integrity of its products. As such, Never-Fail requested Rest-Assured Labs to test its newest nightlight—the Everglo—to determine its life expectancy. The lab determined that the distribution of the life expectancy is exponential with an average life of five years. What is the probability that one of the Everglo units will last:

   a. Less than five years?
   b. More than 30 months?
   c. At least 20 years?

11. Under normal-use conditions, the MTTF of a heating coil can be modeled using a normal distribution with a mean of 20 months and a standard deviation of two months. Determine each of the following:

   a. The probability that a heating coil will wear out before 15 months of service.
   b. The probability that a heating coil will wear out after ten months of service.
   c. The service life that will provide a wear-out probability of 0.10.

12. A hospital conducted focus groups with recently discharged patients to determine what aspects of their interaction with nurses were most important to them. The following items were obtained:

   Empathy
   Caring attitude
   Can get IV in on first try
   Provides information about condition
   Treats family with respect

Explains medical procedures

Dressed appropriately

Takes time with patient

Goes the extra mile for the patient

Is an advocate for the patient with physicians

Responds quickly to patient call light

Asks patient how he or she is feeling

Seems to really care about the patient's recovery

Develop appropriate categories for these items and construct an affinity diagram.

**13.** Develop a tree diagram for an organization with the objectives of improving reliability and cost of their product, a smoke detector for consumer use. Suggest at least two strategies for accomplishing each objective.

**14.** Develop a process decision program chart using the information from your solution to Problem 13. Suggest at least one possible outcome and contingency plan for each strategy.

**15.** A company plans to survey customers about their satisfaction with the current design of their product. They have developed the following list of activities necessary to design the questionnaire for this project along with a listing of which activities must precede which other activities. Create a network (PERT) diagram for this project and determine the critical path.

| Activity by Task(s) | Estimated Task Duration (weeks) | Must Be Immediately Preceded |
|---|---|---|
| 1. Develop questions | 3 | None |
| 2. Test questions | 3 | 1 |
| 3. Prepare questionnaire | 1 | 2 |
| 4. Select test sample of respondents | 1 | None |
| 5. Print questionnaires for sample test | 2 | 3 |
| 6. Print mailing labels | 1 | 4 |
| 7. Label and stuff envelopes | 1 | 5, 6 |
| 8. Mail surveys | 0.5 | 8 |
| 9. Receive responses | 4 | 8 |
| 10. Data entry | 1 | 9 |
| 11. Analyze data | 2 | 10 |
| 12. Revise questionnaire if necessary | 1 | 11 |
| 13. Finalize questionnaire | 1 | 12 |

---

CASE STUDY 3.1:   *Building the Better Mouse*

---

© 2008 Victor E. Sower, Ph.D., C.Q.E.

You are sitting in on a meeting with the Acme Corp. new product development team. The team is comprised entirely of design engineers and is meeting in the engineering conference room. The team leader is the Chief Design Engineer, Michael Carroll, who invited you to sit in today.

Michael addresses the team. "We've been tasked with designing a new mouse to sell with the next generation of personal computers. We have six months to have working prototypes ready to present to marketing and three months after that to have the new mouse in production. It's a very aggressive schedule—we have no time to waste. Let's start by brainstorming ideas for the mouse. Please be as innovative as possible." Michael stepped to the white board prepared to write all of the ideas that emerged from the meeting.

Ideas began to surface:

"Why does a mouse have to have only 2 buttons and a scroller? Why not add an additional button for the thumb that can be programmed to serve as a function key?"

"Why not make the mouse available in many colors rather than just the drab black, grey, and off-white?"

"Why not send power to the mouse using RF rather than using a battery?"

"Why do we need a mouse anyway? Why not implant a chip into users' index fingers?"

"Let's make the mouse a glove. Just move your fingers to move the cursor."

As the ideas were offered, Michael wrote them on the white board. After about 30 minutes the flow of ideas had about stopped. There were a total of 28 ideas generated. Michael divided them loosely into categories: electrical; physical; functional. He asked the team to divide themselves into three groups along functional lines and each group to select a category to develop further. "Please pay particular attention to technical feasibility and manufacturing costs when you evaluate the ideas. Let's plan to meet again in two weeks with each group giving a report on their ideas. We'll try to narrow the ideas down and start rough prototyping the most promising ideas."

After the meeting, Michael asked you for comments about the process he is using to design the new mouse. What comments and suggestions would you make to Michael?

# EXERCISES AND ACTIVITIES

1. Find an example of a product that has redundancy built in. Do all of the components in the product have backups? If not, how do you think the components to have backups were selected?

**2.** Find an example of a service that has redundancy built in. Could you calculate the reliability of a service in the same way as is done for products? What adaptations might need to be made to the analysis methods in order to calculate the reliability of a service?

**3.** Using the class members as representative samples of the student population, conduct a focus group to address the following question: "What are the most important characteristics of a college or university that create quality for the student?" Use an affinity diagram to categorize the responses into meaningful categories. Develop importance weights for each response. Based on that, identify the critical-to-quality characteristics and construct the west wing of the house of quality.

**4.** What are some procedures that would error proof the process by which university students select courses that will count toward their degree? How many of these procedures are used at your university?

## SUPPLEMENTARY READINGS

Akao, Y. (1990). *Quality Function Deployment: Integrating Customer Requirements into Product Design.* Cambridge, MA: Productivity Press.

Gotlow, H., D. Levine, & E. Popovich. (2006). *Design for Six Sigma for Green Belts and Champions.* Upper Saddle River, NJ: Pearson Prentice Hall.

Juran, J. M. (1992). *Juran on Quality by Design: The New Steps for Planning Quality into Goods and Services.* Milwaukee, WI: ASQ Quality Press.

Juran, J. M., & F. Gryna. (1980). *Quality Planning and Analysis,* 2nd edition. New York: McGraw-Hill Book Company.

Krishnamoorthi, K. (1992). *Reliability Methods for Engineers.* Milwaukee, WI: ASQ Quality Press.

Levin, M. (2003). *Improving Product Reliability: Strategies and Implementation.* Milwaukee, WI: ASQ Quality Press.

Mader, D. (2003). "DFSS and Your Current Design Process." *Quality Progress* 36(7), 88–89.

Sinha, M., & W. Willborn. (1985). *The Management of Quality Assurance.* New York: John Wiley & Sons.

Stamatis, D. (2003). *Failure Mode and Effect Analysis: FMEA from Theory to Execution,* 2nd edition. Milwaukee, WI: ASQ Quality Press.

Sullivan, L. (1986). "Quality Function Deployment." *Quality Progress* 19(6), 39–50.

## REFERENCES

AGREE. (1957). "Reliability of Military Electronic Equipment." Report by Advisory Group on Reliability of Electronic Equipment, Office of the Secretary of Defense (R&D) (June). Washington, DC: V.S. Government Printing Office.

Breyfogle, F., J. Cupello, & B. Meadows. (2001). *Managing Six Sigma.* New York: John Wiley & Sons.

"Department of Obscure Information." (2006). *Chemical & Engineering News*, February 13.

Harry, M., & R. Schroeder. (2000). *Six Sigma: The Breakthrough Management Strategy Revolutionising the World's Top Corporations*. New York: Currency/Doubleday.

Hauser, J., & D. Clausing. (1988). "Quality Function Deployment: Integrating Customer Requirements into Product Design." *Harvard Business Review* 66(3), 63–73.

Juran, J. M., & F. M. Gryna. (1980). *Quality Planning and Analysis*, 2nd edition. New York: McGraw-Hill, 209.

Mader, D. (2003). "DFSS and Your Current Design Process." *Quality Progress* 36(7), 88–89.

"Quality Glossary." (2002). *Quality Progress* 35(7), 43–61.

Snee, R., & R. Hoerl. (2003). *Leading Six Sigma*. Upper Saddle River, NJ: Prentice Hall.

Stevenson, W. (2009). *Operations Management*, 8th edition. Boston: McGraw-Hill/Irwin, 147.

Taguchi, G., E. Elsayed, & T. Hsiang. (1989). *Quality Engineering in Production Systems*. New York: McGraw-Hill.

Terninko, J. (2003). "Reliability/Mistake Proofing Using Failure Mode and Effects Analysis (FMEA)." *ASQ's 57th Annual Quality Congress Proceedings*, 515–526.

## CHAPTER FOUR

# Innovation and Creativity in Quality

## CHAPTER OBJECTIVES

After completing this chapter, the reader should be able to:

- discuss the differences between radical and incremental improvement;
- discuss the risks associated with not being creative and innovative;
- discuss ways in which creativity can be improved in an organization;
- discuss the elements of a creative organization;
- understand the relationship between creativity results and individual creativity and organizational factors; and
- discuss the importance of technological forecasting.

In this chapter we will discuss how to increase innovation and creativity in our approach to quality. Continuous incremental improvement is a vital part of the quality management system, but often it is not enough. Sometimes radical improvement is required to satisfy customer needs and to remain competitive. Hiring particularly creative individuals is not enough. Establishing an environment that encourages innovation and creativity is needed as well. That is a strategic issue for organizations. Without the proper environment, often new and innovative ideas that could transform the quality of products and services—indeed the entire organization—will be ignored or given, at best, token attention. At worst, they will be viewed as threats to the status quo—the comfortable ways that we do things now.

Often the ideas and technologies that will have the greatest impact come from outside the organization. In order to take advantage of these new ideas and technologies, organizations must have a defined approach to scanning the external

*Acknowledgment:* Portions of this chapter are derived from Sower & Fair (2005) and are reprinted with permission from ASQ 2005 American Society for Quality. No further distribution without permission.

environment. The external environment must be defined broadly enough to include all possible sources of breakthrough ideas and technologies. Failure to identify breakthroughs that could potentially fundamentally change the way the organization conducts business can result in the failure of the organization because its products and services no longer satisfy customers. Technological forecasting is a vital activity for innovative organizations.

There are approaches and techniques for improving the creativity of individuals, teams, and organizations. Appropriate use of these approaches and techniques can increase the number of innovative and creative ideas and enhance the prospect that they will positively influence the quality of the organization and the products and services it provides.

> Ceativity may be defined as a multi-dimensional process of interaction between organisms and their environment that leads to the creation of unique products or ideas.
>
> (Chambers, 1969)

## BREAKTHROUGH (RADICAL) IMPROVEMENT VERSUS INCREMENTAL IMPROVEMENT

Creative approaches that result in small improvements to existing products and services can be found. There is certainly a need for creativity within the framework of continuous incremental improvement. But if we apply the definition of quality as "meeting customer needs," one need not be elderly to have experienced radical breakthrough improvements that redefined "customer needs." Through the 1960s, the customer need for a means to do complex calculations was fulfilled with slide rules. Beginning in the 1970s, this same need was fulfilled with calculators—slide rules no longer satisfied, much less delighted, customers. During the 1980s, personal computers, while not displacing calculators, provided a new dimension to satisfying customers with a need to do complex calculations.

This use of the term "breakthrough improvement" to describe radical, paradigm-shifting improvement is different from Juran's use of the term. Juran says that the first step in process improvement is to bring the process into a state of statistical control—that is, make the process predictable. Deming said that this step does not constitute improvement; it just makes the process behave as it should in the first place. Juran's concept of breakthrough improvement deals with processes that are in a state of statistical control. An improvement to an in-control process that manifests as a significant shift in performance constitutes a breakthrough improvement. An example of Juran's concept of breakthrough would be a manufacturing process that is stable (in control) and produces product with a mean defective rate of 0.7 percent.

An improvement project that results in a reduction of the mean defect rate to 0.5 percent constitutes a breakthrough according to Juran.

Garvin's transcendent approach to defining quality is most appropriate when thinking in radical, paradigm-shifting improvement terms. Garvin's other approaches (product-based, user-based, manufacturing-based, and value-based) create too many constraints to this type of creative thinking. In the middle of the last century, the railroad industry in the United States declined in part because they defined themselves as being in the railroad business rather than in the people-and-cargo transportation business. They focused on improving various aspects of railroad operations instead of trying to increase the innate excellence of the transportation services they provided to their customers. Eventually, innovative ideas such as piggy back (transporting trailers and containers on railroad flat cars) emerged to help railroads compete.

## Incremental versus Breakthrough Improvement in Aviation

The period from about 1890 to 1901 was marked by stability of outcomes of the many attempts at powered human flight. A breakthrough occurred on December 17, 1903, when the Wright Flyer flew for the first time. The first flight lasted 12 seconds and covered barely 200 feet. The final flight of that day lasted 59 seconds and covered 852 feet (Bradshaw & Wright, ND). This breakthrough improvement paved the way for increasing the quality and changing the paradigm for transportation services.

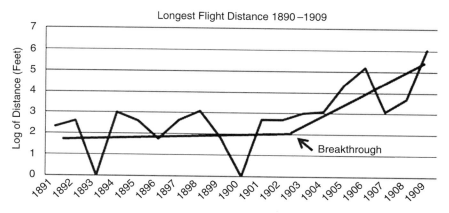

Longest Flight Distance 1890–1909

Recently, Burt Rutan has taken powered human flight a step further. The suborbital flights of SpaceShipOne in 2004, which won Rutan the Ansari X Prize, have paved the way for commercial space transportation. This radical innovation has moved space flight from the exclusive domain of governments to include the private sector.

Quality programs such as Six Sigma, Continuous Quality Improvement (CQI), Zero Defects (ZD), and Total Quality Management (TQM) focus on continuous incremental improvement of quality as defined by the customer—Garvin's user-based approach. Some researchers (Provost, 1996; Plsek, 1998) suggest that these programs contribute little to breakthrough quality and in fact may stifle creativity by subjecting breakthrough products and services to detailed quantitative scrutiny too early. Creative thinking when combined with the critical-thinking processes associated with problem solving and continuous improvement is an essential element for organizational success. "Continuous improvement efforts that do not actively integrate creativity stand to reap only limited benefits. Further, they might even suppress any previously existing creativity in the organization, thus losing out on the associated benefits" (Provost & Sproul, 1996, 102). General Electric is currently working to change its culture to accommodate a new emphasis on innovation while not harming the existing emphasis on continuous improvement using Six Sigma.

But it is important to understand that continuous improvement and radical innovation are not mutually exclusive (Hamel, 2001). In fact both are necessary. Xerox CEO Joe Wilson and VP of Research and Development John Dessauer are the insightful pioneers of xerography who commercialized Chester Carlson's invention and established Xerox as a household name. In later years Xerox was insightful enough to redefine their market as documents rather than imaging. But in the difficult times of the 1970s and 1980s, the company was "rescued by the understanding level of quality as promoted by CEO David Kerns" manifest in their TQM effort known as leadership through quality—a continuous improvement program (Shotmiller, 2004).

## Increasing Creativity

We can find guidance about how to increase creativity in the work of the early philosophers. Plato in the *Republic* introduced the image of the divided line, the segments of which represent forms of awareness and the sorts of things that the form of awareness each has as its objects. Plato's divided line is depicted in Figure 4.1 These forms of awareness are arranged in a hierarchy from weakest to strongest according to how real and unchanging their objects are. At the bottom of the hierarchy are images—representations of concrete things—and "imaging" (*eikasia*) as the corresponding form of awareness. Next in the hierarchy are the concrete things themselves, with perceptual belief (*pistis*) as the corresponding form of awareness. The third segment of the line is where a form of awareness that can be called "understanding" (*dianoia*) is located, and the objects of understanding are "hypotheses." This section of the line contains mathematically formulated general principles that can be applied to understand particular concrete things while the principles are not limited by being only about those particular things. Finally, in the fourth and highest section of the line, the mind is alive with a form of awareness that can be called "insight" (*noesis*). This form of awareness uses the "hypotheses" of the geometers as "stepping stones to take off from, enabling the attainment of the unhypothetical first principle of everything." But having reached this unhypothetical first principle, it is important to note that the mind then returns to consider the geometers' principles (Plato, 1992, 185).

To illustrate the application of the divided line image to creativity, let's use chemistry as an example. In the first, and lowest, stage we have a person learning

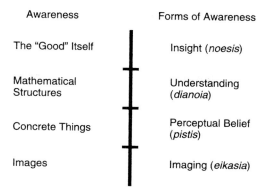

**Figure 4.1.** The Divided Line—Plato's Forms of Awareness. (*Source*: Sower and Fair, 2005. Reprinted with permission from *Quality Management Journal*. © 2005 American Society for Quality. No further distribution allowed without permission.)

chemistry who becomes familiar with textbook representations of chemical phenomena. But even if she memorizes reams of textbook information, such knowledge is not as complete as that which a person has who ascends to the second stage, the stage in which she has hands-on, personal experience in the laboratory. In the laboratory the person sees for herself how things work. But if her experiences are to become more meaningful as knowledge, this in turn must lead to stage three. In stage three, a person is not content simply to accumulate observations in the laboratory. She wants to understand the patterns that she observes, and this means that she will have to spend a great deal of time and effort getting to know and apply the laws and theories of chemistry, most of which are formulated in mathematical language. This is the part of the line where our developing chemist meets the "hypotheses" that Plato wrote about. But if the person's attempts to know chemistry stops at this point, then she is a highly trained, perhaps very capable, technician, but not a genuine chemist. What is lacking is chemical insight, insight which enables her to identify and conceive *valuable* new chemical "hypotheses" that are *worth* being researched. Those who possess chemical insight are capable of creativity and innovation in the field of chemistry, but those without insight are limited to repeating and applying what others have created. In Plato's language, acquaintance with the good itself as it is manifested through fruitful chemical insight is necessary in order to have fully genuine knowledge in chemistry (Sower & Fair, 2005).

It takes individuals and organizations operating at the insight level of Plato's hierarchy to develop truly creative, radical innovations. It is top management's task to bring the organization and its employees to the level of insight. Deming's sixth point "Institute training" provides the stimulus for elevating employees to the perceptual belief level. His thirteenth point "Institute a vigorous program of education" holds the promise for achieving understanding and insight.

Robinson and Stern (1997) discuss the importance of serendipity and sagacity in the creative process associated with paradigm-shifting discoveries. To illustrate their point they use the discovery of Teflon. Teflon was discovered by DuPont in 1938 when researchers working on new refrigerants found some white powder in a tank supposed to contain tetrafluoroethlene gas. This was the serendipitous part—the fortunate accident. Sagacity entered when the researchers were curious about the powder, analyzed it, and found it to be a polymer, polytetrafluoroethlene—trademarked as Teflon in 1944. They went on to determine its properties: it is impervious to most solvents, acids, and other corrosives; it doesn't easily melt or burn; and it won't stick to anything. Next they discovered the conditions under which the powder formed. At this point they recognized that they had discovered a "quality" material. Quality in this case was not adequately defined by customer needs or comparison to other similar materials, or potential applications. This polymer did not dissolve or stick to anything—a detriment when compared to other polymers such as polyurethanes used in paints and coatings. Teflon would not easily melt—a detriment when compared to other polymers like polystyrene used in injection molding. This polymer was rigid and could be machined—a detriment when compared with polyurethanes used for pillow stuffing. However, their insight prepared them to recognize the quality of what they had discovered. Their curiosity led them to follow up on their fortunate accident by characterizing its properties and methods of preparation. Others developed wondrous applications for the product, among them nonstick cookware, rain-proof garments, chemically resistant gaskets, and inert lubricants.

Sagacity means "gifted with acuteness of mental discernment" (*Oxford English Dictionary*, 1997) and is an attribute of insight. Serendipity without sagacity—without insight—does not lead to paradigm-shifting discovery. Accidents are simply accidents without the insight necessary to turn them into fortunate accidents. Robinson and Stern (1997, 192) suggest that serendipity can be increased by creating a "bias for action" within the organization that will promote fortunate accidents. Sagacity can be increased by "expanding the company's human potential beyond its immediate needs." This is diametrically opposed to current trends to downsize—particularly in overhead (including R&D) positions. If one wishes to receive the benefits that derive from achieving Plato's insight level, one must provide the resources. There must be individuals and groups within the organization charged with asking Barker's (1990) fundamental question: "What is it that is impossible today, that if it were possible, would fundamentally change the way we do business?" These people must have the sagacity—indeed the insight—to recognize the value of the answers to that question.

Plsek (1998) identifies successfully fostering creativity and innovation as a differentiating factor between successful and less successful firms. He identifies three dilemmas facing organizations which serve as barriers to creativity. One dilemma is that many leaders believe they lack the creative gift. "Research from the field of cognitive science indicates that this is simply not true" (Plsek, 1998, 22). Robinson and Stern (1997) believe that the need for creativity is as powerful as the need for food in all individuals. Another dilemma is the idea that many creative approaches appear to be frivolous. Leaders are afraid to ask for the creative ideas they need for "fear of being seen as making light of the situation" (Plsek, 1998, 22). The third dilemma is that many leaders are unaware of the many tools available to help in the generation of creative ideas. These tools are designed to move one out of mental ruts and to think in new patterns. These tools include concept fan, morphological analysis, word play, analogies, cinematics, and reversals.

## ORGANIZATIONAL VERSUS INDIVIDUAL CREATIVITY

Creativity can be considered at two levels—organizational creativity and individual creativity. However, these should not be considered as alternative approaches to creativity. In order to achieve creativity in a quality program, both are required. We need highly creative individuals working together in an organization that encourages, supports, and rewards creative behavior.

Clarke (1996) suggests that creative behavior results from a combination of these two conditions: individual creative ability and a work environment that encourages and supports creative behavior. Organizations through their policies, procedures, and cultures can create working environments that either encourage or discourage creativity. All too often this is not a conscious decision. The environment evolves without regard for its impact on creativity.

## DESIGNING THE INNOVATIVE ORGANIZATION

Consider the case of consumer products. Most customers are rather naïve about the technology involved in the products they purchase and use every day. They know quality when they see it, but they generally know little of the technologies involved in cell phones, DVDs, and personal computers. Customers are usually at the images level of Plato's hierarchy. Marketing and quality professionals who obtain inputs from customers about products and then translate them into specific product-based attributes are at the perceptual belief level. Engineers and scientists who create prototypes and test these attributes and their interactions with each other, and on the basis of these tests establish product specifications, are at the understanding level. When scientists and engineers in the research department utilize creativity combined with detailed knowledge of the science involved and the fundamental needs of the customer to create entirely new products, they are at the insight level. An example of this would be where customers describe their need for greater ease of operation for the personal computer (images level). Insightful researchers use creativity to go beyond the keyboard/DOS programming paradigm (which led to the DOS shell—understanding level) to the mouse/graphical user interface paradigm (insight level). Understanding is sufficient for continuous improvement. Insight is required for breakthrough improvement.

If I'd listened to customers, I'd have given them a faster horse. (Henry Ford)

(Mayer, 2006)

Therefore one key to designing a creative organization is to develop individual members so that they move up Plato's hierarchy—ultimately to the insight level from which maximum creativity springs. Deming would say that his sixth point (institute training) and his thirteenth point (institute a vigorous program of education and retraining) address this key. Another key is designing the organization's structure and culture to encourage personal growth and nurture everyone's creative potential. Deming would say his seventh (institute leadership), eighth (drive out fear), and ninth points (break down barriers between staff areas) address this key. Development of more creative individuals is inextricably linked with development of the organizational environment.

## Elements of a Creative Organization

A number of elements have been identified for organizations in which creativity is nurtured and encouraged. Among them are those by Robinson and Stern (1997) and Clarke (1996). These elements are shown in Table 4.1.

Often "thinking outside the box" is perceived to be the main path to creativity. But, in order to be creative, employees need to "understand the context and constraints within which they must work" (Vaisnys, 2000). This is accomplished through the process of *alignment*. Alignment refers to how well the interests and actions of each employee contribute to attainment of organizational goals. Alignment is necessary for employees to understand in which directions to channel their creativity. Some research has shown that only 5 percent of the workforce understands their company's strategy. The keys to achieving alignment involve good communication by management about what the key goals and objectives of the organization are; obtaining commitment from employees to channel their activities toward achievement of those goals and objectives; and holding employees accountable for the results of their activities. The strategic plan (Chapter 2) is the best source of information employees

**TABLE 4.1. Elements of Creative Organizational Environments**

| Robinson & Stern | Clarke |
| --- | --- |
| Alignment | Senior Management Support |
| Self-Initiated Activity | Hire Creative People |
| Unofficial Activity | Long-Term Employment Commitment |
| Serendipity | Allow Freedom & Autonomy |
| Diverse Stimuli | Provide Challenging Assignments |
| Within-Organization Communication | Provide Adequate Resources |
| | Encourage Risk Taking |
| | Provide Reward & Recognition System |
| | Consultative Style of Management |
| | Encourage Effective Timely Communication |
| | Tolerate Nonconformity |

need in order to know what they are to be aligned to. Alignment is the responsibility of senior management and is facilitated by effective communication, a consultative management style, and establishment of a responsive and equitable reward and recognition system.

Which of Deming's 14 Points for Management (Chapter 1) appear to address these responsibilities of top management?

Although hiring creative people can enhance organizational creativity, self-initiated activity recognizes that there is a strong drive for creativity within most people. The problem is helping them unfetter that drive and channel it into creative activities that will aid the organization in attaining its goals and objectives. Idea programs sponsored by the organization are one way to encourage self-initiated activity. Another way is to adopt a policy similar to the 15 percent rule, which is a key aspect of creativity and innovation at 3M. The rule states that 15 percent of an employee's time must be spent in pursuit of self-initiated creative ideas. According to Mayer (2003), although "the rule is more heavily aimed at our technical employees ... the rule applies to any of our employees who have a project they want to pursue to improve business and make 3M company better." Self-initiated activity must be supported and promoted by senior management and is facilitated by allowing freedom and autonomy in decisions about work, encouraging risk taking, and tolerance of nonconformity.

Which of Deming's 14 Points for Management (Chapter 1) appear to address the importance of developing a risk tolerant organization?

*Unofficial activity* recognizes that good ideas sometimes are killed in their infancy because they are made official too soon. When a project is unofficial it is not subject to budgets, timelines, or review by management. That gives the originator of the idea the freedom to develop it. On the other hand, time constraints can result in faster development. Given that only 10 percent or fewer new ideas work out, failing faster—that is, rapidly trying out many new ideas—can increase the chances of success. According to Mayer (2003) it is "important to discover failure fast and abandon it quickly." Tolerance and indeed encouragement of unofficial activity starts with senior management and is facilitated by hiring creative people and allowing freedom and autonomy in decisions about work, encouraging risk taking, providing adequate resources (especially time) and tolerance of nonconformity.

Rex Harvey, a principal engineer at Parker Hannifin Corp.'s gas turbine and fuel systems division, holds 11 patents and is known as an innovator. "We do some of our best work at lunch on napkins ... When you start with computer drawings, it slows you down. You don't want to deviate ... But when you sketch on the back of a napkin, you can be very innovative."

(*Houston Chronicle*, 2006, D1)

Serendipity, discussed briefly earlier in this chapter, refers to discoveries made by accident. Every unexpected event is an opportunity. At Toyota, even quality problems are viewed as opportunities to learn something new. One key to taking advantage of unexpected events is the observers' possession of sagacity—the mental discernment necessary to recognize the opportunity within an unexpected event. Acute mental discernment would be a hallmark of someone at Plato's insight level. Therefore the more the organization can facilitate movement up Plato's hierarchy of awareness, the greater the probability that unexpected events will result in creative new ideas. Often investigation of unexpected events is discouraged by organizations that see this as a nonproductive diversion from the primary mission. *Allowing freedom and autonomy* and *tolerating nonconformity* are important to encouraging the development of an unexpected event into an opportunity to learn something new.

In 1945, the Raytheon Corp. was awarded a patent for the microwave oven. The Raytheon "pioneer" responsible for the discovery was Percy Spencer. Spencer was working with vacuum tubes to produce microwave radiation for use in radar devices. One day he noticed that a candy bar in his pocket had melted (serendipity). For most people, the next step would be to figure out how to clean the melted chocolate from his pocket. But Spencer searched until he found the explanation—the microwaves melted the chocolate. He soon concluded that microwave radiation could be used for cooking (sagacity).

(Raytheon Corp. http://www.raytheon.com)

*Diverse stimuli* recognizes that the more varied the stimuli to which a person is exposed, the more likely that one of these stimuli will result in a creative idea or act. Cross training and using job rotation is one way to add diversity to the stimuli of organization members. Providing opportunities for organization members to attend professional conferences, attend seminars, share ideas with others within and without the organization increases the diversity of stimuli and thus promotes creativity.

*Within-organization communication* requires that not only official but unofficial communication opportunities be encouraged. Promotion of a collegial atmosphere that encourages organization members to share information and discuss ideas freely with other members is necessary for good within-organization communication. Design of work spaces that provide natural gathering areas also encourages within-organization communication. Encouraging organization members to be responsive to requests for information or feedback from other organization members is also important.

Clarke (1996) includes *encouraging risk-taking* as an element of a creative organization. A recent survey (2006) indicates that while two-thirds of U.S. organizations consider innovation to be very important, only about 5 percent reward intelligent risk-taking. Organizations that wish to encourage employee creativity must create an environment where workers can benefit from their mistakes as well as their successes. Mistakes must be treated as learning opportunities. BMW celebrates mistakes with a "creative error of the month" award.

## Tools and Techniques for Increasing Organizational Creativity

Although Robinson and Stern (1997) advocate encouraging creativity in the workplace itself, a number of companies such as Xerox and IBM have established well-equipped creative (research) centers staffed with top research talent separate from their other facilities. In some cases the inability of the company to fully capitalize on the creative ideas developed in their research centers has resulted in criticism. Stix (2004) notes the "inability of Xerox's . . . PARC (research center) to capitalize on computer science innovations." To get around this problem, Microsoft's research division conducts a TechFest where it displays its innovations to the rest of the company. This promotes within-company communication and diverse stimuli.

Brainstorming is a useful tool for developing many new ideas. The facilitator must be careful to prevent any evaluation of the ideas during the brainstorming session. This inhibits the flow of ideas. Affinity diagrams (discussed in Chapter 3) and cause-and-effect diagrams (discussed in Chapter 8) are useful tools for collecting brainstorming ideas into logical categories.

Companies that emphasize new products are necessarily more creative. 3M sets stretch targets based on its goal of achieving at least 30 percent of its sales from products that have been around no longer than four years (Kanter, Kao, & Wiersema, 1997). Michael Dell attributes the success of his company to "taking risk and staying one step ahead of your competitors . . . by introduce(ing) new products continuously and vigorously" (Jain, 2003).

# INCREASING INDIVIDUAL CREATIVITY

## Myths about Individual Creativity

Many believe that some individuals are inherently creative and others are inherently not. Those who subscribe to this belief think that the key to establishing a creative organization is selection of members who are particularly creative and the exclusion of members who are not. This has led to batteries of pre-employment "aptitude" tests to screen potential members for creativity among other traits.

There is no doubt that there are creative geniuses. Michelangelo, da Vinci, Einstein, Bach, Carver, and Edison are examples from the past who are recognized as creative geniuses. No matter how hard others may try, it is an extremely rare individual who will be able to create works of art, science, and music approaching the quality of these masters. However, research has shown that *every* individual has the capacity to be creative. The results of many of the "aptitude" tests for creativity do not correlate well with actual creative performance. There has to be something more than just individual aptitude involved in whether an individual is "creative" or not. That something more is the organizational environment.

> Creativity is often misunderstood. People think of it in terms of artistic work—unbridled, unguided effort that leads to beautiful effect... Creativity, in fact, thrives best when constrained (but the constraints) must be balanced with a healthy disregard for the impossible. The creativity realized in this balance between constraint and disregard for the impossible is fueled by passion and results in... unexpected insights, cleverness, and imagination, (and revolutionary change).
>
> Marissa Mayer
> *V.P. Search Products and User Experience*, Google
>
> (Mayer, 2006)

## THE IMPORTANCE OF TECHNOLOGICAL FORECASTING

Technologies typically follow a growth pattern that may be described as an S-curve. The length of the path varies. High technologies typically have very short S-curves. The risk in relying just on continuous improvement with no regard for where the current technology falls on the S-curve is that a new technology will replace the existing one. As Figure 4.2 illustrates, this lack of awareness of radical new technologies can result in technology leaders becoming technology laggards or, worse yet, technology losers.

Often the new technologies that transform industries come from outside the industry itself. Intense scanning of the technological environment beyond the boundaries of the organization's current technologies is required to prevent it from being blindsided by a paradigm shift from outside the industry. The slide-rule manufacturers of the 1960s failed to detect the technological breakthroughs in the electronics industry that put them out of business. The carbon paper and photographic imaging companies of the 1930s and 1940s rejected Carlson's xerography technology that came from outside their industry. They defined their technological environments too narrowly. What potentially paradigm-shifting technologies are emerging today? Nanocrystals, such as quantum dots, may have applications in areas as diverse as

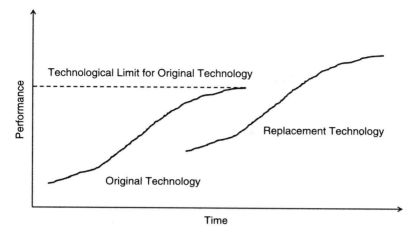

**Figure 4.2.** Technology S-Curves and Technology Discontinuity

medical diagnostics and household lighting (Khalil, 2000). Teraherz (THz) technologies may have applications in medical imaging and chemical analysis (Mallozzi, 2003). Magnetic field nanosensors may revolutionize computer data storage (Solin, 2004). These are examples of technologies that make yesterday's impossibilities tomorrow's mainstream technologies. Lack of awareness of developing technologies such as these could render today's market-leading companies tomorrow's has-beens. Insight is required to develop applications for the key emerging technologies that potentially can disrupt the existing paradigm upon which one's business depends.

There are many ways to approach technological forecasting. Suppliers can be an excellent source of information about developing technologies. Organizations should develop partnering relationships with major suppliers that include information sharing. Assigning responsibility within the organization for staying informed about developments outside the specific domain of the company is another good way to anticipate potential radical shifts in technologies. Including subscriptions to general technology-related periodicals, such as *Scientific American*, in the company library along with publications from a variety of technological fields provides the opportunity to sense radical shifts in technologies. Systematic contact with customers about their future needs and their perceptions about how these needs might be met should be part of the technology-forecasting process.

It is very important to establish as part of the organization's strategy an openness to technological advancement. A major component of this must be broadly defining the purpose of the organization. The railroads in the United States failed to recognize the advances in highway infrastructure and air-and-truck transportation. They defined their business as the "railroad business" rather than the people-and-cargo-moving business. Because of this they were blindsided after World War II and essentially lost their people-moving business, scrambling to preserve market share in the transportation of goods. The Swiss watch makers narrowly defined their business as mechanical watches. Then they were driven out of all but the high-end market by quartz crystal watches—a technology which they themselves discovered.

## Incremental Improvement Loses to Breakthrough in Slide Rule Industry

Imagine being part of the R&D staff at a leading manufacturer of slide rules during the late 1960s. A discussion is underway on ways to improve the quality of the company's slide rule. Customers say they want more accuracy. Providing more accuracy means making longer slide rules. Customers do not want slide rules that are too long. The dilemma is resolved when someone observes that the circumference of a circle is more than three times the diameter. This means that a circular slide rule with a diameter of only 10 inches will have a circumstance (effective length) of over 30 inches.

Another participant observes that much has been happening in the world of microelectronics as a result of the replacement of vacuum tubes with transistors. Radios are now portable and fit in one's pocket. What if the company could develop a portable electronic device programmed to do all that a slide rule can do?

Subject both suggestions to analysis and I suspect that the circular slide rule would get the nod. The investment would be much less, leading to a higher return on investment (ROI); it is responsive to customer input for a more accurate slide rule (did any customer even mention a pocket size calculator?); the development lead time would be less; and the company already possesses command of the required technologies. However, in perfect hindsight, which approach would have prepared the company to compete in the scientific calculating market of the 1970s? It is instructive to note that the only place where slide rules are sold today is in antiques markets while almost everyone owns a pocket calculator.

(Sower & Fair 2005. Reprinted with permission from *Quality Management Journal*. © 2005 American Society for Quality. No further distribution allowed without permission.)

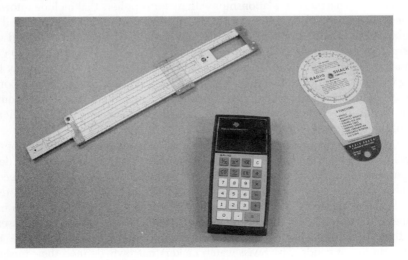

# SUMMARY

Innovation and creativity are more about organizational culture and individual development than about some innate creativity trait in individuals. Although there is certainly a range of creative ability among individuals, even the most creative individual can be beaten down by a poor organizational environment.

Radical innovation is different from incremental improvement. Both are necessary. In order to be creative and develop radical innovations in quality, both the organization and the individuals within must strive to reach Plato's insight level of awareness. It is the combination of individual creative ability and the organizational culture and work environment that results in creative behavior.  .

There are common elements that creative organizations possess. Organizations who wish to become more creative can benefit from finding ways to develop these elements in their own cultures.

Technology forecasting is important for organizations which wish to remain on the quality cutting edge. It is also important just to survive in today's rapidly advancing technological environment.

# DISCUSSION QUESTIONS

1. Of what value is creative thinking to an organization?
2. Discuss the difference between breakthrough (radical) improvement and continuous incremental improvement.
3. What is Juran's definition of breakthrough improvement?
4. Discuss the interrelationship between serendipity and sagacity.
5. Discuss the approach of trying to select and hire only the most creative applicants as an organization's approach to becoming more creative.
6. How does Plato's divided line image relate to creativity?
7. Which of Deming's 14 points (Chapter 1) address issues that might impact creativity in an organization?
8. What are some ways to stimulate creativity within an organization?
9. Why might creative projects benefit from some period of unofficial status?
10. What is meant by alignment? Of what importance is it to a creative organization?
11. What does it mean to be a risk-tolerant organization? How does that relate to the level of creativity that is likely to develop in an organization?
12. Why might technology forecasting be important to commodity industries such as petroleum refining, bottled water, and tax services?
13. What are some sources of information that might be useful in technology forecasting?
14. How does one reconcile the definition of quality as meeting customer needs in cases where customers cannot articulate those needs?

**CASE STUDY 4.1:** *Smallburg Community Bank*

©2006 Victor E. Sower, Ph.D., C.Q.E.

It is September 1990. Mary Roberts, CEO of Smallberg Bank, begins the staff meeting by reviewing the recent findings of a survey of customers conducted for the bank by a professor at the local college. "I asked Professor Sanders to survey our customers to determine how we can improve the quality of service to our existing customers and what we need to do to increase our customer base over the next five years. The findings show that the greatest factor that we need to address is accessibility. According to the professor, accessibility means availability of services. Our customers want 24-hour access."

"We all know that's impossible," offers Jill Summers, operations manager. "Perhaps we can keep our inside banking hours the same but keep the drive through open longer every day and half day on Saturday. That would probably be our lowest cost option."

As the discussion began about how long to extend the drive through banking hours, Bill Wilson, head teller, interrupts. "I've been reading about breakthroughs in automated banking services. Automated teller machines (ATM) are beginning to show up in major markets. There is even talk of online banking—that someday everyone will have a computer in their home connected to the bank. Maybe we should find out more about that."

Mary responds, "That's interesting, Bill, but remember we are in the banking business—not the computer business. Our customers want personal contact. And online banking... I heard that some top manager at IBM predicted that the world only needed 5–10 computers, maximum. A computer in every home; online banking! That will never happen here. Let's focus on the problem at hand."

1. Critique the reaction of Smallberg National Bank to Professor Sanders' survey findings.
2. What are the risks the bank is exposed to due to this reaction?
3. What are the potential risks the bank would be exposed to if they take Bill's comments more seriously?
4. What are the potential risks the bank would be exposed to if they ignore Bill's comments?
5. If you were on the staff of Smallberg National Bank and present in this meeting that took place in 1990, what would you advise them to do?

## EXERCISES AND ACTIVITIES

1. Paper Cup Exercise (based on Robinson & Stern, 1997)
   a. Provide each participant with three paper cups. Give them 4 minutes to come up with as many ideas for the use of the cups as possible.
   b. Have participants count the number of ideas they developed.

c. Have participants count the number of ideas which use the cup as a container. Then calculate the percentage of ideas that use the cup as a container.

d. Plot the results on the creativity grid.

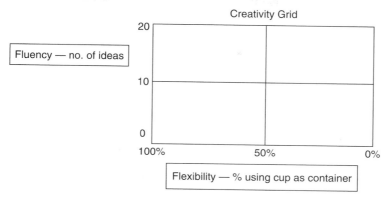

e. Classify participants' creativity based on their position on the grid.

f. Have the students prepare a brief report about what they learned about themselves from this exercise.

g. Discuss the validity of the exercise with the students.

**2.** The Importance of Alignment (*Source:* Joe Kavanaugh, Ph.D.) (This exercise works best with a group of 10–20 participants.)

Part A

a. Appoint a group leader and tie a 20–30 foot rope around the leader's waist and lay the rope on the floor down the center of a room.

b. Divide the remaining group members into two parts with one group lined up along each side of the rope.

c. Have the group members close their eyes and spin in place.

d. After a few seconds of spinning, say "Stop!"

e. Without adjusting their position, have all group members grasp the rope with their hand nearest the rope.

f. On your signal, have all group members move in the direction they are facing, pulling the rope with them. Have the group members observe what happens (or does not happen) to the leader.

Part B

g. Repeat Steps (a) and (b) above.

h. This time, have the leader face the direction in which he or she wishes to move. Have the leader direct the group members to align the rope and themselves in that direction.

i. Repeat Steps (e) and (f) above.

j. Discuss what was learned from the exercise.

# SUPPLEMENTARY READINGS

Barker, J. (1990). *The Business of Paradigms*. Burnsville, MN: Charthouse International Learning Corp.

Kaplan, R., & D. Norton. (2001). *The Strategy-Focused Organization*. Boston: Harvard Business School Press.

Khalil, T. (2000). *Management of Technology*. Boston: McGraw-Hill.

Plsek, P. (1998). "Incorporating the Tools of Creativity into Quality Management." *Quality Progress* 31(3), 21–28.

Provost, L., & R. Sproul. (1996). "Creativity and Improvement: A Vital Link." *Quality Progress* 29(8), 101–107.

Rakich, J. (2000). "Strategic Quality Planning." *Hospital Topics: Research and Perspectives on Healthcare* 78(2), 5–11.

Robinson, A., & S. Stern. (1997). *Corporate Creativity*. San Francisco: Berrett-Koehler.

Sower, V., & F. Fair. (2005). "There is More to Quality than Continuous Improvement: Listening to Plato." *Quality Management Journal* 12(1), 8–20.

Tennant, C., & P. Roberts. (2000). "Hoshin Kanri: a Technique for Strategic Quality Management." *Quality Assurance* 8(2), 77–90.

# REFERENCES

Barker, J. (1990). *The Business of Paradigms*. Burnsville, MN: Charthouse International Learning Corp.

Bradshaw, G., & S. Wright. (ND). http://www.wam.umd.edu/~stwright/WrBr/taleplane.html. (Link is no longer active).

Chambers, J. (1969). "Beginning a Multidimensional Theory of Creativity." *Psychological Reports* 25(3), 779–799.

Clarke, T. (1996). "Organizational Climate, Productivity and Creativity." Paper prepared for the Canadian Government Working Group on Rewards, Recognition and Incentives (November). http://www.stargate-consultants.ca/artcexec.htm.

"Give Employees the Freedom to Fail." (2006). *Inside Supply Management*, September 17 (9), 9.

Hamel, G. (2001). "The Why, What, and How of Management Innovation." *Harvard Business Review* 84(2), February, 72–84. *Houston Chronicle*, January 4, 2006.

Jain, C. (2003). "Benchmarking New Product Forecasting." *The Journal of Business Forecasting* (Fall), 27–28.

Kanter, R., J. Kao, & F. Wiersema. (1997). *Innovation*. New York: Harper Business.

Khalil, T. (2000). *Management of Technology*. Boston: McGraw-Hill, 255.

Mallozzi, J. (2003). "Harnessing THz for Medical Applications." *R&D* 45(10), 28.

Mayer, M. (2006). "Turning Limitations into Innovation." *Business Week Online*, February 1, 1–2.

Mayer, S. (2003). Personal communication.

*Oxford English Dictionary*, quoted in Robinson, A. & S. Stern. (1997), 179.

Plato. (1992). (Original circa 390 BC). *Republic*. Translated by G. M. A. Grube, revised by C. D. C. Reeve. Indianapolis, IN: Hackett.

Plsek, P. (1998). "Incorporating the Tools of Creativity into Quality Management." *Quality Progress* 31(3), 21–28.

Provost, L., & R. Sproul. (1996). "Creativity and Improvement: A Vital Link." *Quality Progress* 29(8), 101–107.

Robinson, A., & S. Stern. (1997). *Corporate Creativity*. San Francisco: Berrett-Koehler.

Shotmiller, J. (2004). Personal communication.

Sidawi, D. (2003). "Nanocrystals Enable Diverse Applications." *R&D* 45(10), 24–25.

Solin, S. (2004). "Magnetic Field Nanosensors." *Scientific American* (June), 71–77.

Sower, V.E., & F. Fair. (2005). "There is More to Quality than Continuous Improvement: Listening to Plato." *Quality Management Journal* 12(1), 8–20.

Stix, G. (2004). "A Confederacy of Smarts." *Scientific American* 290(6), 40–45.

Vaisnys, V. (2000). "Retaining Creative Employees." *Innovative Leader* 9(10), http://www.winstonbrill.com/index.html.

# SECTION III

## QUALITY SYSTEMS TO ASSURE CONFORMANCE TO DESIGN

## CHAPTER FIVE

# Quality Systems and Quality Systems Auditing

## CHAPTER OBJECTIVES

After reading this chapter the reader should be able to:

- list and discuss the elements of a quality management system;
- understand the basic elements of the major quality management systems;
- understand the basics of the ISO 9001 standard;
- understand the basics of the MBNQA process;
- list and discuss the objectives of quality audits;
- list and discuss the types of quality audits;
- discuss the quality system audit process;
- discuss the scope and objectives of quality information systems;
- discuss the importance of ensuring data accuracy and integrity;
- discuss quality documentation systems; and
- understand the basics of a quality information system, document control, and information flows.

The general requirements for a quality management system are to say what you do and do what you say.

(Russell, 2001)

A system can be defined as any set of interdependent parts performing a specific function or set of functions. A quality management system is that part of the organization's overall management system that includes "the collective plans, activities and events that are provided to ensure that a product, process, or service will satisfy given needs" (ANSI/ASQC Q1-1986, 2). It is a "formalized system that documents the structure, responsibilities and procedures required to achieve effective quality management" (Quality Glossary, 2002, 56). A quality system is more than the sum of processes. "To be effective, the quality system needs coordination and compatibility of its component processes, and definition of their interfaces" (ANSI/ASQC Q9000-1-1994, 5).

This chapter examines the development and operation of a quality system for an organization. Included in this chapter are the elements of a quality system, elements of a quality information system, the scope and objectives of quality information systems, techniques for ensuring data accuracy and integrity, management systems for improving quality, quality documentation systems, and problem identification, analysis, reporting, and corrective action systems.

Quality audits are part of the evaluation and assessment process that managers use to uncover areas for improvement. When used appropriately, audit findings can serve to focus the organization on the areas most in need of attention. When used as the basis for punitive measures, they can further divide an already troubled organization.

*ISO 8402* and *ANSI/ASQC Q10011-1-1994* define a quality audit as "[a] systematic and independent examination to determine whether quality activities and related results comply with planned arrangements and whether these arrangements are implemented effectively and are suitable to achieve objectives." *ANSI/ASQC Q1-1986*, (1-2) defines a quality audit as "a systematic examination of the acts and decisions by people with respect to quality in order to independently verify or evaluate and report degree of compliance to the operational requirements of the quality program, or the specifications or contract requirements of the product or service".

Quality audits, then, are by definition a form of performance audit, also referred to as management audit (Arter, 2003). It is also evident that a quality audit cannot be performed unless the desired state has been fully documented. Unless the ideal state has been defined, it is impossible to determine through an audit the degree to which that undefined state has been attained. A quality system is usually defined by the quality manual.

# QUALITY MANAGEMENT SYSTEMS

## Elements of a Quality Management System

A quality management system includes four fundamental activities (Arter, 2003):

- *Planning.* A plan for quality activities including designation of responsibility, accountability, and ownership of the activities. This section of the system defines the customer and other constituents and their requirements.

- *Performance.* The activities should be executed according to the plan, and records should be kept to facilitate measurement of actual versus planned performance.

- *Measurement.* The results of the activities are compared to some defined standard using tools such as audit, inspection, evaluation and review. Customer feedback is a vital component of the measurement process.

- *Improvement.* The process must be continually evaluated for problems and opportunities for improvement.

The primary evidence that a quality system has been designed is the quality manual. This manual, at a minimum, provides evidence that:

- a process has been defined

- the procedures are approved

- the procedures are under document control (ANSI/ASQC Q9000-1-1994).

ISO 9001, the Malcolm Baldrige National Quality Award (MBNQA), and ISO/TS 16949:2002 (which is an equivalent to the QS 9000 standards for the automobile industry) are formal guidelines for quality systems. Each approaches the process from somewhat different perspectives, but with the same goal: to provide a framework through which a quality control program can be identified, designed, developed, implemented, and enhanced to improve the overall performance of an organization.

It is possible for an organization to obtain certification to the ISO 9001 and ISO/TS 16949 standards and to apply for and win the MBNQA. This provides external validation of the conformance of the organization's quality system to the standard.

## ISO 9000

ISO 9000 is the commonly used term to refer to the ANSI/ISO/ASQ Q9000-2008, ANSI/ISO/ASQ Q9001-2008, and ANSI/ISO/ASQ Q9004-2008 standards. This set of standards describes the elements of a quality system but not how a specific organization should implement these elements. The standards are issued jointly by the American National Standards Institute (ANSI), the International Organization for Standardization (ISO), and the American Society for Quality (ASQ). ANSI is the U.S. member body of the ISO. A related standard, ISO 19011, "provides guidance on auditing quality and environmental management systems" (ANSI/ISO/ASQ Q9000-2008, ix).

Organizations may be certified to the ANSI/ISO/ASQ Q9001-2008 *Quality Management Systems—Requirements*. ISO 9000 defines a quality management system very simply as a system "to direct and control an organization with regard to quality" (ANSI/ISO/ASQ Q9000-2008, 8).

**Figure 5.1.** Process-Based Quality Management System Model (*Source*: Adapted from ANSI/ISO/ASQ Q9000-2000-Quality Management System: Fundamentals and Vocabulary.)

The ISO 9000 standard encourages the process approach to managing quality as shown in Figure 5.1. Its standards are based on eight quality management principles (ANSI/ISO/ASQ Q9000-2008):

1. Customer Focus
2. Leadership
3. Involvement of People
4. Process Approach
5. Systems Approach to Management
6. Continual Improvement
7. Factual Approach to Decision Making
8. Mutually Beneficial Supplier Relationships

ISO 9000 specifies eight steps included in the development and implementation of a quality management system (ANSI/ISO/ASQ Q9000-2008):

- determination of the needs and expectations of customers and other constituents
- establishment of a quality policy and quality objectives for the organization
- determination of the processes and responsibilities necessary to attain the quality objectives
- determination and provision of the resources necessary to attain the quality objectives
- establishment of measures for the effectiveness and efficiency of each process
- application of these measures to determine the effectiveness and efficiency of each process
- determination of means of preventing nonconformities and eliminating their causes
- establishment and application of a process for continual improvement of the quality management system

A basic outline of the ISO-9001 quality system requirements is in Figure 5.2.

ASQ defines process as a "set of interrelated work activities characterized by a set of specific inputs and value added tasks that make up a procedure for a set of specific outputs."

ASQ defines effectiveness as the "state of having produced a decided upon or desired effect."

ASQ defines efficiency as the "ratio of the output to the total input in a process."

("Quality Glossary," 2002, 49, 55)

According to ISO 9000, an important role of top management is to "carry out regular systematic evaluations of the suitability, adequacy, effectiveness and efficiency of the quality management system with respect to the quality policy and quality objectives" (ANSI/ISO/ASQ Q9000-2008). This role is commonly fulfilled through a quality system audit. An organization seeking registration to the ISO 9001 standard would typically follow the following path:

Self-Assessment and Improvement:
- Comprehensive self-assessment to review actual processes and results to the quality policy and objectives. This is accomplished through an internal audit conducted either by employees of the organization or by consultants hired by the organization.
- Identification of areas for improvement based on the results of the internal audit.
- Establishment of objectives for the improvement efforts.
- Development of improvement plans.
- Implementation of the improvement plans.
- Re-audit to assure the improvement plans achieved the desired results.

Third Party Audit:
- Engage an accredited registrar to conduct an external audit to determine whether the organization meets the ISO 9001 standards.

## ISO/TS 16949 and QS-9000

QS-9000 is a specialized standard for U.S. automotive suppliers that is interdependent with ISO-9000. The QS-9000 standard includes all the ISO 9000 requirements plus other requirements that are similar to the Malcolm Baldrige National Quality Award concepts. The process of becoming registered to QS-9000 is similar to that for ISO-9000.

Although the ISO/TS 16969:2000(E) technical specification does not replace the QS-9000 standard, many organizations in the automobile industry are transitioning to the new standard. ISO/TS 16969 is an international quality management system specification for the automobile industry. It evolved from Big Three (Daimler-Chrysler, Ford, GM) quality manuals, QS-9000, and ISO 9000. The ISO/TS 16949 provides additional specifications for customer satisfaction and employee

4. Quality Management System
   4.1 General requirements
   4.2 Documentation requirements

5. Management responsibility
   5.1 Management commitment
   5.2 Customer focus
   5.3 Quality policy
   5.4 Planning
   5.5 Responsibility, authority and communication
   5.6 Management review

6. Resource management
   6.1 Provision of resources
   6.2 Human resources
   6.3 Infrastructure
   6.4 Work environment

7. Product realization
   7.1 Planning of product realization
   7.2 Customer-related processes
   7.3 Design and development
   7.4 Purchasing
   7.5 Production and service provision
   7.6 Control of monitoring and measuring devices

8. Measurement, analysis and improvement
   8.1 General
   8.2 Monitoring and measurement
   8.3 Control of nonconforming product
   8.4 Analysis of data
   8.5 Improvement

**Figure 5.2.** Basic Outline of ISO 9001 and ISO/TS 16949 Requirements

motivation, empowerment, and satisfaction compared with QS-9000. "Together with ISO 9001:2000, ISO/TS 16949 specifies the quality system requirements for the design/development, production, installation and servicing of automotive related products" (http://www.bsiamericaas.com). The basic outline of the ISO/TS 16969 requirements is identical to that of ISO 9001 (Figure 5.2).

A survey conducted by the Automotive Industry Action Committee found that the average cost for a supplier to become registered to QS-9000 is $118,100. The average cost for selected certification activities include:

| | |
|---|---|
| • Preparation | $36,900 |
| • Consulting/training | $26,000 |
| • Registrar | $18,300 |
| • Software | $5,100 |

**TABLE 5.1. MBNQA Winners**

| Year | Manufacturing | Service | Small Business | Health Care | Education | Nonprofit |
|---|---|---|---|---|---|---|
| 1988 | Motorola, Inc.<br>Westinghouse Electric Corp. Commercial Nuclear Fuel division | | Globe Metallurgical, Inc. | | | |
| 1989 | Milliken & Co.<br>Xerox Corp., Business Products & Systems | | | | | |
| 1990 | Cadillac Motor Car Co.<br>IBM Rochester | Federal Express Corp. | Wallace Co., Inc. | | | |
| 1991 | Solectron Corp.<br>Zytec Corp. | | Marlow Industries, Inc. | | | |
| 1992 | AT & T Network Systems Group Transmission Systems Business Unit<br><br>Texas Instruments Inc. Defense Systems & Electronics Group | The Ritz-Carlton Hotel Co.<br><br>AT & T Universal Card Services | Granite Rock Co. | | | |
| 1993 | Eastman Chemical Co. | | Ames Rubber Corp. | | | |
| 1994 | | AT & T Consumer Communications Services<br><br>Verizon Information Services | Wainwright Industries, Inc. | | | |

(continued overleaf)

TABLE 5.1. (*continued*)

| Year | Manufacturing | Service | Small Business | Health Care | Education | Nonprofit |
|------|---------------|---------|----------------|-------------|-----------|-----------|
| 1995 | Armstrong World Industries, Inc. | | | | | |
| | Corning, Inc. Telecommunications Products Division | | | | | |
| 1996 | ADAC Laboratories | Dana Commercial Credit Corp. | Custom Research, Inc. | | | |
| | | | Trident Precision Manufacturing, Inc. | | | |
| 1997 | 3M Dental Products Division | Merrill Lynch Credit Corp. | | | | |
| | Solectron Corp. | Xerox Business Services | | | | |
| 1998 | Boeing Airlift & Tanker Programs | | Texas Nameplate Co., Inc. | | | |
| | Solar Turbines, Inc. | | | | | |
| 1999 | STMicroelectronics, Inc. | The Ritz-Carlton Hotel Co., LLC | Sunny Fresh Foods | | | |
| | | BI | | | | |
| 2000 | Dana Corp. Spicer Driveshaft Div. | Operations Management International, Inc. | Los Alamos National Bank | | | |
| | KARLEE Co., Inc. | | | | | |

(*continued*)

**Table 5.1.** (*continued*)

| Year | Manufacturing | Service | Small Business | Health Care | Education | Nonprofit |
|---|---|---|---|---|---|---|
| 2001 | Clarke American Checks, Inc. | | Pal's Sudden Service | | Pearle River School District<br>University of Wisconsin-Stout<br>Chugach School District | |
| 2002 | Motorola Commercial, Government & Industrial Solutions Sector | | Branch-Smith Printing Division | SSM Health Care | | |
| 2003 | Medrad, Inc. | Caterpillar Financial Services Corp.<br>Boeing Aerospace Support | Stoner, Inc. | Baptist Hospital, Inc. | Community Consolidated School District 15 | |
| 2004 | The Bama Companies, Inc. | | Texas Nameplate Co., Inc. | St. Luke's Hospital of Kansas City<br>Robert Wood Johnson University Hospital Hamilton | Kenneth W. Monfort College of Business | |

(*continued overleaf*)

TABLE 5.1. (*continued*)

| Year | Manufacturing | Service | Small Business | Health Care | Education | Nonprofit |
|---|---|---|---|---|---|---|
| 2005 | Sunny Fresh Foods, Inc. | DynMcDermott Petroleum Operations | Park Place Lexus | Bronson Methodist Hospital | Richland College | |
| | | | | | Jenks Public Schools | |
| 2006 | | Premier, Inc. | Mesa Products, Inc. | North Mississippi Medical Center | | |
| 2007 | | | PRO-TEC Coating Co. | Mercy Health System | | City of Coral Springs |
| | | | | Sharp HealthCare | | U.S. Army Armament Research, Development, and Engineering Center (ARDEC) |
| 2008 | Cargill Corn Milling (CCM) | | | Poudre Valley Health System | Iredell-Statesville Schools | |

The suppliers estimated the average benefit of being registered to be $304,300 (*Quality Digest*, 1997).

## Malcolm Baldrige National Quality Award (MBNQA)

The Malcolm Baldrige National Quality Award (MBNQA) is unlike the ISO 9001 and ISO/TS 16969 in that it is a competition, not an accreditation standard. The award was created in 1987 and is "the highest level of national recognition for performance excellence that a U.S. organization can receive" (*Baldrige Award Application Forms*). No more than three awards are given each year in each of six categories: manufacturing, service, small business, education, health care, and nonprofit. The American Society for Quality (ASQ) assists the National Institute of Standards and Technology (NIST) in administrating the MBNQA program. Many of the state quality awards use the MBNQA criteria. Winners of the MBNQA are listed in Table 5.1.

The MBNQA criteria consist of seven categories that differ slightly among the business, education, health care, and nonprofit criteria. These categories provide an outline for the components of a quality management system that will meet the award standards. A listing of these categories is contained in Figure 5.3.

Organizations interested in applying for the MBNQA should obtain the *Criteria for Performance Excellence* package for their specific category. This document contains information about the MBNQA criteria for the category, a self-analysis worksheet, the scoring system and guidelines, the application process and associated fees, and eligibility guidelines. The first formal step in the application process

| Category Number | Business | Education | Health Care |
|---|---|---|---|
| 1 | Leadership | Leadership | Leadership |
| 2 | Strategic Planning | Strategic Planning | Strategic Planning |
| 3 | Customer and Market Focus | Student, Stakeholder, and Market Focus | Focus on Patients, Other Customers, and Markets |
| 4 | Measurement, Analysis, and Knowledge Management | Measurement, Analysis, and Knowledge Management | Measurement, Analysis, and Knowledge Management |
| 5 | Human Resource Focus | Faculty and Staff Focus | Staff Focus |
| 6 | Process Management | Process Management | Process Management |
| 7 | Business Results | Organizational Performance Results | Organizational Performance Results |

**Figure 5.3.** MBNQA Categories

is to submit an Eligibility Certification Package to NIST. This is followed by submission of the *Baldrige Award Application Forms*, background information about the organization (e.g., organization chart, organizational profile), and a self-evaluation against the MBNQA criteria. Applications are first subjected to independent review. Those selected for consensus review are evaluated by judges who determine whether to move to the next step: site visit review. Those organizations selected for a site visit are audited by a team of judges who make recommendations for award of the MBNQA. No matter how far an application progresses in this process, a feedback report is provided to the applicant.

Robert Wood Johnson (RWJ) University Hospital in Hamilton, New Jersey, won the 2004 Malcolm Baldrige National Quality Award (MBNQA). They had a quality program in place in 1999 that was based on their "five pillars of excellence"—service, finance, quality, people, and growth. But looking for ways to better serve its customers, the hospital's management decided to use the MBNQA criteria as a "framework . . . for leadership and acceleration of our quality journey." One of their achievements is best-in-class service in their Emergency Department (ED). Their 15/30 Program guarantees that every patient will be seen by a nurse within 15 minutes and by a doctor within 30 minutes of entering the ED. They back this program with an extraordinary guarantee—if they fail to do so, the ED portion of the bill will be waived upon patient request. This program has contributed to overall hospital success since 70 percent of the hospital's inpatients enter through the ED. Patient satisfaction in the ED was crucial to the hospital's success. Their payout is less than 1 percent indicating that they have a process in place to achieve the desired results. Patient satisfaction with ED increased from 85 percent in 2001 to 90 percent in 2004.

(Nelsen, 2005, 69–79)

## Other Approaches

There are many other approaches to quality management systems other than those discussed above. These might be loosely grouped under the heading of total quality management (TQM) systems. ASQ defines TQM as "a management approach to long-term success through customer satisfaction" (Quality Glossary, 2002). There are many approaches to implementing TQM but all are "based on the participation of all members of an organization in improving processes, products, services and the culture in which they work" (Quality Glossary, 2002). These approaches revolve around the teachings of quality gurus such as Deming, Juran, Crosby, Feigenbaum, among others discussed in Chapter 1. The overall focus of TQM is as broad as the more structured quality systems such as the MBNQA and ISO 9000.

## Six Sigma

Six Sigma is "a methodology that provides businesses with the tools to improve the capability of their business processes. This increase in performance and decrease in process variation lead to defect reduction and improvement in profits, employee morale and quality of product" (Quality Glossary, 2002). Developed at Motorola, Six Sigma quality programs have been adopted at many major corporations, including GE, Dow Chemical, and AlliedSignal. When used as a metric, Six Sigma means doing things right more than 99.9996 percent of the time (fewer than 3.4 defects per million opportunities). Six Sigma is more narrowly focused than ISO 9001, MBNQA, or TQM. It is a project-based system that uses the tools of quality in conjunction with experimental design and statistical analysis to investigate and resolve problems and optimize processes to improve quality and reduce costs. The process used in these processes is the define-measure-analyze-improve-control or DMAIC process. Project leaders are usually certified as "black belts" in the Six Sigma methodologies.

Like the other quality management systems, Six Sigma stresses leadership, communication, training, and teamwork. It can fit very well into any approach to quality system management. In fact, Motorola, which developed the Six Sigma approach, was one of the first winners of the MBNQA.

Six Sigma has been criticized by some as being "just a repackaging of long-cherished quality techniques" (Franco, 2001). But David Silverstein of Breakthrough Management Group disagrees. He says, "What is special about Six Sigma is that it puts all of the elements together in a comprehensive system that's structured and disciplined and includes many points of accountability" (Franco, 2001).

Other critics of Six Sigma suggest that it doesn't go far enough. According to Thomas Pyzdek (1999), Six Sigma programs focus on nonconformances and defects that can only result in a "not dissatisfied" customer. Six Sigma programs must be adapted (such as the Dow Chemical approach) to focus on "critical to quality (CTQ)" characteristics that can create satisfied customers. But Pyzdek claims that customer satisfaction is not enough. Perfection in the CTQ will not assure the viability of the firm in the long run.

The Dow Chemical approach to Six Sigma attempts to "focus on the determinants of customer satisfaction and drive them back to the businesses they touch" (McCoy, 1999). Dow started the process from the top, focusing on major projects and breakthrough goals, and establishing those goals in Six Sigma metrics. Kathleen Bader, Dow Chemical's corporate vice president for quality and business excellence, says that "Six Sigma is a cultural change program that accelerates perfection," and expects the program to add "a cumulative $1.5 billion to the company's earnings before interest and taxes by the end of 2003" (McCoy, 2001). One project initiated by a Six Sigma black belt at Dow cost $75 for a monitor to measure moisture and saved $713,000 in the first quarter of the year (McCoy, 2001).

Lean Six Sigma is a combination of Six Sigma's process for reducing process variation and eliminating defects with lean operations' methodologies for identifying unnecessary costs and nonvalue adding process steps and reducing cycle times (George, 2002). There are many examples in both manufacturing and service of quality improvements resulting from the "leaning up" of processes. The synergistic combination of these two methodologies often results in improved quality, reduced costs, less customer waiting, and more efficient operations.

## QUALITY AUDITING

Quality audits may be either internal (Q10011-1-1994, 3.4a) or external (Q10011-1-1994, 3.4b-d). Internal audits (first-party audits) are performed within the auditee's own organization. Internal auditors may be organizational employees or outsiders hired by the organization. External audits include supplier certification, regulatory compliance (e.g., FDA regulations), standards compliance (e.g., UL standards), and registration audits (e.g., ISO 9001 registration). External auditors may be either employees of the client organization (second party) or employees of an independent agency (third party) authorized to perform the audit.

The knowledge gained from an independent internal audit of a quality system can provide management with information necessary to improve that program. That same knowledge can be gained through an independent external audit. However, because an outside party conducts an external audit, they often are viewed in a more negative light and sometimes create a defensive reaction. There often is much at stake in an external audit.

Successfully navigating one's way through a quality audit is important to organizations. ANSI/ISO/ASQ Q-9001 2008 registration, accreditation by an industry body (e.g., AACSB or JCAHO), or remaining on the preferred supplier list of a major customer may hang in the balance. This can sometimes lead to a defensive posture on the part of the auditee. Management must take appropriate measures to avoid such a reaction.

ASQ defines an **audit** as the inspection and examination of a process or quality system to ensure compliance to requirements. An audit can apply to an entire organization or may be specific to a function, process, or production step.

ASQ defines a **quality audit** as a systematic, independent examination and review to determine whether quality activities and related results comply with planned arrangements and whether these arrangements are implemented effectively and are suitable to achieve the objectives.

(Quality Glossary, 2002, 44, 56)

### Specific Types of Quality Audits

There are several different approaches to classifying audits. Tunner (1990) describes three generic types of quality audit:

1. Policy audit

2. Practice audit

3. Product audit

A policy audit compares written policies and procedures against standards and specifications. A practice audit checks actual practices against established procedures. A product audit evaluates the performance of a product relative to its specifications.

Mills (1989) subdivides quality audits based upon four dimensions:

1. The purpose of the audit — "Why?"
   a. Suitability quality audit.
   b. Conformity quality audit.

2. The object of the audit — "What?"
   a. Quality program audit.
   b. Quality system audit.

3. The nature of the audit — "Who?"
   a. Internal quality audit.
   b. External quality audit.

4. The method of the audit — "How?"
   a. Comprehensive quality system audit.
   b. Selected quality program element audit.

Various permutations and combinations of these dimensions constitute specific types of audits (see Mills, Chapter 2, pp. 25–34). For example, an ANSI/ISO/ASQ Q-9001 2008 audit is a comprehensive suitability and conformity quality audit of a quality system by an external auditor.

ANSI/ISO/ASQ Q9000-2008 and Arter (2003) characterize audits based upon the identity of the auditor (the individual performing the audit) and auditee (the organization being audited):

1. First-party audit

2. Second-party audit

3. Third-party audit

A first-party audit is an internal audit—the auditor and auditee are in the same organization. They are performed "for internal purposes and can form the basis for an organization's self-declaration of conformity" (ANSI/ISO/ASQ Q9000-2008). A second-party audit would be an external audit if your organization is the auditor. An example would be where your organization conducts an audit of a supplier. A second-party audit would be an external audit if your organization is the auditee. An example would be where your organization is audited by a customer. A third-party audit is performed by someone other than either the customer or the supplier. An example of a third-party audit would be an ISO 9001 audit performed by an accredited registrar.

## Performing a Quality System Audit

*ANSI/ASQC Q1-1986* lists the responsibilities of the auditor, the client (the individual requesting the audit), and the auditee (ANSI/ASQC Q1-1986, 2–4). It also provides a flowchart documenting the entire audit process (ANSI/ASQC Q1-1986, 29-13).

The audit client responsibilities include (ANSI/ASQC Q1-1986, 3):

Initiate audit, define reference standards, receive audit report

Abstain from an undue interference with audit activities

Determine follow-up action

Auditee responsibilities include (ANSI/ASQC Q1-1986, 31):

Appointing a responsible person to accompany the auditor(s)

Provide access to facilities and evidential material requested by the auditor

Provide adequate working facilities at the audit site

Cooperate with the auditors

Attend meetings called by the auditor

Review audit findings to ensure a factual report

Take corrective action when required by the client

Abstain from any undue interference with the audit

Auditor responsibilities include (ANSI/ASQC Q1-1986, 2):

Comply with applicable audit standards

Clarify and articulate the audit objective

Effectively and efficiently plan and implement the audit

Report the audit results

Audit results of corrective action(s), if requested by the client

Retain and safeguard audit working papers

Maintain independence from the organization being audited

The steps involved in performing a quality audit, as defined by *ANSI/ISO/ASQ QE19011S* (2004), are:

1. Initiating the Audit
2. Conducting Document Review
3. Preparing for the On-Site Audit Activities
4. Conducting the On-Site Audit Activities
5. Preparing, Approving, and Distributing the Audit Report
6. Completing the Audit
7. Conducting the Audit Follow-up

The Eli Lilly internal audit process is defined somewhat differently (Bishara & Wyrick, 1994). Lilly's approach defines auditing as a cycle consisting of five basic steps:

Preparation
>  Audit Plan
>  Audit Program

Conduct
>  Opening Meeting
>  Fieldwork, Examination, Daily Update
>  Closing Meeting

Writing/Review
>  Draft Detailed Audit Report

Reporting
>  Audit Report

Follow-up
>  Follow-up Audit (when applicable)

Lilly has found this approach facilitates understanding, cooperation, and partnership between the quality assurance function and its customers while providing management with unbiased information.

Particular attention must be directed to the proper conduct of internal audits. Internal quality audits performed by representatives of the quality assurance department can perpetuate the "quality department as policeman" stereotype. Rice (1994) suggests that attention to establishing and maintaining clear lines of communication between auditor and auditee is key. This includes discussing deficiencies with the auditee prior to making a decision that will impact the auditee's organization. Proper preparation so that the auditor understands the auditee's procedures prior to the start of the audit is also important. An auditor's ability to see things from the auditee's perspective is helpful in heading off potential conflict. Focusing on problems and not individuals helps avoid defensive responses to audit findings. Taking the time to build a good working relationship will help assure that even differences of opinion can be handled in an objective manner, and that the audit will have the desired effect of helping the auditee improve the operation.

## QUALITY INFORMATION SYSTEMS

Information systems are systems designed to collect, process, store, and transmit data and information for future access and retrieval. Information systems may be manual or electronic. For instance, both a filing cabinet and a computer hard disk are forms of data storage and retrieval systems. E-mail, Web sites, memos, notices, and Post-it™ notes are all methods of information transmission.

Quality information systems (QISs) may be entirely electronic, entirely manual, or some combination of the two. They range from formal, detailed systems, to informal systems of verbal feedback. The size and type of quality information system required by a particular organization is determined by the people who will use it. The best system in the world, unused, is no better than having no system at all. Therefore, it is important that the people in an organization who will use the QIS are involved in the identification, recommendation, selection, and implementation of the quality system.

QISs are part of and support the overall quality system in ensuring that desired quality is being achieved in an organization. To develop an effective system, we must analyze the quality needs of the organization and define an information system to meet those needs. This analysis and design process is driven from an organizational perspective, is an organizational improvement process, and is based on an understanding of the organization's objectives, structure, and processes with regard to quality.

There are three key components to the development of a QIS:

- data: raw facts about things
- data flows: data in motion from one place in the system to another
- processing logic: steps by which data are transformed or moved and a description of the events that trigger these steps

Each component must be designed and analyzed so that the right information is provided to the right person at the right time and in the right format to ensure that a quality product/service is provided to the customer.

To ensure proper design of the system, a systems development life cycle (SDLC) was developed for the analysis and design of information systems. There are several different versions of the SDLC. One is the six-step process defined in Figure 5.4. Utilizing this process ensures that users design a system capable of meeting the needs of the quality assurance process.

## Data Accuracy and Security

QISs must be checked and verified on a regular basis. The data contained in a QIS must be accurate and secure. Data accuracy can be improved by using automated data entry approaches such as bar codes, RFID tags, and automated measurement systems. Direct entry minimizes errors in data entry that can result from manually transcribing data from a report to a data base. Data security is addressed by limiting access to data files and strictly controlling who has the authority to modify data sets. Periodic audits also help assure the accuracy and integrity of the QIS.

A survey of 385 senior IT professionals conducted by CFO Research Services and Deloitte Consulting finds that fewer than half are happy with the quality of the management information they receive. Respondents reported spending considerable time building special reports and analyses because of the lack of effective information quality (IQ) reporting.

(Myers, 2005)

---

1. **Identifying the Project**
   Purpose: Develop a preliminary understanding of the business situation.
   Deliverable: A formal request to conduct a project to design and develop an information system solution to the business problem identified.

2. **Project Initiation and Planning**
   Purpose: State business situation and how information systems might help solve a problem or make an opportunity possible.
   Deliverable: Written request to study possible changes to an existing system or development of a new system.

3. **Analysis**
   Purpose: Analyze the business situation thoroughly to:
   - determine requirements for a new or enhanced IS
   - structure requirements for clarity and consistency
   - select among competing systems features those that best meet user requirements within development constraints
   
   Deliverable: Functional specifications for a system that meets user requirements and is feasible to develop and implement.

4. **Logical Design**
   Purpose: To elicit and structure all information requirements for the new system
   Deliverable: A detailed and highly structured set of functional specifications for the system (includes all data, forms, reports, computer displays, and processing rules for all aspects of the system). Must be agreed to by all affected parties (stakeholders).

5. **Physical Design**
   Purpose: To develop all technology and organizational specifications for the new information system.
   Deliverables: Program and database structures, technology purchases, physical site plans, and organizational redesigns.

6. **Implementation and Maintenance**
   Purpose: To program the system, build all data files, test the new system, install system components, convert and cease operation of prior systems, train users, and turn over the system to operations.
   Deliverables: Programs that work accurately and which meet specifications, documentation, training materials, and project reviews.

---

**Figure 5.4.**  Steps in the Systems Development Life Cycle

## QUALITY DOCUMENTATION SYSTEMS

Quality documentation systems begin with the quality manual and include all process documentation and procedures and end on the production floor with such things as color-coded stickers that, when placed on a product, indicate the type and seriousness of defects found (see Chapter 6). Regardless of the size, complexity, or formalization of the program, each quality documentation system must be designed to provide an audit trail that can be used to verify that quality defects are being identified and noted, and that corrective action is being taken and followed up on to ensure the continuous improvement of the product and process.

> Documentation is important for quality improvement. When procedures are docu-
> mented, deployed, and implemented, it is possible to determine with confidence how
> things are done currently and to measure current performance. Then reliable measure-
> ment of the effect of a change is enhanced. Moreover, documented standard operating
> procedures are essential for maintaining the gains from quality-improvement activities.
> (ANSI/ASQC Q9000-1-1994, vii)

Most systems utilize a series of standard forms for reporting quality problems. Figure 5.5 shows an example of a quality control reporting form. Note that Part 1 of the form has a place to report the type of defect, the time, date, and location where the defect occurred, a place for comments from the person who identified the defect, and a place for that person to sign.

Once Part 1 of the form is completed it is filed in the quality information system and routed to the appropriate party for action. Part 2 of the form provides places for the time and date when the form was received, the person to whom the problem was assigned, the corrective action taken, when, where, and by whom.

Part 3 of the form allows for a follow-up check on the problem area to ensure that the corrective action is having the desired effect. Once again it notes the time and date of the follow up, who performed it, and what they found.

Document control is an important aspect of a quality management system. Personnel using documents that are part of the quality management system must be assured that the documents are properly approved and current. Quality problems can result if, for example, a procedure is modified but the documentation for the outmoded procedure remains in the system. If someone uses the outmoded procedure instead of the newly modified one, the output will not be as expected. According to ISO 9001, document control procedures should be defined in a quality management system for:

- approval of documents for adequacy prior to issue
- review and update as necessary and re-approve documents
- ensure that changes and the current revision status of documents are identified
- ensure that relevant versions of applicable documents are available at points of use
- ensure that documents remain legible and readily identifiable
- ensure that documents of external origin are identified and their distribution controlled
- prevent the unintended use of obsolete documents.

---

PART 1:  DEFECT REPORT

Date:_____  Time: _____        Location: _____

Type of           ☐ non-conformance to spec           ☐ damaged parts
Defect:           ☐ process out of control            ☐ incorrect raw material

Comments: _____
_____
_____
_____

Signature: _____ Date:_____

---

PART 2:  CORRECTIVE ACTION REPORT

Date Received: _____        Time Received:_____

Assigned Person: _____

Type of           ☐ non-conformance to spec           ☐ damaged parts
Defect:           ☐ process out of control            ☐ incorrect raw material

If different than in Part 1, please comment: _____
_____

Corrective Action Taken: _____
_____
_____

By Whom: _____

Date:  _____        Time:_____        Location: _____

Signature: _____ Date:_____

---

PART 3:  FOLLOW UP

Date:_____        Time: _____        Location: _____

Assigned Person: _____

Findings:_____
_____
_____
_____

Signature:_____        Date:_____

---

**Figure 5.5.**  Sample Quality Control Reporting Form (*Source*: M.J. Savoie & Associates, Dallas, Texas. Used with permission.)

Common features of document control systems include central control of documents, required approval authority before issue, issue of documents by serial number to authorized users, prohibition of unauthorized copying of any controlled document, and methods to recover outmoded documents when revisions are issued.

Increasingly, documents are written, maintained, and disseminated in electronic form. The use of electronic documents simplifies control in some respects and complicates it in other respects. If everyone uses *only* the electronic document (i.e., does not print a copy for actual use), the job of keeping documents up to date is greatly simplified. There is no need to have methods for recovering outmoded documents. Approval, access, and control are more complicated in that systems for electronic signatures, passwords, and restricted access are required.

## MAKING DATA USEFUL—INFORMATION FLOWS

With the advent of computerized data collection and storage, vast amounts of data are available for analysis. However, the ability to turn this data into useable information is dependent on our ability to:

- understand and accurately track the data
- analyze the data using statistical analysis to determine its significance
- report our findings in a clear, concise manner that is understandable by the intended recipient
- formulate and implement corrective actions that fix nonconformance and enhance the overall quality of the system.

The larger and more complex the systems being investigated, the more formal this system should be. Superfluous reports need to be identified and eliminated so that critical information can be received, analyzed, and acted on in a timely manner. The ability to quickly respond to quality control issues can minimize and, in some cases, eliminate the problem.

Reporting can take either a vertical or horizontal path through the organization. On a vertical path, reports are "sent up the chain" so that supervisors, managers, and executives can be made aware of the quality issues in the facility. This reporting sequence is critical to the strategic quality management process. Only by knowing what problems are occurring, what action is being taken to correct the problem, and the results of this action can management truly plan for improving the overall quality of the organization and its processes.

A horizontal path allows quality issues to be passed "up and down the line" to those people who will be directly affected by the nonconformance. By sharing data horizontally, problems can be addressed at the root cause of occurrence, and the effects of the nonconformance can be seen by all affected parties. Quality circles were an initial attempt to address quality issues at the line level. They have evolved into the quality teams of today that may be either functional or cross-functional. In many cases, these teams have evolved to include customers as well as suppliers in order to obtain the best possible quality across the "cradle-to-grave" life cycle of the product.

## SUMMARY

This chapter has looked at quality systems, quality management systems, quality audits, quality information systems, and their various elements. We began by discussing the key elements of a quality system so as to better understand what is meant by the term quality management system. Next, we identified some of the key functional elements required in order to have a comprehensive quality management system. ISO 9000, ISO/TS 16949, and MBNQA were discussed as frequently used formal guidelines for quality management systems.

We then discussed quality auditing as a management tool to systematically determine compliance to requirements. The types of audits and basic steps for performing a quality system audit were discussed. Quality audits are a form of management audit. Effective quality audits can be an invaluable tool to managers for improving quality. Care must be taken to ensure that the audits are properly conducted and that the findings are appropriately utilized. Poorly executed audits provide incomplete or inaccurate information upon which to base future decisions. Using audit results in a punitive fashion can result in a nonproductive, defensive reaction instead of quality improvement. The ISO 9000 and MBNQA standards and criteria are the two most frequently used audit standards in the United States.

The last section of the chapter discussed the scope and objectives of quality information systems and the techniques used to ensure data accuracy and integrity. Finally, quality documentation systems and turning data into useful information flows were addressed. A sample quality reporting form was provided as an example of the type of data collection required to ensure an accurate and complete assessment of a quality control issue.

## DISCUSSION QUESTIONS

1. Define the term system.
2. List and discuss the key elements of a quality management system.
3. What is the purpose of a quality manual in a quality system?
4. What guidance does ISO 9000 provide for developing and implementing a quality management system?
5. What are the main differences between ISO 9000 and the MBNQA?
6. What are the key components of Six Sigma?
7. Discuss some of the criticisms of Six Sigma.
8. What does Pyzdek mean when he says that Six Sigma programs can only result in a "not dissatisfied" customer?
9. Discuss the differences between a first-party, second-party, and third-party audit.
10. Might there be differences in the reception by managers and employees of an internal versus an external audit report? Discuss.

11. Discuss the differences in responsibilities of client, auditor, and auditee in performing a quality system audit.

12. Discuss the similarities and differences between the audit steps in *ANSI/ASQC Q1-1986* and those used by Eli Lilly.

13. Discuss ways that an internal auditor might avoid the "quality department as policeman" stereotype.

14. Compare and contrast the ANSI/ISO/ASQ Q9000-2000 standards and the Malcolm Baldrige National Quality Award criteria. Are the purposes of these two frameworks the same?

15. List and discuss the three key components for developing a quality information system.

16. Discuss the importance of data accuracy and integrity in a quality information system.

17. What are ways of assuring data accuracy and integrity in a QIS?

18. List the steps of the systems development life cycle (SDLC).

19. What are the purposes of quality documentation systems?

20. What document control procedures are prescribed by ISO 9001?

---

## CASE STUDY 5.1: *The First Audit*

© 2006 Victor E. Sower, Ph.D., C.Q.E.

The family business has grown faster than anyone ever anticipated. From 3 family members 10 years ago, the company now employs 175 workers in the production of specialty electronic components for the consumer electronics industry. John, son of the founder and chief operating officer (COO) has just left a meeting with the other directors—who are also family members. They are concerned that the business has expanded so rapidly that their quality management system has not kept up. Since attending a quality conference a few years ago, John has been educating himself on ISO 9001 and thinks it would be a good framework to use to do an internal audit of the company's quality management system.

He has started collecting documentation that he needs to conduct the audit. The company has long claimed to "provide excellent quality in everything we do." Many but not all of the production processes are documented, but that documentation is scattered throughout the company. Some of the processes that are not documented are run by operators who have been with the company for a long time and know more about the processes than anyone else in the company. The quality control department inspects all finished products before they are shipped. Defective products are sent back to production for repair. As far as John can tell, no records are kept of the failure rate or rework costs.

1. Can John conduct an audit of his company's quality management system given its present state? Discuss.

2. What are some of the documentation requirements that John must address in order to develop his quality management system so that they comply with ISO 9001?

3. Use Tunner's, Mills', and the ANSI/ISO/ASQ Q9000 classification systems to describe the type of audit that John proposes to conduct.

## EXERCISES AND ACTIVITIES

1. Identify an organization in your area that has been certified to the ISO 9001 standard. Meet with a member of that organization or arrange for a representative to meet with your class to discuss why they decided to seek certification, how they approached meeting the standard, and the benefits they obtained from being certified.

2. Examine advertisements in trade publications to determine what percentage of companies include in their advertisements a notice that they are ISO 9001 certified. Research these companies to determine where they rank in their industries. Does there appear to be a competitive advantage associated with being ISO 9001 certified?

3. Select an organization that has won the Malcolm Baldrige National Quality Award from the list at http://www.quality.nist.gov/Contacts_Profiles.htm. Use the links to contact that organization and inquire about the award process. Based on input obtained from the organization, prepare a report on the costs and benefits of winning the award.

4. Select an organization that has won the Malcolm Baldrige National Quality Award from the list at http://www.quality.nist.gov/Contacts_Profiles.htm. Compare the performance and reputation of that organization to comparable organizations in the same field that have not won the award. What differences do you observe between award winners and nonwinners?

5. Access the 2005 MBNQA Application Summary for MBNQA winner Bronson Methodist Hospital from http://www.bronsonhealth.com/AboutUs/BaldrigeAppSummary05.pdf.pdf. Select one MBNQA category and discuss how they demonstrated excellence in that category. Include a discussion of Bronson's objectives, improvement process, and metrics.

## SUPPLEMENTARY READINGS

*ANSI/ASQC Q1-1986. American National Standard Generic Guidelines for Auditing of Quality Systems.*

*ANSI/ASQC Q10011-1, 2, 3-1994. Guidelines for Auditing Quality Systems.*

*ANSI/ISO/ASQ QE 19011S-2004. Guidelines for Quality and/or Environmental Management Systems Auditing—U.S. Version with Supplemental Guidance Added.*

*ANSI/ISO/ASQ Q9000-2008. Quality Management Systems—Fundamentals and Vocabulary.*

*ANSI/ISO/ASQ Q9001-2008. Quality Management Systems—Requirements.*

*ANSI/ISO/ASQ Q9004-2008. Quality Management Systems—Guidelines for Performance Improvements.*

Arter, D. R. (2003). *Quality Audits for Improved Performance*, 3rd edition. Milwaukee, WI: ASQ Quality Press.

Bishara, R., & M. Wyrick. (1994). "A Systematic Approach to Quality Assurance Auditing." *Quality Progress* 27(12), 67–70.

Fiorentino, R., & M. Perigord. (1994). "Going From an Investigative to a Formative Auditor." *Quality Progress* 27(10), 61–65.

Hoffer, J., J. George, & J. Valacich. (1996). *Modern Systems Analysis and Design*. Reading, MA: The Benjamin/Cummings Publishing Company, Inc.

Juran, J., F. Gryna, & J. DeFeo. (2007). *Quality Planning and Analysis*, 5th edition. New York: McGraw-Hill.

*Malcolm Baldrige National Quality Award 2009-2010 Education Criteria for Performance Excellence*. Milwaukee, WI: ASQ.

Pyzdek, T. (2003). *The Six Sigma Handbook*. New York: McGraw-Hill.

Rice, C. (1994). "How to Conduct an Internal Quality Audit and Still Have Friends." *Quality Progress* 27(6), 39–41.

Russell, J. (2003). *Process Auditing Techniques Guide*. Milwaukee, WI: ASQ Quality Press.

The British Standards Institution. http://www.bsigroup.com.

## REFERENCES

*ANSI/ASQC Q1-1986. American National Standard Generic Guidelines for Auditing of Quality Systems.*

*ANSI/ASQC Q9000-1-1994. American National Standard Quality Management and Quality Assurance Standards—Guidelines for Selection and Use.*

*AOSI/ISO/ASQ Q9000-2000. Quality Management Systems Fundamentals and Vocabulary.*

*ANSI/ISO/ASQ Q9000-2008. American National Standard Quality Management Systems—Fundamentals and Vocabulary.*

*ANSI/ISO/ASQ QE 19011S-2004. Guidelines for Quality and/or Environmental Management Systems Auditing—U.S. Version with Supplemental Guidance Added, 17.*

Arter, D. R. (2003). *Quality Audits for Improved Performance*, 3rd edition. Milwaukee, WI: ASQ Quality Press.

*Baldrige Award Application Forms*. (2009–2010). Gaithersburg, MD: NIST, 1.

Bishara, R., & M. Wyrick. (1994). "A Systematic Approach to Quality Assurance Auditing." *Quality Progress* 27(12), 67–70.

http://www.bsiamerica.com/en-us/Assessment-and-certification-services/Management-systems/Standards-and-schemes/ISO-TS-16949/ISOTS-169492002-Questions-and-Answers/. British Standards Institution. (2007). "ISO/TS 16949:2002 Questions and Answers."

Franco, V. (2001). "Adopting Six Sigma." *Quality Digest* 21(6), 28–32.

George, M. (2002). *Lean Six Sigma*. New York: McGraw-Hill.

McCoy, M. (1999). "Six Sigma Gaining as Improvement Method." *Chemical & Engineering News* 77(45), 11–12.

McCoy, M. (2001). "Dow Chemical." *Chemical & Engineering News* 79(25), 21–26.

Mills, C. (1989). *The Quality Audit: A Management Evaluation Tool*. Milwaukee, WI: ASQC Quality Press, 25–34.

Myers, R. (2005). "IQ Matters: Senior Finance and IT Executives seek to Boost Information Quality." Report by CFO Research Services and Deloitte Consulting LL? (November). Bostom, MA: CFO Publishing Corp. http://www2.deloitte.com/assets/Dcom-Canada/Local%20Assets/Documents/IAMatters.pdf. See also "Information Quality still Eludes Companies." *Quality Digest* (February 2006). http://www.qualitydigest.com/feb06/news.shtml.

Nelson, D. (2005). "Baldrige—Just What the Doctor Ordered." *Quality Progress* 38(10), 69–79.

Pyzdek, T. (1999). "Why Six Sigma is Not Enough." *Quality Digest*. 26(11)

"QS 9000 Trivia." (1997). *Quality Digest* 17(8), 10.

"Quality Glossary." (2002). *Quality Progress* 35(7), 43–61.

Rice, C. (1994). "How to Conduct an Internal Quality Audit and Still Have Friends." *Quality Progress* 27(6), 39–41.

Russell, J. P. (2001). *ISO 9001 Conspectus*. Milwaukee, WI: ASQ Quality Press.

Tunner, J. R. (1990). *A Quality Technology Primer for Managers*. Milwaukee, WI: ASQC Quality Press.

## CHAPTER SIX

# Product, Process, and Materials Control

## CHAPTER OBJECTIVES

After reading this chapter the reader should be able to:

- discuss the importance of work instructions;
- understand how to use various classifications of quality characteristics and defects;
- discuss approaches to identification of materials and status;
- discuss approaches to lot traceability;
- understand the importance of lot traceability;
- discuss the importance of materials segregation practices;
- discuss materials review board criteria and procedures; and
- understand the principles of supplier management.

Work instructions are important in ensuring that everyone understands how to perform an operation properly. They minimize variation in the system by standardizing operations, and they also provide a basis for auditing an operation.

Characteristics and defects may be classified according to a number of schemes. One reason for such classifications is to segregate characteristics and defects according to their importance. This allows appropriate focus to be placed upon each characteristic and defect.

Identification of materials and status (e.g., awaiting inspection, accepted for use) is important to ensuring the quality of manufactured products. Properly identified materials are more likely to be used only where and as intended. Lot traceability is the ability to match a particular lot of material to a particular lot of product. Although there are a number of internal reasons for ensuring lot traceability, there are also many instances where traceability is required by customers or regulatory bodies.

Materials segregation practices ensure that lots of materials that are not approved for use are safeguarded in a separate area from approved materials. Material review boards are responsible for the disposition of nonconforming lots. Good supplier management can minimize problems caused by nonconforming purchased materials.

## WORK INSTRUCTIONS

Work instructions, in their base form, are nothing more than written instructions on how to perform a particular job or function. They contain the basics of how the work associated with an operation is to be performed, and how the performance of that job will be measured. Quality audit systems, including ISO 9000, rely heavily upon work instructions as the standard by which to judge the completeness and quality of an operation. For example, *ANSI/ASQC Q1-1986* defines a quality system audit as "a documented activity performed to verify, by examination and evaluations of objective evidence, that applicable elements of the quality system are appropriate and have been developed, ***documented***, and effectively implemented in accordance and in conjunction with specified requirements." And *ANSI/ASQC Q9000-1-1994* states that

> Documentation is important for quality improvement. When procedures are documented, deployed, and implemented, it is possible to determine with confidence how things are done currently and to measure current performance. Then reliable evidence of the effect of a change is enhanced. Moreover, documented standard operating procedures are essential for maintaining the gains from quality-improvement efforts.

Work instructions take a variety of forms. There are engineering specifications that are comprised of engineering drawings (see Figure 6.1) showing materials, dimensions, tolerances, surface finish, and other key attributes of a part. Bills of materials document, usually by part number, all parts and subassemblies required to produce one unit of a product. There are assembly drawings that are schematic drawings showing how parts are assembled into a subassembly or finished product. There are flow charts that show the order in which a product is to be assembled. There are standard process sheets that provide detailed instructions for the process of making a part. Route sheets provide instructions for the route that a part takes through the manufacturing process. Sometimes these are combined with the standard process sheets. There are job tickets that authorize the performance of individual operations in a manufacturing process. All of these forms of work instructions must be clearly stated and complete. There also must be a document control system in place to ensure that the most up-to-date versions of the work instructions are being used (Amrine, et al., 1993).

In job shop or custom manufacturing, each job will require its own unique work instructions. In batch and repetitive manufacturing operations, the work instructions listed above are routine. Engineering change orders (ECO) or engineering change notices (ECN) are nonroutine work instructions that amend standard work

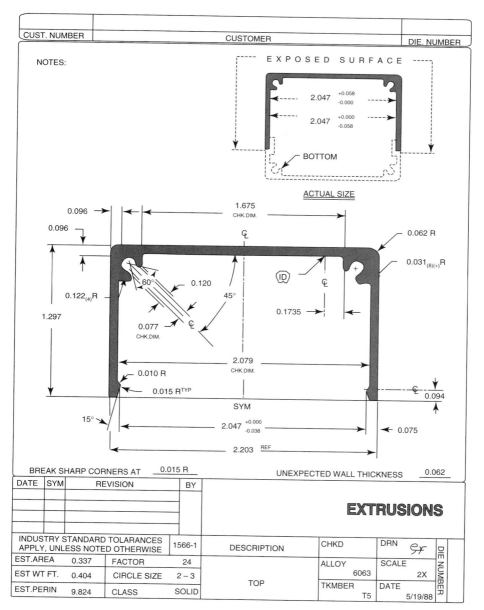

**Figure 6.1.** Engineering Drawing

instructions. Care should be taken to limit the number of ECOs and to carefully control their use to assure that the work is carried out as specified.

Shingo (1986) includes work instructions under the planning function. To link the planning function to the control and execution functions, management must "compile standard work process manuals and standard operations manuals." According to Shingo (1986), defects may occur during the execution stage where:

- Standards devised in the planning stage are flawed.
- Control or execution is not carried out in accordance with standards set during the planning stage because those standards were imperfect or improperly understood.
- Standards established by plans are observed, but deviations from permissible tolerances occur.
- Standards set by the planning function are correctly understood, but inadvertent mistakes occur.

Clearly defined work instructions used as the basis for training and evaluation can reduce confusion among employees, increase morale by clearly stating job requirements and methods of evaluation, and reduce variation in the system. Reducing variation reduces the incidence of nonconformancies or defects; it is a key aspect of quality improvement. Improvement in work instructions and greater attention to their consistent application can be important contributors to a quality improvement program.

## CLASSIFICATION OF QUALITY CHARACTERISTICS AND DEFECTS

Some quality characteristics are "serious," that is, of critical importance to the fitness for use of the product or service. Most have relatively minor effects on fitness for use. The more important or serious the characteristic, the greater the attention it should receive from the quality system. Many companies utilize formal systems to classify the seriousness of the characteristic. These systems use inspection, quality planning, and written specifications, among others, to determine the classification level of the characteristic in question.

There are two lists that need to be classified: quality characteristics derived from the specifications, and defects due to nonconformance during manufacturing and field failures during use. Normally one system of classification can be applicable to both lists. However, the lists are usually published separately because their usage in an organization may differ significantly between departments. Regardless of how a specific organization sets up its classification scheme, the overriding concern is the grouping of characteristics and defects into categories that reflect the seriousness or priority of the characteristics or defects.

The basic system of definitions was developed in the 1920s in the Bell System. One system classifies defects as Class A, B, C, or D (Dodge, 1928):

Class A Defects—Very serious, and will surely cause operating failure of the unit in service which cannot be readily corrected on the job.

Class B Defects—Serious, and will probably, but not surely, cause Class A operating failure of the unit in service.

Class C Defects— Moderately serious, and will probably cause operating failure of the unit in service.

Class D Defects— Not serious, and will not cause operating failure of the unit in service.

A similar commonly used system for classifying defects according to their seriousness is contained in *MIL STD 105E* (1989). This method classifies defects into three classes:

Critical Defect    "a defect that judgment and experience indicate is likely to result in hazardous or unsafe conditions for individuals using, maintaining, or depending upon the product ... "

Major Defect    "a defect, other than critical, that is likely to result in failure, or to reduce materially the usability of the unit or product for its intended purpose."

Minor Defect    "a defect that is not likely to reduce materially the usability of the unit or product for its intended purpose, or is a departure from established standards having little bearing on the effective use or operation of the unit."

A similar classification scheme (Feigenbaum, 1983) adds a fourth classification as follows:

Incidental Defect    a defect which "will have no unsatisfactory effect on customer quality."

The ASQ Statistics Division's classification system (American Society for Quality, 1983) is also based upon the seriousness of the defect:

Class 1 Very Serious:    "Leads directly to severe injury or catastrophic economic loss."

Class 2 Serious:    "Leads directly to significant injury or significant economic loss."

Class 3 Major:    "Related to major problems with respect to intended normal, or reasonably foreseeable, use."

Class 4 Minor:    "Related to minor problems with respect to intended normal, or reasonably foreseeable, use."

The *MIL STD 105E* goes on to classify defectives according to the defect classification system (i.e., a critical defective contains one or more critical defects).

Classification can be a long, tedious process, but is one that must be performed. By-products of this effort include identification of misconceptions and confusion among departments, and recognition of potential characteristics or defects that would otherwise remain undiscovered.

A key problem area that may arise involves the reluctance of personnel to "downgrade" characteristics and defects. In some people's eyes, every characteristic or defect is critical. Care must be taken to properly categorize the seriousness of each item; otherwise the list will be useless as the critical category will contain the majority, if not all, of the identified characteristics and defects. The better the classification scheme, the shorter the inspection time, resulting in faster turnarounds, quicker delivery to customers, and reduced costs.

## IDENTIFICATION OF MATERIALS AND STATUS

Materials can be identified either as discrete units, that is, an engine, a washing machine, and so on; or as a collection of discrete units—a lot. Material can also exist in bulk such as food or chemicals. In the case of bulk items, we usually refer to some or all of the bulk as a lot, while a unit is referred to as a specimen.

An important aspect of material packaging is content identification, tracking, and handling instructions (Bowersox & Closs, 1996). Typical information included on a package is manufacturer, product, type of container, count, customer identification, manufacturer lot number, and special handling instructions. Other information can include the date, shift, and machine on which the material was produced. Increasingly this information is provided in scannable (e.g., bar code) or machine readable (RFID) format. Large commercial purchasers frequently specify exactly where the label is to be placed and what information it is to contain. Some customers require that the contents be identified by a code designation for proprietary purposes.

Some information is often made part of the product itself. Plastic molded parts frequently have part number, cavity number, and manufacturing date molded into the part. Formed metal parts sometimes have similar information stamped into the piece. In other cases serial numbers and other information are included either as an integral part of the unit or on labels affixed to the units.

Customers increasingly demand that suppliers provide quality information with lots of material. In some cases this consists of control charts documenting the state of the process during production of the lot. In other cases it is documentation of inspection under a specified sampling plan to an agreed upon acceptable quality level (AQL) or lot tolerance percent defective (LTPD). A certificate of conformance to specifications may also be required. The standards for lot quality are usually contained in the inspection plans and sampling criteria published by the organization's quality control department. Chapter 11 contains a detailed discussion of sampling plans and procedures.

The status of all materials in a facility must be evident. For example, it should be evident to everyone that a particular lot of materials is awaiting inspection before being released for use in production. There are a number of approaches to material control, and usually more than one approach is used in an organization. For uncertified or new suppliers, incoming materials are usually segregated into a separate holding area until they pass incoming inspection. Once they pass this inspection, a label or stamp is affixed to the packages (see Figure 6.2) and a move ticket authorizes the material to be stocked. Materials that fail the incoming inspection should be marked and held in a separate secured storage area pending final disposition. For

 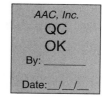

**Figure 6.2.** Examples of Material Status Labels

certified suppliers, materials may bypass incoming inspection and move directly to the materials warehouse or production area.

Material identification, control, handling, storage, packaging, preservation, and delivery are explicit parts of the ANSI/ISO/ASQ Q-9000 standards. This is a further indication of the importance of these topics in maintaining and improving the performance of a quality system.

## LOT TRACEABILITY

Product traceability systems provide the ability to identify and track the genealogy of a product or part backwards to its point of origin. Traceability is needed to ensure lot uniformity in materials, to avoid mix-ups of look-alike materials, to aid in proper sequential usage of perishable materials, to simplify investigation of nonconforming material; and to aid in the location of material involved in product recalls. Traceability is also an explicit part of the ANSI/ISO/ASQ Q-9000 standards.

### ANSI/ISO/ASQ Q9001-2000

7.5.3 Identification and traceability

Where appropriate, the organization shall identify the product by suitable means throughout product realization.

The organization shall identify the product status with respect to monitoring and measurement requirements.

Where traceability is a requirement, the organization shall control and record the unique identification of the product (see 4.2.4).

NOTE: In some industry sectors, configuration management is a means by which identification and traceability are maintained.

Although there are instances where complete traceability is required (e.g., aircraft, pharmaceuticals), most commercial products limit traceability to safety-oriented qualities and to those components that are indispensable in achieving overall fitness for use. Traceability is accomplished using part identification numbers (for unique identification), date codes, or lot numbers, where specific identification is either unwarranted or not possible (i.e., drug lots). Traceability is facilitated when relevant information is included in a machine readable format (e.g., bar code or RFID tag).

## THE BENEFITS OF TRACEABILITY

The recent product recalls of toys which contained excessive amounts of lead involved all toys of specified types manufactured in specified factories in China. It was sufficient to be able to trace specific toys to their manufacturing locations. Other recent recalls, however, affect just certain lots of production at specified locations. In these cases, traceability to specific lots or dates of manufacture is required in order to recall just the affected products.

In early 2009, specified lots of Philips Senseo One-Cup Coffeemakers were recalled because of a possible burn hazard. Lots 0727 through 0847 made in China and lots 0627 through 0847 made in Poland are affected. Other lots of the same product are not subject to the recall.

(CPSC, 2009)

Three lots of WOW Thai Peanut Wing Sauce and Dressing were recalled in early 2009 due to potential contamination with *Salmonella*. Only jugs of the product with codes 3247, 1718, and 2138 are subject to the recall.

(FDA, 2009)

In 2005 two lots of Pagoda Egg Rolls were recalled due to possible contamination with glass fragments. Only packages with date codes 384314 and 384315 were subject to the recall.

(FDA, 2005)

Because these products were traceable through lot numbers and date codes, the affected products could be identified and recalled. Consumer safety was assured without recalling products which were not subject to the contamination or hazard.

## MATERIALS SEGREGATION PRACTICES

Any time an inspector determines a lot of materials to be nonconforming, the material should be clearly labeled to clearly identify it as such. This often involves placing a red "hold" tag on the lot. The material should then be moved to a secured area of the facility reserved for nonconforming material. All reasonable effort should be taken to ensure that nonconforming material is segregated, labeled, and secured to ensure it will not be accidentally used in the process.

The inspector prepares a nonconforming report that is distributed to various departments and personnel. Distribution should, at a minimum, include purchasers and schedulers who may have to make up for the lost material, and an investigator who is assigned to collect the type of information needed as inputs for the fitness-for-use decision maker. The final disposition decision for nonconforming materials is frequently made by a materials review board.

## MATERIALS REVIEW BOARD CRITERIA AND PROCEDURES

Nonconformities may occur at any stage of a process, from incoming materials, work in progress, to finished product. Organizations should have an effective and efficient process to provide for the review and disposition of indentified nonconformities (ANSI/ISO/ASQ Q9004-2008). Often a materials review board (MRB) is charged with the disposition of nonconforming product. A board may consist of a quality engineer, process engineer, purchasing representative, marketing representative, and a production representative. It is important that the MRB members have "the competency to evaluate the total effects of the nonconformity and should have the authority and resources to disposition the nonconformity and to define appropriate corrective action" (*ANSI/ISO/ASQ Q9004 2000* 41). The board generally has four choices available to it relative to the nonconforming material: ship (or use as is); don't ship (or don't use as is); corrective action or regrade for alternative applications. *ANSI/ISO/ASQ Q9004* condenses these to three actions that may be taken for the control of nonconforming product into the following: (a) take action to eliminate the detected nonconformity (e.g., rework to meet the specified requirements); (b) authorize its use, release or acceptance under concession from relevant authority or customer; (c) take action to preclude its original intended use or application.

The decision to "ship or use as is" manifests itself in several different ways. First, the designer may allow a waiver in the specifications for the material in question, thereby allowing the lot to be used or shipped as is. Second, the intended customer may allow a waiver, which in essence supersedes the material specifications. Third, for noncritical items, the quality control department may grant a waiver based on fitness-for-use decision criteria. Fourth, the MRB may grant a waiver. This waiver is based on the facts and conclusions of the investigator and requires the unanimous consent of the members of the MRB. A special case of a waiver involves approving the material for use for other than the original intended purpose or as a substitute for a lower grade of material. Finally, a waiver may be granted by upper management in conjunction with a recommendation from the MRB. Upper management becomes involved in cases of a critical nature where human safety or large sums of money are involved. Note that in none of the cases is the material designation changed from nonconforming to conforming. Rather a "waiver" is granted to the nonconforming lot allowing it to be used. This should be noted in the traceability system in case of future problems. In the case of purchased materials, the decision to waive certain quality requirements should always be promptly communicated to the supplier and a report of corrective action to prevent recurrence requested.

A "don't ship or don't use as is" decision may result from the investigation of the nonconforming material. When a "don't ship" decision is made, the MRB must determine the most economical way to dispose of the nonconforming material. Choices for materials manufactured in house include sort, repair, downgrade, and scrap. Purchased materials are usually returned to the supplier for credit or replacement.

The third MRB decision alternative is "corrective action" (sometimes called rework). Sometimes the most economical decision is to accept the material and to initiate actions to correct the nonconformancies. Sometimes this involves sorting; in other cases additional processing is required. The additional processing may take the form of replacing defective components, tightening loose connections, adding an additional spot weld, or similar actions. Usually the cost of rework of purchased materials is billed to the supplier.

Sometimes it may be appropriate to regrade a material for use in an alternative application. Example 6.1 illustrates such a situation. When purchased material is regraded (or downgraded), negotiations must be conducted with the supplier to obtain agreement with the proposed course of action. It is appropriate to hold the supplier responsible for any difference in value of the regraded material as well as any costs associated with extra testing and administrative expense associated with the MRB.

---

### EXAMPLE 6.1

A hardware distributor recently received an order of machine screws designed for use in high-stress environments. The cost of the screws is $15.00 per thousand. Receiving inspection determined that the screws do not meet tensile strength requirements for high-stress applications. The inspector has marked the shipment "QC Hold," has placed it in a secure holding area, and has reported the nonconformance to the QC manager. The QC manager convenes an MRB to review the test information. The MRB agrees that the shipment does not conform to the specifications for high-stress applications. Because the shipment does meet the standard application specifications and there is an open order with this supplier for this grade of screw, the MRB recommends that the shipment be regraded for standard applications.

The purchasing manager and QC manager make a conference call to the supplier. They fax the test results and offer to ship samples for retesting at the supplier's location. Upon reviewing the test data, the supplier agrees that the material is nonconforming. The purchasing manager offers the supplier two options. The first option is the distributor will return the entire shipment for credit plus cost of shipping both ways, plus the cost for convening the MRB. The second option is the distributor will regrade the shipment to standard application and retain it for that use. The supplier will bill the distributor for cost of standard application screws which is $10.00 per thousand. In addition, the supplier will reimburse the distributor for the cost of convening the MRB. In either case, in order to retain their preferred supplier status, the supplier must submit a report in a timely fashion documenting the cause of the nonconforming shipment and the actions taken to prevent recurrence.

The supplier elects option two—regrading of the shipment. The QC manager reports this to the MRB which authorizes the action. The MRB report is provided to the inspector who properly labels the product as standard application grade and releases the shipment to the materials warehouse. Copies of the MRB action report are filed with quality control, purchasing, accounts payable, and materials control. A copy is also provided to the supplier. When the supplier's corrective action report is received, the MRB reviews it to determine whether to recommend that the supplier retain its preferred supplier status.

Purchasing involvement in MRB actions is important because they are principal contacts between the organization and its suppliers. Purchasing is also usually responsible for negotiating the allocation of costs associated with nonconforming purchased materials (Leenders & Fearon, 1997). Usually the supplier of nonconforming materials will be held responsible for transportation costs to and from the rejection point, testing costs, and rework costs associated with nonconforming lots. In some cases, contingent costs (e.g., production downtime, overtime) are also charged to the supplier.

In addition to the need to disposition nonconforming material, there is a need to prevent reoccurrence. The prevention process usually takes one of two paths, depending on the type of nonconformance. The first path involves nonconformance that occurs in some isolated, sporadic way within a traditionally well-behaved process. These problems, for example, may be due to human error or incorrect calibration of equipment. For such cases, it is usually possible to identify the cause of the nonconformance and restore the process to its normal mode of operation. In statistical process control, this type of problem is referred to as an "assignable cause" and no changes to the fundamental nature of the process are required. The second path involves "repeat offenders." These cases point to fundamental stability problems in the process that require root cause analysis and correction if the nonconformance is to be eliminated. When the nonconformance involves purchased material, it is common to require the supplier to provide a report of their investigation into the cause(s) of the nonconformance and actions taken to prevent recurrence.

## SUPPLIER MANAGEMENT

Evidence for the changing nature of the purchasing function is everywhere. From Deming's point number 4—end the practice of awarding business on the basis of price tag alone—to moving purchasing from a tactical function to a strategic function, to moving to strategic sourcing and supply chain management, the change is evident. Because high-quality inputs are required in order to produce high-quality outputs from any productive system, quality is inextricably linked to the strategic purchasing function.

## Supplier Selection

The trend today is toward doing business with a smaller number of suppliers who are carefully selected and with whom close ties are established. Partnering arrangements—"explicit or implicit arrangement by which selected parties gain more benefits by cooperating in a long-term, win-win relationship than by pursuing a short-term, win-lose arrangement" (Hutchins, 1992)—with suppliers are becoming more common.

The focus of such partnerships is on obtaining the *best buy* (Leenders & Fearon, 1997). Best buy is a multidimensional concept that involves selecting the product for purchase that has the best combination of technical factors (e.g., specifications, reliability) and procurement factors (e.g., price, delivery, service). It reflects the total cost of ownership (TCO) of a purchased item over its useful life. Total cost of ownership includes not only the purchase price but also the expected cost of installation, maintenance, operation, downtime, and so forth, over the expected life of the equipment. Life cycle costing is an approach to measuring the total cost of ownership.

The basic approach to determining the TCO is to determine the initial delivered and installed cost of the equipment. Then estimate all costs associated with the operation of the equipment during its lifetime, including such costs as power consumption, routine maintenance, MTBF and mean cost to repair, and labor requirements. Finally, estimate any salvage value the equipment might have at the end of its life. Project costs to the future dates at which they will be incurred and discount these costs to their present values. This yields a TCO expressed in net present value (NPV) terms.

$$\text{TCO} = \text{Initial cost} + \text{NPV}_{\text{Life Cycle Costs}} - \text{NPV}_{\text{Salvage Value}}$$

Comparison of alternatives using TCO instead of initial cost will protect the purchaser from the purchase of items that are not best buys when viewed over their entire useable life cycle.

Selection of suppliers who can provide the best buy frequently is based upon four major factors (Leenders & Fearon, 1997):

1. Technical or engineering capability
   Level of engineering technology
   R&D capability

2. Manufacturing or distribution capability
   Supplier location
   Quality systems
   Cleanliness of facility

3. Financial strength
    Ability to finance activities over long term

4. Management capability
    Progressive management
    Management stability
    Management attitudes

These factors are usually addressed using a formal supplier evaluation procedure that is designed to answer the questions (Leenders & Fearon, 1997):

1. Is this supplier capable of supplying the purchaser's requirements satisfactorily in both the short and long run?

2. Is this supplier motivated to supply these requirements in the way the purchaser expects in the short and long term?

Sometimes third-party audits are used in addition to or instead of on-site supplier audits. Registration to the ISO 9001 standard is required by many European companies. The big three automobile manufacturers require certification to the QS 9000 or ISO/TS 16949 standards. After winning the Malcolm Baldrige National Quality Award in 1988, Motorola required that their suppliers apply for the award.

Careful selection of long-term supplier-partners is just the first step. Blindly staying with a supplier that is not continuously improving the value they add to the relationship is not effective. The effectiveness of the relationship must be evaluated, the results of the evaluation must be shared, and both parties must work to continuously improve the relationship.

## Supplier Evaluation

Evaluation of existing suppliers is a continuous process and is conducted using a variety of methods. Incoming inspection of purchased products is one commonly used means of ensuring that raw materials and purchased products meet specifications. Routinely recording by supplier the results of incoming inspections provides one way of evaluating supplier performance over time.

However, the modern view of incoming inspection is that none should be necessary. Emphasis should be placed on selecting suppliers that are capable of doing things right the first time and requiring those suppliers to provide documentation (e.g., SPC control charts and process capability reports) showing that their processes are in control and that their products meet specifications.

Formal supplier evaluation systems recognize that supplier performance is multi-dimensional. The Institute for Supply Management (formerly the National Association for Purchasing Management) (Juran & Gryna, 1988) recommends rating suppliers in three areas of performance: quality, price, and service. Each area is weighted depending on market conditions. Hickman and Hickman (1992) recommend a similar system using: delivery performance, quality performance, and cost containment.

These rating systems focus on the suppliers' output. Many modern companies go beyond evaluation of output to evaluation of the suppliers' system. This is frequently done using a supplier audit. A quality audit is a formal and systematic assessment of suppliers and is covered in Chapter 5. The reason for evaluating the suppliers' system is that a capable system, operating in control and under good management, is very likely to produce acceptable products on time and at the lowest possible price.

## SUMMARY

Inadequate work instructions or work instructions that are not adhered to are sources of defects and worker confusion and dissatisfaction. Clearly defined work instructions are therefore important aspects of the quality system. All defects do not result in the same risk. Defect classification schemes provide ways to classify defects according to the seriousness of their likely consequences. Clear identification of materials and their status helps ensure that materials will be used appropriately. The ability to trace a product back to its constituent components provides a means of troubleshooting problems and also provides a rational basis for product recalls. The proper handling of nonconforming materials is important. Materials segregation practices and materials review boards are key components of the system to handle nonconforming materials. One key to reducing quality problems is to properly control the quality of parts and components. A good system for the evaluation and management of suppliers will help assure the quality of purchased parts and components.

## DISCUSSION QUESTIONS

1. What are work instructions and why are they important?
2. What would be the foremost characteristics of an acceptable sampling plan for critical defects?
3. Should sampling procedures differ for critical, major, and minor defects? Discuss.
4. A manufacturer approaches a customer and asks which of the 237 dimensions on the blueprint are critical. The customer replies that he or she expects the product to be in conformance to all of the dimensional specifications— therefore they are all critical. Is there a better approach the manufacturer could have taken with the customer? Discuss.
5. What are some of the categories of information that might be important to include on product packaging? When would it be appropriate and desirable to include this information on the product itself?
6. Why might lot traceability be more important in pharmaceutical manufacturing than in writing instrument manufacturing?
7. An inspector determines at receiving inspection that a lot of raw materials is nonconforming. Discuss the actions that should be taken next.

8. What are the responsibilities of a materials review board?

9. Discuss some of the actions that a materials review board should *not* take.

10. Why is it important to inform the supplier of the actions recommended by an MRB?

11. What actions might an MRB require a supplier to take in conjunction with a decision to regrade a lot of material?

12. Discuss what is meant by the term best buy.

13. Define total cost of ownership. How is TCO helpful in determining the best buy?

14. List and discuss the four major factors in supplier selection.

## Case Study 6.1: *The Case of the Missing Lot*

©2005 Victor E. Sower, Ph.D., C.Q.E.

Ed Jones, the materials manager, enters your office obviously greatly disturbed. "You remember that lot of PN 77-305 that your inspectors rejected last week? I negotiated their return to the supplier. We just received the replacement shipment and I signed the authorization to return the defective lot to the supplier for credit. My materials handler just told me he cannot find the defective lot in the receiving area. What happened to it?"

"What!" you respond. "What do you mean you can't find it? My inspectors marked it as 'QC Hold' right after they finished the inspection. It should still be in the receiving area."

You convene a meeting with the operations manager, the materials manager, and yourself (the quality manager). The operations manager admits that he had his night shift supervisor overrule the QC Hold status and use the material a few nights ago. "Look, it was do that or shut the plant down. We have quotas to meet," says Sue Hanson, operations manager. "I checked with the QC inspector on duty. He told me the lot was rejected for a few minor defects—nothing major. I figured it would be better to use it than to shut the plant down. I told my guys to watch for defects and discard any that looked bad."

1. What are the major material control issues here?

2. Recommend changes to the procedures for dealing with defective lots of material.

3. How do you suggest that the materials manager deal with the issue of the supplier expecting to receive a defective lot and being told that it was used anyway? What message does that send to the supplier?

# EXERCISES AND ACTIVITIES

1. Select a relatively simple product with which students are familiar (e.g., lawn mower or hair dryer). Use the *MIL STD 105 E* classification system to create a list of three to five potential defects in each class: critical, major, minor.

2. Collect several samples of assembly drawings and instructions from consumer products such as toys, inexpensive book cases, etc. Critique the drawings and instructions for simplicity, clarity, and completeness. If these drawings and instructions were part of the work instructions for your organization, how would you improve them?

# SUPPLEMENTARY READINGS

Amrine, H., J. Ritchey, C. Moodie, & J. Kmec. (1993). *Manufacturing Organization and Management*, 6th edition. Englewood Cliffs, NJ: Prentice Hall.

*ANSI/ISO/ASQC Q10011-1994 Series: Guidelines for Auditing Quality Systems.*

ASQ Statistics Division. (2005). *Glossary & Tables for Statistical Quality Control*, 4th edition. Milwaukee, WI: ASQ Quality Press.

Bowersox, D. J., & D. J. Closs. (1996). *Logistical Management, The Integrated Supply Chain Process*. New York: McGraw-Hill.

Feigenbaum, A. V. (1993). *Total Quality Control*, 3rd edition. New York: McGraw-Hill.

Leenders, M. R., & H. E. Fearon. (1997). *Purchasing and Supply Management*, 11th edition. Chicago: Irwin.

*MIL STD 105E.* (1989). *Sampling Procedures and Tables for Inspection by Attributes.* Washington, DC: U.S. Government Printing Office.

*Quality System Requirements QS-9000*, 2nd edition, February 1995 (fourth printing July 1996).

# REFERENCES

Amrine, H., J. Ritchey, C. Moodie, & J. Kmec. (1993). *Manufacturing Organization and Management*, 6th edition. Englewood Cliffs, NJ: Prentice Hall.

*ANSI/ASQC Q1-1986. American National Standard Generic Guidelines for Auditing of Quality Systems.*

*ANSI/ASQC Q9000-1-1994. American National Standard Quality Management and Quality Assurance Standards–Guidelines for Selection and Use.*

*ANSI/ISO/ASQ Q9001-2000. Quality Management Systems—Requirements.*

*ANSI/ISO/ASQ Q9004-2000. Quality Management Systems—Guidelines for Performance Improvements.*

ASQC Statistics Division. (1983). *Glossary & Tables for Statistical Quality Control*. Milwaukee, WI: ASQC Quality Press.

Bowersox, D., & D. Closs. (1996). *Logistical Management, The Integrated Supply Chain Process*. New York: McGraw-Hill.

CPSC. (2009). "Senseo One-Cup Coffeemakers Recalled by Philips Consumer Lifestyle Due to Burn Hazard." Press release by U.S. Consumer Product Safety Commission (April 15). http://www.cpsc.gov/CPSCPUB/PREREL/prhtml09/09194.html.

Dodge, H. F. (1928). "A Method of Rating Manufactured Product." *The Bell System Technical Journal* 7(2), 350.

FDA. (2009). "Allegro Fine Foods, Inc. Recalls Wow Thai Peanut Wing Sauce & Dressing Because of Possible Health Risk." Press release by U.S. Food and Drug Administration (February 3). http://www.fda.gov/Safety/Recalls/ArchiveRecalls/2009/ucm228341.htm.

FDA. (2005). "Texas Firm Initiates a Voluntary Recall of Egg and Spring Rolls That May Contain Pieces of Glass." Press release by U.S. Food and Drug Administration (February 8). http://www.fda.gov/Safety/Recalls/ArchiveRecalls/2005/ucm111757.htm.

Feigenbaum, A. V. (1983). *Total Quality Control*, 3rd edition. New York: McGraw-Hill.

Hickman, T. K., & W. M. Hickman. (1992). *Global Purchasing*. Homewood, IL: Business One Irwin.

Hutchins, G. (1992). *Purchasing Strategies for Total Quality*. Homewood, IL: Business One Irwin.

Juran, J. M., & F. M. Gryna. (1988). *Quality Control Handbook*, 4th edition. New York: McGraw-Hill.

Leenders, M., & H. Fearon. (1997). *Purchasing and Supply Management*, 11th edition. Chicago: Irwin.

*MIL STD 105E*. (1989). *Sampling Procedures and Tables for Inspection by Attributes*. Washington, DC: U.S. Government Printing Office.

Shingo, Shigeo. (1986). *Zero Quality Control: Source Inspection and the Poka-yoke System*. Cambridge, MA: Productivity Press.

## CHAPTER SEVEN

# Experimental Design

## CHAPTER OBJECTIVES

After completing this chapter, the reader should be able to:

- understand the basic concepts and definitions of experimental design;
- discuss the characteristics of experimental design;
- understand the use of full and fractional factorial experimental designs;
- understand the use of analysis of variance (ANOVA) in analyzing experimental results; and
- discuss Taguchi Methods for experimental design.

Even relatively simple systems are affected by a number of variables. For example, some of the factors that may affect the quality of a hole drilled into a block of wood include the type of drill bit, the sharpness of the bit, the rotational speed of the bit, the feed rate of the bit into the work, the type of wood, and the moisture content of the wood. To really optimize the performance of this process, the quality manager or engineer would need to determine the best settings for these six variables. Many industrial processes involve hundreds of variables, any or all of which can affect the quality of the output. Determining which of these variables are most important, how they may interact with each other, and how to adjust them for optimal performance is the domain of experimental design. In our example, designed experiments can assist the quality professional in determining which type of drill bit to use, how long to use it before resharpening, how many revolutions per minute (rpm) to run the bit, how fast to feed the bit into the work, adjustments necessary for different types of wood being drilled, and how dry the wood should be before processing in order for the drilling process to produce consistent, top-quality holes.

An experiment where one variable is studied while the other variables are held constant can be inefficient and suffers from the inability to assess interactions among the variables. Factorial designs allow for the efficient testing of the main effects of the variables as well as the interaction effects among the variables. Interpretation

**153**

of the data obtained from factorial designs is often accomplished using analysis of variance (ANOVA). Factorial designs coupled with analysis using ANOVA enable the experimenter to determine all main effects (i.e., the effect on the process of changing one variable) and all interaction effects (the effect on the process of the interaction of several variables).

Genichi Taguchi made a significant contribution by adapting fractional factorial orthogonal arrays (balanced both ways) to experimental design so that the time and cost of experimentation is reduced while validity and reproducibility are maintained. Taguchi's approach is disciplined and structured to make it easy for quality managers and engineers to apply. A full factorial design with seven factors at two levels would require $2^7 = 128$ experiments while Taguchi's $L_8$ orthogonal array requires only eight experiments.

- Is this process operating in a way that quality is maximized and cost is minimized?
- What can we do to improve the performance of this process?
- Will this change to the process create undesired effects on other aspects of the process?

Questions such as these are often asked but frequently dealt with using just intuition, assumptions, and experience. They may be addressed best by use of carefully designed experiments in conjunction with technical knowledge about the processes and experience in working with the processes. The result of a program of process improvement using experimental design is a process that performs optimally with a minimum of variation. Process owners also will better understand the relationships among the many variables in the process and the performance that they desire. Ultimately this translates into higher quality, improved customer satisfaction, and increased profits.

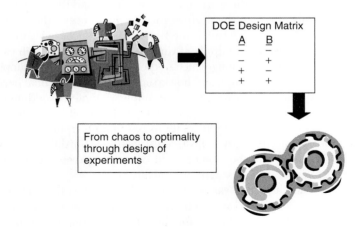

DOE Design Matrix

| A | B |
|---|---|
| − | − |
| − | + |
| + | − |
| + | + |

From chaos to optimality through design of experiments

# BASIC CONCEPTS AND DEFINITIONS

Experimental design is defined as "a formal plan that details the specifics for conducting an experiment, such as which responses, factors, levels, blocks, treatments, and tools are to be used" (Quality Glossary, 2002, 49). Designed experiments are important tools for optimizing processes, identifying interactions among process variables, and reducing variation in processes.

In design of experiments (DOE) the experimenter changes the inputs to a process in a systematic way and evaluates resulting changes in the outputs. The inputs are called the independent variables (X-variables) and the outputs are called the dependent variables (Y-variables). A *dependent variable* is the variable of primary interest in an experiment. *Independent variables* are those we believe that affect the measurements obtained on the dependent variable for a given experiment. It is possible for several independent variables to be under investigation simultaneously. *Environmental variables* are those which may or may not affect experimental results but which are not easily controlled by the experimenter. Examples of environmental variables would be ambient temperature and humidity.

In an experimental investigation, each independent variable that is assumed to influence the dependent variable of interest is called a *factor*. The various logical categories or intensities of the factors being investigated are referred to as *levels* or *treatments*. In a given experiment, several independent variables, or factors, might be under investigation simultaneously. A specific combination of factor levels imposed on a single unit of experimental material is called a treatment combination. The experiment in Figure 7.1 consists of three levels (0.2%, 0.4%, and 0.65%) of one factor, chlorination. The commonly used notation is to show the number of factors as the exponent for the number of levels. For example, an experiment that examines two factors at two levels would be referred to as a $2^2$ full-factorial design. One with three factors at two levels would be referred to as a $2^3$ full-factorial design (see Figure 7.4).

Three basic concepts of experimental design are replication, randomization, and local control (Fisher, 1958). When two or more identical experimental units are subjected to the same treatment, the experiment is said to be replicated. *Replication* is necessary in an experiment in order to provide a measure of experimental error and thus "to increase the precision of the estimates of the effects" (Montgomery, 2005). When two identical experimental units receive the same treatment or treatment combination (replication) and yield different responses or measurements, the difference between what statistical analysis of a sample says a value should be and the actual value based on the population as a whole is defined as *error*. Error arises due to random forces and due to other variables that contribute to variation (such as environmental variables), but which are not singled out for investigation (i.e., not included as factors in the experiment). The experiment in Figure 7.1 consists of three replications.

*Randomization* is a requirement for the statistical methods (ANOVA and regression) used to analyze the results of designed experiments and also minimizes the effect of procedural bias. Randomization is achieved through the use of random

| Trial | Chlorination Level | Bacterial Count |
|-------|--------------------|-----------------|
| 1 | 1 | 150 |
| 2 | 2 | 100 |
| 3 | 1 | 145 |
| 4 | 1 | 160 |
| 5 | 2 | 140 |
| 6 | 3 | 25 |
| 7 | 2 | 130 |
| 8 | 3 | 35 |
| 9 | 3 | 40 |

Chlorination Levels: 1 - 0.2%
2 - 0.4%
3 - 0.6%

A simple analysis of this experiment can be done using a scatter diagram.

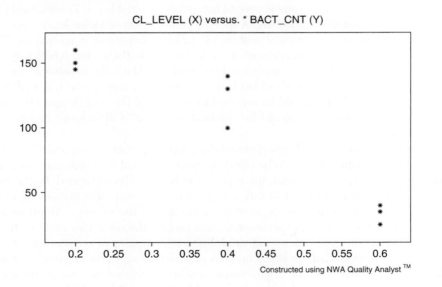

It appears that the relationship between chlorination levels and bacterial counts is fairly linear, and that as chlorine levels are increased, bacterial counts decrease.

**Figure 7.1.** Single Factor Experiment

numbers to determine the order of experimental trials and to assign the order for specific inputs. The experiments in Figure 7.4 do not show randomization. Before running the experiment, the order of the four trials for the $2^2$ design and the eight trials for the $2^3$ design should be randomly assigned.

*Local control* refers to the use of *blocks*. Blocks are a "subdivision of the experiment space into relatively homogeneous experimental units between which the experimental error can be expected to be smaller than would be expected should a similar number of units be randomly located within the entire experimental space" (ASQC Statistics Division, 1983, 62). An example of the use of blocking would be the testing of fertilizers by applying the different treatments to test plots within a small block of the field. The external variables (e.g., amount of sunlight, basic soil fertility, drainage) within the block would be expected to vary less than over the entire field. This provides for "a more homogeneous experiment subspace" (ASQC Statistics Division, 1983, 62). Blocking may be used as an alternative to a completely randomized experiment.

Consider a case of testing the hardness of material used in a metal stamping process. The experimenter has been provided several different stamping tools—that is, different designs, materials, weights, and so forth. The experimenter wants to determine which of various stamping tools will provide the best impact on the metal plates being stamped. In a completely randomized design, each tool would be used to stamp randomized pieces of stamping material and the results compared. Although this sounds okay, a closer examination would reveal that random variations in the stamping material could introduce a bias to the experiment that may skew the test results. In order to minimize this bias, a randomized block design is used. In this case, a number of pieces of stamping material are randomly selected. All tools are tested at random points on each piece of material. By using this method, we have minimized the potential bias from variations in the stamping material and thus have a more robust data set for comparing the various stamping tools.

Experiments can be performed by anyone wishing to answer a question. We all perform experiments of one kind or another. For example, we may conduct an experiment to determine the quickest way to get from our house in the suburbs to a point in the central business district. We may consider three alternative modes of travel (independent variable): personal vehicle (car), city bus, and light rail. We may collect our data by randomly selecting a mode on each of the nine days so that each mode is taken three times. Our decision could be made based on the average travel time (dependent variable) for each mode.

We may find that the decision made based on this simple experiment does not provide the expected outcome. The process may be more complicated than we thought when we designed this simple experiment. This might be due to one or more uncontrolled variables in this process. Among the possible uncontrolled variables would be time of day and weather. Weather would be a difficult, but not impossible, variable to incorporate into your experiment. Time of day is much more easily included, and based upon your prior knowledge of the process, is very likely to influence travel time. Time of day might interact with the mode selected. During rush hour, travel time for a car might be the highest, while during non-rush hour it might be the lowest. Time of day might interact less with bus travel time since buses may be able to use high occupancy vehicle lanes. Time of day might not interact at all with rail travel times since rail should not be affected by highway congestion. In order to understand this interaction effect, a new experiment must be designed that incorporates time of day as an independent variable.

## EXPERIMENTAL DESIGN CHARACTERISTICS

In addition to replication, randomization, and local control, it is important to consider balance, efficiency, and fit when designing experiments. *Balance* refers to having equal numbers of observations, n, in each cell. Balance is important because it facilitates the use of more multiple comparison procedures. It can also prevent certain forms of bias from affecting the experimental results. An *orthogonal design* provides both horizontal and vertical balancing—that is, all pairs of factors at particular levels appear together an equal number of times.

*Efficiency* has to do with how focused or precise the experimental design is. For example, because a higher order full factorial design requires the running of a large number of trials, we may use a fractional factorial design (i.e., look at a specific set of variables, while ignoring others). The selection of variable for a fractional factorial design would be based on technical knowledge and experience with the process. The fractional factorial design would be more efficient than a full k-factorial design, but it would not take into account all factors and their possible interactions. So we may miss a relationship that we did not expect, as only those factors previously identified as pertinent are being evaluated.

*Fit* refers to how well the experimental design fits the actual population. Fit is usually calculated using error, which measures the difference between what our experimental analysis tells us the outcome should be and what the actual outcome is using the entire population.

The process of designing and conducting an experiment consists of seven steps (Montgomery, 2005, 14):

1. Recognize and define the problem to be addressed by the experiment.
2. Select the response variable(s).
3. Select the factors, levels, and ranges.
4. Select and appropriate experimental design.

**5.** Perform the experiment.

**6.** Statistically analyze the data.

**7.** Form conclusions and recommendations.

## TYPES OF DESIGN

There are various types of experimental designs. When there are several factors of interest in an experiment and all main effects and interaction effects are to be examined, a factorial design should be used. In a *full-factorial design* or experiment, all possible combinations of the levels of the factors are investigated in each complete trial of the experiment. Thus if there are two factors, A and B, with j levels of factor A and k levels of factor B, then each replicate contains all jk possible combinations. In a *fractional factorial design*, a subset of the factors is evaluated.

### Single-Factor Design

When we desire information on the relationship between a single input factor and the output factor in the experiment, a *one-factor or single-factor design* is appropriate. A single-factor design saves time and effort because it focuses on a single item rather than all possible combinations of many factors, yet it may result in a suboptimal solution for the same reason. A full-factorial design is best used when we are concerned about the effects of the interactions of the multiple factors because single factor experiments cannot assess these interaction effects. A full-factorial design is best used when the need for a complete data set outweighs the potential cost savings of a smaller, more focused experiment.

An example of a single-factor experiment would be the analysis of the effect of input concentration of a chlorinator on bacterial counts in a stream of water. Three levels of chlorination are to be evaluated, and the trials are to be replicated three times. Using the random number table in Appendix A results in the sequence of trials shown in Figure 7.1.

### One-Factor-at-a-Time Design

When multiple factors are to be considered, a simplistic approach is to vary one factor at a time and hold the other factors constant. This is a very inefficient experimental design, and, unless all possible combinations are run, does not allow for the estimation of interaction effects among the variables. Therefore this design is only useful if no factor interactions exist.

Consider a chemical process with three independent variables (factors)— temperature, pressure, and time—and one dependent variable, yield. A possible one-factor-at-a-time experiment is shown in Figure 7.2. The one-factor-at-a-time experimental design provides incomplete and possibly misleading information. With the addition of two more runs (four more with replication), complete information can be obtained by using the $2^3$ full-factorial design.

2a. Hold everything constant except time. Run two replications of two different levels of time and select the time with the highest yield.

| Run | Time | Temp. | Pressure |
|---|---|---|---|
| 1 | − | + | + |
| 2 | + | + | + |
| 1 | − | + | + |
| 2 | + | + | + |

Assume that the results show that the longer time (+) is better.

2b. Then fix time at the "optimum level", hold pressure constant, and run two replications of two different levels of temperature.

| Run | Time | Temp. | Pressure |
|---|---|---|---|
| 1 | + | − | + |
| 2 | + | + | + |
| 1 | + | − | + |
| 2 | + | + | + |

Assume that the results show that the lower temperature (−) is better.

2c. Then fix time and temperature at the "optimum levels," and run two replications of two different levels of pressure.

| Run | Time | Temp. | Pressure |
|---|---|---|---|
| 1 | + | − | − |
| 2 | + | − | + |
| 1 | + | − | − |
| 2 | + | − | + |

Assume that the results show that the higher pressure (+) is better.

The experimenter now believes that the optimum conditions for this process are long time (+), low temperature (−), and high pressure (+). However, since all possible combinations of these variables have not been assessed, this conclusion may very well be erroneous.

To arrive at this conclusion, the experimenter executed six runs—with replication, a total of 12 trials. Had the experimenter used a $2^3$ full-factorial design, she would need to execute eight runs—with replication, a total of 16 trials. But, with the full-factorial design, she would be able to assess all main effects and all interaction effects. This provides a much greater likelihood of identifying the true optimal settings for the three factors.

2d. Full-factorial design.

| Run | Time | Temp. | Pressure |
|---|---|---|---|
| 1 | − | − | − |
| 2 | + | − | − |
| 3 | − | + | − |
| 4 | + | + | − |
| 5 | − | − | + |
| 6 | + | − | + |
| 7 | − | + | + |
| 8 | + | + | + |

Runs 9–16 would be a replication of the above.

**Figure 7.2.** Comparison of One-Factor-at-a-Time with Full-Factorial Design

An engineer is interested in finding the values of temperature and time that maximize yield. Suppose we fix the temperature at 160°F (the current operating level) and perform five runs at different levels of time. The results of this series of runs are shown in the table below.

| Run Time (Hour) | Yield (%) |
|:---:|:---:|
| 0.5 | 42 |
| 1.0 | 50 |
| 1.5 | 62 |
| 2.0 | 70 |
| 2.5 | 66 |

This experiment indicates that maximum yield is achieved at approximately 2.0 hours of reaction time. To optimize the temperature, the engineer fixes the time at 2.0 hours (the apparent optimum) and performs five runs at different temperatures.

| Temperature (°F) | Yield (%) |
|:---:|:---:|
| 140 | 36 |
| 150 | 44 |
| 160 | 76 |
| 170 | 62 |
| 180 | 31 |

Based on the data from the second experiment, maximum yield occurs at 160°F.

Therefore, we would conclude that running the process at 160°F and 2.0 hours is the best set of operating conditions, resulting in a yield of about 73 percent $[(70 + 76)/2]$.

The downside of one-factor design is that it fails to detect possible interactions between the two factors (in this case time and temperature). For the example above, a full factorial experimental design indicates that optimal yield is really around 95 percent at a temperature of between 180°F and 190°F and a time of around 0.5 hours.

## Full-Factorial Design

A full-factorial design involves testing all possible combinations of the factors in an experiment at a number of levels. A full-factorial design allows for the estimation of all main effects and all interaction effects. The difficulty is that this design requires a considerable investment of time and resources. This becomes of increasing importance as the number of factors increases. A full-factorial design for two levels of three factors ($2^3$) is shown in Figure 7.2d and in Figure 7.3.

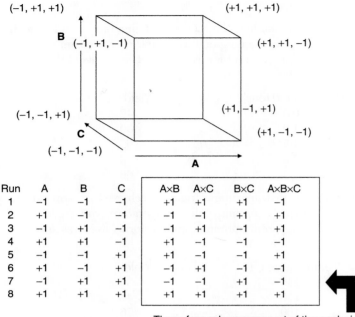

| Run | A | B | C | A×B | A×C | B×C | A×B×C |
|-----|-----|-----|-----|-----|-----|-----|-----|
| 1 | −1 | −1 | −1 | +1 | +1 | +1 | −1 |
| 2 | +1 | −1 | −1 | −1 | −1 | +1 | +1 |
| 3 | −1 | +1 | −1 | −1 | +1 | −1 | +1 |
| 4 | +1 | +1 | −1 | +1 | −1 | −1 | −1 |
| 5 | −1 | −1 | +1 | +1 | −1 | −1 | +1 |
| 6 | +1 | −1 | +1 | −1 | +1 | −1 | −1 |
| 7 | −1 | +1 | +1 | −1 | −1 | +1 | −1 |
| 8 | +1 | +1 | +1 | +1 | +1 | +1 | +1 |

These four columns are part of the analysis matrix and show the interactions that can be assessed. The three columns following the Run column constitute the design matrix.

Note that this design examines only the corners of the cube. If there is an indication that the relationships may be nonlinear, it would be advantageous to examine the center points as well as the corners.

**Figure 7.3.** $2^3$ Full-Factorial Design

| | $2^2$ | | | $2^3$ | | |
|-----|-----|-----|-----|-----|-----|-----|
| Run | Factor A | Factor B | Run | Factor A | Factor B | Factor C |
| 1 | − | − | 1 | − | − | − |
| 2 | − | + | 2 | + | + | − |
| 3 | + | − | 3 | − | + | − |
| 4 | + | + | 4 | + | + | − |
| | | | 5 | − | − | + |
| | | | 6 | + | − | + |
| | | | 7 | − | + | + |
| | | | 8 | + | + | + |

**Figure 7.4.** Some Full-Factorial Designs

The design in Figure 7.3 assumes a linear relationship among the factors. The corners of the cube represent the two levels of the factors, that is, −1 (minimum setting) and +1 (maximum setting). If a nonlinear relationship is suspected, it would be necessary to run the center points of the cube shown. A $3^3$ factorial design that examines three levels of the three factors will provide more complete evidence of the linearity of the relationships. But this comes at the cost of the need to make 27 runs rather than eight runs.

Students running a $2^3$ full-factorial-designed experiment to optimize the settings on the catapult to maximize the distance that the ball is thrown. [Exercise 1]

## FRACTIONAL FACTORIAL DESIGN

When there are many factors, the number of runs required for a full-factorial design becomes unmanageable. A fractional factorial design involves testing an orthogonal (balanced) subset of all possible combinations of the factors. A fractional factorial design allows for the estimation of all main effects and selected interaction effects. The sacrifice in information obtained is balanced by the reduced resource requirements compared with a full-factorial design. A $2^{3-1}$ fractional factorial design for the example in Figure 7.1 is shown in Figure 7.5. The run number is the number these runs would be in a full-factorial design.

Often fractional factorial designs are used for *screening experiments* to identify critical factors, to identify the direction and magnitude of the main effects, and to estimate factor interactions. This could lead to additional experiments examining only the critical factors. The results of a screening experiment might also be helpful in identifying critical factors to monitor more closely in order to better control a process.

| Run | A | B | C | A × B | A × C | B × C | A × B × C |
|-----|-----|-----|-----|-----|-----|-----|-----|
| 2 | +1 | −1 | −1 | −1 | −1 | +1 | +1 |
| 3 | −1 | +1 | −1 | −1 | +1 | −1 | +1 |
| 5 | −1 | −1 | +1 | +1 | −1 | −1 | +1 |
| 8 | +1 | +1 | +1 | +1 | +1 | +1 | +1 |

**Figure 7.5.** $2^{3-1}$ Fractional Factorial Design

## ANALYSIS OF RESULTS

As discussed earlier, design of experiments is used to study the product or process. Once we have the data from the experiment, however, it must be analyzed. Analysis of variance (ANOVA) is used to interpret the experimental data. ANOVA partitions the total variance into two components: between-group variation and within-group variation. We use sum of squares (SS) to represent the partitioned variation. The null hypothesis for ANOVA is that there is no difference among the levels of the dependent variable due to variation in the independent variable(s). By calculating the sum of squares and the appropriate degrees of freedom (DF) for each component of variation, the null hypothesis can be tested using the F distribution. It is common to see the sum of squares presented in an ANOVA table that gives all the pertinent data to test the null hypothesis using the F ratio as the test statistic. For single-factor experiments, one-way ANOVA is used. Example 7.1 shows the ANOVA results for the experiment illustrated in Figure 7.1.

---

**EXAMPLE 7.1:  One-way ANOVA: Bacterial Count versus Chlorine (Cl) Level**

```
Source      DF      SS      MS      F       P
Cl Level    2     22906   11453   62.47   0.000
Error       6      1100     183
Total       8     24006


S = 13.54    R-Sq = 95.42%    R-Sq(adj) = 93.89%


                         Individual 95% CIs For Mean Based on
                         Pooled StDev
Level   N    Mean   StDev   ------+---------+---------+---------+---
0.2     3  151.67    7.64                                (----*----)
0.4     3  123.33   20.82                       (----*----)
0.6     3   33.33    7.64   (---*----)
                            ------+---------+---------+---------+---
                               40        80       120       160


Pooled StDev = 13.54
```

---

The large F statistic indicates that there is a highly significant difference (p <
0.001)[*] among the chlorination levels. The adjusted R-Sq indicates that 93.89%
of the variation in the bacterial counts is accounted for by variation in the
chlorination levels. The 95% confidence intervals indicate that the 0.6 level of
chlorination yields bacterial counts that are significantly lower than the other
two levels of chlorination.

[*]Note that the value of p on the printout does not mean that p is equal to
0.000. p approaches 0 but never reaches it. It is correct to say that p is less than
the smallest value in the last place shown to the right of the decimal. In this
case, p is smaller than 0.001.

Analysis using Minitab™

Example 7.2 shows the results of a $2^3$ full-factorial design with two replications
for a chemical process. The dependent variable is Yield. The factors are reaction time
(Time), catalyst concentration (Catalyst), and reactant concentration (Reactant).

## EXAMPLE 7.2: Analysis of Variance for Yield, Using Adjusted SS for Tests

| Source | DF | Seq SS | Adj SS | Adj MS | F | P |
|---|---|---|---|---|---|---|
| Time | 1 | 6252.9 | 6252.9 | 6252.9 | 8.67 | 0.019 |
| Catalyst | 1 | 6508.5 | 6508.5 | 6508.5 | 9.03 | 0.017 |
| Reactant | 1 | 61.2 | 61.2 | 61.2 | 0.08 | 0.778 |
| Time*Catalyst | 1 | 895.5 | 895.5 | 895.5 | 1.24 | 0.297 |
| Time*Reactant | 1 | 0.2 | 0.2 | 0.2 | 0.00 | 0.988 |
| Catalyst*Reactant | 1 | 2.8 | 2.8 | 2.8 | 0.00 | 0.952 |
| Time*Catalyst*Reactant | 1 | 383.2 | 383.2 | 383.2 | 0.53 | 0.487 |
| Error | 8 | 5767.4 | 5767.4 | 720.9 | | |
| Total | 15 | 19871.6 | | | | |

S = 26.8500    R-Sq = 70.98%    R-Sq(adj) = 45.58%

Main Effects: The ANOVA table shows that the factors Time and Catalyst
concentration are significant (p < 0.05) while Reactant concentration is not.

The main effects plot shows the same information graphically. As the levels
of Time and Catalyst concentration vary, Yield varies. As the Reactant level is
changed, Yield is relatively unaffected.

Interaction effects: The ANOVA table shows that none of the interactions
are significant.

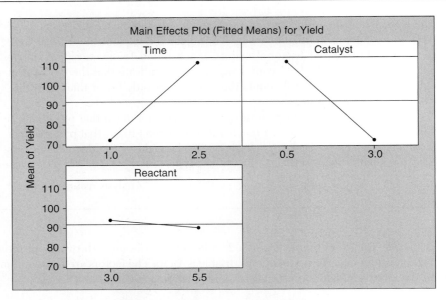

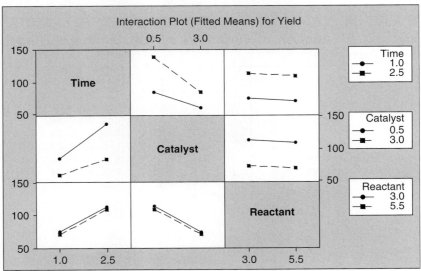

The interaction plot shows the same information graphically. Perfectly parallel plots show no interaction. The slight deviations from parallel for these plots are not significant according to the F ratios in the ANOVA table.

Analysis using Minitab™

A regression analysis can be conducted using the significant factors only. The regression equation in Example 7.3 shows that Yield increases as Time increases and Catalyst decreases. Based on the combined ANOVA and regression analysis, the high level of Time and low level of Catalyst should be used with the most economical level of Reactant in order to increase yield. Based on the regression equation, further experimentation with lower levels of Catalyst and longer times might result in even higher yields.

---

### EXAMPLE 7.3: Regression Analysis: Yield versus Time, Catalyst

```
The regression equation is
Yield = 73.8 + 26.4 Time - 16.1 Catalyst
Predictor      Coef  SE Coef      T      P
Constant      73.82    16.95   4.35  0.001
Time         26.358     7.796   3.38  0.005
Catalyst    -16.135     4.677  -3.45  0.004


S = 23.3869    R-Sq = 64.2%    R-Sq(adj) = 58.7%


Analysis of Variance

Source            DF       SS      MS      F      P
Regression         2  12761.3  6380.7  11.67  0.001
Residual Error    13   7110.3   546.9
Total             15  19871.6
```

Analysis using Minitab™

---

# TAGUCHI METHODS OF EXPERIMENTAL DESIGN

In the early 1980s Professor Genichi Taguchi introduced his approach to using experimental design for:

1. designing products or processes so that they are robust to environmental conditions;

2. designing/developing products so that they are robust to component variation; and

3. minimizing variation around a target.

Taguchi refers to these three activities as quality engineering. They flow in order from system design to tolerance design. System design occurs in the initial or idea phase of product or process development. Parameter design is the middle component of the three, where the system is "fine tuned" to ensure that it consistently functions as intended. Tolerance design determines the acceptable variations around the nominal settings determined in parameter design.

Taguchi took assumptions from engineering knowledge and used them to reduce the size of experiments, thereby speeding up the experimental process. One of the areas he looked at involved random noise and its effect on variability. Taguchi focused on minimizing the effect of the causes of variation. By inserting a second orthogonal array into the experiment, Taguchi added the capability of determining those combinations of controllable factors that minimize the effect of the sources of experimentation variability. He defined this ability as *robustness*. In other words, the product or process performs consistently on target and is relatively insensitive to factors that are difficult to control.

The purpose of experimentation using Taguchi methods is to identify the key factors that have the greatest contribution to variation and to ascertain those settings or values that result in the least variability. Dr. Taguchi adapted orthogonal arrays for designing and analyzing experimental data. Orthogonal arrays are used to control experimental error. Taguchi methods use orthogonal arrays to measure the effect of a factor on the average result, and also to determine the variation from the mean. The primary advantage of orthogonal arrays is the relationship among the factors under investigation. For each level of any one factor, all levels of the other factors occur an equal number of times. This constitutes a balanced experiment and permits the effect of one factor under study to be separable from the effects of other factors. The result is that the findings of the experiment are reproducible. This compares with full-factor analysis in which the effect of each and every variable on each and every other variable must be determined (adding significantly to the time and cost of the experiment), and single-factor analysis in which factors not of interest are eliminated (jeopardizing the reproducibility of the study). Figure 7.6 shows an example of an orthogonal array.

To enhance the flexibility of the arrays, Dr. Taguchi used linear graphs to represent the arrays. By using these graphs and the triangular tables provided by Taguchi, the experimenter can effectively study the interactions between experimental factors as well as the effects of the individual factors (main effects) themselves. Linear graphs make this possible by providing a logical scheme for assigning interactions to the

This design may be used for three factors at two levels.

| Run | A | B | C |
|-----|-----|-----|-----|
| 1 | $-1$ | $-1$ | $-1$ |
| 2 | $-1$ | $+1$ | $+1$ |
| 3 | $+1$ | $-1$ | $+1$ |
| 4 | $+1$ | $+1$ | $-1$ |

Note that this design consists of runs 1, 7, 6, and 4 of the $2^3$ full-factorial design.

**Figure 7.6.** $L_4$ ($2^3$) Orthogonal Array

| Experimental Runs | Factors Column | | | | | | |
|---|---|---|---|---|---|---|---|
| | A | B | C | D | E | F | G |
| 1 | 1 | 1 | 1 | 1 | 1 | 1 | 1 |
| 2 | 1 | 1 | 1 | 2 | 2 | 2 | 2 |
| 3 | 1 | 2 | 2 | 1 | 1 | 2 | 2 |
| 4 | 1 | 2 | 2 | 2 | 2 | 1 | 1 |
| 5 | 2 | 1 | 2 | 1 | 2 | 1 | 2 |
| 6 | 2 | 1 | 2 | 2 | 1 | 2 | 1 |
| 7 | 2 | 2 | 1 | 1 | 2 | 2 | 1 |
| 8 | 2 | 2 | 1 | 2 | 1 | 1 | 2 |

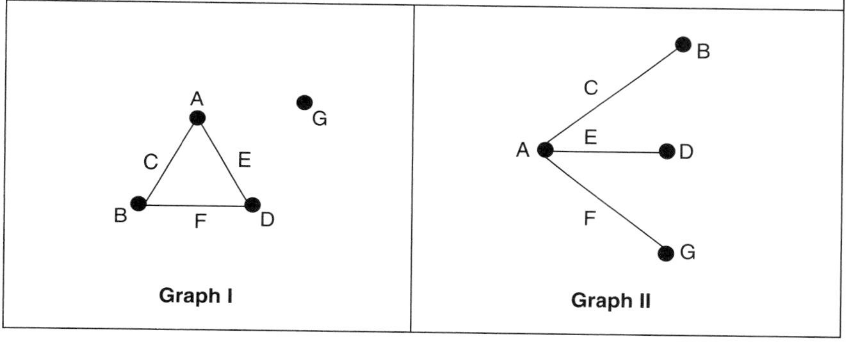

**Graph I**    **Graph II**

**Figure 7.7.** Example of an $L_8$ $(2^7)$ Orthogonal Array and Linear Graphs

orthogonal array without confounding the effects of the interactions with the effects of the individual factors being studied.

Figure 7.7 shows two linear graphs for the $L_8$ array. Graph II (on the right) shows the graph for the situation where all interactions of interest involve a common factor, A. Graph I (on the left) shows the graph for a design that requires the study of three interactions (A × B, B × C, and A × C), involving the same three main effect factors (A, B, and C). No interaction effects involving G are included in this design.

The graphs are constructed of interconnecting dots, with each dot representing a column within the array in which a factor (main effect) can be assigned. The connecting line represents the interaction between the two dots (factors) at each end of the line segment. The number accompanying the line segment represents the column within the array to which the interaction should be assigned.

Dr. Taguchi's concept of robustness was earlier defined as the product or process performing consistently on target and is relatively insensitive to factors that are difficult to control. Robustness applies to both product and process. From a product standpoint, we can further define robustness as "the ability of the product to perform consistently as designed with minimal effect from changes in uncontrollable operating influences" (Peace, 1993, 5). For processes, we can define robustness as "the ability of the process to produce consistently good product with minimal effect from changes in uncontrollable manufacturing influences" (Peace, 1993, 5). These definitions recognize that we cannot always control some of the things that create variation within the process or the product. Walter Shewhart referred to this as random or common variation and recognized its existence in all processes. Similar to Shewhart, Dr. Taguchi's approach is to use designed experiments to identify and control those factors that are significant causes of variation and to do so in a way that minimizes the effect of those variables that cannot be controlled, or that it is not practical to control.

## SUMMARY

This chapter has provided a brief overview of experimental design. Experimental design can be important in optimizing processes and solving problems. The different types and methodologies associated with experimental design were introduced in this chapter. Full-factorial designs permit the assessment of all main effects and all interaction effects at the expense of efficiency. To increase efficiency, screening experiments using fractional factorial designs can identify critical variables for further experimentation. ANOVA is used to analyze the data obtained from designed experiments. Genichi Taguchi's contributions to the field of experimental design were discussed and his approach to DOE using orthogonal arrays was introduced.

## DISCUSSION QUESTIONS

1. Discuss what is meant by factor, level, and treatment.
2. What is meant by the term replication? What role does it play in DOE?
3. Define and discuss the term blocking. When might blocking be useful?
4. Discuss the advantages and disadvantages of full-factorial design over one-factor-at-a-time experimentation.
5. What is meant by a $2^3$ experimental design?
6. How is variance broken down in ANOVA?
7. How do Taguchi's orthogonal arrays compare to full-factorial designs?
8. What is meant by the term orthogonal array?
9. Define and discuss Taguchi's concept of robustness.
10. What is meant by the term interaction effect?
11. How might the use of fractional factorial designs be useful in increasing the efficiency of an experimental design?

# PROBLEMS

1. The yield from a chemical process is thought to be affected by two process conditions: temperature and pressure. Process engineering has determined that reasonable operating ranges are 120°C and 150°C for temperature and 800 psi and 1000 psi for pressure. Develop a $2^2$ full-factorial design with two replications.

2. Use the random number table in Appendix A to determine the order for completely randomizing the experimental runs in Problem 1.

3. You have conducted a single-factor experiment for a chemical process investigating the effect of three levels of catalyst on reaction rate. You used three replications and randomized the order of the runs. You obtained the following output from Minitab. Interpret the results and make a recommendation for the level of catalyst given that maximum reaction rate is desired.

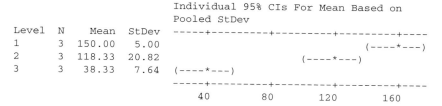

```
One-way ANOVA: Rate versus Catalyst

Source      DF     SS     MS      F       P
Catalyst     2   19872   9936   57.69   0.000
Error        6    1033    172
Total        8   20905

S = 13.12    R-Sq = 95.06%    R-Sq(adj) = 93.41%


                                 Individual 95% CIs For Mean Based on
                                 Pooled StDev
Level   N    Mean   StDev   -----+---------+---------+---------+----
1       3  150.00    5.00                                 (----*---)
2       3  118.33   20.82                        (----*---)
3       3   38.33    7.64    (----*---)
                            -----+---------+---------+---------+----
                              40        80       120       160

Pooled StDev = 13.12
```

4. You have conducted a $2^3$ full-factorial experiment with two replications on a chemical process evaluating the effects on hardness of two levels of temperature, pressure, and relative humidity. You obtained the following output from Minitab. Interpret the results and make a recommendation for the levels of temperature, pressure, and relative humidity, given that maximum hardness is desired.

```
General Linear Model: Hardness versus Temp, Press, RH

Factor   Type   Levels  Values
Temp     fixed       2  160, 200
Press    fixed       2  120, 150
RH       fixed       2  30, 50


Analysis of Variance for Hardness, using Adjusted SS for Tests

Source        DF   Seq SS   Adj SS   Adj MS      F      P
Temp           1   324.00   264.14   264.14  16.62  0.003
Press          1     0.02    28.12    28.12   1.77  0.216
RH             1   408.00   302.29   302.29  19.02  0.002
Temp*Press     1     0.16     2.00     2.00   0.13  0.731
Temp*RH        1     2.45     0.14     0.14   0.01  0.927
Press*RH       1    10.12    10.12    10.12   0.64  0.445
Error          9   143.00   143.00    15.89
Total         15   887.75

S = 3.98609   R-Sq = 83.89%   R-Sq(adj) = 73.15%
```

5. You have obtained the following main effects plot for the experiment in Problem 4. Explain what you can deduce from the plot.

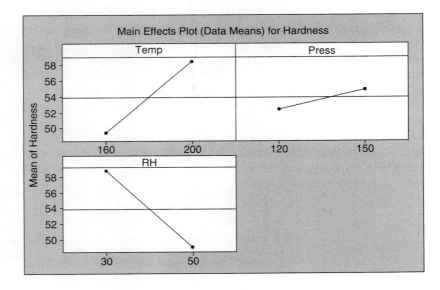

6. You have obtained the following interaction effects plot for a $2^3$ experiment you have conducted. Based on the plot, which interactions might be significant? Explain your answer.

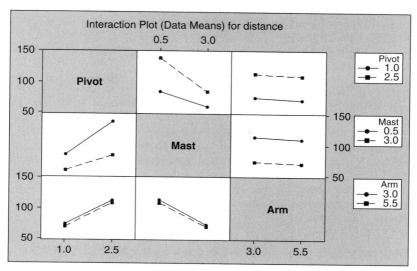

7. The yield from a chemical process is thought to be affected by three process conditions: temperature, pressure, and time. Process engineering has determined that reasonable operating ranges are 120°C and 150°C for temperature, 800 psi and 1,000 psi for pressure, and 15 minutes and 20 minutes. for time. Develop a $2^3$ full-factorial design with one replication.

8. Develop an $L_4$ Taguchi orthogonal array as an alternative to the full-factorial design in Problem 7. Discuss the tradeoffs in using the $L_4$ design rather than the $2^3$ design.

## CASE STUDY 7.1: *The Case of the Variable Laminates*

©2006 Victor E. Sower, Ph.D., C.Q.E.

A plywood manufacturer has asked for your assistance in solving a problem in the log-peeling operation. The peeling process consists of soaking de-barked logs in a hot bath, fixing the logs in chucks, and rapidly spinning them while shaving off a continuous thin section called a lamination with a sharp knife blade. The laminations are then cut into sheets to be laid up, glued, and pressed into plywood sheets. The manufacturer is having difficulty maintaining a controlled thickness when peeling laminations from a log.

Discussions with engineering and the process operators indicate that four variables are related to laminate thickness: soak time, soak temperature, knife pressure, and knife setting. The knife setting is pretty straight forward and is not felt to be a source of variation in the process. Specifications call for logs to be soaked for 60 minutes, but no process control for this process is in place. Some logs are peeled after as little as 30 minutes soak time.

The operators believe that this causes some of the variation, but they are under the gun to keep the peeler busy, even if it means compromising on the soak time. The engineers feel that knife pressure may contribute to the thickness variation. Knife pressure setting is not standardized—operators set it between 250 psi and 300 psi based on their experience. Soak temperature varies between 150 degrees and 200 degrees, depending upon how much bark has accumulated around the heating coils.

Thickness measurements are made every 15 minutes on the laminate. The variation does not seem to follow a particular pattern.

Design an experiment that will assist the process engineers in determining what actions to take to reduce laminate thickness variation. Provide them with your assessment of the causes of the variation and how to use the results of the experiment to define the optimal operating conditions for the process.

## EXERCISES AND ACTIVITIES

1. The Catapult Exercise

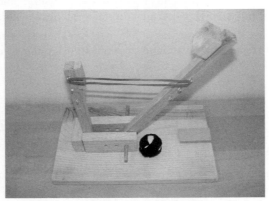

A catapult can be used to teach experimental design in the classroom. The one shown in this exercise was built from half-inch thick red oak. The mast is 7.5 inches tall and the arm is 11 inches long. The base is 12 inches by 7 inches. The brakes are two layers of self-adhesive weather stripping. The cradle is a piece of oak with a 1.25-inch hole that does not go completely through the piece. Plans for the catapult may be found in Deane & Burgess (1998). The balls are ping pong balls covered with self-adhesive Velcro. There are three positions for the rubber band on the arm and the mast. These are partially opened eye bolts. There are three positions for the hinge location. The hinge is a hardwood dowel. Construction time is approximately one hour using a table saw and a hand drill or drill press.

Design a $2^3$ full-factorial experiment with two replications using the extreme positions for the three variables: mast attachment, arm attachment, and hinge position. Use a random number table to randomize the order of the experiments. For each run, measure the distance that the ball travels.

Analyze the results using ANOVA and interpret the results. What are the optimal settings to maximize the distance that the ball travels?

Discussion points:

A. What are some environmental variables in this experiment? How might they be controlled?
B. If you suspect that some of the relationships among the variables are nonlinear, how would you redesign the experiment?
C. What are the tradeoffs of running the $2^3$ experiment using the extreme points (levels) for each independent variable versus running the $3^3$ experiment that would examine all possible levels for the independent variables?

**2.** The Airplane Exercise

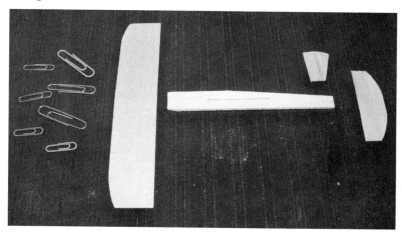

This exercise can be used in two ways:

A. Do the exercise prior to discussing the material in this chapter. Students are most likely to use one-variable-at-a-time experimentation or just trial and error. Use this as a motivation to learn more structured and efficient approaches to experimentation (e.g., screening experiments, factorial design).
B. Do the exercise after discussing the material in this chapter to reinforce learning with regard to screening experiments and factorial design of experiments.

Provide small groups with identical, small balsa wood airplane model kits. Use the ones that are gliders, not the rubber band powered ones.

Remove from the kits the weight that is designed to go on the front of the planes. Instead of the weight, provide a selection of paper clip of various sizes. Have the students design a plane using the materials provided and the fewest number of experimental trials possible that will fly the longest distance. Inform the students that experimental trials cost $1,000 each. The winner will be determined based on the distance the plane flies and the total cost of the designed experiments. (Hints: Among the variables that may be significant are the amount of weight on the nose; position of the wings; position of the tail; position of the rudder; and warp of the wings. Students may determine that other variables are significant.)

Have each team fly its plane in random order in a large room. Measure and record the distance flown for each flight. Allow at least two flights per team with no alterations to the plane's design between flights. Determine a winner.

Have the students discuss environmental variables that may have affected the flight of their planes. How might they control these variables?

## SUPPLEMENTARY READINGS

Barrentine, L. (1999). *An Introduction to Design of Experiments—A Simplified Approach.* Milwaukee, WI: ASQ Quality Press.

Montgomery, D. C. (2005). *Design and Analysis of Experiments*, 3rd edition. Hoboken, NJ: John Wiley & Sons.

Roy, R. (1990). *A Primer on the Taguchi Method.* New York: Van Nostrand Reinhold.

Taguchi, G., (1986). *Introduction to Quality Engineering.* White Plains, NY: Asian Productivity Organization UNIPUB.

Taguchi, G., & S. Konishi, (1987). *Orthogonal Arrays and Linear Graphs.* Dearborn, MI: American Supplier Institute.

Taguchi, G., S. Chowdhury, & Y. Wu. (2005). *Taguchi's Quality Engineering Handbook.* Hoboken, NJ: John Wiley & Sons.

## REFERENCES

ASQC Statistics Division. (1983). *Glossary & Tables for Statistical Quality Control.* Milwaukee, WI: ASQC Quality Press.

Deane, R., & R. Burgess. (1998). "Experiential Teaching Techniques in Quality Management: The Roman Catapult." *Quality Management Journal* 5(2), 58–66.

Fisher, R. A. (1958). *Statistical Methods for Research Workers*, 13th edition. Edinburgh: Oliver & Boyd.

Montgomery, D. (2005). *Design and Analysis of Experiments.* Hoboken, NJ: John Wiley & Sons.

Peace, G. S. (1993). *Taguchi Methods: A Hands On Approach.* Reading, MA: Addison-Wesley.

"Quality Glossary." (2002). *Quality Progress* 35(7), 43–61.

# SECTION IV

# CONTROL
# AND IMPROVEMENT
# OF QUALITY

## CHAPTER EIGHT

# Quality Improvement Tools

## CHAPTER OBJECTIVES

After completing this chapter, the reader should be able to:

- understand and use the problem-solving process;
- understand and use the seven tools of quality; and
- understand the use of the PDSA and DMAIC cycles for continuous improvement.

Quality managers and engineers are often engaged in a process that is called *problem solving*. This chapter discusses a systematic approach to problem solving based on the work of Osborn (1963), Parnes, et al. (1977), and Kepner and Tregoe (1965). There are a number of tools available to the quality engineer that are effective in addressing problems. This chapter will focus on seven quality tools (the seven tools of quality) and how they can be used in each stage of the problem-solving process.

Usually, instead of seeing a problem, a quality manager or engineer is confronted with a mess. The mess consists of one or more symptoms that indicate that there is a problem of some sort somewhere. There is a difference between a symptom and a problem. Healthwise, a headache is usually a symptom. The cause of a headache (e.g., drinking too much alcohol or a brain tumor) is the problem. Addressing the symptom (headache) with a pain-relieving drug (aspirin) can be dangerous in that it allows the problem (tumor) to continue to grow. In business, poor employee morale is usually a symptom (not a problem)—perhaps of poor supervision, inadequate working conditions among others. High rates of scrap and rework are usually symptoms of a process problem (e.g., defective lot of material, a malfunctioning machine, an inadequately trained operator). In order to have any meaningful and lasting impact, the problem-solving process must focus on the problem (root cause) rather than the symptom. Healthwise, an aspirin might temporarily relieve the headache, but the headache will recur because the root cause (tumor) has been ignored. Holding a company picnic will have little lasting impact on employee morale if the cause of poor morale (poor supervision) is ignored. Effective quality professionals use a structured approach to problem solving that is focused on root causes rather than a haphazard or seat-of-the-pants approach.

There are three general types of errors that can occur in problem solving. A Type I error involves solving a problem that does not exist. An example of this would be admonishing an employee for variation that is due to random causes. A Type II error involves failing to recognize that a problem exists. An example of this would be the failure to use tools such as control charts to identify when a special cause of variation has occurred in a process. A Type III error occurs when the wrong problem is solved. An example of this would be redecorating the break room to improve employee morale when the real problem is poor supervision.

Problems and opportunities are but two sides of the same coin. Solving a problem is an opportunity to improve the process. The basic problem-solving process can be applied to continuous-improvement activities in conjunction with the Deming (or Shewhart) Cycle (plan—do—study—act) or the Six Sigma DMAIC process (define—measure—analyze—improve—control).

Organizations need not go it alone when working to improve their processes. Benchmarking enables organizations to learn from what others have done. When approached properly, benchmarking can increase the quality of the final result and dramatically reduce the time required for the improvement project.

## THE PROBLEM-SOLVING PROCESS

The more complex the problem, the less likely a lasting solution can be developed off the cuff. A structured approach is more likely to lead to an optimal or near-optimal, lasting solution to complex problems. An eight-step creative problem-solving process adapted from the work of Kepner & Tregoe (1965), Osborn (1963), and Parnes, et al.(1977) has proven to be effective in addressing complex problems. Figure 8.1 illustrates this model.

*Symptom recognition/Mess finding* involves recognizing a problem through the observation of one or more symptoms. A symptom is an inconsistency between how the system is expected to perform and how it is actually performing. Tools that are useful in the recognition of symptoms are flow charts, run charts, and process-control charts. Evans (1990, 94) suggests that creative managers take a proactive approach to this step by actively seeking messes rather than waiting for them to appear on their own.

In the *fact finding/specify deviation* step data must be collected for analysis to provide insight into the nature of the problem that is creating the symptoms. In this step the nature of the deviation between actual and desired performance is defined and factors that may affect the problem are identified by asking questions such as What? Where? When? Extent? Check sheets are useful in this step.

*Problem identification* involves sorting out the real problem from the symptoms created by that problem as shown in Figure 8.2. Initially, flow charts, check sheets, and Pareto analysis are useful in this step. The data are used in order to better

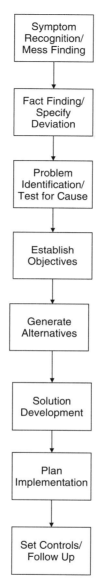

**Figure 8.1.** Problem-Solving Process

understand the causal system and relationships involved in the problem (root-cause analysis). Cause-and-effect diagrams and scatter diagrams are useful in this step.

*Objectives are established* to define what an acceptable solution to the problem must accomplish. An objective might include several aspects, including process performance, time, and financial. These objectives are used to evaluate alternative solutions to the problem.

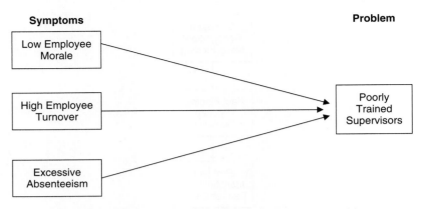

**Figure 8.2.** The Relationship between Symptoms and Problems

Next, *alternative solutions to the problem are generated.* Brainstorming is an effective tool during this step. Affinity diagrams, discussed in Chapter 3, can be useful in the brainstorming process.

In the *solution development step* the alternative ideas for addressing the problem are evaluated and the best course of action is selected based on the objective criteria established in Step 4. Tree diagrams and PDPC charts discussed in Chapter 3 can be useful in this step.

*Plan implementation* addresses issues such as resources required, project planning, and acceptance of the solution. In this step the selected course of action is actually put into effect. Activity networks discussed in Chapter 3 can be useful in this step.

Implementation of the plan does not complete the problem-solving process. Because "the best laid schemes o' mice an' men gang aft agley" (Burns, 1785), *setting controls and follow up* are important to ensure that the solution implemented has had the desired effect and will be a lasting solution to the problem. Control charts and run charts can be useful in this step.

## THE SEVEN TOOLS OF QUALITY

The seven tools of quality are relatively simple but very powerful tools that every quality manager and engineer should master. Indeed, these tools are routinely used by individuals and groups throughout organizations to address all sorts of problems. The tools, shown in Figure 8.3, are:

Flow Chart

Run Chart

Process-Control Chart

Check Sheet

Pareto Diagram

Cause-and-Effect Diagram

Scatter Diagram

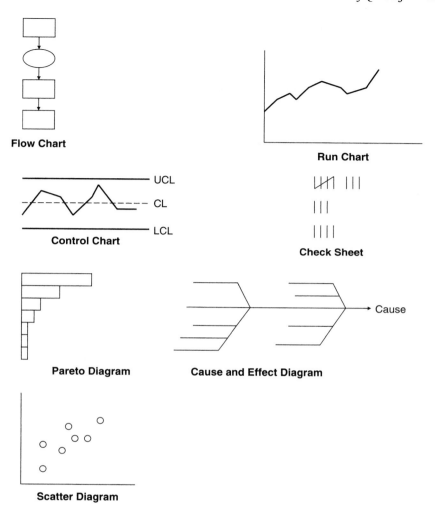

Flow Chart

Run Chart

Control Chart

Check Sheet

Pareto Diagram

Cause and Effect Diagram

Scatter Diagram

**Figure 8.3.** The Seven Tools of Quality

The seven tools of quality can assist the quality professional in addressing problems and opportunities for improvement. They are simple but powerful tools that can be of significant value throughout the problem-solving and continuous-improvement processes. The Mystery Chemical example in this chapter (Figures 8.4–8.10) shows a simple example of how the seven tools of quality can be utilized in a systematic way to address a problem. With the exception of process-control charts, they do not require any knowledge of statistics to be used effectively. And these tools are equally effective in both service and manufacturing environments. Training in the use of these tools can be incorporated into the early phases of employee-empowerment training programs. Management cannot expect employees to effectively participate in problem-solving and continuous-improvement programs (i.e., to be empowered) unless they are provided training in how to address problems.

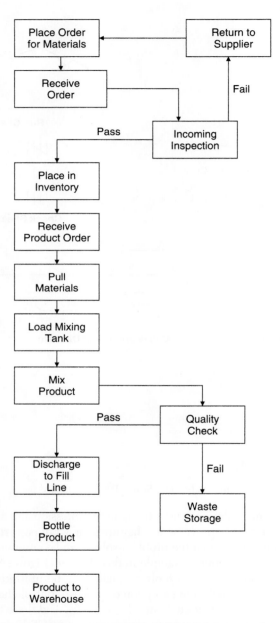

**Figure 8.4.** Mystery Chemical Inc. Mixing Process

*Flow charts* are used to define and to understand a process. ASQ defines a flow chart as "a graphical representation of the steps in a process. Flowcharts are drawn to better understand processes. The flowchart is one of the 'seven tools of quality'" (Quality Glossary, 2002, 50). There are conventions for the use of flow chart symbols (for example, see Galloway, 1994); however, the consistent use of a given convention contributes more to understanding than the selection of a particular convention.

Flow charts can be produced easily by hand using templates, although most modern presentation software and word processors enable the creation of professional-looking flow charts quickly and with little effort. Specialized software packages are also available for all seven tools of quality.

## FLOW CHART FOR THE MANUFACTURE OF PLYWOOD

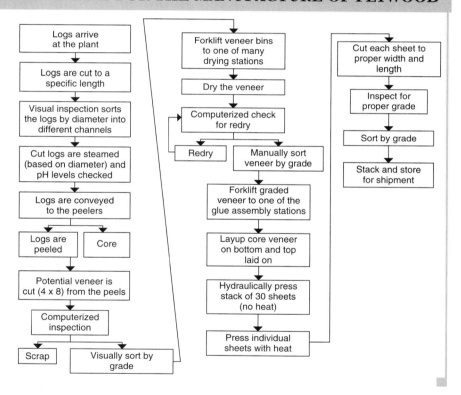

Flow charts are equally useful in services. When they focus on moments of truth—when customers form an opinion about the quality of service—they are often called service blueprints. This is a flow chart for the admissions process for the Honors Program at Sam Houston State University.

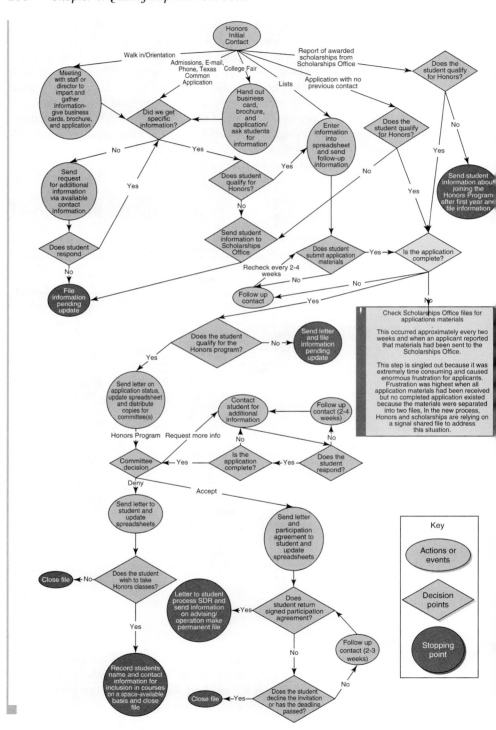

Flow charts facilitate an analysis of the steps in a process to determine relationships between the steps in the process. An example would be the precedence relationship between steps—which step(s) must precede which other step(s). Flow charts provide a means of visually depicting the steps and interrelationships without the user struggling through a lengthy textual description of each step. This becomes more important the more complex the process becomes.

Flow charts facilitate the process of continuous improvement. Questions about which steps are value-adding and which are not are clarified by a flow chart. "Why is this step here?" and "What can we do to eliminate the need for this step?" are questions that flow charts facilitate. Figure 8.4 is a flow chart of a chemical batch process. Someone working to improve the process might question whether the (nonvalue-adding) incoming material inspection could be eliminated by using supplier certification. Could improved control of the mixing process reduce the number of batches sent to waste storage? Figure 8.5 shows a process that was improved by analysis with a flow chart and the addition of technology to eliminate nonvalue-adding activities and reduce the risk of error.

A *run chart* is a graphical representation of the variation in a measurable characteristic over time. The measurable characteristic is represented on the vertical axis, and the time periods are represented on the horizontal axis. Run charts are useful in providing an indication of a possible shift in the characteristic being plotted. Figure 8.6 shows a run chart that Mystery Chemical uses to track rejections of materials at incoming inspection. The run chart provides evidence of a troubling rising trend in the percentage of chemical batches that are rejected and consigned to the waste storage tank. The use of the run chart alone provides no statistical evidence that the apparent trend is due to anything other than random variation alone.

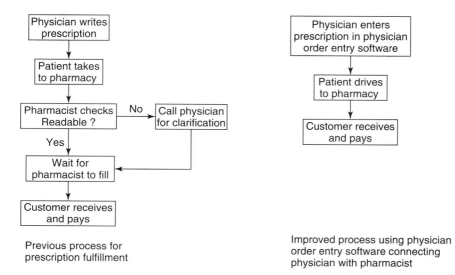

**Figure 8.5.** Eliminating Nonvalue-Adding Activities Using Flow Charts and Technology

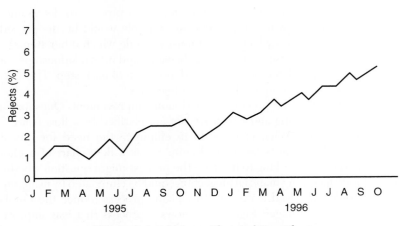

**Figure 8.6.** Mystery Chemical Run Chart

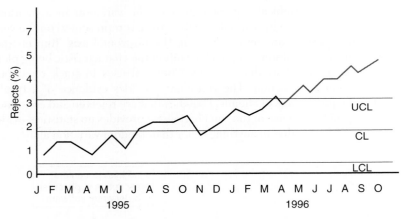

**Figure 8.7.** Mystery Chemical Control Chart

The same data plotted on a *process-control chart* (Figure 8.7—in this case, a proportion defective or p-chart) provide clear evidence that the manufacturing process is out of control. The control chart (which is discussed in more detail in Chapter 10) is a tool that provides a means of determining the type of variation present in a process and whether the process is performing predictably. It looks much like the run chart but with additional lines. These lines are the upper control limit (UCL), lower control limit (LCL), and center line (CL). These lines define the average (CL) and extreme (UCL and LCL) performance of the process when it is behaving as designed (i.e., only random variation is present). Readings outside the UCL or LCL or unnatural patterns occurring within the UCL and LCL indicate that some new source of variation is affecting the process.

*Check sheets* are useful during data collection. They provide a simple means for recording data by categories and enable the analyst to determine the relative

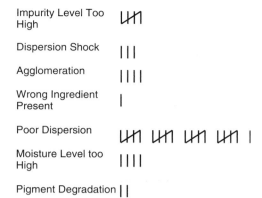

**Figure 8.8.**   Mystery Chemical Check Sheet. Causes for Rejected Batches

frequency of occurrence of the various categories of the data. Mystery Chemical may start collecting data about the causes for rejected batches. The check sheet used for this purpose is in Figure 8.8.

From the check sheet it is possible to easily determine that the most frequent reason for a defective batch is *poor dispersion. Wrong ingredient present* and *pigment degradation* are the least frequent reasons for a defective batch.

Another way to analyze data is by use of a *Pareto diagram*. Like the check sheet, the Pareto diagram provides the same type of insight into the most and least frequent occurrences. But the Pareto diagram provides a better organization of the data than does the check sheet, and it also provides a more polished presentation. Frequently the results from a check sheet are transferred to a Pareto diagram for presentation.

The Pareto diagram sorts the data categories from highest to lowest and also shows the cumulative frequencies. This information is helpful in focusing attention on the highest-priority category. The Pareto diagram for the data in Figure 8.8 is in Figure 8.9.

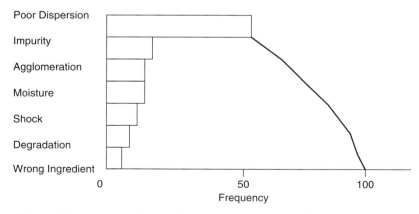

**Figure 8.9.**   Mystery Chemical Pareto Diagram. Causes for Rejected Batches

The Pareto diagram clearly shows that Mystery Chemical could reduce the incidence of rejected batches by 52 percent if they could identify the cause(s) of poor dispersion. Resources directed toward this one reason for rejected batches would have the highest potential payoff.

A manufacturer of electrical wire observed that the amount of defective wire being produced as evidenced by increasing material usage variances on the monthly profit and loss statements. The quality control records were examined using a Pareto diagram which determined that two categories of defect accounted for almost two-thirds of the rejects. Programs were instituted to determine the root causes of these two defects.

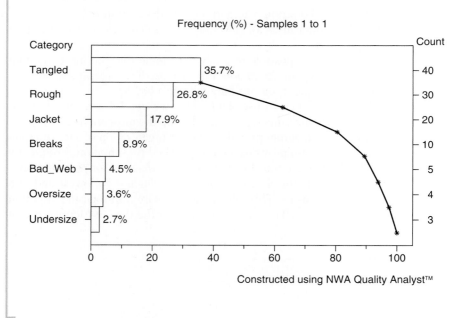

In order to reduce the incidence of rejected batches due to poor dispersion Mystery Chemical must understand why poor dispersion occurs. *Cause-and-effect diagrams* are helpful at this stage. Mystery Chemical invited representatives from operations, quality control, process engineering, and development engineering to a meeting to brainstorm potential causes for poor dispersion. They used a cause-and-effect diagram, shown in Figure 8.10, to organize the ideas generated during the meeting.

A manufacturer of electrical wire was having difficulty with excessive variation in the outside diameter (OD) of the wire. A brainstorming session was conducted with representatives from engineering, operations (including several machine operators), quality, and maintenance to determine possible causes for the problem. A cause-and-effect diagram was developed which was instrumental in determining the root cause of the problem.

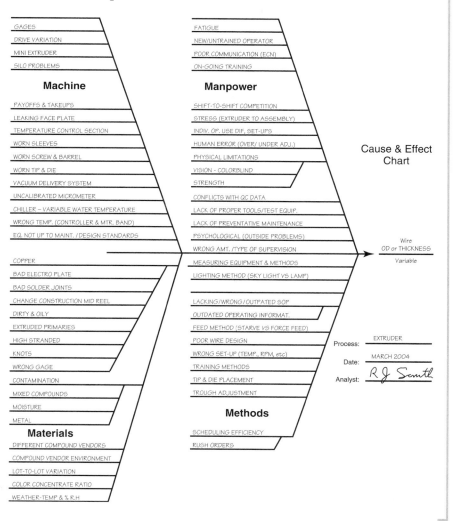

At the end of the meeting the development engineer was assigned to investigate the methods, the quality engineer was assigned to investigate materials, the production

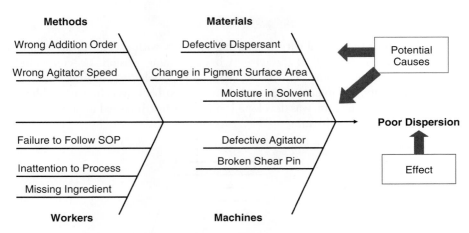

**Figure 8.10.** Mystery Chemical Cause-and-Effect Diagram. Potential Causes for Poor Dispersion

supervisor was assigned to investigate the workers, and the process engineer was assigned to investigate the machines. Using the cause-and-effect diagram facilitated the logical assignment of responsibilities.

At the next team meeting, the quality engineer reported that a defective stack vent on one of the solvent tanks was allowing moisture to seep into the tank. Using a *scatter diagram* (Figure 8.11), she demonstrated the results of a series of experiments she conducted to document the relationship between the two variables—moisture content and dispersion quality. A scatter diagram can provide visual evidence for a possible relationship between two variables. The scatter diagram in Figure 8.11

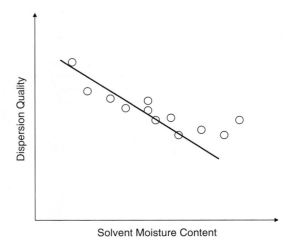

**Figure 8.11.** Mystery Chemical Scatter Diagram. Solvent Moisture Content versus Dispersion Diagram

indicates that from low to moderate levels of solvent moisture content, dispersion quality decreases as moisture content increases. This is referred to as a negative correlation between solvent moisture content and dispersion quality.

The problem cannot be listed as solved until there is appropriate follow-up to ensure that the solution implemented has the desired effect. Run charts and process control charts are useful in the follow-up stage.

## APPROACHES TO CONTINUOUS QUALITY IMPROVEMENT

The American Society for Quality (ASQ) defines *kaizen* as a "Japanese term that means gradual unending improvement by doing little things better and setting and achieving increasingly higher standards" (Quality Glossary, 2002, 52). Although *kaizen* is attributed to Masaaki Imai, the idea of a formal approach to continuous quality improvement can be traced back to Walter Shewhart. Continuous quality improvement is at the heart of all modern quality systems from total quality management (TQM), to Six Sigma, to Zero Defects.

## DISCOVERING A "SLEEPER" BENEFIT

Allan Kempert, assistant production supervisor at a metal stamping plant, tells a great *Quick & Easy Kaizen* story. Metal stamping involves lubricating oil. Allan tells this tale in classic *Quick & Easy Kaizen* lingo: *Before Improvement, After Improvement, and Effect.*

### Before Improvement

"Our operators use cotton rags to clean lubricant off dies. Operators collect rags in a fireproof can and periodically during the week will come to a central location in the plant to count out their rags, one by one. One operator submitted and had approved a *Quick & Easy Kaizen* idea to put a small counter on his fire proof can. As he was putting rags into the can, he simply toggled off how many rags went into the can. When he went to drop off the rags at the central location, all he had to do was dump the rags."

"A second operator liked it and wanted to incorporate it in his area. Instead, I encouraged him to first speak to our purchasing manager, who orders rags, about the need to count them. It turns out that we are on a recycling program with the supplier of the rags. Approximately 15 years ago, there was a discrepancy in the count. The supplier and my company decided that we would both keep count for a period of time to determine what was happening. It turns out that the issue was resolved within a short period of time but nobody told the operators to stop counting rags."

**After Improvement**

"All operators in the plant have been asked to discontinue counting rags (14 plus years after the fact)."

**Effect**

"Operator jobs are easier and our company has just found in excess of 150 more hours per year to be more productive."

(Dewar, 2005. Used with permission.)

## PDSA

The plan-do-check-act (PDCA) cycle of continuous improvement was developed by Shewhart. Deming, who referred to this as the Shewhart Cycle, later revised the cycle by changing *check* to *study* because he thought study better reflected the depth of analysis needed at this step in the cycle. The resulting PDSA cycle, as shown in Figure 8.12, is often referred to as the Deming Cycle.

**4. Act**     **1. Plan**

**3. Study**     **2. Do**

**Figure 8.12.** The PDSA Cycle

PDSA represents a spiral of actions taken to continuously improve processes. In the *plan* step, the process is studied to determine changes that might be made to improve performance. A team is formed to address information requirements, tests that might be conducted to generate needed data, and develop plans for obtaining that data. In the *do* step, improvement ideas are tested on a pilot scale. In the *study* step, data generated during the do step are analyzed to determine the effects of the ideas on the process. In the *act* step the results are thoroughly analyzed to determine what was learned from the tests. If the results were favorable and no unexpected side effects are observed, the new process is implemented. Because there is always room for further improvement in a process, the PDSA cycle can then be applied to the new process to create further improvement.

## DMAIC

The measure-analyze-improve-control cycle was developed as part of the Six Sigma approach to quality at Motorola. Later, General Electric added another step to the process, creating the define-measure-analyze-improve-control (DMAIC) cycle for continuous improvement. DMAIC, as shown in Figure 8.13, is applied after a problem has been selected as a Six Sigma project. All of the tools of the Six Sigma approach are integrated into the DMAIC framework.

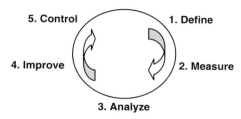

**5. Control**        **1. Define**

**4. Improve**        **2. Measure**

**3. Analyze**

**Figure 8.13.**   The DMAIC Cycle

In the *define* step, goals for the project are defined based on direct input from constituents. In the *measure* step, metrics are developed and applied to the existing system to develop a baseline. The same metrics are used to monitor progress toward the goals. A gap analysis is performed on the existing system in the *analyze* step to identify ways to achieve the goals. In the *improve* step, the improvement ideas are implemented to create a new system. Finally, in the *control* step the new system is institutionalized as the "new way that we do business" (Pyzdek, 2003). As is the case with the PDSA cycle, DMAIC can then be applied to the new process to create further improvement.

## Benchmarking

Benchmarking is an improvement process in which an organization measures its strategic operations or internal process performance against that of best-in-class organizations within or outside its industry; determines how those organizations achieved their performance levels; and uses that information to improve its own performance. Benchmarking can be a valuable tool in moving beyond national average performance to best-in-class performance.

True benchmarking is not simply comparing outcome measures against industry averages. This is more like a scoreboard answering the question "Who is winning?" or "Am I above or below average?" The answers to these questions are not very instructive about how to improve operations. This approach may be of interest to some constituents but are of limited value as input to an organization's process of continuous quality improvement (CQI). They fail to provide insight into what must be done to improve. Ask yourself which is more instructive to your CQI program: (a) knowing that your hospital is slightly above average nationally in controlling infections, or (b) understanding the processes that a particular hospital used to achieve best-in-class infection control?

There is value to comparisons to national averages. Customers can use these comparisons to judge the quality of their suppliers compared to national averages. The organization's quality manager and quality-improvement teams can use this information to determine areas that are most in need of improvement. Progress of the improvement efforts can be monitored over time to determine whether the actions taken are effective in "closing the gaps."

However, for all its usefulness, comparison to national averages is insufficient. Meeting the national average does not equate to excellence. It may not equate even to sufficiency. Without information about the processes used by the best organizations, we must approach improvement by reinventing the wheel. We are doomed to make the same mistakes that other organizations have made and learned from. Another problem with national averages is that we don't even know which organizations are the best performers and we don't know what that best-in-class performance is (Sower, 2007).

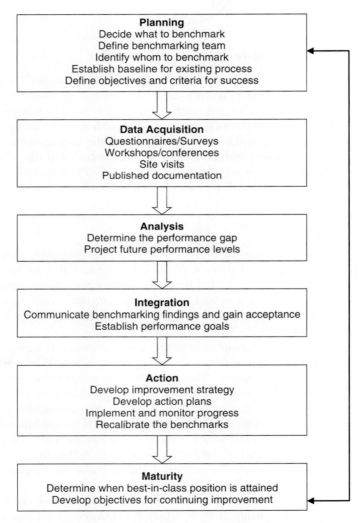

**Figure 8.14.** Six-Phase Benchmarking Process (*Source*: Sower et al., 2007. Reprinted with permission from ASQ Quality Press. © 2007 American Society for Quality. No further distribution without permission.)

National averages provide no measure of variation in performance and no information about the level for best-in-class performers. Variation in performance can be a bigger problem than average performance. The Nebraska Medical Center's interventional radiology department undertook to improve major problems in delays in treatment that created patient dissatisfaction and loss of patients. They found that it took an average of 1.4 calls to schedule an appointment. Further analysis revealed that the standard deviation was 0.989 calls with a maximum of seven calls. After several improvement projects had been completed, the average was still 1.4 calls. However, the standard deviation had been reduced to 0.52 calls with a maximum of three calls. If they had used a comparison to national averages, the significant improvement in this process would not be visible (Sower, 2007).

A systematic approach to benchmarking is necessary in order for the organization to adapt, not just adopt, best-in-class processes to its particular strategic and environmental factors. The six-phase benchmarking process shown in Figure 8.14 is an adaptation by Sower, Duffy, & Kohers (2008, 18) of Robert Camp's (1995, 21) five-phase benchmarking process and QAP's seven-phase general approach to benchmarking (Keley, et al., ND, 4).

## SUMMARY

Problem solving is a key activity engaged in by quality managers and engineers. Problem solving is made easier by the utilization of a structured approach such as those proposed by Osborn, Parnes, and Kepner and Tregoe. There are many tools that can be helpful in both the problem-solving and continuous-improvement processes. Among these tools are the seven quality tools that are simple but powerful tools for understanding processes and analyzing data. These tools should be in every quality manager and engineer's tool box. PDSA and DMAIC are continuous-improvement models that have found widespread application in many organizations. Benchmarking can be helpful in reducing the time required to complete improvement projects and increase the quality of the improved process. But, in order to be effective, benchmarking cannot be seen as just copying what another company does.

## DISCUSSION QUESTIONS

1. Discuss the difference between a symptom and a problem.

2. Would you classify excessive employee absenteeism as a symptom or a problem? Discuss.

3. Discuss the three types of errors that can occur during the problem-solving process.

4. Discuss the proactive approach to mess finding.

5. List the steps in the problem-solving process.

6. What are the main purposes of a flow chart? Why might creating flow charts of the major processes for which you are responsible be a good idea when you start a new job?

7. Compare the use of check sheets and Pareto diagrams. Discuss the advantages and disadvantages of each and under which circumstances each would be preferred.

8. Discuss the differences between a run chart and a control chart.

9. Which of the tools of quality might be most helpful in the setting controls/follow-up step in the problem-solving process? Discuss how they would be helpful in this step.

10. Compare the PDSA and DMAIC approaches to continuous improvement. What are their key similarities and differences?

11. Discuss the difference between benchmarking and comparison to national averages.

12. Discuss the difference between benchmarking and copying what some other organization has done.

## PROBLEMS

1. Use a cause-and-effect diagram to develop a list of potential causes for each of the following:

   a. Failure to earn an A on an examination.
   b. You consistently arrive late for class or work.
   c. You consistently slice when hitting a golf ball with your driver.
   d. Your table lamp fails to light when you turn the switch on.

2. Prepare a flow chart for getting to work or school in the morning. Discuss areas for improvement revealed by the flow chart.

3. You have collected the following data from customer comment cards at your restaurant. Construct a Pareto diagram to show which of the problems should be investigated first. Show the cumulative frequency line on your diagram.

| Comment | Frequency |
|---|---|
| Dirty Dishes | 11 |
| Dirty Silverware | 18 |
| Inattentive Service | 98 |
| Cold Food | 23 |
| Wrong Order | 5 |

| Comment | Frequency |
|---|---|
| Overpriced | 35 |
| Long Wait | 4 |

4. Use the following data to construct a scatter diagram. Does there appear to be a relationship between hours of overtime and number of rejects? Discuss.

| Hours of Overtime | Number of Rejects |
|---|---|
| 127 | 33 |
| 90 | 25 |
| 95 | 23 |
| 160 | 40 |
| 10 | 9 |
| 80 | 19 |
| 27 | 14 |
| 103 | 28 |
| 48 | 19 |
| 65 | 31 |

5. Your boss has asked you to evaluate the reject percentage for the past year on one of the production lines. Use the following data to construct a run chart. Does there appear to be a pattern in the change in the reject rate over the year?

| Month | Reject (%) |
|---|---|
| January | 3.7 |
| February | 3.3 |
| March | 3.1 |
| April | 3.5 |
| May | 3.3 |
| June | 2.7 |
| July | 3.0 |
| August | 2.3 |
| September | 2.5 |
| October | 2.2 |
| November | 1.6 |
| December | 1.7 |

6. An analyst measured the length of 30 peanuts for grading purposes. She obtained the following measurements:

| 997 | 1002 | 998 | 1000 | 999 |
|-----|------|-----|------|-----|
| 999 | 999 | 1000 | 1001 | 998 |
| 1003 | 1000 | 999 | 1000 | 1001 |
| 1000 | 1002 | 997 | 1002 | 997 |
| 1000 | 1001 | 1001 | 1003 | 998 |
| 1001 | 998 | 1000 | 999 | 1001 |

Prepare a check sheet and a Pareto diagram of the peanut diameters. What conclusions can you draw? Discuss.

7. Prepare a flow chart of the process you use to prepare a pot of coffee. Do you believe that someone could use your flow chart to prepare coffee that would taste the same as yours? Can you see ways to improve your coffee-making process?

8. The manager of the Billing Department has collected some information about the causes of billing errors. Construct a Pareto diagram with cumulative frequency line and advise the manager about her next step in reducing billing errors.

| Cause | Frequency |
|-------|-----------|
| Typing Error | 81 |
| Wrong Address | 13 |
| Calculation Error | 27 |
| Wrong Account | 20 |
| Wrong Product Entered | 5 |
| Others | 6 |

9. A fraternity collected information about study habits and grades of members of their fraternity enrolled in the same course. Construct a scatter diagram with study time as the x-variable and grade as the y-variable. Does there appear to be a relationship between time spent studying and grade received on the mid-term examination? Discuss.

| Study Time (Hours) | Grade |
|--------------------|-------|
| 1 | 62 |
| 8 | 94 |
| 3 | 75 |

| Study Time (Hours) | Grade |
|---|---|
| 2 | 65 |
| 2 | 77 |
| 4 | 80 |
| 7 | 98 |
| 1 | 55 |
| 3 | 77 |
| 5 | 86 |

10. Roll two dice 100 times. Use a check sheet to record the frequency with which the numbers 2 through 12 occur. Use the same data to construct a Pareto diagram.

11. Use an appropriate data base to access sales and profits for a five- to 10-year period for a publicly traded company. Construct a run chart for both sales and profits. What can you conclude from the charts?

12. Use the data you collected in problem 11 to construct a scatter diagram. What can you conclude about the relationship between sales and profits?

## CASE STUDY 8.1: *Sour Grape Ice Cream*
© 1996, Victor E. Sower, Ph.D., C.Q.E.

The Quality Ice Cream Company has recently introduced a new flavor, Sour Grape Ice Cream. They have not been able to meet demand for this new product due to quality problems—many batches have been discarded. They have collected a lot of data but are at a loss about how to use it. They are overwhelmed with numbers. They have asked you to help them address the problems. What do you recommend? *[Be specific.]*

## PROCESS DESCRIPTION:

1. Pull ingredients from warehouse.
2. Blend ingredients in mixer.
3. Pump mixture to freeze machine.
4. Run freeze machine until consistency is correct.
5. Extrude ice cream into package.
6. Inspect and test ice cream.
7. Transfer packages to Finished Good storage.

## REJECT LOG

| Date | Ice Crystals | Number of Rejects by Cause Soupy | Too stiff | Tastes Bad | Off Color |
|------|------|------|------|------|------|
| 2/1 | 1 | 7 | 0 | 0 | 1 |
| 2/2 | 0 | 2 | 0 | 0 | 0 |
| 2/3 | 2 | 4 | 0 | 1 | 0 |
| 2/4 | 1 | 6 | 1 | 0 | 0 |
| 2/5 | 0 | 5 | 0 | 1 | 1 |
| 2/6 | 1 | 4 | 0 | 1 | 0 |
| 2/7 | 0 | 3 | 0 | 1 | 0 |
| 2/8 | 0 | 5 | 0 | 0 | 0 |
| 2/9 | 1 | 2 | 0 | 1 | 0 |
| 2/10 | 2 | 4 | 0 | 1 | 0 |

Ice crystals seem to be related to the mixing process. Soupy and Too Stiff refer to consistency (soupy is viscosity below 5000 cps; too stiff is viscosity above 6000 cps). Tastes Bad and Off Color seem to be related to raw materials.

One of the production operators believes that the consistency of the ice cream (measured by the ice cream's viscosity) is related to the length of time in the freeze machine. She has collected some data but doesn't know what to do with it.

| Run Time (min.) | Viscosity (cps) | Run Time (min.) | Viscosity (cps) |
|------|------|------|------|
| 93 | 5500 | 97 | 5750 |
| 90 | 5100 | 77 | 3000 |
| 89 | 4950 | 83 | 4200 |
| 94 | 5375 | 95 | 5600 |
| 93 | 5400 | 81 | 4300 |

## CASE STUDY 8.2: *The Westover Wire Works*

© 1996, Victor E. Sower, Ph.D., C.Q.E.

As a new business graduate, you feel good about your first week as management trainee at Westover Wire Winding, Inc. You have been given an office area to yourself equipped with the latest personal computer but no secretary. You have not yet developed any technical knowledge about the manufacturing process, but you have toured the entire facility and have met many people in various areas of the operation.

Westover is a medium-sized manufacturer of wire windings used in transformer manufacturing. These windings are produced in Westover's manufacturing plant that uses a process-type layout. Bill, the production control manager, described the windings as being of standardized design. Your plant tour followed the manufacturing sequence for the windings: drawing, extrusion, winding, inspection, and packaging. After inspection, good product is packaged and sent to finished product storage; defective product is stored separately until it can be reworked. You sketched the layout (Figure A) after your plant tour so that you could find your way around the plant.

Westover Wire Winding, Inc.

**Figure A.** Plant Layout

This morning, Maria Espania, Westover's general manager and your boss, stopped by your office and asked you to attend the staff meeting to be held at 1:00 pm today. "Let's get started with the business at hand," Maria said, opening the meeting. "You all have met <your name>, our new management trainee. <Your name> studied operations management during the last year of their university studies, so I feel she/he is competent to help us with a problem we have been discussing for a long time without resolution. I'm sure that each of you on my staff will give <your name> your full cooperation."

You are a little surprised and apprehensive to hear that you are about to receive a high-profile, important assignment so early in your career. However, you are confident in your own ability and in the education you received in operations management.

Maria continues, "Joe Wilson, our operations manager, has experienced an increasing problem with rejected product found during the manufacturing operation."

"Yeah, I'm not sure where to begin," says Joe, "but we know you covered quality control in your BBA studies. Rejects in the Winding Department have been killing us the past two months. Nobody in operations has any idea why. I would like you to take a look at the situation and make recommendations about how we can find out what is going on. I know that you haven't been here long enough to become a 'technical expert' in our processes, so I don't expect you to make technical recommendations—just see if you can point us in the right direction."

After the meeting your first stop was the production floor. Your discussions with the production supervisors in the Winding Department indicated they had no real grasp of what the problem(s) was or what to do to correct it. They did give you a more detailed tour of the winding operation and a copy of the Winding Department layout (Figure B). There were three machines that wound wire onto plastic cores to produce the primary and secondary transformer windings. After inspection by quality control (QC), these windings then went to the Packaging Department. Packaging personnel inspect their own work and make corrections on the spot to any packaging defects they find. The problem is, too many windings are found to be defective by QC and require reworking before they can be sent to Packaging.

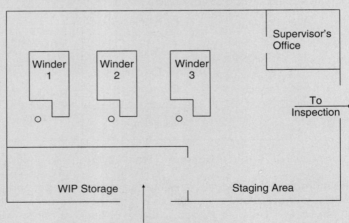

**Figure B.** Winding Department Layout

Your next stop was the Quality Control Department where you obtained the records for the past month's Winding Department rejects (Figure C). You then retired to your office area to decide how to approach this project.

NOTE: Your recommendations *with justification* should be presented in the first page of a report to Maria. Your detailed analysis should be contained in the subsequent pages of that report so that she can understand how you arrived at your recommendations. Any charts, graphs, computer printouts, etc., you used should be included in the report.

**Figure C.** Transformer Reject Log—Winding Process (January)

| Date | No. Inspected | Winder No. | Bad Wind | Twisted Wire | Broken Leads | Abraded Wire | Wrong Core | Wrong Wire | Failed El. Test |
|------|------|------|------|------|------|------|------|------|------|
| 1 | 100 | 1 | 1 | 0 | 4 | 1 | 0 | 0 | 1 |
| | 100 | 2 | 2 | 1 | 0 | 0 | 1 | 5 | 0 |
| | 100 | 3 | 0 | 0 | 0 | 5 | 0 | 0 | 3 |
| 2 | 100 | 1 | 0 | 1 | 3 | 0 | 0 | 0 | 0 |
| | 100 | 2 | 3 | 1 | 0 | 0 | 2 | 3 | 0 |
| | 100 | 3 | 0 | 0 | 1 | 6 | 0 | 0 | 0 |
| 3 | 100 | 1 | 1 | 0 | 0 | 2 | 0 | 0 | 0 |
| | 100 | 2 | 0 | 0 | 0 | 0 | 0 | 3 | 0 |
| | 100 | 3 | 0 | 0 | 1 | 4 | 0 | 0 | 3 |
| 4 | 100 | 1 | 0 | 0 | 3 | 0 | 0 | 0 | 0 |
| | 100 | 2 | 0 | 0 | 0 | 0 | 0 | 2 | 0 |
| | 100 | 3 | 0 | 0 | 0 | 3 | 1 | 0 | 3 |
| 5 | 100 | 1 | 0 | 1 | 5 | 0 | 0 | 0 | 0 |
| | 100 | 2 | 0 | 0 | 0 | 0 | 0 | 2 | 1 |
| | 100 | 3 | 0 | 0 | 0 | 3 | 0 | 0 | 2 |
| 8 | 100 | 1 | 0 | 0 | 2 | 0 | 0 | 0 | 0 |
| | 100 | 2 | 0 | 0 | 0 | 0 | 0 | 1 | 0 |
| | 100 | 3 | 0 | 0 | 0 | 3 | 0 | 0 | 3 |
| 9 | 100 | 1 | 0 | 1 | 2 | 0 | 0 | 0 | 0 |
| | 100 | 2 | 0 | 0 | 0 | 0 | 0 | 1 | 0 |
| | 100 | 3 | 0 | 0 | 0 | 3 | 0 | 0 | 4 |
| 10 | 100 | 1 | 0 | 0 | 5 | 0 | 0 | 0 | 0 |
| | 100 | 2 | 1 | 0 | 0 | 0 | 1 | 0 | 0 |
| | 100 | 3 | 0 | 0 | 0 | 5 | 0 | 0 | 4 |
| 11 | 100 | 1 | 0 | 0 | 4 | 0 | 0 | 0 | 0 |
| | 100 | 2 | 0 | 0 | 0 | 0 | 0 | 0 | 0 |
| | 100 | 3 | 0 | 0 | 0 | 4 | 0 | 0 | 4 |
| 12 | 100 | 1 | 0 | 0 | 3 | 0 | 1 | 0 | 0 |
| | 100 | 2 | 1 | 0 | 1 | 0 | 0 | 0 | 0 |
| | 100 | 3 | 0 | 0 | 0 | 5 | 0 | 0 | 4 |
| 15 | 100 | 1 | 0 | 0 | 2 | 0 | 0 | 1 | 0 |
| | 100 | 2 | 0 | 0 | 0 | 0 | 0 | 1 | 0 |
| | 100 | 3 | 0 | 0 | 0 | 3 | 0 | 0 | 3 |
| 16 | 100 | 1 | 0 | 0 | 6 | 0 | 0 | 0 | 0 |
| | 100 | 2 | 0 | 0 | 0 | 0 | 0 | 0 | 0 |
| | 100 | 3 | 0 | 0 | 0 | 3 | 0 | 0 | 3 |
| 17 | 100 | 1 | 0 | 1 | 1 | 0 | 0 | 0 | 0 |
| | 100 | 2 | 0 | 0 | 0 | 0 | 0 | 0 | 1 |
| | 100 | 3 | 0 | 0 | 0 | 3 | 0 | 0 | 3 |
| 18 | 100 | 1 | 1 | 0 | 2 | 0 | 0 | 0 | 0 |
| | 100 | 2 | 0 | 0 | 0 | 0 | 0 | 1 | 0 |
| | 100 | 3 | 0 | 0 | 0 | 4 | 0 | 0 | 1 |

(*continued overleaf*)

**(continued)**

| Date | No. Inspected | Winder No. | Bad Wind | Twisted Wire | Broken Leads | Abraded Wire | Wrong Core | Wrong Wire | Failed El. Test |
|------|---------------|------------|----------|--------------|--------------|--------------|------------|------------|-----------------|
| 19 | 100 | 1 | 0 | 0 | 2 | 0 | 0 | 0 | 0 |
|    | 100 | 2 | 0 | 0 | 0 | 0 | 0 | 0 | 0 |
|    | 100 | 3 | 0 | 0 | 0 | 3 | 0 | 0 | 1 |
| 22 | 100 | 1 | 0 | 1 | 4 | 0 | 0 | 0 | 0 |
|    | 100 | 2 | 0 | 0 | 0 | 0 | 0 | 0 | 0 |
|    | 100 | 3 | 0 | 0 | 0 | 3 | 0 | 1 | 2 |
| 23 | 100 | 1 | 0 | 0 | 4 | 0 | 0 | 0 | 0 |
|    | 100 | 2 | 0 | 0 | 0 | 0 | 0 | 0 | 1 |
|    | 100 | 3 | 0 | 0 | 0 | 4 | 0 | 0 | 3 |
| 24 | 100 | 1 | 0 | 0 | 2 | 0 | 0 | 1 | 0 |
|    | 100 | 2 | 0 | 1 | 0 | 0 | 0 | 0 | 0 |
|    | 100 | 3 | 0 | 0 | 0 | 4 | 0 | 0 | 3 |
| 25 | 100 | 1 | 0 | 0 | 3 | 0 | 0 | 0 | 0 |
|    | 100 | 2 | 0 | 0 | 0 | 1 | 0 | 0 | 0 |
|    | 100 | 3 | 0 | 0 | 0 | 2 | 0 | 0 | 4 |
| 26 | 100 | 1 | 0 | 0 | 1 | 0 | 0 | 0 | 0 |
|    | 100 | 2 | 0 | 1 | 0 | 1 | 0 | 0 | 0 |
|    | 100 | 3 | 0 | 0 | 0 | 2 | 0 | 0 | 3 |
| 29 | 100 | 1 | 0 | 0 | 2 | 0 | 0 | 0 | 0 |
|    | 100 | 2 | 0 | 0 | 1 | 0 | 0 | 0 | 0 |
|    | 100 | 3 | 0 | 0 | 0 | 2 | 0 | 0 | 3 |
| 30 | 100 | 1 | 0 | 0 | 2 | 0 | 0 | 0 | 0 |
|    | 100 | 2 | 0 | 0 | 0 | 0 | 1 | 0 | 0 |
|    | 100 | 3 | 0 | 0 | 0 | 2 | 0 | 0 | 3 |

## EXERCISES AND ACTIVITIES

1. The Peanut M&M® Exercise (adapted from Morrow & McNeese, 2002, 257–267)

   Divide the class or training group into small teams. If the team size is at least five, provide each member with one small bag (approximately 22 pieces per bag) of Peanut M&M®s plus one for the team. If the teams are smaller than five, provide two bags to each member. Also provide each team with large sheets of paper, markers, and masking tape to mount the paper on the wall.

### Flow Chart

Have each group prepare a flow chart for opening a bag of M&M®s. Have the teams display their flow charts using the large sheets of paper.

Students preparing a flow chart for opening a bag of M&Ms™.

After all teams have completed their flow charts, the instructor should use each team's flow-charted process to demonstrate to the class the results of using each flow chart to open a bag of M&M®s.

1. How many flow charts resulted in a process that was capable of successfully opening a bag of M&M®s? Discuss any problems that occurred.
2. Were there differences in the flow charts? Why?

## Check Sheet/Pareto Diagram

Have each member of the teams open one or two bags of M&M®s. You should try to have at least six open bags per group.

Have each member use a check sheet to determine the number of M&M®s of each color in each bag.

Have each team prepare a check sheet and a Pareto diagram for the combined results of their team. Have them include a cumulative frequency line and the percentage of each color on the Pareto diagram. In addition, have each team prepare a check sheet for the number of M&M®s in each bag.

Make copies of both team check sheets for each participant.

Debrief:

1. What did you learn from your check sheet and Pareto diagram?
2. Which color appeared most and least frequently?
3. Why don't all the check sheets and Pareto diagrams look the same?
   The team members may now eat their M&M®s.

## Distribution Analysis

Ask each participant to construct a master check sheet that shows the cumulative results for all the teams on the total number of M&M®s in a bag using the information on the team check sheets.

Debrief:
1. What is the maximum and minimum number in a bag?
2. What is the mode (the most representative common value)?
3. What does the shape of the distribution look like?

## Cause and Effect Diagram

Have each team brainstorm possible causes of variation in the number of M&M®s in a bag. If convenient, have the class access www.m-ms.com to find information about the manufacturing process for M&M®s. Have each team develop a cause-and-effect diagram from the brainstorming session.

Debrief:
1. Have each team briefly present their cause and effect diagrams to the class.
2. Save the check sheets for use in future exercises.

2. The Letter Game Exercise (adapted from Chen & Roth (2005))
   Divide the class or training group into small teams. Provide each team with large sheets of paper, markers, and masking tape to mount the paper on the wall.
   Put the letter tiles from a Scrabble® board game into a bag. Select 10 letters at random from the bag. Write the letters on the board. Give the teams 30 seconds to create as many words as possible from the letters using the following rules:

   • All words must have three or more letters.
   • Each of the 10 letters may be used only once.
   • Words may not be proper nouns, slang, derogatory, or crude (decision of instructor is final).
   • Only a single list from each team will be scored.

   Run several iterations of the game, giving each team the opportunity to show its words. Stop the game and discuss the variation that exists between teams and within teams from iteration to iteration. Then ask which team is winning.
   The teams may make several suggestions about ways to identify the winner:

   • The most words.
   • The fewest unused letters.
   • The highest score using the Scrabble® letter values.

Make the point that metrics must be established with input from the internal or external customer. Discuss who is the customer for the teams' process in this exercise. It is the instructor. After this discussion, select the second metric—fewest unused letters—to judge who is winning. Use this metric to determine winners of the previous iterations.

Have each team flow chart its process for forming words. Have several teams present their process to the class or training group. Discuss whether the process changed from iteration to iteration. Then have the teams identify ways the process might be improved further.

Conduct several additional iterations using the improved processes, making sure that a Q shows up at least once without a U. Discuss the impact of uncontrollable factors (a Q without a U) in process performance. Identify the winning group.

## SUPPLEMENTARY READINGS

Camp, R. (1995). *Business Process Benchmarking: Finding and Implementing Best Practices*. Milwaukee, WI: ASQC Quality Press.
Evans, J. (1990). *Creative Thinking in the Decision and Management Sciences*. Cincinnati, OH: Southwestern.
Galloway, D. (1994). *Mapping Work Processes*. Milwaukee, WI: ASQ Quality Press.
Kepner, C., & B. Tregoe. (1965). *The Rational Manager: A Systematic Approach to Problem Solving and Decision Making*. New York: McGraw-Hill.
Oakes, D., & R. Westcott (eds.). (2001). *The Certified Quality Manager Handbook*, 2nd edition. Milwaukee, WI: ASQ Quality Press.
Osborn, A. (1963). *Applied Imagination*, 3rd edition. New York: Scribner's.
Parnes, S., R. Noller, & A. Biondi (eds.). (1977). *Guide to Creative Action*. New York: Scribner's.
Homepage of Pyzdek Institute, http://www.pyzdek.com.
Sower, V.E. (2007). "Benchmarking in Hospitals: When You Need More than a Scorecard." *Quality Progress* 40(8), 58–60.
Sower, V.E., J. Duffy, & G. Kohers. (2008). *Benchmarking in Hospitals: Achieving Best-In-Class Performance without Having to Reinvent the Wheel*. Milwaukee, WI: ASQ Quality Press.
Walton, M. (1986). *The Deming Management Method*. New York: Perigee Books.

## REFERENCES

Burns, Robert. (1785). *To a Mouse*.
Camp, R. (1985). *Business Process Benchmarking: Finding and Implementing Best Practices*. Milwaukee, WI: ASQC Quality Press.
Chen, C., & H. Roth. (2005). *The Big Book of Six Sigma Training Games*. New York: McGraw-Hill.
Dewar, D. (2005). *Timely Tips for Teams*. E-newsletter of CQI International, April 2005.

Evans, J. (1990). *Creative Thinking in the Decision and Management Sciences*. Cincinnati, OH: Southwestern.

Galloway, D. (1994). *Mapping Work Processes*. Milwaukee, WI: ASQ Quality Press.

Keley, E., J. Ashton, & T. Bornstein. (ND). "Applying Benchmarking in Health." *Quality Assurance Project*. Bethesda, MD: Center for Human Services. http://www.qaproject.org/pubs/PDFs/Benchfinal.pdf.

Kepner, C., & B. Tregoe. (1965). *The Rational Manager*. New York: McGraw-Hill.

Morrow, C., & L. McNeese. (2002). "A Simple Way to Digest SPC." *2002 Proceedings of the ASQ Annual Quality Congress*.

Osborn, A. (1963). *Applied Imagination*, 3rd edition. New York: Scribner's.

Parnes, S., R. Noller, & A. Biondi (eds.). (1977). *Guide to Creative Action*. New York: Scribner's.

Pyzdek, T. (2003). "DMAIC and DMADV." http://www.pyzdek.com.

"Quality Glossary." (2002). *Quality Progress* 35(7), 43–61.

Sower, V.E., (2007). Benchmarking in Hospitals: When You Need More than a Scorecard. *Quality Progress* 40 (8), 58–60.

Sower, V.E., J. Duffy, & G. Kohers. (2008). *Benchmarking in Hospitals: Achieving Best-In-Class Performance without Having to Reinvent the Wheel*. Milwaukee, WI: ASQ Quality Press.

## CHAPTER NINE

# Metrology, Inspection, and Testing

## CHAPTER OBJECTIVES

After completing this chapter, the reader should be able to:

- define metrology;
- discuss the fundamentals of metrology;
- differentiate between accuracy and precision;
- differentiate among accuracy, reproducibility, and repeatability;
- discuss types of gauges;
- conduct a gauge repeatability and reproducibility (R&R) study; and
- understand nondestructive testing concepts.

When technicians use a gauge to take a measurement, the value they obtain really consists of two components: (1) the actual value of the dimension being measured and (2) errors relating to the ability of the gauging system to measure that dimension. Unless the second component is assessed, it is impossible to determine how well the reported measurement reflects the true value of the dimension. Metrology is the science of measurement (Quality Glossary, 2002, 53). The focus of metrology and of this chapter is how to minimize the contribution of the second component to the total reported measurement value—that is, how to ensure that the reported value really reflects the true value.

These issues are of far more than passing interest. Considerable expense can result from measurement errors. Acceptable product may be labeled as defective and scrapped; defective product may be labeled as acceptable and shipped to customers. Process capability studies and projects to implement statistical process control are often extensive, time consuming, and expensive. It is foolish to begin such studies without first assessing the accuracy and precision of the measurement systems to be used.

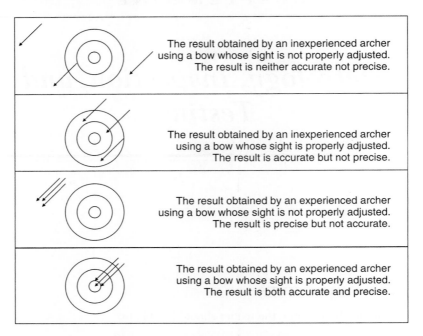

**Figure 9.1.** Accuracy versus Precision

## METROLOGY

The measurement value determined by use of a gauge or instrument can be considered to be a function of four terms:

$$MV = f[(TV) + (Ac) + (Rep) + (Rpr)]$$

where MV = measured value; TV = true value; Ac = gauge accuracy; Rep = gauge repeatability; and Rpr = gauge reproducibility.

Gauge accuracy is the ability of the gauge to provide a measurement that is free of bias. The accuracy of a gauge is addressed through calibration. Gauge repeatability is the ability of a single operator to obtain the same measurement value multiple times using the same measuring device on the same part. Gauge reproducibility is the ability of separate operators to obtain the same measurement value using the same gauge on the same part. Reproducibility and repeatability together are referred to as precision. The precision of a gauging system is addressed through gauge repeatability and reproducibility (gauge R&R) studies. The relationship of accuracy and precision is shown in Figure 9.1. The goal is to have a measurement system that is both accurate and precise.

**Accuracy** is the characteristic of a measurement that tells how close an observed value is to a true value.

**Precision** is the aspect of measurement that addresses repeatability or consistency when an identical item is measured several times.

(Quality Glossary, 2002, 48–49)

## TYPES OF GAUGES

Measurement instruments come in all shapes, sizes, and types to measure everything from chemical properties (e.g., pH) to electrical parameters (e.g., volt meters). The focus of this section will be on instruments designed to enable the measurement of physical dimensions.

*Variable gauges* are adjustable gauges used to measure part dimensions. Variable gauges include line-graduated gauges, such as rulers and vernier calipers, dial gauges, digital gauges, height gauges, and optical gauges. Figure 9.2 illustrates three types of variable gauges: vernier calipers, dial calipers, and digital calipers. All three of these calipers can be used to measure inside and outside dimensions as well as depth dimensions.

Figure 9.3 illustrates a digital micrometer. Micrometers tend to be able to measure dimensions to more significant digits—i.e., a higher resolution—than calipers. The digital caliper shown in Figure 9.2 has a resolution of 0.01 mm while the micrometer shown in Figure 9.3 has a resolution of 0.001 mm. A good rule of thumb is to select a gauge that has a resolution that is at least 10 times the last significant digit of your tolerance. For example, if your tolerance is ± 0.01 mm, you should select a gauge with a resolution of at least 0.001 mm.

Figure 9.4 shows a height gauge. The resolution of this gauge is 0.001 inches.

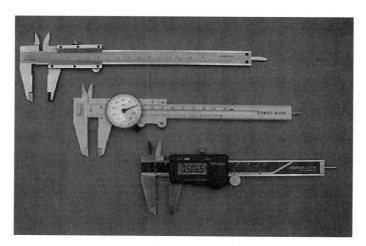

**Figure 9.2.** Vernier, Dial, and Digital Calipers

**Figure 9.3.** Digital Micrometer

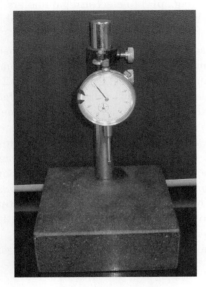

**Figure 9.4.** Height Gauge

Figure 9.5 illustrates a simple optical gauge. The calibrations on the reticule of this portable instrument enable the measurement of linear dimensions. More complex optical gauges magnify the part to be measured and project the profile on a screen for measurement.

*Fixed gauges* are designed to measure a particular dimension and are not adjustable. Examples include go/no-go gauges, feeler gauges, ring gauges, and plug gauges. Feeler gauges are thin metal strips or wires used to measure gap dimensions. Ring gauges are used to measure outside diameters, while plug gauges measure inside diameters. Both ring and plug gauges are forms of go/no-go gauges. Figure 9.6 shows set-up blocks which are an example of fixed gauges.

*Automated Gauging and Inspection.* The preceding gauge types are normally considered to be manual inspection gauges. The digital gauges can, however, be adapted to partial automation by adding a data collection device. Figure 9.7 shows digital gauges used with data collection devices that are capable of sophisticated

**Figure 9.5.**   Optical Gauge

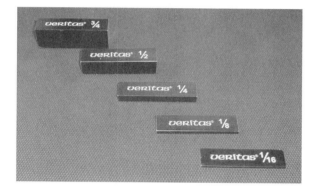

**Figure 9.6.**   Set-up Blocks

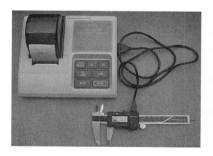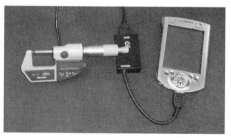

**Figure 9.7.**   Digital Caliper and Digital Micrometer with Two Different Automated Data Collection Systems

analysis of the data on-site. Additional analysis can be performed by down loading the data from the data collection device to a personal computer.

Fully automated on-line gauging and inspection can be accomplished using a variety of sensors linked to data collection and display units. Examples of sensors used for on-line dimensional measurement include contact gauges such as linear potentiometers (illustrated in Figure 9.8), and noncontact gauges such as pixel

**Figure 9.8.** Linear Potentiometer—A Type of Contact Gauge for Automated Inspection

cameras (vision systems). Coordinate measuring machines (CMM) are fully auto-mated measurement systems designed for off-line dimensional measurement.

## ACCURACY AND PRECISION

The *accuracy* of a gauge is "the closeness of agreement between an observed value and an accepted reference value" (ASQ Statistics Division, 1983, 1). The accuracy of a gauge is determined by calibration. Use of an instrument whose calibration is unknown results in measurement data that are of questionable validity. Decisions based upon questionable data can be no more valid than the data upon which they are based.

One means of calibrating dimensional gauges is by the use of *gauge blocks*. Gauge blocks are a type of fixed gauge. They are especially machined to close tolerances, and their accuracy can be traced in the United States to reference standards at the National Institute of Standards and Technology (NIST). Traceability of a gauge's accuracy through working standards to NIST reference standards is an important aspect of ensuring the accuracy of a measurement system.

Calibration records should be maintained in the laboratory and on the instrument, and recalibration schedules should be established and adhered to. An example of a calibration label that would be affixed to a gauge is shown in Figure 9.9. Gauges with labels showing they are overdue for calibration should be taken out of service until the calibration is performed. Increasingly, calibration records are being maintained in a computer database.

*Repeatability and reproducibility (R&R) studies* are designed experiments to evaluate the precision of a measurement system. The measurement system should be properly calibrated prior to the gauge R&R study. The following process for conducting a gauge R&R study is based on the procedure established by the ASQ Automotive Division (1986).

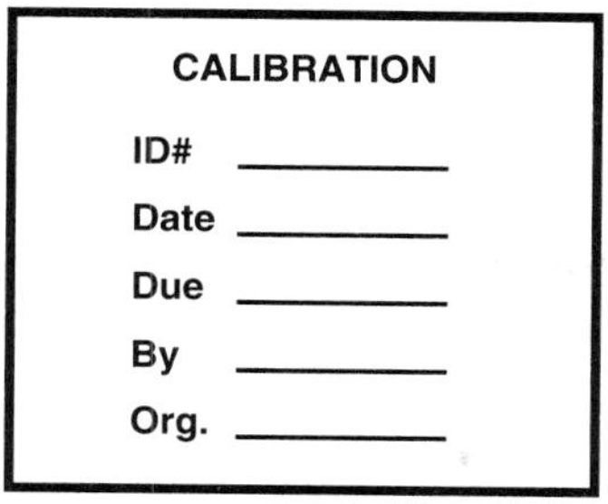

**CALIBRATION**

ID# _____

Date _____

Due _____

By _____

Org. _____

**Figure 9.9.**   Gauge Calibration Label

1. Verify that the gauge to be studied is properly calibrated.

2. Select at least two ($m$) properly trained operators and at least 10 ($n$) parts to be measured. Identify each part with a number that is not visible to the operator.

3. Present the parts to the operator for measurement in random sequence and record each measurement ($M$). Repeat this process until each part has been measured at least two ($r$) times.

4. Compute the average measurement ($\overline{x}_i$) for each operator ($i$) where $M_{ijk}$ represents operator $i$'s kth measurement on part $j$:

$$\overline{x}_i = \frac{\left(\sum\limits_{j}\sum\limits_{k} M_{ijk}\right)}{nr} \tag{9.1}$$

5. Compute the difference between the largest and smallest average ($\overline{x}_D$):

$$\overline{x}_D = \max(\overline{x}_i) - \min(\overline{x}_i) \tag{9.2}$$

6. Compute the range ($R_{ij}$) for each part ($j$) and each operator ($i$):

$$R_{ij} = \max(M_{ijk}) - \min(M_{ijk}) \tag{9.3}$$

7. Compute the average range ($\overline{R}_i$) for each operator ($i$):

$$\overline{R}_i = \frac{\sum\limits_{j} R_{ij}}{n} \tag{9.4}$$

8. Compute the overall range ($\overline{\overline{R}}$):

$$\overline{\overline{R}} = \frac{\sum\limits_{i} \overline{R}_i}{m} \tag{9.5}$$

9. Compute the control limit on the individual ranges $(R_{ij})$. The constant $D_4$ may be found in Table 10.1 in Chapter 10 using the number of trials $(r)$ for n.

$$\text{Control Limit} = D_4 \overline{\overline{R}} \qquad (9.6)$$

Compare each range to the control limit. Any range that exceeds the control limit should be investigated for some assignable cause. Typical assignable causes include measurements which have been recorded incorrectly, digits which have been reversed, and ranges which have been incorrectly calculated. If the assignable cause can be identified and is correctable, make the correction and redo the calculations beginning with Step 4. If no assignable cause can be found, eliminate the values beyond the control limit and redo the calculations beginning with Step 4.

10. Compute the equipment variation (EV):

$$EV = K_1 \overline{\overline{R}} \qquad (9.7)$$

where $K_1$ is a constant found in Table 9.1 and is based on the number of trials $(r)$.

11. Compute the operator variation (OV):

$$OV = \sqrt{(K_2 \overline{x}_D)^2 - (EV^2/nr)} \qquad (9.8)$$

where $K_2$ is a constant found in Table 9.1 and is based on the number of operators $(m)$. If the expression under the radical is negative, set OV equal to 0.

12. Compute the overall gauge repeatability and reproducibility (RR):

$$RR = \sqrt{(EV)^2 + (OV)^2} \qquad (9.9)$$

**TABLE 9.1. Constants for Use in Gauge R&R Studies**

| $K_1$ for Calculating EV | | | |
|---|---|---|---|
| Trials (r) | 2 | 3 | 4 |
| $K_1$ | 4.56 | 3.05 | 2.50 |

| $K_2$ for Calculating OV | | | |
|---|---|---|---|
| Operators (m) | 2 | 3 | 4 |
| $K_2$ | 3.65 | 2.70 | 2.30 |

| Part # | Operator 1 | | | Operator 2 | | | Operator 3 | | |
|---|---|---|---|---|---|---|---|---|---|
| | 1 | 1 | Range | 1 | 2 | Range | 1 | 2 | Range |
| 1 | 0.71 | 0.69 | 0.02 | 0.56 | 0.57 | 0.01 | 0.52 | 0.54 | 0.02 |
| 2 | 0.98 | 1.00 | 0.02 | 1.03 | 0.96 | 0.07 | 1.04 | 1.01 | 0.03 |
| 3 | 0.77 | 0.77 | 0.00 | 0.76 | 0.76 | 0.00 | 0.81 | 0.81 | 0.00 |
| 4 | 0.86 | 0.94 | 0.08 | 0.82 | 0.78 | 0.04 | 0.82 | 0.82 | 0.00 |
| 5 | 0.51 | 0.51 | 0.00 | 0.42 | 0.42 | 0.00 | 0.46 | 0.49 | 0.03 |
| 6 | 0.71 | 0.59 | 0.12 | 1.00 | 1.04 | 0.04 | 1.04 | 1.00 | 0.04 |
| 7 | 0.96 | 0.96 | 0.00 | 0.94 | 0.91 | 0.03 | 0.97 | 0.95 | 0.02 |
| 8 | 0.86 | 0.86 | 0.00 | 0.72 | 0.74 | 0.02 | 0.78 | 0.78 | 0.00 |
| 9 | 0.96 | 0.96 | 0.00 | 0.97 | 0.94 | 0.03 | 0.84 | 0.81 | 0.03 |
| 10 | 0.64 | 0.72 | 0.08 | 0.56 | 0.52 | 0.04 | 1.01 | 1.01 | 0.00 |
| Average = | 0.7980 | | 0.0320 | 0.7710 | | 0.0280 | 0.8255 | | 0.0170 |
| XD = | 0.0545 | | | | | | | | |
| Avg Rbarbar = | 0.0257 | | | | | | | | |
| D4 = | 3.267 | | | | | | | | |
| Control Limit = | 0.08385 | | | | | | | | |
| | | | | | | | Percent of Tolerance | | |
| EV = | 0.11704 | | Lower Tolerance = | 0.49 | | | 23.4% | | |
| OV = | 0.1448 | | Upper Tolerance = | 0.99 | | | 29.0% | | |
| RR = | 0.18619 | | | | | | 37.2% | | |
| | | | Enter your tolerances here | | | | | | |

**Figure 9.10.** Spreadsheet Template for Gauge R&R Study (Thanks to Dr. Gerald Kohers for creating this template.)

The operator variation (OV), equipment variation (EV), and overall gauge repeatability and reproducibility (RR) are usually reported as a percentage of the total allowed tolerance range. The smaller the OV, EV, and RR variations as a percentage of the total tolerance, the more precise is the gauging system. A rule of thumb is that a RR that is less than 10% of the tolerance range is acceptable; a RR that is 10–25% of the tolerance range may be acceptable under certain circumstances; a RR that is greater than 25% of the tolerance range is not acceptable (Griffith, 2003, 500).

An example of gauge R&R calculations using a spreadsheet is shown in Figure 9.10. In this example, three ($m$) operators are used with each operator measuring 10 ($n$) parts two ($r$) times. The measurement instrument used in this example has been properly calibrated. The average measurement ($\bar{x}_i$) for each operator ($i$) is shown below the first trial columns. The range ($R_{ij}$) for each part ($j$) is shown in the range column for each operator ($i$). The EV, OV, and RR are reported in absolute terms and as a percentage of the total tolerance.

The same example of the gauge R&R as shown in Figure 9.10 but with the calculations done by hand is shown in Example 9.1. The calculations to determine EV, OV, and RR as a percentage of tolerance are in Example 9.2.

## EXAMPLE 9.1: Calculating RR by Hand

**Step 1.** The gauge is properly calibrated.

**CALIBRATION**
**ID#** MC-045-328
**DATE** 1/15/04
**DUE** 1/15/05
**BY** *VES*
**ORG.** *SHSU*

**Step 2.** Three $(m)$ properly trained operators are selected to measure 10 $(n)$ parts.

**Step 3.** The facilitator presents the 10 parts to each operator twice $(r)$ in random sequence without any identification apparent to the operator. Each operator measures each part and gives the value to the facilitator who records it on the data sheet.

**Step 4.** Compute the average measurement $(\overline{x_i})$ for each operator using Equation 9.1.

$$\text{Operator 1: } \overline{x_1} = \frac{15.96}{10x2} = 0.7980$$

$$\text{Operator 2: } \overline{x_2} = \frac{15.42}{10x2} = 0.7710$$

$$\text{Operator 3: } \overline{x_3} = \frac{16.51}{10x2} = 0.8255$$

**Step 5.** Compute the difference between the largest and smallest average $(\overline{x_D})$ using Equation 9.2.

$$\overline{x_D} = 0.8255 - 0.7710 = 0.0545$$

**Step 6.** Compute the range $(R_{ij})$ for each part $(j)$ and each operator $(i)$ using Equation 9.3.

| Part No. | Operator 1 Range | Operator 2 Range | Operator 3 Range |
|---|---|---|---|
| 1 | 0.02 | 0.01 | 0.02 |
| 2 | 0.02 | 0.07 | 0.03 |
| 3 | 0.04 | 0.00 | 0.00 |
| 4 | 0.08 | 0.04 | 0.00 |
| 5 | 0.00 | 0.00 | 0.03 |
| 6 | 0.08 | 0.04 | 0.04 |
| 7 | 0.00 | 0.03 | 0.02 |
| 8 | 0.00 | 0.02 | 0.00 |
| 9 | 0.00 | 0.03 | 0.03 |
| 10 | 0.08 | 0.04 | 0.00 |

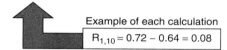

Example of each calculation

$R_{1,10} = 0.72 - 0.64 = 0.08$

**Step 7.** Compute the average range $(\overline{R}_i)$ for each operator $(i)$ using Equation 9.4.

$$\text{Operator 1: } \overline{R}_1 = \frac{0.320}{10} = 0.0320$$

$$\text{Operator 2: } \overline{R}_2 = \frac{0.280}{10} = 0.0280$$

$$\text{Operator 3: } \overline{R}_3 = \frac{0.170}{10} = 0.0170$$

**Step 8.** Compute the overall range $(\overline{\overline{R}})$ using Equation 9.5.

$$\overline{\overline{R}} = \frac{0.0320 + 0.0280 + 0.0170}{3} = 0.0257$$

**Step 9.** Compute the control limit on the individual ranges $(R_{ij})$. The constant $D_4 = 3.267$ was found in Table 10.1 in Chapter 10 using the number of trials $(r = 2)$ for $n$.

$$\text{Control Limit} = 3.267 \times 0.0257 = 0.08396$$

None of the individual ranges exceed the control limit.

**Step 10.** Compute the equipment variation (EV) using Equation 9.8. $K_1 = 4.56$ from Table 9.1 using the number of trials $(r) = 2$.

$$EV = K_1 \times \overline{\overline{R}} = 4.56 \times 0.0257 = 0.1172 \quad \text{(difference due to rounding)}$$

**Step 11.** Compute the operator variation (OV) using Equation 9.8. $K_2 = 2.70$ from Table 9.1 using the number of operators $(m) = 3$.

$$OV = \sqrt{(2.70x0.0545)^2 - (0.1172^2/10x2)} = 0.1448$$

**Step 12.** Compute the overall gauge repeatability and reproducibility (RR) using Equation 9.9.

$$RR = \sqrt{(0.1172)^2 + (0.1448)^2} = 0.18619$$

---

## Example 9.2: Calculating EV, OV, and RR as Percentage of Tolerance

To calculate EV, OV, and RR as a percentage of tolerance:

$$\text{Tolerance} = 0.99 - 0.49 = 0.50$$

$$EV = \frac{0.1172}{0.50} \times 100\% = 23.44\%$$

$$OV = \frac{0.1448}{0.50} \times 100\% = 29.0\%$$

$$RR = \frac{0.18619}{0.50} \times 100\% = 37.2\%$$

Since RR exceeds 25% of tolerance, this measurement system is not acceptable. Since EV and OV both are high as a percent of tolerance, both operator training and gauge suitability should be examined.

---

"The tendency to accept whatever figure is presented . . . is very dangerous."

(Traver, 1962)

Prior to using any measurement system it is important that the gauge is properly calibrated and that a gauge R&R study is performed. Otherwise it is impossible to determine whether systematic bias exists in the reported value or how much of the variation in reported values is due to variation in the parts being measured and how much is due to variation in the measurement system itself. One should use a measurement system that has proven accuracy and reliability—not a rubber ruler.

## NONDESTRUCTIVE TESTING AND EVALUATION

Testing is defined as "appraising characteristics of supplies, components, and so forth, that involves the application of established scientific and laboratory methods mostly functional" (Griffith, 1986, 148). Nondestructive testing and evaluation (NDT/NDE) is the name given to "testing and evaluation methods that do not damage or destroy the product being tested" (Quality Glossary, 2002, 54). NDT/NDE is often used to inspect a part for internal defects or microscopic defects on the surface of a part. This section briefly discusses some of the more common types of nondestructive testing procedures.

One type of NDT is surface-finish measurement. The symbol used to specify surface-finish specifications on an engineering drawing is $\sqrt{}$. A common instrument used to measure surface finish is a profilometer. A modern profilometer may be either a contact type (using a stylus) or a noncontact type.

Another type of NDT is hardness testing. Common hardness tests (e.g. Rockwell, Brinell, and Vickers) measure the penetration of a probe into the surface under test. The Scleroscope hardness test measures hardness by the height of the rebound of a diamond-tipped hammer after it strikes the surface under test.

NDT of welds and castings can be accomplished by a variety of NDT means. In X-ray and gamma ray inspection, defects such as cracks, holes, or inclusions show up clearly on a film image called a radiograph. Ultrasonic inspection looks for the same types of defects using sound waves instead of radiography.

Microscopic surface defects can be located using dye-penetrant inspection. A dye is spread on the surface under test and wiped off. After spraying the surface with a developer, surface defects such as cracks show up clearly under white light or ultraviolet light depending on the type of dye used.

NDT is an important and growing area of testing. With NDT, parts can be inspected for critical defects without incurring the time and cost associated with destructive tests. NDT also offers the prospect of 100% inspection, which is infeasible with destructive tests.

## SUMMARY

A measured value is subject to bias error due to lack of calibration of the instrument being used. It is also subject to precision error due to poor gauge repeatability and reproducibility. It is important that gauges be calibrated and the measurement system subjected to a gauge R&R study before use. Otherwise it is impossible to determine whether the measurement system is accurate and precise or a "rubber ruler."

This chapter provided an introduction to the types of gauges and nondestructive testing. There are entire books on these topics—some of which are listed in the Reference and Supplementary Readings sections—which are available for more thorough study.

## DISCUSSION QUESTIONS

1. Why is there a difference between the value determined by the use of a gauge and the true value of the dimension?

2. What is the difference between precision and accuracy?

3. How is gauge accuracy assessed?

4. How is gauge precision assessed?

5. What is the difference between a fixed gauge and a variable gauge?

6. What calibration information should be included on the calibration label?

7. Discuss appropriate actions to take if you find that a gauge you are planning to use to make a measurement has not been calibrated as scheduled.

8. What is the difference between repeatability and reproducibility?

9. Discuss the purpose of conducting a gauge R&R study.

10. What is considered to be acceptable as total RR for a measurement system?

11. List four different types of nondestructive tests and discuss their usefulness.

## PROBLEMS

1. A quality engineer is conducting a gauge R&R study of a new measurement system. He has had two operators measure 10 parts two times and has recorded the following data:

$$\overline{x_D} = 0.060$$

$$\overline{\overline{R}} = 0.018 \text{ (none of the individual ranges exceed the control limit)}$$

Calculate the EV, OV, and RR. If the specification is $0.750 \pm 0.250$, would the gauging system be considered to be acceptable? Would your answer change if the part being measured was a component of an emergency fire suppression system whose functioning depended on this part being within tolerance?

2. A gauge R&R study has been conducted on a measuring system. Three trained operators measured five parts three times using a properly calibrated instrument. The tolerance for the parts is 0.750 ± 0.150.

$$\overline{x_D} = 0.060$$

$$\overline{\overline{R}} = 0.018 \text{ (none of the individual ranges exceed the control limit)}$$

Calculate EV, OV, and RR in absolute terms and as a percentage of tolerance.

3. A gauge R&R study has determined the following:

$$EV = 0.0212$$

$$OV = 0.0925$$

Calculate RR. Given that the tolerance for this measurement is 1.50 ± 0.25, would this gauging system be considered to be acceptable? What action would you recommend to improve RR?

4. You have obtained the following data from a gauge R&R study. The gauge is properly calibrated and the operators are trained.

| Part | Operator 1 Trial 1 | Operator 1 Trial 2 | Operator 2 Trial 1 | Operator 2 Trial 2 |
|------|------|------|------|------|
| 1 | 1.005 | 1.004 | 1.004 | 1.004 |
| 2 | 1.006 | 1.003 | 1.003 | 1.005 |
| 3 | 1.008 | 1.010 | 1.009 | 1.008 |
| 4 | 1.015 | 1.013 | 1.012 | 1.012 |
| 5 | 1.014 | 1.014 | 1.012 | 1.014 |
| 6 | 1.007 | 1.005 | 1.006 | 1.005 |
| 7 | 1.015 | 1.013 | 1.015 | 1.016 |
| 8 | 1.005 | 1.002 | 1.004 | 1.005 |
| 9 | 1.008 | 1.007 | 1.008 | 1.008 |
| 10 | 1.010 | 1.012 | 1.014 | 1.013 |

a. Calculate EV.
b. Calculate OV.
c. Calculate RR.
d. Given that the tolerance for the measurement is 1.010 ± 0.015, calculate RR as a percentage of tolerance.
e. Is the measurement system acceptable? Explain.

5. You have obtained the following data from a gauge R&R study. The gauge is properly calibrated and the operators are trained. You carefully observed the process and did not observe any assignable causes for error.

| Part | Operator 1 Trial 1 | Operator 1 Trial 2 | Operator 2 Trial 1 | Operator 2 Trial 2 |
|---|---|---|---|---|
| 1 | 1.005 | 1.004 | 1.004 | 1.004 |
| 2 | 1.025 | 1.003 | 1.003 | 1.005 |
| 3 | 1.008 | 1.010 | 1.009 | 1.008 |
| 4 | 1.015 | 1.013 | 1.012 | 1.012 |
| 5 | 1.014 | 1.014 | 1.012 | 1.014 |
| 6 | 1.007 | 1.005 | 1.006 | 1.005 |
| 7 | 1.015 | 1.013 | 1.015 | 1.016 |
| 8 | 1.005 | 1.002 | 1.004 | 1.005 |
| 9 | 1.008 | 1.007 | 1.008 | 1.008 |
| 10 | 1.010 | 1.012 | 1.014 | 1.013 |

   a. Calculate EV.
   b. Calculate OV.
   c. Calculate RR.
   d. Given that the tolerance for the measurement is $1.010 \pm 0.015$, calculate RR as a percentage of tolerance.
   e. Is the measurement system acceptable? Explain.

**6.** Match the type of test, inspection, or measurement to the type of gauge.

| Test | | Gauge |
|---|---|---|
| A. | Actual length of nominal 1 inch part to the nearest 0.001 inch. | 1. Ruler |
| B. | Internal cracks in a cast metal part | 2. Height gauge |
| C. | Surface finish | 3. Plug gauge |
| D. | Diameter of a dot on a printed page | 4. Micrometer |
| E. | Quick check that a hole is of the proper diameter. | 5. Caliper |
| | | 6. Profilometer |
| F. | Spark plug gap | 7. Feeler gauge |
| G. | Actual width of a nominal 6 inch part to nearest 1/16 th of an inch. | 8. Optical gauge |
| | | 9. X-ray inspection |
| | | 10. Rockwell gauge |

## CASE STUDY 9.1:  *Somebody's Got a Problem*

©2006 Victor E. Sower, Ph.D., C.Q.E.

"I'll look into the problem right away and call you back before noon." John Wilson, customer service manager for Tweedle's Widgits, finished a high-stress conversation with Jim Johnson, QC manager for Dumm Industries. Dumm is one of Tweedle's newest customers who potentially could develop into one the highest volume purchasers of Tweedle's products. Johnson claims that the first shipment of parts from Tweedle fails to meet a number of dimensional specifications. This is not the way that Wilson wanted to start his day.

After informing the general manager of the problem, Wilson meets with Dee Barnes, QA manager for Tweedle's Widgits. "I don't understand it," Dee says. "We all knew how important this first shipment was. There are three critical dimensions on the RT-101 part that we make for Dumm: (1) Length of the tab (specification is 0.490 inches ±0.004); (2) Width of the tab (specification is 0.250 inches ±0.004); (3) Thickness of the tab (specification is 0.050 inches ±0.004). I had two of our best technicians inspect all three critical dimensions on every part in this first lot. We used micrometers with a precision of 0.001. Our records show that they all are within tolerance."

What actions would you recommend that Dee take in her investigation to determine the root cause of this problem?

# EXERCISES AND ACTIVITIES

1. Purchase a bag of jellybeans. Locate two different types of measurement systems that can be used to determine the length of a jellybean (e.g., a micrometer, a caliper, or a ruler graduated at least in millimeters or 64ths of an inch). With the help of two friends, conduct gauge R&R studies of the two measurement systems. Measure the length of the jellybeans. Determine R&R for each measurement system. (Provide your raw data to the instructor who will provide the specification range you need to complete your gauge R&R study. (*Note:* The specification will vary depending upon the size of jelly bean selected for this exercise.) Discuss the results you obtained. Which is the better system? Explain.

2. Using members of the class as subjects, conduct a study of the precision of a set of bathroom scales. Select at least four subjects in various weight ranges and weigh each subject at least 10 times in random order. Does it appear that the precision of the scale varies by weight range?

## SUPPLEMENTARY READINGS

*ANSI/ASQC M1-1996*. American National Standard for Calibration Systems.

ASQ Measurement Quality Division. (2004). *The Metrology Handbook*. Milwaukee, WI: ASQ Quality Press.

ASQ Statistics Division. (2005). *Glossary & Tables for Statistical Quality Control*, 4th edition. Milwaukee, WI: ASQ Quality Press.

Barrentine, L. B. (2003). *Concepts for R&R Studies*, 3rd edition, Milwaukee, WI: ASQC Quality Press.

Duncan, A. J. (1986). *Quality Control and Industrial Statistics*, 5th edition. Homewood, IL: Irwin, Chapter 31.

Farago, F. T. (1994). *Handbook of Dimensional Measurement*, 3rd edition. New York: Industrial Press.

Griffith, G. (2003). *The Quality Technician's Handbook*. Englewood Cliffs, NJ: Prentice Hall.

*ISO 10012:2003*. Measurement Management Systems—Requirements for Measurement Processes and Measuring Equipment.

*ISO 5725-1,2,3-1994*. Accuracy (Trueness and Precision) of Measurement Methods and Results.

Morris, A. S. (1991). *Measurement and Calibration for Quality Assurance*. Englewood Cliffs, NJ: Prentice Hall.

Pennella, C. R. (2004). *Managing the Metrology System*, 3rd edition. Milwaukee, WI: ASQ Quality Press.

Suntag, C. (1993). *Inspection and Inspection Management*. Milwaukee, WI: ASQC Quality Press.

## REFERENCES

*ASQC Automotive Division Statistical Process Control Manual*. (1986). Milwaukee, WI: ASQC Quality Press.

ASQC Statistics Division. (1983). *Glossary & Tables for Statistical Quality Control*. Milwaukee, WI: ASQC Quality Press.

Griffith, G. (1986). *Quality Technician's Handbook*. New York: Wiley.

Griffith, G. (2003). *The Quality Technician's Handbook*. Upper Saddle River, NJ: Prentice Hall.

"Quality Glossary." (2002). *Quality Progress* 35(7), July 2002, 43–61.

Traver, R. W. (1962). "Measuring Equipment Repeatability–The Rubber Ruler." *1962 ASQC Annual Convention Transactions*. Milwaukee, WI: ASQC Quality Press.

## CHAPTER TEN

# Statistical Process Control

## CHAPTER OBJECTIVES

After completing this chapter, the reader should be able to:

- discuss the two types of variation and who has the responsibility to address each type;
- explain the concept of the control chart;
- identify out-of-control signals on a control chart;
- determine when it is appropriate to reevaluate the control limits on a control chart;
- select the appropriate control chart for specific applications and data types;
- construct variable control charts: x-bar, range, S, individual/moving range, and Delta charts;
- construct attribute control charts: p, np, c, and u charts; and
- select the appropriate measure for process capability and assess the capability of the in-control process to meet specifications.

Quality as a concept can be subdivided into quality of design and quality of conformance. Quality of design is determined by the extent to which products and services are designed with the needs and desires of the customers in mind. Quality of conformance is determined by the extent to which the intent of the designer is actually built into the product or service.

Statistical process control (SPC) is concerned with quality of conformance. Organizations that have properly designed their products or services (i.e., quality of design is assured), and who use SPC to assure quality of conformance can answer the question "How are things going?" very simply and precisely. If things are going very well, it means that all processes are capable and are operating in control. This question is not so easily answered by organizations that do not use SPC.

# SPC AND VARIATION

Statistical process control (SPC) is defined as "the application of statistical techniques to control a process"(Quality Glossary, 2002, 59). Walter Shewhart (1931) is credited with creating the concept of the control chart and statistical process control during the late 1920s and early 1930s. Shewhart recognized that variation is the enemy of quality. He determined that variation in a process may be partitioned between "common causes" and "assignable causes" (also referred to as "special causes").

Common cause variation is inherent in a process when it is operating as designed. Assignable cause variation is unnatural variation in a process. A thermostat is designed to maintain room temperature within ±2 degrees of the set point. Temperature readings taken at random intervals when the thermostat is operating correctly will vary over the *normal* 4 degree temperature range. This is common cause variation. If the thermostat malfunctions so that it only maintains the temperature within ±4 degrees of the set point, the excessive variation is assignable cause variation.

The primary function of a control chart is to determine which type of variation is present. When only common cause variation is present the process is said to be in a state of statistical control—or simply "in control." When assignable cause is present, the process is said to be out of control.

The control chart provides input about whether adjustments need to be made to the process. It can be just as damaging to adjust a process that is operating in control (only common cause variation present) as it is to fail to adjust a process operating out of control (assignable cause variation present). Over-adjusting a process (sometimes referred to as "tinkering") by reacting to every small swing in the value of a measured parameter will actually increase the amount of variation in the process. It is therefore important to be able to determine what type of variation is present in a process and make adjustments only when assignable cause variation is present. W. Edwards Deming's Funnel Experiment shows the increase in variation that results from over-adjusting a process. In the experiment, a funnel is suspended over a target and balls are dropped through the funnel. If the funnel is left alone, the distribution of the balls' final resting place will center on the center of the target with moderate variation. If the funnel is adjusted after each ball is dropped, depending upon where that ball comes to rest, the variation increases dramatically.

Deming (1993) contended that only management can address common cause variation as it is inherent in the process as designed by management. If, for example, the current machines cannot hold the required tolerance when operating properly, management must decide to upgrade or replace the machines. Workers can address assignable cause variation as it occurs as a result of special causes not naturally inherent in the process. Examples of special causes include dull cutting blades, incorrect machine settings, and misaligned dies.

Deming's Red Bead Experiment illustrates the consequences of treating common cause variation as if it were within the control of the operators. In this experiment, four operators use a paddle with holes in it to randomly select beads from a mixture of red and white beads. Deming would task the operators with producing only white beads. Deming would chastise the operator that produced the most red beads for failing to follow instructions. Likewise he would praise the operator who produced the fewest red beads. Because only common cause variation is present in this process, the production of red beads is a random process out of the operators' control. Only management can reduce the production of red beads by finding a source of beads that contains only white beads.

Control charts by themselves tell us nothing about whether the process, when operating with only common cause variation present (in statistical control), is capable of producing a product that meets specifications for the characteristic being measured. The process capability study, discussed later in this chapter, is designed to enable this determination to be made.

SPC addresses the quality control process of Juran's (1986) quality trilogy. The trilogy of quality planning, quality control, and quality improvement is central to Juran's quality philosophy. The quality-control process consists of the process for meeting quality goals during operations. SPC is designed to be used as an in-process or "real time" tool for monitoring a process. SPC, then, can be said to be a tool for preventing the production of defective products by ensuring that the process is both in control and capable.

## TYPES OF DATA

The key to selecting the correct control chart for a particular situation is recognizing the type of data that is needed to evaluate the state of control of the process. For the purpose of control charting, there are two basic types of data: variables and attributes. Variables data are data that can be measured on a continuous scale. Examples include measurements such as height, length, width, wavelength, and pressure. Attributes data are data that are discrete. One type of attributes data is count data where the number is theoretically unbounded. An example of count data would be the number of defects in a sample. Another type of attributes data can take on only one of two possible states. An example of this type of attributes data would be whether an individual unit meets specifications or fails to meet specifications. These are the only two states that are considered for binomial classification data. Figure 10.1 shows the types of data and the specific control chart that are appropriate for use with each type.

## VARIABLES CONTROL CHARTS

Variables data are plotted on a combination of two charts—usually an x-bar ($\overline{X}$) chart and a range (R) chart. However, an s-chart should be used in place of a range chart for large sample sizes (n > 10). This is because the range method loses efficiency relative to $S^2$ as sample size increases (Duncan, 1986, 503). For a sample size of two, the two methods are equivalent. For a sample size of 10 the range method efficiency is only 0.85 relative to $S^2$ (Montgomery, 1996, 184–185).

The x-bar chart plots sample means. It is a measure of between-sample variation and is used to assess the centering and long-term variation of the process. The range chart and the s-chart measure the within-sample variation and assess the short-term variation of the process.

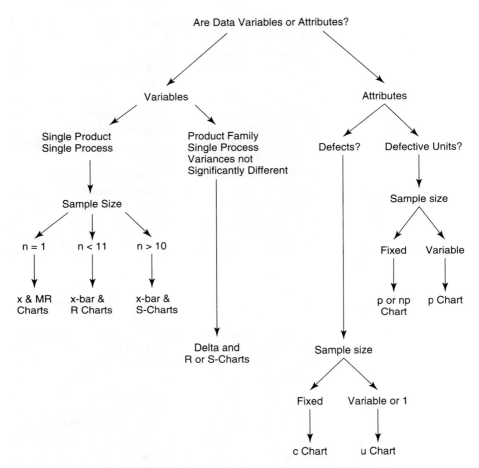

**Figure 10.1.** Selecting the Proper Basic Control Chart(s)

## Concept of the Control Chart

All control charts discussed in this chapter (x-bar, R, Individual/Moving Range, S, Delta, p, np, c, u) operate on the basis of the same basic concept. The differences among the types of control charts revolve around the type of data being plotted and its underlying distribution. The concept of the control chart will be illustrated here using the x-bar chart.

The construction of an x-bar chart begins with the collection of a series of samples (sometimes called subgroups) from a process. The samples consist of two or more observations [sample sizes of 3–10 are best (Evans & Lindsay, 2005, 694)] each. The individual observations are averaged for each sample to determine the sample mean ($\bar{x}$). The average of at least 25 to 30 sample means is called the grand mean or x-double bar ($\bar{\bar{x}}$). The standard deviation of the sample means is $\sigma_{\bar{x}}$ (sigma sub-x-bar).

The underlying distribution for the x-bar chart is the normal distribution. However, Shewhart (1931) and Burr (1967) demonstrated through simulation that the x-bar chart is robust to non-normality in the distribution of the sample means. It is wise to check the data for normality when constructing individual/moving range charts as individual values are plotted rather than sample means.

An x-bar chart is shown in Figure 10.2. The centerline (CL) of the x-bar chart is $\bar{\bar{x}}$ (x double bar). The upper control limit (UCL) is set at $\bar{\bar{x}} + 3\sigma_{\bar{x}}$ (+3 sigma); the lower control limit (LCL) is set at $\bar{\bar{x}} - 3\sigma_{\bar{x}}$ (−3 sigma).

The 25 to 30 sample means are then plotted on the control chart. If none of the points fall outside the control limits and there are no discernible patterns in the plot, the process is said to be in control (as in Figure 10.2). The chart then represents a form of statistical model of the process and can then be used to plot subsequent sample means.

Control charts are sometimes created using fewer than 25 samples. In this case the control limits should be considered to be trial control limits. After at least 25 samples have been obtained, they are considered to be final control limits for the process.

## Out of Control Signals

One point falling outside the control limits on an x-bar control chart indicates the process mean may have shifted from $\bar{\bar{x}}$. This shift is due to some assignable cause that must be identified and corrected. The probability of a point outside the control limits actually coming from the distribution upon which the control chart was developed is

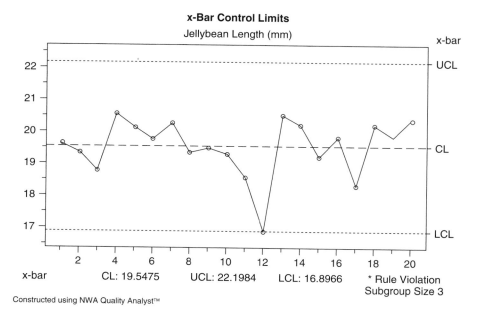

**Figure 10.2.** X-Bar Control Chart

very small ($p < 0.0027$ for 3 sigma control limits). Because this probability is so low, quality engineers often say that the process *is out of control* rather than using the statistically correct terminology *may be out of control* when they observe a signal.

The risk of unnecessarily taking action based upon a point outside the control limits when the process is actually in control is a Type I error. The risk of the control chart failing to produce a signal when the process is actually out of control is a Type II error. The probability of a Type II error must be assessed for each individual sample.

The probability of a Type I error may be decreased by expanding the control limits from, for example, 3 sigma to 4 sigma. However, this increases the probability of a Type II error. The probability of a Type II error may be decreased by decreasing the control limits from, for example, 3 sigma to 2 sigma. However, this increases the probability of a Type I error. Setting the control limits depends on the relative consequences of a Type I and a Type II error. In the case of a nuclear power plant where a missed signal might have catastrophic consequences and the cost of investigating a signal is relatively low, the quality engineer may elect to set the control limits at 2 sigma. In the case of a cardboard container manufacturer where the cost of investigating a signal is large relative to the consequences of missing a real signal, the quality engineer may elect to set the control limits at 4 sigma. The combination of 3 sigma control limits and the use of the pattern rules provides a compromise that addresses both Type I and Type II errors.

There are other ways that a control chart can signal an out-of-control condition. These are referred to as *pattern rules*. A run of seven or eight points falling on one side of the centerline (CL) is an indication that the process mean has shifted. This might be the result of a change in operator or a change in raw material lots. Similarly, a run of seven or eight points on a rising or falling trend indicates that the process is out of control. This could be due to gradual tool wear, temperature buildup, or operator fatigue.

Points observed to be hugging the centerline are an indication that the control limits are too wide. This can result from a reduction in process variation that has occurred since the limits were calculated. If this is the case, new control limits should be calculated. This can also be a signal that the control limits were miscalculated.

Points observed to be changing on a regular, cyclical basis may be an indication of shift-to-shift variation. This could be the result of differences in training and experience of the operators or set-up technicians from shift to shift.

Figure 10.3 shows examples of out-of-control signals observed in practice and the assignable causes associated with those signals. An excellent discussion of out of control signals is contained in the Western Electric Corporation's *Statistical Quality Control Handbook* (1956).

### Patterns Leading to Modifying Control Limits

A run of seven or eight points in a row above or below the centerline (CL) is an indication of a possible shift in the mean on an x-bar chart. For other charts it is also an indication of a possible shift in the statistic being plotted. The appropriate action to take depends upon whether the shift is an indication of improvement or degradation in the process.

a. One point outside the control limit

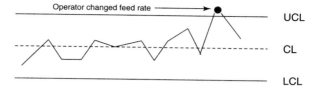

b. Eight points on one side of the centerline

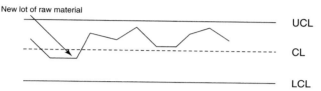

c. Eight points on a rising (or falling) trend

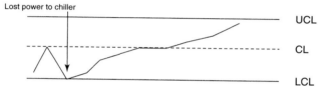

d. Hugging the centerline

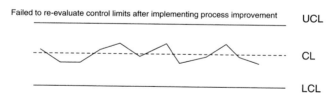

**Figure 10.3.** Examples of Out of Control Signals

For example, an upward shift in the mean on an x-bar chart plotting yield in ounces of gold from a refining operation would represent an improvement. The quality manager should determine what changed in the process that created the improvement, verify that it is an appropriate change, document the change, and institutionalize the change so that it becomes the new process. The control limits for the process should then be changed to reflect the new process. An upward shift in the proportion defective plotted on a p-chart would be an indication of process degradation. In this case the cause of the degradation should be found and corrected to bring the process back into control using the existing control limits.

A manufacturer of jellybeans uses an x-bar chart to monitor the length of the jellybeans produced by an extrusion machine. There is no industry specification for jellybean length, but the manufacturer would like the mean length to be as consistent as possible and to be smaller rather than larger.

Recently the manufacturer undertook a capital project to upgrade the extrusion machine. Upon the start-up of the upgraded extruder, the quality manager observed a signal of eight samples in a row whose means were below the centerline. She investigated and was able to attribute the shift to the upgrade in the machine. Since this is a desirable shift, she recalculated the control limits for the x-bar chart to reflect the new process.

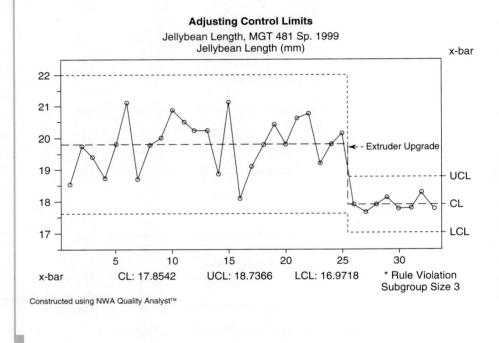

## Constructing Variables Control Charts

The first step in constructing variables control charts is to determine the variable to be measured. This is usually the most critical dimension of a product or a dimension that is highly sensitive to changes in the process. The second step is to evaluate the process to ensure that it is being operated as designed. Among the things to look for would be the use of incorrect procedures, off-specification materials, or worn parts. If nonstandard conditions are found they should be adjusted to design standards.

### x-Bar and Range Charts

After the process is brought up to design standards, 25 to 30 samples (k) consisting of three to 10 observations (n) are taken. The dimension of interest is measured using a system that is known to be accurate and reliable. The mean ($\bar{x}$) and range (R) are calculated for each sample. These values are used to calculate the grand mean ($\bar{\bar{x}}$) and average range ($\bar{R}$).

$$\bar{x} = \frac{\sum\limits_{i=1}^{n} x_i}{n} \tag{10.1}$$

$$\bar{\bar{x}} = \frac{\sum\limits_{i=1}^{k} \bar{x}_i}{k} \tag{10.2}$$

$$R = x_k(\text{largest}) - x_k(\text{smallest}) \tag{10.3}$$

$$\bar{R} = \frac{\sum\limits_{i=1}^{k} R_i}{k} \tag{10.4}$$

The centerline (CL) for the x-bar chart is $\bar{\bar{x}}$. The upper control limit (UCL) and lower control limit (LCL) are calculated using Equations 10.5 and 10.6, respectively. The constant $A_2$ is found in Table 10.1.

$$\text{UCL} = \bar{\bar{x}} + A_2\bar{R} \tag{10.5}$$

$$\text{LCL} = \bar{\bar{x}} - A_2\bar{R} \tag{10.6}$$

The centerline for the range chart is $\bar{R}$. The UCL and LCL are calculated using Equations 10.7 and 10.8, respectively. The constants $D_3$ and $D_4$ are found in Table 10.1.

$$\text{UCL} = D_4\bar{R} \tag{10.7}$$

$$\text{LCL} = D_3\bar{R} \tag{10.8}$$

The range chart is evaluated first. If it is in control, then the x-bar chart can be evaluated. An out-of-control signal on either chart is an indication that the process is out of control.

**TABLE 10.1.   Factors for Variables Control Charts**

| n | $A_2$ | $A_3$ | $c_4$ | $B_3$ | $B_4$ | $D_3$ | $D_4$ | $d_2$ |
|---|---|---|---|---|---|---|---|---|
| 2 | 1.880 | 2.659 | 0.7979 | 0 | 3.267 | 0 | 3.267 | 1.128 |
| 3 | 1.023 | 1.954 | 0.8862 | 0 | 2.568 | 0 | 2.575 | 1.693 |
| 4 | 0.729 | 1.628 | 0.9213 | 0 | 2.266 | 0 | 2.282 | 2.059 |
| 5 | 0.577 | 1.427 | 0.9400 | 0 | 2.089 | 0 | 2.115 | 2.326 |
| 6 | 0.483 | 1.287 | 0.9515 | 0.030 | 1.970 | 0 | 2.004 | 2.534 |
| 7 | 0.419 | 1.182 | 0.9594 | 0.118 | 1.882 | 0.076 | 1.924 | 2.704 |
| 8 | 0.373 | 1.099 | 0.9650 | 0.185 | 1.815 | 0.136 | 1.864 | 2.847 |
| 9 | 0.337 | 1.032 | 0.9693 | 0.239 | 1.761 | 0.184 | 1.816 | 2.970 |
| 10 | 0.308 | 0.975 | 0.9727 | 0.284 | 1.716 | 0.223 | 1.777 | 3.078 |
| 11 | 0.285 | 0.927 | 0.9754 | 0.321 | 1.679 | 0.256 | 1.744 | 3.173 |
| 12 | 0.266 | 0.886 | 0.9776 | 0.354 | 1.646 | 0.284 | 1.716 | 3.258 |
| 13 | 0.249 | 0.850 | 0.9794 | 0.382 | 1.618 | 0.308 | 1.692 | 3.336 |
| 14 | 0.235 | 0.817 | 0.9810 | 0.406 | 1.594 | 0.329 | 1.671 | 3.407 |
| 15 | 0.223 | 0.789 | 0.9823 | 0.428 | 1.572 | 0.348 | 1.652 | 3.472 |
| 16 | 0.212 | 0.763 | 0.9835 | 0.448 | 1.552 | 0.364 | 1.636 | 3.532 |
| 17 | 0.203 | 0.739 | 0.9845 | 0.466 | 1.534 | 0.379 | 1.621 | 3.588 |
| 18 | 0.194 | 0.718 | 0.9854 | 0.482 | 1.518 | 0.392 | 1.608 | 3.640 |
| 19 | 0.187 | 0.698 | 0.9862 | 0.497 | 1.503 | 0.404 | 1.596 | 3.689 |
| 20 | 0.180 | 0.680 | 0.9869 | 0.510 | 1.490 | 0.414 | 1.586 | 3.735 |
| 21 | 0.173 | 0.663 | 0.9876 | 0.523 | 1.477 | 0.425 | 1.575 | 3.778 |

(Adapted from ASTM STP 15D (1976), Table 27.)

**Where Do the Factors in Table 10.1 Come From?**

Some of the mystery surrounding the factors in Table 10.1 can now be unraveled. The UCL of the x-bar chart is defined as

$$UCL = \bar{\bar{x}} + 3\sigma_{\bar{x}}$$

$\sigma_x$ can be estimated by using Equation 10.34

$$\hat{\sigma}_x = \frac{\bar{R}}{d_2}$$

$\sigma_{\bar{x}}$ can be estimated by using Equation 10.33

$$\hat{\sigma}_{\bar{x}} = \frac{\hat{\sigma}_x}{\sqrt{n}}$$

So, the equations for calculating the UCL

$$UCL = \bar{\bar{x}} + 3\frac{\hat{\sigma}_x}{\sqrt{n}}$$

and

$$UCL = \bar{\bar{x}} + A_2\bar{R} \text{ (see Equation 10.5)}$$

where

$$A_2 = \frac{3}{d_2\sqrt{n}}$$

are equivalent.

See Duncan (1986, 1026) for a more detailed discussion.

---

## EXAMPLE **10.1**

An analyst collects seven samples of three observations during a production shift. She measures and records the length in centimeters of each part and uses this data to construct x-bar and range charts.

| Sample | Observations 1 | 2 | 3 | $\bar{x}$ | Range |
|--------|------|------|------|--------|-------|
| 1 | 1.000 | 1.014 | 1.005 | 1.0063 | 0.014 |
| 2 | 1.000 | 1.010 | 1.012 | 1.0073 | 0.012 |
| 3 | 1.021 | 1.008 | 1.011 | 1.0113 | 0.013 |
| 4 | 1.005 | 1.010 | 1.005 | 1.0067 | 0.005 |
| 5 | 1.010 | 1.005 | 1.006 | 1.0070 | 0.005 |
| 6 | 1.001 | 1.016 | 1.007 | 1.0080 | 0.015 |
| 7 | 1.004 | 1.007 | 1.010 | 1.0070 | 0.006 |
| | | | | $\bar{\bar{x}} = 1.008$ | |
| | | | | $\bar{R} = 0.010$ | |

The sample mean ($\bar{x}$) for Sample 1 is:

$$\frac{1.000 + 1.014 + 1.005}{3} = 1.0063 \text{ (see Equation 10.1)}$$

The range for Sample 1 is $1.014 - 1.000 = 0.014$ (see Equation 10.3)

The sample means and ranges for Samples 2–7 are calculated similarly.

$\bar{\bar{x}}$ is the mean of the sample means (Equation 10.2), and $\bar{R}$ is the mean of the sample ranges (Equation 10.4).

The control limits of the x-bar and range charts are calculated (n = 3):

$$\text{UCL} = \bar{\bar{x}} + A_2\bar{R} = 1.008 + 1.023(0.01) = 1.0182 \text{ (see Equation 10.5)}$$

$$\text{LCL} = \bar{\bar{x}} - A_2\bar{R} = 1.008 - 1.023(0.01) = 0.9978 \text{ (see Equation 10.6)}$$

$$\text{UCL} = D_4\bar{R} = 2.574(0.01) = 0.02574 \text{ (see Equation 10.7)}$$

$$\text{LCL} = D_3\bar{R} = 0(0.01) = 0 \text{ (see Equation 10.8)}$$

The control charts are constructed and the seven sample means and ranges are plotted:

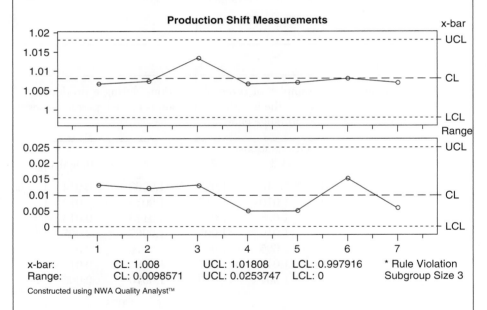

| x-bar: | CL: 1.008 | UCL: 1.01808 | LCL: 0.997916 | * Rule Violation |
| Range: | CL: 0.0098571 | UCL: 0.0253747 | LCL: 0 | Subgroup Size 3 |

Constructed using NWA Quality Analyst™

Because the number of samples taken is less than 25, these should be considered trial control limits for the process.

## INTERPRETING CONTROL CHART PATTERNS IN ACTION

The injection molding division of a major company had recently instituted statistical process control for the molding operation producing plastic housings for personal computers. The process defied all their efforts to bring it under statistical control. The control charts showed a cyclical pattern of a brief period of stability, a period of instability, then stability again but at another level.

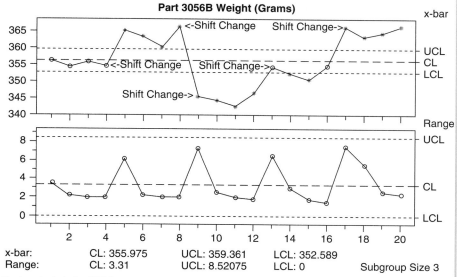

**Part 3056B Weight (Grams)**

x-bar: CL: 355.975  UCL: 359.361  LCL: 352.589
Range: CL: 3.31    UCL: 8.52075  LCL: 0    Subgroup Size 3

Chart constructed using NWA Quality Analyst™

The plant operated on a 24-hour basis. The quality engineer began his investigation by interviewing operating personnel on all shifts. When he asked the set-up technician on the evening shift what he thought the biggest problem was, he replied, "The first shift technician doesn't know how to run the process." The technicians on the other shifts had similar comments about the technician on the preceding shift. All three technicians had considerable experience in molding operations. The engineer found that each technician felt that he knew ways to improve the process by making small changes in the set-up. None had bothered to share this information with anyone else. The engineer met with the technicians as a group, they studied the process together and produced a standard set-up sheet that all agreed was the right way to run the process. Once the standard set-up was approved and implemented, the patterns due to this assignable cause disappeared.

## x-Bar and s-Charts

When the sample size (n) exceeds 10, x-bar and s-charts should be used instead of x-bar and range charts. For larger sample sizes, the range is not a good measure of the spread within each sample.

As with the x-bar and range charts, 25 to 30 samples (k) are required to construct the x-bar and s-charts. The dimension of interest is measured using a system that is known to be accurate and reliable. The mean ($\bar{x}$) and standard deviation (s) are calculated for each of the k samples. These values are used to calculate the grand mean ($\bar{\bar{x}}$), using Equation 10.2, and the average standard deviation ($\bar{s}$), using Equation 10.10.

$$s = \sqrt{\frac{\sum x^2 - \left(\sum x\right)^2 / n}{n-1}} \qquad (10.9)$$

$$\bar{s} = \frac{\sum s}{k} \qquad (10.10)$$

The centerline (CL) for the x-bar chart is $\bar{\bar{x}}$. The upper control limit (UCL) and lower control limit (LCL) are calculated using Equations 10.11 and 10.12, respectively. The constant $A_3$ is found in Table 10.1.

$$UCL = \bar{\bar{x}} + A_3\bar{s} \qquad (10.11)$$

$$LCL = \bar{\bar{x}} - A_3\bar{s} \qquad (10.12)$$

The centerline (CL) for the s-chart is $\bar{s}$. The upper control limit (UCL) and lower control limit (LCL) are calculated using Equations 10.13 and 10.14, respectively. The constants $B_3$ and $B_4$ are found in Table 10.1.

$$UCL = B_4\bar{s} \qquad (10.13)$$

$$LCL = B_3\bar{s} \qquad (10.14)$$

Interpretation of the x-bar and s-charts is the same as with the x-bar and range charts.

---

### EXAMPLE 10.2

An analyst collects seven samples each consisting of 20 observations during a production shift. She measures and records the weight in ounces of each part. She calculates the mean using Equation 10.1 and the standard deviation using Equation 10.9 for each sample. Since the sample size (n) exceeds 10, she must construct x-bar and s-charts rather than x-bar and range charts.

| Sample | $\bar{x}$ | s |
|--------|-----------|------|
| 1 | 1.001 | 0.014 |
| 2 | 1.000 | 0.010 |
| 3 | 1.021 | 0.008 |
| 4 | 1.005 | 0.010 |
| 5 | 1.010 | 0.005 |
| 6 | 1.001 | 0.016 |
| 7 | 1.004 | 0.007 |
| | $\bar{\bar{x}} = 1.006$ | $\bar{s} = 0.010$ |

$\bar{\bar{x}}$ is the mean of the sample means (Equation 10.2), and $\bar{s}$ is the mean of the sample standard deviations (Equation 10.10).

The control limits of the x-bar and s-charts are calculated (n = 20):

$$\text{UCL} = \bar{\bar{x}} + A_3\bar{s} = 1.006 + 0.680(0.010) = 1.0128 \text{ (see Equation 10.11)}$$

$$\text{LCL} = \bar{\bar{x}} - A_3\bar{s} = 1.006 - 0.680(0.010) = 0.9992 \text{ (see Equation 10.11)}$$

$$\text{UCL} = B_4\bar{s} = 1.490(0.010) = 0.0149 \text{ (see Equation 10.13)}$$

$$\text{LCL} = B_3\bar{s} = 0.510(0.010) = 0.0051 \text{ (see Equation 10.14)}$$

The control charts are constructed and the seven sample means and standard deviations are plotted:

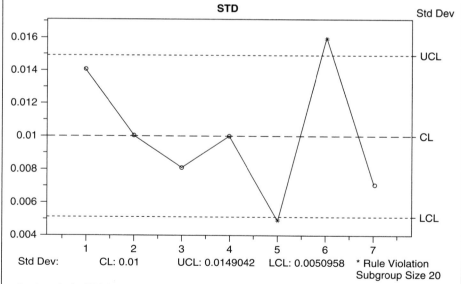

Constructed using NWA Quality Analyst™

Because the s-chart is out of control the x-bar chart cannot be interpreted and is not shown.

## Individual/Moving Range Charts

There are instances when it is desirable to construct control charts where the sample size is 1 (n = 1). Examples would include breweries monitoring daily production of beer in gallons, chemical manufacturers monitoring daily production of polymer in pounds, and track athletes monitoring the time to run a specific distance each day. The appropriate control charts to use in these situations are the individual (or x) and moving range charts.

In the case of a track athlete monitoring the time taken to run 800 meters each day, 25 to 30 (k) daily times would be accumulated for construction of the control charts. The average of the collected times is $\bar{x}$. The absolute value of the difference between successive samples is the moving range, R. Because the first observation has no preceding observation, no moving range can be calculated and the total number of moving ranges will be k-1. The average moving range is $\bar{R}$. An estimate of the standard deviation of the individual measurements is calculated using Equation 10.15, where $d_2$ is a constant found in Table 10.1.

$$\sigma_i = \frac{\bar{R}}{d_2} \tag{10.15}$$

As the moving range is calculated using two successive observations, n = 2 and the value of $d_2$ is 1.128. This results in Equation 10.15a.

$$\sigma_i = \frac{\bar{R}}{1.128} \tag{10.15a}$$

The centerline of the individual chart is $\bar{x}$. The upper and lower control limits may be calculated using Equations 10.16 and 10.17, respectively.

$$UCL = \bar{x} + 3\sigma_i \tag{10.16}$$

$$LCL = \bar{x} - 3\sigma_i \tag{10.17}$$

Substituting $\bar{R}/d_2$ for $\sigma_i$ in Equations 10.16 and 10.17 results in the following equations for calculating the UCL and LCL for the individual chart:

$$UCL = \bar{x} + 3\frac{\bar{R}}{d_2} \tag{10.18}$$

$$LCL = \bar{x} - 3\frac{\bar{R}}{d_2} \tag{10.19}$$

The centerline of the moving range chart is $\bar{R}$, and the UCL and LCL are calculated using Equations 10.7 and 10.8, respectively. Interpretation of the individual and moving range charts is the same as for x-bar and range charts. However, control charts for individuals require that the underlying distribution be checked for normality. Serious departures from normality in the distribution of the individuals renders the control chart limits invalid.

---

### EXAMPLE 10.3

A manager wishes to determine whether the daily production volume for a chemical process is in control. He collects data on the amount of chemical produced in gallons for the previous 10 days. In this case since we have individual measurements the control charts to use are the individual/moving range charts.

| Day | Output (gallons), x | Moving Range, R |
|-----|---------------------|-----------------|
| 1 | 9056 | – |
| 2 | 8645 | 411 |
| 3 | 9100 | 455 |
| 4 | 8800 | 300 |
| 5 | 8557 | 243 |
| 6 | 8900 | 343 |
| 7 | 8600 | 300 |
| 8 | 8900 | 300 |
| 9 | 9150 | 250 |
| 10 | 8800 | 350 |
| | $\bar{x} = 8{,}850.8$ | $\bar{R} = 328$ |

$\bar{x}$ is the mean of the individual values and $\bar{R}$ is the mean of the moving ranges.

The control limits of the individual and moving range charts are calculated where $d_2$ is found using a sample size of 2 (two ranges are used to calculate each range):

$$\text{UCL} = \bar{x} + 3\frac{\bar{R}}{d_2} = 8850.8 + 3\frac{328}{1.128} = 9{,}723.1 \text{ (see Equation 10.18)}$$

$$\text{LCL} = \bar{x} - 3\frac{\bar{R}}{d_2} = 8850.8 - 3\frac{328}{1.128} = 7{,}978.5 \text{ (see Equation 10.19)}$$

$$\text{UCL} = D_4\bar{R} = 3.267(328) = 1{,}071.6 \text{ (see Equation 10.7)}$$

$$\text{LCL} = D_3\bar{R} = 0(0.070) = 0 \text{ (see Equation 10.8)}$$

The control charts are constructed and the 10 individual values and moving ranges are plotted:

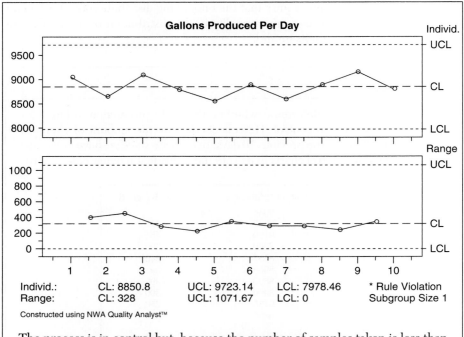

Constructed using NWA Quality Analyst™

The process is in control but, because the number of samples taken is less than 25, these should be considered trial control limits for the process.

## A Special Form of the x-bar Control Chart for Short Production Runs

Many manufacturing organizations feel that they cannot use variables control charts because their average production run length is too short. Short production runs, which are the norm for job shops, do not lend themselves to the usual x-bar chart (and its companion range chart) because short runs sometimes allow for only two or three samples to be taken during the run. Then the process is set-up for the next run and a new pair of charts is needed.

A delta (Sower, et al., 1994) chart [also referred to as deviation from nominal chart (Montgomery, 1996, 314), DNOM chart (Farnum, 1992), Nom-I-Nal chart (Bothe, 1988), or code value chart (Pyzdek, 1993)] can often be used for short run process variables measurements. The delta chart plots the deviation from a nominal value instead of plotting the measured value directly. Consider a specialty shop that fills bottles with cleaning solution in small lots. The automatic bottle-filling equipment can be adjusted to fill 1-pint, 1-quart, and half-gallon sizes of the cleaning solution. A run of a given size might last 1 to 2 hours. If it has been shown that the variance in fill volume does not change significantly with the setting, instead of using the actual fill volume for control charting purposes, the difference from the nominal fill volume can be used. A reading of 1.003 quarts becomes a delta statistic of 0.003

(1.003 − nominal of 1.000). A reading of 1.003 pints also becomes a delta statistic of 0.003. X-bar and range charts can now be created based on the delta statistics rather than the actual measurements. One delta chart (special form of an x-bar chart) can now be used for all three fill volumes.

$$\text{Delta Statistic} = \text{Measured Value} - \text{Nominal Value} \qquad (10.20)$$

---

## EXAMPLE 10.4

An analyst collects six samples of three observations during a production shift from a bottle filling line. Three of the samples are 1-liter bottles and three are half-liter bottles. She measures and records the actual volume of liquid in each bottle. The target values for 1-liter bottles and half-liter bottles are 1.0 and 0.5 liters respectively. She has verified that the variances of the fill volumes for the two sizes are nearly equal.

| Sample | Observations 1 | 2 | 3 |
|---|---|---|---|
| 1 | 1.001 | 1.014 | 1.005 |
| 2 | 1.000 | 1.010 | 1.012 |
| 3 | 1.021 | 1.008 | 1.011 |
| 4 | 0.505 | 0.510 | 0.505 |
| 5 | 0.510 | 0.505 | 0.506 |
| 6 | 0.499 | 0.516 | 0.507 |

She transforms her raw observations into Delta statistics by subtracting the target value from each observation and calculates the Mean Delta and $\overline{R}$.

| Sample | Observations 1 | 2 | 3 | $\overline{Delta}$ | $\overline{R}$ |
|---|---|---|---|---|---|
| 1 | 0.001 | 0.014 | 0.005 | 0.0067 | 0.013 |
| 2 | 0.000 | 0.010 | 0.012 | 0.0073 | 0.012 |
| 3 | 0.021 | 0.008 | 0.011 | 0.0133 | 0.013 |
| 4 | 0.005 | 0.010 | 0.005 | 0.0067 | 0.005 |
| 5 | 0.010 | 0.005 | 0.006 | 0.0070 | 0.005 |
| 6 | −0.001 | 0.016 | 0.007 | 0.0073 | 0.017 |

$$\overline{\overline{Delta}} = 0.00805$$
$$\overline{R} = 0.0108$$

The control limits of the Delta and range charts are calculated (n = 3):

$$\text{UCL} = \overline{\overline{Delta}} + A_2\overline{R} = 0.00805 + 1.023(0.0108) = 0.0191 \text{ (see Equation 10.5)}$$

$$LCL = \overline{Delta} - A_2\overline{R} = 0.00805 - 1.023(0.0108) = -0.00300 \text{ (see Equation 10.6)}$$

$$UCL = D_4\overline{R} = 2.574(0.0108) = 0.02780 \text{ (see Equation 10.7)}$$

$$LCL = D_3\overline{R} = 0(0.0108) = 0 \text{ (see Equation 10.8)}$$

The control charts are constructed and the seven sample means and ranges are plotted:

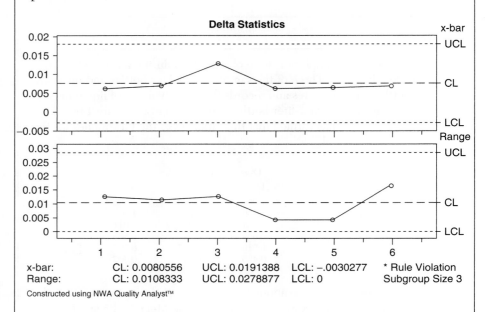

x-bar:  CL: 0.0080556  UCL: 0.0191388  LCL: −.0030277  * Rule Violation
Range:  CL: 0.0108333  UCL: 0.0278877  LCL: 0  Subgroup Size 3

Constructed using NWA Quality Analyst™

The process is in control but, because the number of samples taken is less than 25, these should be considered trial control limits for the process.

# DELTA CHART IN ACTION

The Metals Fabrication Division of a major corporation uses cut-off saws to produce different length aluminum housings for multiple-outlet surge protectors. The length of the housings varies from 6 to 14 inches. All lengths are cut from the same aluminum extrusions using the same cut-off saw. To change from one length to another, the operator adjusts a hard stop. The tolerance limits for all lengths of the housing are the same, ±0.020 inches. A process capability study found that the variance in length was constant regardless of the length being cut.

The plant initially tried to use x-bar and range charts to control the process. Because the run lengths were short (<8 hours), they seldom plotted more than four or five samples before they had to change set-ups and run a different length using separate control charts. Using a delta chart enabled the plant to use just one set of charts for the process simplifying the SPC process.

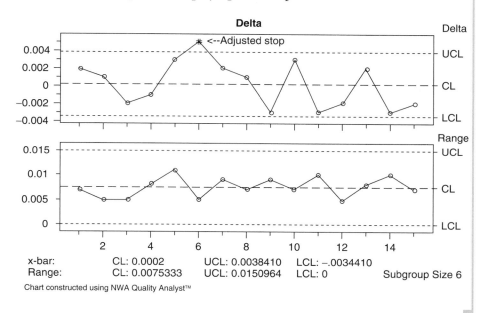

| x-bar: | CL: 0.0002 | UCL: 0.0038410 | LCL: –.0034410 | |
| Range: | CL: 0.0075333 | UCL: 0.0150964 | LCL: 0 | Subgroup Size 6 |

Chart constructed using NWA Quality Analyst™

## ATTRIBUTES CONTROL CHARTS

Variables control charts provide more information about a process than attribute control charts because variables charts show actual measurement data while attribute charts show only count data. But it is often preferable to use attribute control charts instead of variables control charts. Attributes control charts are required when there are multiple possible causes for rejecting a product and the parameter of interest is the proportion of rejected products from the process or the average number of defects per sample or product. Attributes control charts are also required when the test used is a "go–no–go" type of test (e.g., meets specification or fails to meet specification) rather than a continuous measurement (e.g., length, width, weight).

The concept of attributes control charts is the same as for the x-bar chart. However, instead of being based upon the normal distribution (a continuous distribution), attribute control charts are based upon some discrete distribution (e.g., binomial, Poisson). The interpretation of out-of-control signals is the same for both attributes and variables control charts.

## Control Charts for Nonconforming Units

The *proportion defective chart* (p-chart) is used to control the proportion of defective product in samples taken from a process. This chart is also referred to as the fraction-nonconforming or fraction-defective chart. The underlying distribution for the p-chart is the binomial. Although the sample size for a p-chart may vary, in practice it is desirable to hold the sample size constant. If the sample size varies, it is necessary to recalculate the control limits for each sample (see Figure 10.4).

The sample size required for a p-chart is usually larger than for a variables control chart. Typically, sample sizes vary from about 30 to more than 100. Duncan (1986) provides a complete discussion of the procedure for determining the appropriate sample size based upon the degree of variation in proportion defective expected in the process.

As in the construction of variables control charts, 25 to 30 samples are taken from the process after the process has been inspected and determined to be operating as designed. The proportion defective (p) is calculated for each sample by dividing the number of defective units by the sample size. Control limits for the p-chart are calculated as follows, where k = the number of samples, and n = the number of observations in each sample. The centerline for the p-chart is $\bar{p}$.

$$\bar{p} = \frac{\sum_{i=1}^{k} p_i}{k} \tag{10.21}$$

$$\text{UCL} = \bar{p} + 3\sqrt{\frac{\bar{p}(1-\bar{p})}{n}} \tag{10.22}$$

$$\text{LCL} = \bar{p} - 3\sqrt{\frac{\bar{p}(1-\bar{p})}{n}} \tag{10.23}$$

When the LCL formula yields a value that is negative, the LCL is set to 0.

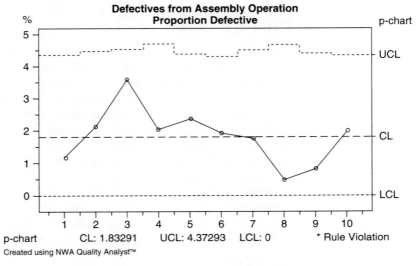

**Figure 10.4.** Example of p-chart with Variable Sample Size

## EXAMPLE 10.5

An analyst collects 10 samples of 200 observations during a production shift. The number of defective units in each sample is determined and recorded. A proportion defective (p-chart) is constructed.

| Sample | Number of Defective Units |
|--------|---------------------------|
| 1 | 5 |
| 2 | 3 |
| 3 | 7 |
| 4 | 2 |
| 5 | 1 |
| 6 | 4 |
| 7 | 10 |
| 8 | 4 |
| 9 | 1 |
| 10 | 6 |

$$\bar{p} = \frac{5+3+7+2+1+4+10+4+1+6}{10(200)} = 0.0215 \text{ (see Equation 10.21)}$$

or 2.15%.

The control limits for the p-chart are calculated:

$$\text{UCL} = \bar{p} + 3\sqrt{\frac{\bar{p}(1-\bar{p})}{n}} = 0.0215 + 3\sqrt{\frac{0.0215(1-0.0215)}{20}} = 0.052268$$

(see Equation 10.22)

or 5.2268%.

$$\text{LCL} = \bar{p} - 3\sqrt{\frac{\bar{p}(1-\bar{p})}{n}} = 0.0215 - 3\sqrt{\frac{0.0215(1-0.0215)}{20}} = -0.00927$$

(see Equation 10.23)

Since <0, set LCL equal to 0. The control chart is constructed and the data points are plotted.

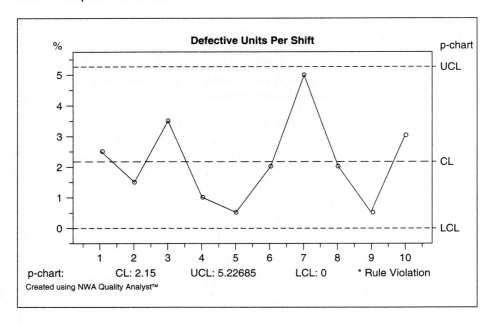

p-chart:      CL: 2.15      UCL: 5.22685      LCL: 0      * Rule Violation

Created using NWA Quality Analyst™

The *number defective chart* (np-chart) is an alternative chart that may be substituted for the p-chart. The underlying distribution for the np-chart is the binomial. In the case of the np-chart, the sample size must be constant. Rather than calculating the proportion of defective items in a sample for plotting on a p-chart, the np-chart allows the actual number of defective units to be plotted directly. This eliminates the need for one calculation (p), thereby decreasing the probability of an error. The np-chart also is somewhat easier for production operators to understand. No power is lost by using the np-chart instead of the p-chart.

As in the construction of the p-chart, 25 to 30 samples are taken from the process after the process has been inspected and determined to be operating as designed. The number of defective units (np) is recorded for each sample. For calculation of the control limits, $\bar{p}$ must also be calculated for these 25–30 samples. Control limits for the np-chart are calculated as follows, where k = the number of samples. The centerline for the np-chart is $n\bar{p}$.

$$n\bar{p} = \frac{\sum_{i=1}^{k} np_i}{k} \tag{10.24}$$

$$UCL = n\bar{p} + 3\sqrt{n\bar{p}(1 - \bar{p})} \tag{10.25}$$

$$LCL = n\bar{p} - 3\sqrt{n\bar{p}(1 - \bar{p})} \tag{10.26}$$

When the LCL formula yields a value that is negative, the LCL is set to 0.

## EXAMPLE 10.6

Using the same data from Example 10.4, an np-chart is constructed.

$$n\bar{p} = \frac{\sum_{i=1}^{k} np_i}{k} = \frac{5+3+7+2+1+4+10+4+1+6}{10} = 4.30$$

(see Equation 10.24)?

$$\text{UCL} = n\bar{p} + 3\sqrt{n\bar{p}(1-\bar{p})} = 4.3 + 3\sqrt{4.3(1-.0215)} = 10.4537$$

(see Equation 10.25)?

$$\text{LCL} = n\bar{p} - 3\sqrt{n\bar{p}(1-\bar{p})} = 4.3 - 3\sqrt{4.3(1-.0215)} = -1.8537$$

(see Equation 10.26)?

Since < 0, set LCL equal to 0.
The control chart is constructed and the data points are plotted.

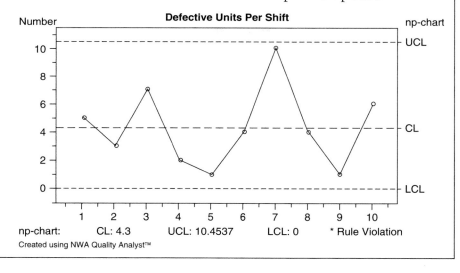

Number — Defective Units Per Shift — np-chart
np-chart: CL: 4.3    UCL: 10.4537    LCL: 0    * Rule Violation
Created using NWA Quality Analyst™

## Control Charts for Nonconformities (Defects)

The *c-chart* is used to control the average number of defects per inspection unit in samples of fixed size. The inspection unit may be one item or multiple items. The underlying distribution for the c-chart is the Poisson. Initial data are collected in the same way as for the previously discussed control charts. For each sample the number of defects (c) is recorded. The centerline for the c-chart is $\bar{c}$, and the control limits for the c-chart are calculated as follows.

$$\bar{c} = \frac{\text{Total\_Defects}}{\text{No.\_of\_samples}} \qquad (10.27)$$

$$\text{UCL} = \bar{c} + 3\sqrt{\bar{c}} \qquad (10.28)$$

$$\text{LCL} = \bar{c} - 3\sqrt{\bar{c}} \qquad (10.29)$$

When the LCL formula yields a value that is negative, the LCL is set to 0.

---

### EXAMPLE 10.7

An analyst takes 10 samples of 100 jelly beans from a production line over a shift. The number of minor defects in each sample is recorded.

| Sample | Number of Defects |
|--------|-------------------|
| 1 | 4 |
| 2 | 7 |
| 3 | 2 |
| 4 | 8 |
| 5 | 6 |
| 6 | 3 |
| 7 | 5 |
| 8 | 4 |
| 9 | 2 |
| 10 | 6 |

A c-chart is constructed:

$$\bar{c} = \frac{4 + 7 + 2 + 8 + 6 + 3 + 5 + 4 + 2 + 6}{10} = 4.7 \text{ (see Equation 10.27)}$$

$$\text{UCL} = \bar{c} + 3\sqrt{\bar{c}} = 4.7 + 3\sqrt{4.7} = 11.204 \text{ (see Equation 10.28)}$$

$$\text{LCL} = \bar{c} - 3\sqrt{\bar{c}} = 4.7 - 3\sqrt{4.7} = -1.804 \text{ (see Equation 10.29)}$$

Since <0, set LCL equal to 0.

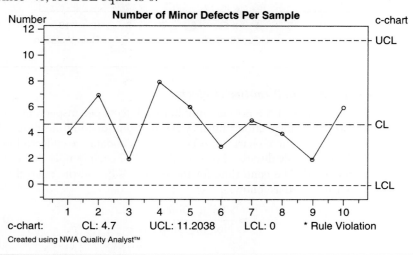

c-chart:  CL: 4.7  UCL: 11.2038  LCL: 0  * Rule Violation

Created using NWA Quality Analyst™

The *u-chart* is used to control the average number of defects per sample when the sample size varies and the inspection unit is one unit. The underlying distribution for the u-chart is the Poisson. Initial data are collected in the same way as for the previously discussed control charts. For each sample the number of defects (u) is recorded. Control limits for the u-chart are calculated as follows where k = the number of samples and n = the number of observations in each sample. The centerline for the u-chart is $\bar{u}$.

$$\bar{u} = \frac{\sum\limits_{i=1}^{k} u_i}{k} \tag{10.30}$$

$$\text{UCL} = \bar{u} + 3\sqrt{\frac{\bar{u}}{n}} \tag{10.31}$$

$$\text{LCL} = \bar{u} - 3\sqrt{\frac{\bar{u}}{n}} \tag{10.32}$$

When the LCL formula yields a value that is negative, the LCL is set to 0.

---

### EXAMPLE 10.8a

(a) Sample Size = 1 unit
An analyst examines five plywood sheets taken at random times during a production shift and records the number of defects in each sheet.

| Sample | Number of Defects |
|--------|-------------------|
| 1 | 1 |
| 2 | 4 |
| 3 | 5 |
| 4 | 3 |
| 5 | 6 |

A u-chart is constructed:

$$\bar{u} = \frac{1+4+5+3+6}{5} = 3.8 \text{ (see Equation 10.30)?}$$

$$\text{UCL} = \bar{u} + 3\sqrt{\frac{\bar{u}}{n}} = 3.8 + 3\sqrt{\frac{3.8}{1}} = 9.64808 \text{ (see Equation 10.31)?}$$

$$\text{LCL} = \bar{u} - 3\sqrt{\frac{\bar{u}}{n}} = 3.8 - 3\sqrt{\frac{3.8}{1}} = -2.048 \text{ (see Equation 10.32)?}$$

Since <0, set LCL equal to 0.

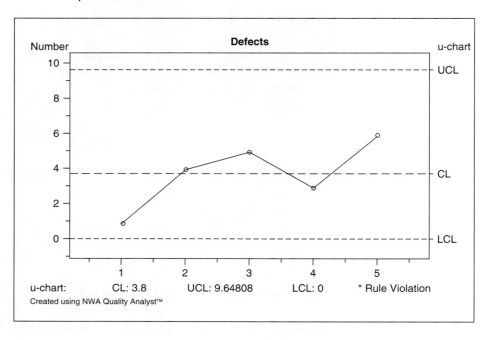

Number                     **Defects**                    u-chart

u-chart:      CL: 3.8      UCL: 9.64808      LCL: 0      * Rule Violation
Created using NWA Quality Analyst™

## EXAMPLE 10.8b

(b) Sample Size is Variable
An analyst examines each shift's production of plywood sheets and records the number sheets of plywood produced and the number of defects in each sheet. The inspection unit is one sheet of plywood.

| Shift | Number of Sheets | Total Number of Defects | Number of Defects Per Sheet |
|-------|------------------|-------------------------|-----------------------------|
| A | 250 | 300 | 1.20 |
| B | 270 | 310 | 1.15 |
| C | 230 | 290 | 1.26 |
| D | 245 | 310 | 1.27 |
|  | 995 | 1,210 |  |

A u-chart is constructed.

$$\bar{u} = \frac{1210}{995} = 1.216$$

Control limits would be calculated as follows:

| Shift | Number of Inspection Units, n | UCL (Eq. 10.31) | LCL (Eq. 10.32) |
|-------|-------------------------------|-----------------|------------------|
| A | 250 | 1.425 | 1.007 |
| B | 270 | 1.417 | 1.015 |
| C | 230 | 1.434 | 0.998 |
| D | 245 | 1.427 | 1.005 |

**Number of Defects in each Shift's Plywood** — u-chart

u-chart: CL: 1.21608  UCL: 1.42744  LCL: 1.00472  * Rule Violation

Other control charts exist for a variety of specialized situations. These are thoroughly discussed in the books contained in the Suggested Readings at the end of this chapter.

## PROCESS CAPABILITY

Thus far we have concerned ourselves with assessing whether the process is in control (i.e., predictable). Another important question is whether the in-control process is capable of meeting the specifications for the item being produced. This is determined through process-capability study.

Process capability is defined as "a statistical measure of the inherent process variability for a given characteristic. The most widely accepted formula for process capability is $6\sigma$" (Quality Glossary, 2002, 55). The process-capability index is defined as "the value of the tolerance specified for the characteristic divided by the process capability. The several types of process capability indexes for variables data include the widely used $C_{pk}$ and $C_p$" (Quality Glossary, 2002, 55). A process-capability index only has meaning when calculated from data collected while the process is in control.

When using attributes control charts for defective units, the measure of process capability is $\bar{p}$ —the average proportion defective produced by the process when it is operating in control. Therefore, a $\bar{p} = 0.0023$ would indicate that on average 99.77 percent of the product produced by this process when it is operating in control is acceptable ($0.0023 \times 100\% = 0.23\%$ defective).

When using variables control charts, the appropriate measure of process capability is $C_p$, when the process average is centered on the nominal value (centerline or target value) of the specification, or $C_{pk}$, when the process average is off-center relative to the nominal value (centerline or target value) of the specification. These two situations are illustrated in Figure 10.5.

$C_p$ compares the spread of the specification (upper specification limit–lower specification limit) to the process capability as measured by $6\sigma$. In order for the calculated value of $C_p$ to have any meaning, the data used to calculate the process capability must have been taken when the process was operating in control.

The sigma ($\sigma$) used to calculate the process capability is not the same as the sigma used to calculate the "3-sigma control limits" on the x-bar chart. The control limits are calculated using an estimate of $\sigma_{\bar{x}}$, the standard deviation of the sample means. Process capability is calculated using an estimate of $\sigma_x$, the standard deviation of the individual measurements. These two "sigmas" are related as shown in Equation 10.33. It can be seen from the equation that $\sigma_x$ is larger than $\sigma_{\bar{x}}$.

$$\sigma_{\bar{x}} = \frac{\sigma_x}{\sqrt{n}} \tag{10.33}$$

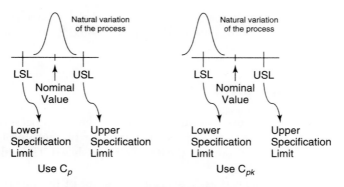

**Figure 10.5.** Centering of Process on the Nominal Value

In practice, $\sigma_x$ is often estimated from the range using Equation 10.34, where $d_2$ is a constant obtained from Table 10.1.

$$\hat{\sigma}_x = \frac{\overline{R}}{d_2} \tag{10.34}$$

When the process mean is centered on the nominal value of the specification, $C_p$ may be used as the process capability index. $C_p$ is calculated using Equation 10.35, where USL and LSL are the upper and lower specification limits, respectively.

$$C_p = \frac{\text{USL} - \text{LSL}}{6\sigma_x} \tag{10.35}$$

A value of $C_p$ that is greater than or equal to 1.33 is usually used as the indicator that the process is capable. Note that a value of 1.00 for $C_p$ indicates that the specification range and the $\sigma_x$ range are exactly the same. In such a case, 0.0027 (or 0.27 percent) of the output from the process when it is operating in control would be expected to fail to meet specifications.

When the process mean is not centered on the nominal value of the specification, $C_{pk}$ must be used instead of $C_p$ as the process capability index. $C_{pk}$ is calculated using Equation 11.36.

$$C_{pk} = \min(C_{pl}, C_{pu}) \tag{10.36}$$

$$\text{where } C_{pl} = \frac{\mu - \text{LSL}}{3\sigma_x} \tag{10.37}$$

$$\text{and } C_{pu} = \frac{\text{USL} - \mu}{3\sigma_x} \tag{10.38}$$

As is the case with $C_p$, a value of $C_{pk}$ that is greater than or equal to 1.33 is usually used as the indicator that the process is capable. Note that when the process mean is centered on the nominal value of the specification, $C_p = C_{pk}$.

Both $C_p$ and $C_{pk}$ are based on the assumption that the distribution of the individual values is normal or approximately so. When using these measures of process capability, it is always advisable to at least construct a histogram to confirm that the data are distributed approximately normal (see Figure 10.6). Some appropriate ways of addressing process capability for non-normally distributed data are discussed in Rodriguez (1992).

Sometimes it is convenient to think of process capability in terms of parts per million (ppm) defective or the number of defective parts per million opportunities. This is prevalent in organizations using Six Sigma quality programs. Table 10.2 shows the comparison of $C_p$ and ppm for a process whose output is distributed normally and is centered on the target value.

Motorola's definition of Six Sigma quality allows the process to be off-center by as much as 1.5 sigma. Using this definition, Six Sigma quality results in 3.4 ppm defective rather than the 0.002 ppm shown in Table 10.2.

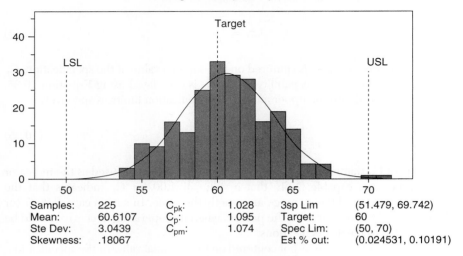

**Locking Pin for Assembly CYF-23**
**Weight of Pin (Grams)**

| | | | | | |
|---|---|---|---|---|---|
| Samples: | 225 | $C_{pk}$: | 1.028 | 3sp Lim | (51.479, 69.742) |
| Mean: | 60.6107 | $C_p$: | 1.095 | Target: | 60 |
| Ste Dev: | 3.0439 | $C_{pm}$: | 1.074 | Spec Lim: | (50, 70) |
| Skewness: | .18067 | | | Est % out: | (0.024531, 0.10191) |

**Figure 10.6.**  Process Capability Histogram

**TABLE 10.2.  $C_p$ and ppm Defective**

| Quality Level | $C_p$ | ppm Defective |
|---|---|---|
| 3 sigma | 1.0 | 2,700 |
| 4 sigma | 1.33 | 63 |
| 5 sigma | 1.67 | 0.57 |
| 6 sigma | 2.0 | 0.002 |

(Adapted from Tadikamalla, 1994, 83–85.

# SPC in the Service Industry

Huntsville Memorial Hospital

SPC is not just for the manufacturing industry. Service organizations also use SPC effectively. One example is Huntsville Memorial Hospital. During the late 1990s they developed a process to measure patient satisfaction using patient surveys. They recorded each month's survey data on x-bar and s control charts—one set for each of the eight dimensions of service quality that they measure. They then constructed a p-chart showing the number of patients rating the hospital below the neutral midpoint on the scale for any of the 60 items comprising the eight quality dimensions.

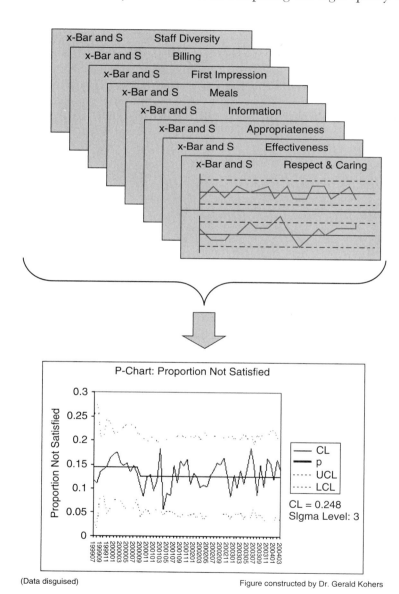

(Data disguised)                                            Figure constructed by Dr. Gerald Kohers

The p-chart provided an economic measure of overall patient satisfaction while the eight x-bar and s-charts provided detailed information about patient satisfaction with each key quality dimension. The detailed information was most useful in the hospital's continuous quality improvement program. The control charts enabled the hospital to differentiate between random variation and assignable cause variation in patient satisfaction scores. This helped to insure that the appropriate action was taken to identify assignable causes and that inappropriate action was not taken as a result of common cause variation.

Control charts were also used in other areas of the hospital. One example was the use of p and u-charts to monitor the frequency of indicator events in the Anesthesiology Department. The p-charts tracked the proportion of procedures with an indicator event. The u-charts tracked the number of indicator events per procedure (it is possible to have more than one indicator event per procedure).

## SUMMARY

The goals of an SPC system are to have processes that are predictable (in control) and capable of meeting specifications. Control charts are used to determine the state of control of a process. Control charts for variables data include x-bar, range, s, individual/moving range, and Delta charts. Control charts for attributes data include p, np, c, and u charts.

The measure of process capability for attributes data is the centerline value for the control chart. Two measures of process capability for variables data are $C_p$, if the process is centered on the target value, and $C_{pk}$, if the process is not centered on the target value. In order to obtain a valid measure of process capability, the process must be in control.

## DISCUSSION QUESTIONS

1. Discuss the difference between assignable cause variation and common cause variation.
2. Discuss the difference between variables and attributes data.
3. Discuss how it is possible for a process to be in control and yet produce a large percentage of nonconforming product.
4. Discuss the difference between a Type I error and a Type II error.
5. Under what circumstances might it be more appropriate to use 2 sigma control limits on a control chart rather than 3 sigma limits?

6. Discuss what the term "out of control" means.

7. How does a control chart signal that the process being monitored may be out of control?

8. When is it preferable to use an attributes control chart instead of a variables control chart?

9. What is the difference between the p-chart and the np-chart?

10. What are the circumstances that require the use of $C_{pk}$ rather than $C_p$ as a measure of process capability?

11. Under what circumstances would $C_p$ and $C_{pk}$ be the same?

12. How does a delta chart differ from an x-bar chart? Under what conditions should a delta chart be used instead of an x-bar chart?

13. When should an s-chart be used instead of a range chart?

14. What is the appropriate control chart(s) to use to track the number of gallons of gasoline produced on a daily basis in a petroleum refinery?

15. Does being in control always mean that a process is producing few defective items?

16. What would be some possible explanations for a rising trend on an x-bar chart used to monitor moisture content in product emerging from a drying oven?

17. How might shift-to-shift variation in the set-up of a process manifest itself in a control chart?

# PROBLEMS

1. Samples consisting of six observations have been taken from a process. Use the following data to construct x-bar and range charts using 3-sigma control limits. Does the process appear to be in control?

| Sample | $\bar{x}$ (inches) | Range (inches) |
|--------|--------------------|----------------|
| 1 | 27.2 | 1.5 |
| 2 | 28.1 | 1.2 |
| 3 | 28.0 | 1.3 |
| 4 | 27.6 | 1.0 |
| 5 | 27.5 | 1.1 |

2. The specification for the product in Problem 1 is $27.5 \pm 1.0$ inches.

a. Calculate $C_p$ and $C_{pk}$ for the process.

   b. Which measure is appropriate for this process?
   c. Is the process capable?

3. Ten samples of 200 observations were taken from a stamping machine. The samples were inspected and the number of defective units in each sample was recorded.

   a. Use the following data to construct a proportion defective chart. Does the process appear to be in control?
   b. Use the following data to construct a number defective chart. Does the process appear to be in control?

| Sample | Number of Defective Units in Sample |
|--------|-------------------------------------|
| 1 | 12 |
| 2 | 9 |
| 3 | 11 |
| 4 | 3 |
| 5 | 0 |
| 6 | 5 |
| 7 | 9 |
| 8 | 7 |
| 9 | 11 |
| 10 | 8 |

4. An inspector takes samples of 20 painted panels from a painting line at random intervals. She records the number of minor defects in each sample. Use the following data to construct a c-chart. Does the process appear to be in control?

| Sample | Number of Minor Defects in Sample |
|--------|-----------------------------------|
| 1 | 2 |
| 2 | 0 |
| 3 | 0 |
| 4 | 3 |
| 5 | 1 |
| 6 | 2 |
| 7 | 2 |
| 8 | 1 |
| 9 | 0 |
| 10 | 3 |

**5.** A drilling process produces two similar products in short runs. Product A has a 1-inch hole drilled in the center. Product B has a 3/4-inch hole drilled in the center. The quality engineer has determined that the variances for the two hole diameters are equal. Construct a delta chart and range chart for the data provided.

| Sample | Observation 1 | Observation 2 | Observation 3 |
|--------|---------------|---------------|---------------|
| 1 | 1.001 | 1.003 | 1.001 |
| 2 | 1.000 | 1.002 | 1.002 |
| 3 | 1.003 | 1.002 | 1.001 |
| 4 | 0.753 | 0.753 | 0.752 |
| 5 | 0.751 | 0.753 | 0.752 |
| 6 | 0.752 | 0.751 | 0.750 |

**6.** One automobile each hour is selected at random for inspection of its paint finish. The finish may have as many as five minor defects and is still considered to be acceptable. The inspector records the number of defects in each automobile inspected. Use the following data to create a u-chart. Does the process appear to be in control?

| Sample | Number of Minor Defects in Sample |
|--------|-----------------------------------|
| 1 | 2 |
| 2 | 2 |
| 3 | 4 |
| 4 | 3 |
| 5 | 12 |
| 6 | 1 |
| 7 | 0 |
| 8 | 0 |
| 9 | 2 |
| 10 | 3 |

**7.** A track star is preparing for the next Olympic Games. She has recently altered her training program beginning with day 11, and she thinks that it has improved her performance. Her coach has asked you to evaluate the times for her daily 1500-meter run and confirm that the new program is more effective than the old program. The times are listed below. Construct individual and moving range charts and prepare an answer for the runner and her coach.

| Day | Time | Day | Time |
|-----|------|-----|------|
| 1 | 5.25 | 11° | 5.14 |
| 2 | 5.03 | 12 | 5.01 |
| 3 | 4.98 | 13 | 4.95 |
| 4 | 5.29 | 14 | 4.98 |
| 5 | 5.25 | 15 | 5.09 |
| 6 | 5.16 | 16 | 5.12 |
| 7 | 5.03 | 17 | 4.97 |
| 8 | 5.23 | 18 | 5.02 |
| 9 | 5.15 | 19 | 4.95 |
| 10 | 5.20 | 20 | 4.99 |

*A new training program was implemented on day 11.

8. A production process for jellybean manufacturing has been studied. Ten samples each consisting of 100 jellybeans have been inspected. The following table shows the number of defective jellybeans in each sample. Construct the appropriate control chart(s) and determine whether the process is in control.

|  | Sample |  |  |  |  |  |  |  |  |  |
|--|---|---|---|---|---|---|---|---|---|---|
|  | 1 | 2 | 3 | 4 | 5 | 6 | 7 | 8 | 9 | 10 |
| Number of Defective JellyBeans | 1 | 2 | 2 | 0 | 2 | 1 | 2 | 0 | 2 | 7 |

9. A process produces 4′ × 8′ sheets of custom walnut plywood. Ten sheets of plywood are selected at random times during the production shift and examined for defects. The results are tabulated below. Construct the appropriate control chart(s) and determine whether the process is in control.

|  | Sample |  |  |  |  |  |  |  |  |  |
|--|---|---|---|---|---|---|---|---|---|---|
|  | 1 | 2 | 3 | 4 | 5 | 6 | 7 | 8 | 9 | 10 |
| Number of Defects | 2 | 5 | 2 | 1 | 2 | 1 | 3 | 0 | 2 | 7 |

10. A process produces power cords for home computers. Every hour five cords are selected at random for length measurement. The means and ranges for 10 samples are shown below. Construct the appropriate control chart(s) and determine whether the process is in control.

|  | Sample |  |  |  |  |  |  |  |  |  |
|--|---|---|---|---|---|---|---|---|---|---|
|  | 1 | 2 | 3 | 4 | 5 | 6 | 7 | 8 | 9 | 10 |
| $\bar{X}$ | 3.25 | 3.10 | 3.22 | 3.39 | 3.07 | 2.86 | 3.05 | 2.65 | 3.02 | 2.85 |
| R | 0.71 | 1.18 | 1.43 | 1.26 | 1.17 | 0.32 | 0.53 | 1.13 | 0.71 | 1.13 |

**11.** A process is in control and the distribution of the individual values is approximately normal. The process mean is 25.5 and the process standard deviation is 0.10. The specification for the product being produced is 26 ± 1.

   a. Which measure of process capability is most appropriate for this process?
   b. Calculate the process capability.
   c. Is the process considered to be capable? Explain.

**12.** Which one of these processes appears to be in control? Discuss.

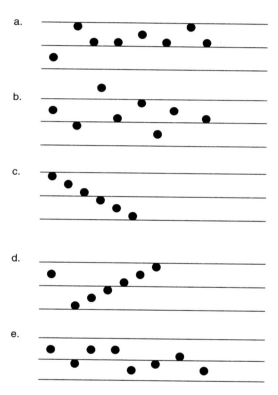

**13.** A randomly selected sample of 100 insurance claim forms filed are inspected each day over 12 working days and the number of forms with errors have been recorded in the following table.

| Sample | Number Defective |
|--------|------------------|
| 1      | 3                |
| 2      | 2                |
| 3      | 0                |

| | |
|---|---|
| 4 | 1 |
| 5 | 7 |
| 6 | 2 |
| 7 | 0 |
| 8 | 1 |
| 9 | 0 |
| 10 | 3 |
| 11 | 2 |
| 12 | 1 |

Construct the appropriate control chart(s) for these data. Determine if the process is in control. Explain your answers.

14. Samples consisting of 15 observations have been taken from a process. Use the following data to construct x-bar and s-charts using 3-sigma control limits. Does the process appear to be in control?

| Sample | $\bar{x}$ (inches) | s (inches) |
|---|---|---|
| 1 | 27.2 | 1.5 |
| 2 | 28.1 | 1.2 |
| 3 | 28.0 | 1.3 |
| 4 | 27.6 | 1.0 |
| 5 | 27.5 | 1.1 |

15. Samples consisting of three observations are taken from a process.

   a. Use the following data to construct x-bar and range charts. Does the process appear to be in control?

| Sample | Observation 1 | Observation 2 | Observation 3 |
|---|---|---|---|
| 1 | 12.0 | 12.1 | 12.1 |
| 2 | 11.8 | 11.9 | 11.8 |
| 3 | 12.0 | 11.9 | 12.0 |
| 4 | 12.0 | 11.9 | 12.1 |
| 5 | 12.0 | 12.1 | 11.9 |

   b. The specification for the process is $12.0 \pm 0.2$ mm. Calculate $C_{pk}$. Is the process capable?

16. An accounting manager reviews all invoices paid each day for defects. A single invoice may have multiple defects. Use the following data to construct

the appropriate control chart. Does the invoice payment process appear to be in control?

| Day | Number of Invoices | Number of Defects |
|---|---|---|
| 1 | 24 | 1 |
| 2 | 27 | 3 |
| 3 | 19 | 1 |
| 4 | 16 | 0 |
| 5 | 18 | 1 |
| 6 | 26 | 4 |
| 7 | 16 | 2 |
| 8 | 17 | 1 |
| 9 | 21 | 1 |
| 10 | 26 | 0 |

**17.** Samples consisting of four parts each have been taken from a machining process. The length of each part was measured in millimeters using a calibrated measuring device. The following data were obtained.

| Time | Length (mm) | | | |
|---|---|---|---|---|
| | Part 1 | Part 2 | Part 3 | Part 4 |
| 8:00 | 20.10 | 19.97 | 20.03 | 20.05 |
| 9:00 | 20.00 | 20.11 | 19.98 | 20.09 |
| 10:00 | 20.10 | 20.06 | 19.99 | 20.03 |
| 11:00 | 19.94 | 20.09 | 20.02 | 20.01 |
| 12:00 | 20.08 | 20.08 | 20.00 | 20.12 |
| 13:00 | 20.06 | 20.10 | 19.95 | 20.05 |
| 14:00 | 20.11 | 20.03 | 20.09 | 20.00 |
| 15:00 | 20.06 | 20.09 | 20.08 | 20.00 |
| 16:05 | 19.88 | 19.94 | 20.02 | 19.96 |
| 17:00 | 20.03 | 20.01 | 19.98 | 19.92 |
| 18:00 | 19.88 | 20.01 | 19.98 | 19.96 |
| 19:00 | 19.87 | 19.97 | 19.96 | 19.99 |
| 20:00 | 20.01 | 19.97 | 19.96 | 19.89 |
| 21:00 | 19.92 | 20.01 | 19.97 | 19.97 |
| 22:00 | 19.96 | 20.00 | 19.90 | 19.90 |
| 23:00 | 20.05 | 20.02 | 19.96 | 20.00 |

Construct x-bar and range charts for the process. Is the process in control? Discuss.

## CASE STUDY 10.1: *Middle County Hospital*

Katie Bent, CEO of Middle County Hospital (MCH), had invited you to her Monday morning meeting with her management staff. You assumed that the invitation was just to introduce you as the new management intern at the hospital. This she did at the beginning of the meeting. "Please welcome <your name> to our staff. <Your name> recently graduated from State University with a BBA degree and will be working for me for the next several months on a variety of projects. Please make <your name> feel welcome." Turning to you, she said "Usually the junior member of the staff makes the coffee. Since you didn't know about this, I came in early and made a fresh pot." Everyone laughed as she finished by saying, "You owe me one."

Katie then proceeded with the meeting. "This weekend I met with the Hospital Board. They asked that I make a presentation at their next meeting on the status of our program of continuous quality improvement (CQI). They are well aware of how important this program is to the operations of the hospital as well as to our continued accreditation by JCAHO." You noticed Nathan Walker, director of quality, shift uneasily in his seat.

Katie continued, "Look upon this as an opportunity to show the Board we're serious about CQI and to enlist their support for the program. Let's be sure we do this right".

"Nathan, I'm assigning <your Name>, our new management intern, to assist you in upgrading the proposal. <your name> has studied quality management at State University and can provide you with some extra technical horsepower. You have until <deadline> to complete the report upon which I will base my presentation. Make every minute count."

The meeting adjourned after about another hour. Nathan invited you to join him for a cup of coffee. "Frankly, I'm still learning the technical aspects of quality. I've joined the American Society for Quality and I'm beginning to study for my certification exam, but I'm fairly new to all of this. I think we have made some great progress—the CQI program is the best thing that has happened to MCH in a long time. Did you study quality when you were a student at State University?"

You paused for a minute, frantically trying to remember where you stored your quality management text—the one your professor said you should hang onto. "Sure. I took quality management as part of my study of operations management. That material is still pretty fresh in my mind and I have been considering preparing for the ASQ Certified Quality Improvement Associate examination," you said. While you weren't as confident as you sounded, you were sure you could re-read the quality management text and it would all come back to you.

"That's great!" said Nathan. "I've been collecting a lot of data, but haven't had time to do anything with it on a systematic basis. Follow me to my office and let me give you a couple of sets of data (in Appendices) and see what you can do with them." Off you both went to Nathan's office.

"One CQI project we implemented at the beginning of last month involves reducing the number of redos in our imaging area. The imaging area does X-ray, MRI, CT scans, ultrasounds, and the like. A redo means that the first image was found to be unsatisfactory by the attending physician who then orders a redo of the image. That creates dissatisfaction in the patient and adds cost both for the hospital and for the patient. Redos could also result in delays in necessary treatment for the patient. Because of its importance, we implemented a new set of procedures at Day 31 on the data table (Appendix 1). Days 1–30 are with the old procedure; Days 31–60 are with the new procedure. I take a random sample of 50 imaging procedures each day and calculate the number of redos. I warn Imaging when they have a bad day and compliment them when they have a good day. I'm not sure how effective this is. I have reported improvement with the new procedure but don't have a way to really show the level of the improvement. Could you develop a good way to show the improvement?"

"Certainly," you say with more confidence than you actually feel as you grow more concerned with locating your old quality management text.

"There is another area in which we are planning a CQI project," Nathan continues. "We use comment cards filled out by our patients to determine their satisfaction with the quality of our food service. Of course, we understand that patients on bland diets won't rate the Jell-O™ and soup that they receive as being as good as the chicken fried steak they really would like to have. That alone results in reduced patient satisfaction and more complaints about food service and is largely unavoidable. We would like to determine some ways of dealing with this factor as well as identifying one or more project objectives to initiate to improve patient satisfaction with our food service. I have put together a summary of our food service process (Appendix 2) and a summary of the comments received from patients about food service (Appendix 3). See what you can do with this".

"I think two projects are enough to show how we are doing with the CQI program. I'm really happy that Katie assigned you to help us out with this. The CQI program is really important. I want to be sure that we have a high quality written report for her to present to the Board. I'm counting on you to analyze the redo data and present it with your conclusions in Part 1 of your report. Then in Part 2 present your analysis of the food service comment card data and propose a project to make the biggest improvement possible in this area. Can you have the work breakdown structure and Gantt chart for this project to me by <deadline>?" You respond that you can meet that deadline. "Great! I'm counting on you," you said.

With that, you retired to your office, found your quality management text (thankfully), refreshed your cup of coffee, and started reading. The more you read, the more that you remembered from class and the greater your confidence became in your ability to do a good job for Nathan. Also, you thought, a top quality report should repay Katie for making the coffee this morning.

## APPENDIX 1: IMAGING REDO DATA FOR LAST TWO MONTHS

| Day | Number of Redos | Comments | Day | Number of Redos | Comments |
|---|---|---|---|---|---|
| 1 | 7 | Warned Imaging | 31 | 5 | |
| 2 | 5 | | 32 | 3 | |
| 3 | 6 | | 33 | 4 | |
| 4 | 5 | | 34 | 3 | |
| 5 | 5 | | 35 | 3 | |
| 6 | 3 | | 36 | 2 | Complimented Imaging |
| 7 | 7 | Warned Imaging | 37 | 1 | Complimented Imaging |
| 8 | 4 | | 38 | 4 | |
| 9 | 8 | Warned Imaging | 39 | 3 | |
| 10 | 2 | Complimented Imaging | 40 | 5 | |
| 11 | 3 | | 41 | 2 | Complimented Imaging |
| 12 | 2 | Complimented Imaging | 42 | 0 | Complimented Imaging |
| 13 | 4 | | 43 | 2 | Complimented Imaging |
| 14 | 6 | | 44 | 1 | Complimented Imaging |
| 15 | 4 | | 45 | 3 | |
| 16 | 7 | Warned Imaging | 46 | 2 | Complimented Imaging |
| 17 | 3 | | 47 | 4 | |
| 18 | 7 | Warned Imaging | 48 | 6 | |
| 19 | 6 | | 49 | 2 | Complimented Imaging |
| 20 | 6 | | 50 | 3 | |
| 21 | 7 | Warned Imaging | 51 | 4 | |
| 22 | 5 | | 52 | 2 | Complimented Imaging |
| 23 | 8 | Warned Imaging | 53 | 2 | Complimented Imaging |
| 24 | 4 | | 54 | 0 | Complimented Imaging |
| 25 | 5 | | 55 | 1 | Complimented Imaging |
| 26 | 3 | | 56 | 3 | |
| 27 | 6 | | 57 | 2 | Complimented Imaging |
| 28 | 7 | Warned Imaging | 58 | 2 | Complimented Imaging |
| 29 | 4 | | 59 | 3 | |
| 30 | 5 | New System Introduced Here | 60 | 2 | Complimented Imaging |

Sample size = 50

## APPENDIX 2: FOOD SERVICE WORK FLOW

Obtain list of patients and room numbers to be fed for each meal.

Check physician's directives for each patient's diet.

Prepare standard menus for each category of dietary directive for each meal.

Prepare food in kitchen.

Prepare individual trays with patient name and room number.

Place comment card on each tray.

Place food on tray.

Cover food to preserve temperature.

Deliver to room within 30 minutes of plating (goal).

Allow 1 hour for meal.

Pick up trays from patient rooms within 1 hour to 1.5 hours of delivery.

Separate comment cards from trays.

Return dirty trays to dishwashing area.

Return comment cards to head dietician.

Head dietician reviews comment cards and takes immediate action where appropriate.

Comment cards delivered to director of quality.

## APPENDIX 3: SUMMARY OF MEAL COMMENTS LAST 30 DAYS

| Day | Wrong Temp. | No Choice | Tastes Bad | Late Delivery | Late Pickup | Other |
|-----|-------------|-----------|------------|---------------|-------------|-------|
| 1 | 1 | 5 | 6 | 2 | 0 | 2 |
| 2 | 2 | 5 | 8 | 3 | 1 | 0 |
| 3 | 2 | 7 | 9 | 2 | 2 | 3 |
| 4 | 0 | 6 | 9 | 0 | 1 | 1 |
| 5 | 3 | 5 | 7 | 4 | 1 | 2 |
| 6 | 1 | 6 | 9 | 1 | 2 | 0 |
| 7 | 0 | 3 | 7 | 1 | 1 | 1 |
| 8 | 1 | 6 | 9 | 2 | 3 | 3 |
| 9 | 1 | 4 | 7 | 1 | 1 | 1 |
| 10 | 1 | 5 | 8 | 0 | 0 | 0 |

*(continued)*

**APPENDIX 3:** *(continued)*

| Day | Wrong Temp. | No Choice | Tastes Bad | Late Delivery | Late Pickup | Other |
|-----|-------------|-----------|------------|---------------|-------------|-------|
| 11 | 3 | 7 | 10 | 2 | 1 | 1 |
| 12 | 0 | 5 | 7 | 1 | 1 | 0 |
| 13 | 1 | 3 | 6 | 1 | 0 | 0 |
| 14 | 3 | 4 | 7 | 3 | 0 | 1 |
| 15 | 3 | 5 | 7 | 4 | 1 | 2 |
| 16 | 1 | 6 | 9 | 1 | 2 | 0 |
| 17 | 0 | 3 | 7 | 1 | 1 | 1 |
| 18 | 1 | 6 | 9 | 2 | 3 | 3 |
| 19 | 1 | 4 | 7 | 1 | 1 | 1 |
| 20 | 1 | 5 | 8 | 0 | 0 | 0 |
| 21 | 3 | 7 | 10 | 2 | 1 | 1 |
| 22 | 0 | 5 | 7 | 1 | 1 | 0 |
| 23 | 2 | 5 | 8 | 3 | 1 | 0 |
| 24 | 2 | 7 | 9 | 2 | 2 | 3 |
| 25 | 0 | 6 | 9 | 0 | 1 | 1 |
| 26 | 3 | 5 | 7 | 4 | 1 | 2 |
| 27 | 1 | 6 | 9 | 1 | 2 | 0 |
| 28 | 0 | 3 | 7 | 1 | 1 | 1 |
| 29 | 1 | 6 | 9 | 1 | 2 | 0 |
| 30 | 0 | 3 | 7 | 1 | 1 | 1 |

## CASE STUDY 10.2: *Precise Molded Products, Inc.*

©2008 Victor E. Sower, Ph.D., C.Q.E.

You were just finishing an important report when, as you turned from your computer to your desk, you accidentally knocked over your half-full cup of coffee. As you raced to mop it up before your papers were ruined, Bob Thomas walked into your office. "Did I catch you at a bad time?" he asked.

"No, Bob," you lied. "I'm just feeling a little stupid that I knocked over my coffee cup. I just finished a report about how everyone needs to be more careful to avoid accidents, and then I create a small accident myself while putting the report on my desk." Smiling, Bob says "Well, I guess you didn't learn everything at State University. I thought they would have a class on avoiding spills." You both laugh.

"They only teach that to the basketball players," you reply. "By the way, have you noticed how well they are doing this year? I'll have to take you to a game sometime." Bob only nods—something is obviously on his mind.

Bob is the quality manager at Precise Molded Products (PMP). In truth he is 25 percent of the entire Quality Department. He has an assistant and two inspectors—one on the day shift and one on the evening shift—in his department. "I'd like you to look at something," Bob begins, opening a folder. "We just set up a new molding process to make the F-106B computer housing. Engineering and Maintenance have made sure that the machinery and process are in good shape. I double checked the quality of the raw materials and Gloria, the production manager, assigned her best operator to the job. I waited until the process stabilized then had my technicians collect data from the process during its two days of operation. (He hands you Exhibit A.)

"We have two critical parameters we must maintain for our customer. These are Part Length and Part Width (see attached part drawing). We make these measurements with a set of calipers that are accurate to 0.001 inch. My technicians collect 4 parts each hour, measure both dimensions, and record the values in Exhibit A.

"Each part is also inspected by the operator for conformance to the other dimensional and cosmetic specifications. The operator records the number of rejected parts and the reason for the rejection on Exhibit B.

"Here's where I need your help. I need a way to analyze these data to determine how well the process is performing. In addition, I would like a way to monitor the process to be sure it continues to work right in the future. I am particularly concerned about the rise in the number of rejects. We have had many days where the number of rejects is low and then some when it is high. I have been spending a lot of time trying to find out what we are doing differently on the good and bad days—so far with no luck.

"I know that they have a great quality management course at State University that you completed just before we hired you last fall. We talked about that course during your interview trip and I was very impressed by how much you knew about my field, quality. Can you take these data and perform some statistical mumbo jumbo and give me a report that makes sense?"

"No problem," you reply. "My professor told me to keep my quality management book and I did. Let me spend a little time with it and your data and I think I can come up with something that will meet your needs."

"Thanks," replies Bob. "I know that we hired you as a management trainee and this falls outside your normal responsibility, but your work since you joined the company has really impressed a lot of people. Just between the two of us, Bill Otis, the plant manager, doesn't put a lot of emphasis on the Quality Department. It sometimes seems that he thinks my job is to stop Production from shipping product on time. Anyway, I think if you produce the report, he will be more likely to pay attention to it than if I did it myself. And to be honest, I never really understood that statistics stuff. My girlfriend helped me get through that course in college 10 years ago. I took my C− and ran, never thinking I would ever actually need to use statistics. I have spent the five years that I have had this job trying to teach myself what I should have learned in that course. I wish I could go back in time. I would tell my younger self that you never know what course will be essential to your success. It pays to do your best in all of them."

After Bob departs and you get your desk cleaned up, you begin the search for your quality management text. You find it in a box you haven't gotten around to unpacking yet, open it up, and begin reading. "Yeah, I remember this stuff. I can do this," you think to yourself.

**Exhibit A   PRECISE MOLDED PRODUCTS**

| | | | Length | | | | Width | | |
|---|---|---|---|---|---|---|---|---|---|
| Date | Time | Part 1 | Part 2 | Part 3 | Part 4 | Part 1 | Part 2 | Part 3 | Part 4 |
| 1 | 8:00 | 20.10 | 19.97 | 20.03 | 20.05 | 12.10 | 12.14 | 12.10 | 12.04 |
| | 9:00 | 20.00 | 20.11 | 19.98 | 20.09 | 12.07 | 12.10 | 12.11 | 12.15 |
| | 10:00 | 20.10 | 20.06 | 19.99 | 20.03 | 12.14 | 12.10 | 12.06 | 12.10 |
| | 11:00 | 19.94 | 20.09 | 20.02 | 20.01 | 12.05 | 12.09 | 12.15 | 12.12 |
| | 12:00 | 20.08 | 20.08 | 20.00 | 20.12 | 12.10 | 12.13 | 12.07 | 12.15 |
| | 13:00 | 20.06 | 20.10 | 19.95 | 20.05 | 12.15 | 12.09 | 12.13 | 12.14 |
| | 14:00 | 20.11 | 20.03 | 20.09 | 20.00 | 12.14 | 12.06 | 12.08 | 12.10 |
| | 15:00 | 20.06 | 20.09 | 20.08 | 20.00 | 12.10 | 12.00 | 12.06 | 12.15 |
| | 16:05 | 19.88 | 19.94 | 20.02 | 19.96 | 12.19 | 12.08 | 12.13 | 12.14 |
| | 17:00 | 20.03 | 20.01 | 19.98 | 19.92 | 12.00 | 12.02 | 12.04 | 12.09 |
| | 18:00 | 19.88 | 20.01 | 19.98 | 19.96 | 12.02 | 11.98 | 12.08 | 12.09 |
| | 19:00 | 19.87 | 19.97 | 19.96 | 19.99 | 12.02 | 12.00 | 12.05 | 12.10 |
| | 20:00 | 20.01 | 19.97 | 19.96 | 19.89 | 12.05 | 12.12 | 12.03 | 12.05 |
| | 21:00 | 19.92 | 20.01 | 19.97 | 19.97 | 12.14 | 12.08 | 12.05 | 12.09 |
| | 22:00 | 19.96 | 20.00 | 19.90 | 19.90 | 12.08 | 12.06 | 12.14 | 12.11 |
| | 23:00 | 20.05 | 20.02 | 19.96 | 20.00 | 12.08 | 12.16 | 12.05 | 12.07 |
| 2 | 8:00 | 19.95 | 20.09 | 20.06 | 20.07 | 12.07 | 12.10 | 12.11 | 12.15 |
| | 9:00 | 19.99 | 20.10 | 20.08 | 20.06 | 12.05 | 12.09 | 12.15 | 12.12 |
| | 10:00 | 20.09 | 19.98 | 20.06 | 20.05 | 12.14 | 12.06 | 12.08 | 12.10 |
| | 11:00 | 20.00 | 20.11 | 19.99 | 20.00 | 12.07 | 12.10 | 12.11 | 12.15 |
| | 12:00 | 20.08 | 20.06 | 19.99 | 20.05 | 12.10 | 12.13 | 12.07 | 12.15 |
| | 13:00 | 20.00 | 20.13 | 20.07 | 20.06 | 12.14 | 12.06 | 12.08 | 12.10 |
| | 14:00 | 20.05 | 20.06 | 20.00 | 20.09 | 12.10 | 12.13 | 12.07 | 12.15 |
| | 15:00 | 20.04 | 20.13 | 20.07 | 20.08 | 12.15 | 12.09 | 12.13 | 12.14 |
| | 16:05 | 20.02 | 20.05 | 19.94 | 19.99 | 12.02 | 12.00 | 12.05 | 12.10 |
| | 17:00 | 20.00 | 19.89 | 20.08 | 20.00 | 12.14 | 12.08 | 12.05 | 12.09 |

*(continued)*

**EXHIBIT A**   *(continued)*

| | | Length | | | | Width | | | |
|---|---|---|---|---|---|---|---|---|---|
| Date | Time | Part 1 | Part 2 | Part 3 | Part 4 | Part 1 | Part 2 | Part 3 | Part 4 |
| | 18:00 | 19.98 | 20.09 | 19.91 | 20.02 | 12.08 | 12.16 | 12.05 | 12.07 |
| | 19:00 | 20.05 | 19.99 | 19.95 | 20.00 | 12.08 | 12.06 | 12.14 | 12.11 |
| | 20:00 | 20.00 | 19.90 | 19.98 | 19.92 | 12.02 | 12.00 | 12.05 | 12.10 |
| | 21:00 | 19.90 | 19.99 | 19.97 | 19.97 | 12.14 | 12.08 | 12.05 | 12.09 |
| | 22:00 | 19.88 | 19.99 | 20.01 | 20.02 | 12.00 | 12.02 | 12.04 | 12.09 |
| | 23:00 | 20.00 | 19.89 | 19.96 | 19.95 | 12.02 | 11.98 | 12.08 | 12.09 |

**EXHIBIT B   PRECISE MOLDED PRODUCTS**

| | | | | Causes | | | | | | | |
|---|---|---|---|---|---|---|---|---|---|---|---|
| Date | Time | Sample Size | Total Rejected Parts | Sh. Shot | Inclus. | Discol. | Warp. | Stain | Scuff | Burr | Flash |
| 1 | 8:00 | 200 | 5 | 1 | | 2 | | 1 | | 1 | |
| | 9:00 | 200 | 6 | | 1 | 1 | 2 | | | | 2 |
| | 10:00 | 200 | 2 | | | | 1 | | | | 1 |
| | 11:00 | 200 | 3 | | | | 2 | | | | 1 |
| | 12:00 | 200 | 8 | | 3 | | 3 | | 1 | | 2 |
| | 13:00 | 200 | 5 | | 1 | 1 | 1 | | | | 2 |
| | 14:00 | 200 | 4 | 1 | | | | 1 | 1 | 1 | |
| | 15:00 | 200 | 6 | 2 | | 2 | | 1 | 1 | | |
| | 16:05 | 200 | 2 | 1 | | 1 | | | | | |
| | 17:00 | 200 | 4 | 1 | | 1 | | 1 | 1 | | |
| | 18:00 | 200 | 3 | | | | 1 | | | | 2 |
| | 19:00 | 200 | 4 | | | | 3 | | | | 1 |
| | 20:00 | 200 | 8 | | 2 | 1 | 3 | | | | 2 |
| | 21:00 | 200 | 7 | | | | 4 | | 1 | | 2 |
| | 22:00 | 200 | 5 | | 1 | 1 | | | 2 | 1 | |
| | 23:00 | 200 | 4 | | 2 | 1 | 1 | | | | |
| 2 | 8:00 | 200 | 1 | | | | | 1 | | | |
| | 9:00 | 200 | 5 | 2 | | 1 | | 1 | 1 | | |
| | 10:00 | 200 | 7 | 1 | 2 | 2 | | 2 | | | |
| | 11:00 | 200 | 3 | 1 | | 2 | | | | | |

*(continued)*

Exhibit B *(continued)*

| | | | | | Causes | | | | | | |
|---|---|---|---|---|---|---|---|---|---|---|---|
| Date | Time | Sample Size | Total Rejected Parts | Sh. Shot | Inclus. | Discol. | Warp. | Stain | Scuff | Burr | Flash |
| | 12:00 | 200 | 5 | 2 | | | 1 | | | | |
| | 13:00 | 200 | 7 | | | | 3 | | | | 4 |
| | 14:00 | 200 | 2 | | | | 2 | | | | |
| | 15:00 | 200 | 5 | | | | 2 | | | | 3 |
| | 16:05 | 200 | 6 | 3 | 2 | | 1 | | | | |
| | 17:00 | 200 | 7 | 1 | 2 | 2 | | | | 2 | |
| | 18:00 | 200 | 5 | 1 | 3 | 1 | | | | | |
| | 19:00 | 200 | 8 | | | | 3 | 1 | 1 | | 3 |
| | 20:00 | 200 | 9 | | | | 6 | | | | 3 |
| | 21:00 | 200 | 4 | 2 | | | 2 | | | | |
| | 22:00 | 200 | 7 | 2 | 1 | | | 1 | 2 | 1 | |
| | 23:00 | 200 | 6 | 1 | 2 | 2 | | 1 | | | |

# EXERCISES AND ACTIVITIES

1. Purchase a bag of jellybeans. Take 25 samples each containing three jelly-beans from the bag. Using the most accurate measuring device available (calipers or micrometer preferred—a ruler graduated in 64ths will do) measure and record the length of each jellybean. Calculate sample averages and ranges for each of the 25 samples. Construct x-bar and range charts and plot the data on the charts. Is the jellybean length in control? Explain.

2. Purchase a bag of jellybeans. Take 12 random samples, each containing 10 jellybeans from the bag. Consider that a red jellybean is a defective unit; all other colors are acceptable. Record the number of defective units in each sample. Construct both a p-chart and an np-chart. Is the jellybean process in control? Explain.

3. Use the jellybean length data collected in Exercise 1 to determine the capability of the jellybean manufacturing process. Be sure to first eliminate any out-of-control points from your data. Set the specification for jellybean length at the grand average ±1/8th of an inch. Calculate both $C_p$ and $C_{pk}$. Do you obtain different values for process capability? Explain.

# SUPPLEMENTARY READINGS

Duncan, A. (1986). *Quality Control and Industrial Statistics*, 5th edition. Homewood, IL: Irwin.

Montgomery, D. (2005). *Introduction to Statistical Quality Control*, 5th edition. New York: John Wiley & Sons.

Shewhart, W. "Excerpts from Economic Control of Manufactured Product." Reprinted in Sower V. E., J. Motwani, & M. J. Savoie (1995). *Classic Readings in Operations Management*. Ft. Worth, TX: Dryden.

Shewhart, W. (1939). "Excerpts from Statistical Method from the Viewpoint of Quality Control." Reprinted in Sower V. E., J. Motwani, & M. J. Savoie (1995). Classic Readings in Operations Management. Ft. Worth, TX: Dryden.

Tadikamalla, P. (1994). "The Confusion over Six-Sigma Quality." *Quality Progress* 27(11), 83–85.

# REFERENCES

*ASTM, ASTM STP 15D ASTM Manual on Presentation of Data and Control Chart Analysis.* (1976). Philadelphia: American Society for Testing and Materials.

Bothe, D. R. (1988). "SPC for Short Production Runs." *Quality* 27(12), 58–59.

Burr, I. (1967). "The Effect of Non-Normality on Constants for X-bar and R Charts." *Industrial Quality Control* 23(9), 563–568.

Deming, W. E. (1993). *The New Economics*. Cambridge, MA: MIT Center for Advanced Engineering Study.

Duncan, A. (1986). *Quality Control and Industrial Statistics*, 5th edition. Homewood, IL: Irwin.

Evans, J., & W. Lindsay. (2005). *The Management and Control of Quality*, 6th edition. Mason, OH: Thomson South-Western, 694.

Farnum, N. R. (1992). "Control Charts for Short Runs: Nonconstant Process and Measurement Error." *Journal of Quality Technology* (July), 138–144.

Juran, J. M. (1986). "The Quality Trilogy." *Quality Progress* 19(8), 19–24. Reprinted in Sower V. E., J. Motwani, & M. J. Savoie (1995). *Classic Readings in Operations Management*. Ft. Worth: Dryden, 277–287.

Montgomery, D. C., (1996). *Statistical Quality Control*, 3rd edition. New York: John Wiley & Sons.

Pyzdek, T. (1993). "Process Control for Short and Small Runs." *Quality Progress* 26(4), 51–60.

"Quality Glossary." (2002). *Quality Progress* 35(7), 43–61.

Rodriguez, R. N. (1992). "Recent Developments in Process Capability Analysis." *Journal of Quality Technology* 24(4), 176–187.

Shewhart, W. (1931). *Economic Control of Quality of Manufactured Product*. New York: Van Nostrand Co.

Sower, V. E., J. Motwani, & M. J. Savoie. (1994). "Delta Charts for Short Run Statistical Process Control." *International Journal of Quality & Reliability Management* 11(6), 50–56.

Western Electric. (1956). *Statistical Quality Control Handbook*. Indianapolis, IN: Western Electric Co.

## CHAPTER ELEVEN

# Acceptance Sampling

## CHAPTER OBJECTIVES

After completing this chapter, the reader should be able to:

- determine when acceptance sampling is appropriate;
- understand how to use sampling theory to properly take samples from a process;
- assess the risks in sampling plans and interpret the operating characteristic (OC) curve;
- determine the type of sampling plan to use in particular situations;
- understand how to use *ANSI/ASQ Z1.4* and *ANSI/ASQ Z1.9* sampling plans; and
- understand how to use Dodge-Romig sampling plans.

It often is impossible to inspect every unit comprising a lot in order to determine whether to accept or reject the lot. Acceptance sampling is an approach to sampling a lot to determine whether the lot should be accepted or rejected (sometimes referred to as lot sentencing). Acceptance sampling is not designed to enable an inspector to estimate the quality of the lot. A lot is a "defined quantity of product accumulated under conditions that are considered uniform for sampling purposes" (Quality Glossary, 2002, 53).

Acceptance sampling is by design an "end-of-line" inspection process. Although it is not a substitute for process control, acceptance sampling does have its place in the quality system (Sower, et al., 1993).

## WHEN ACCEPTANCE SAMPLING IS APPROPRIATE

There are a number of reasons why 100 percent inspection is often not practical. Montgomery (1996, 608) lists six situations in which acceptance sampling is likely to be useful:

1. When testing is destructive. Imagine testing every firecracker in a lot for functionality.

2. When the cost of 100 percent inspection is extremely high. Some tests require considerable time on expensive equipment. Imagine having to inspect every part in a lot of 1000 units on a coordinate measuring machine.

3. When 100 percent inspection is not technologically feasible or would require so much calendar time that production scheduling would be seriously impacted. Imagine having to verify the diameter, length, and thread type and size of every machine screw in a lot of 100,000 units.

4. When there are so many items to be inspected and the inspection error rate is sufficiently high that 100 percent inspection might cause a higher percentage of defective units to be passed than would occur with the use of a sampling plan. The quality of video tapes used by television studios is critical. Imagine having someone watch each tape from end to end in real time on a TV monitor to inspect for defects. How long do you think an inspector could stay focused on the task without missing any defects?

5. When the vendor has an excellent quality history and some reduction in inspection from 100 percent is desired, but the vendor's process capability is sufficiently low so that no inspection is an unsatisfactory alternative. Consider a paint manufacturer who purchases pigment from a supplier whose process runs at a process capability of 1.0 (0.27 percent long-run defective rate). The pigment surface area is critical to the paint-manufacturing process. A paint manufacturer who has never received an off-specification lot of pigment from a supplier may elect to use acceptance sampling rather than testing every drum of each lot received.

6. When there are potentially serious product liability risks, and although the vendor's process is satisfactory, a program for continuously monitoring the product is necessary. The manufacturer of implantable left ventricular assist devices (heart pumps) must assure that every component used in the manufacture of the devices is perfect because the consequences of a defective component could be the death of the recipient.

Acceptance sampling has been condemned by some in the quality field. Deming (1996) criticized acceptance sampling plans as techniques that "guarantee that some customers will get defective product." He recommended an "all or nothing" policy. If the process is in statistical control, no inspection is necessary. If the process is not in statistical control, 100 percent inspection should be implemented. Most, however, concede that acceptance sampling has a legitimate and useful role to play in a quality system. Figure 11.1 shows an approach for the appropriate integration of acceptance sampling and statistical process control in a quality system.

Acceptance sampling assumes that the upstream process is not in statistical control and that the proportion of defective product produced by that process can vary widely without warning. Gitlow, Oppenheim, and Oppenheim (1995, 439–442) show that acceptance sampling is invalid for stable processes—those that are in statistical control. As illustrated in Figure 11.1, there are frequent

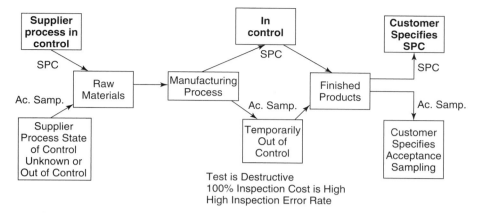

**Figure 11.1.** Integration of SPC and Acceptance Sampling. (*Source*: Sower, V.E., J. Motwani, & M. Savoie, 2009. Reprinted with permission from *Quality Progress* © 1993 American Society for Quality. No further distribution allowed without permission.)

situations where the state of control of the upstream process is unknown or known to be out of statistical control where the use of acceptance sampling is appropriate:

- A new supplier with no history with your company.
- An existing supplier known not to use SPC.
- An existing supplier who uses SPC and whose control charts show that the process was out of control during the time in which the lot was produced.
- A process in your company which uses SPC and which goes out of control, and the material produced since the process was last known to be in control is segregated for further evaluation.

## FUNDAMENTALS OF SAMPLING THEORY

In acceptance sampling a decision about a population is made based upon the results of an inspection of a sample taken from that lot. As Figure 11.2 illustrates, the population is the universe of all possible individuals (for a lot of incoming parts, the population is all of the individual parts comprising the lot) and a sample is a subset of that population. In order for a statistically valid decision to be made, the sample must be selected from the population using some random process.

The term *statistically valid* (as in *this is a statistically valid sampling plan*) does not mean that the decision dictated by the results of the sampling inspection will always be the correct decision. Statistically valid in this context means the probabilities of making the wrong decision can be assessed (calculated). This cannot be done for a statistically *invalid* sampling plan.

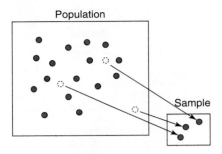

**Figure 11.2.** Population versus Sample

There are two types of errors (or wrong decisions) that can result from sampling inspection. We can incorrectly reject a lot that should be accepted or we can incorrectly accept a lot that should be rejected. The former is referred to as a Type I or $\alpha$ error; the latter is referred to as a Type II or $\beta$ error. The risk of making a Type I error is referred to as the producer's risk; the risk of making a Type II error is referred to as the consumer's risk.

## Assessing Risk in Sampling Plans

A single-sampling plan (where the accept/reject decision is based upon the results of a single sample) is defined by two parameters: the sample size $(n)$ and the acceptance number $(c)$. A sample of size $n$ is randomly selected from a lot of size $N$. The lot is accepted if the number of defective units in the sample is $c$ or smaller.

Each sampling plan has an operating characteristic (OC) curve associated with it that is uniquely defined by $n$ and $c$. The OC curve can be used to estimate the probability of making either a Type I or a Type II error. Figure 11.3 shows the general form of an OC curve. The vertical axis shows the probability of accepting the lot. The horizontal axis shows the true fraction of defective items in the lot. From the OC curve in Figure 11.3 we can estimate the probability of, for example, accepting a lot (using this sampling plan) that has a true fraction defective $(p)$ of 0.025. The probability of accepting $(P_{ac})$ this lot is approximately 0.50. If a lot that contains 0.025 fraction defective is considered to be a rejectable lot, then there is a 0.50 probability (consumer's risk) of accepting this lot. If a lot that contains 0.015 fraction defective is considered to be an acceptable lot, we can estimate the probability of rejecting this lot (producer's risk) as approximately 0.15 $(1 - 0.85)$.

Figure 11.4 shows the ideal operating characteristic curve for a situation where a lot containing a fraction defective of 0.02 or less is considered to be acceptable and greater than 0.02 to be unacceptable. This sampling plan has 0 producer's and 0 consumer's risk. All lots with a fraction defective of 0.02 or less will be accepted with a $P_{ac} = 1.00$. Lots with a fraction defective greater than 0.02 will be rejected with a $P_{ac} = 0$.

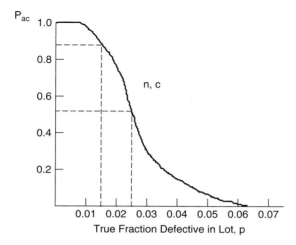

**Figure 11.3.**  General Form of the Operating Characteristic (OC) Curve

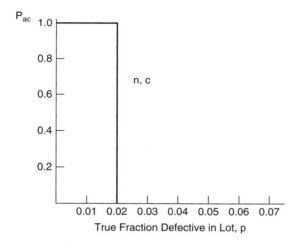

**Figure 11.4.**  Idealized Form of the Operating Characteristic (OC) Curve

The OC curve of a sampling plan can be made to resemble the idealized form more closely by changing the sample size, $n$, or the acceptance number, $c$. By increasing the sample size and keeping the acceptance number proportional to $n$, the OC curve becomes steeper indicating the sampling plan is more discriminating. Decreasing the acceptance number while holding $n$ constant has the same effect — the shape of the OC curve becomes more like the ideal.

## HOW IS THE OC CURVE DETERMINED?

The sampling plans in Z1.4 are based on the binomial distribution. The probability density function for the binomial distribution is:

$$p(x) = \left[\begin{array}{c} n \\ x \end{array}\right] p^x (1-p)^{n-x}$$

This equation may be used to calculate the probability of acceptance ($P_{ac}$) for given sample outcomes and lot quality. For example, to calculate the probability of accepting a lot using Z1.4 sampling plan code letter G, an AQL of 1.5 percent, and a lot true fraction defective of 5.19 percent is done as follows.

1. From Figure 11.12, the sample size, n, is 32. We accept the lot when we get zero or one defective unit in the sample. We reject the lot when we get two or more defective units in the sample.

2. We calculate the probability of getting zero defective units (x) in a sample of 32 (n) where the true fraction defective (p) is 0.0519.

$$p(0) = \left[\begin{array}{c} 32 \\ 0 \end{array}\right] 0.0519^0 (1-0.0519)^{32-0} = 0.1817$$

3. We calculate the probability of getting one defective unit (x) in a sample of 32 (n) where the true fraction defective (p) is 0.0519.

$$p(1) = \left[\begin{array}{c} 32 \\ 1 \end{array}\right] 0.0519^1 (1-0.0519)^{32-1} = 0.3183$$

4. Add these two probabilities together to get $P_{ac}$, the probability of accepting the lot.

$$0.1817 + 0.3183 = 0.500$$

Looking at Table X-G-1 in Figure 11.11, you can see that this is the probability listed there of accepting the lot. This process is done for a number of true fraction defectives to generate a number of points on the OC curve. Connecting these points yields the OC curve shown in Chart G in Figure 11.11.

Sampling plans are often selected based upon the acceptable quality level (AQL). The AQL is the highest proportion defective that is considered acceptable as a long-run average for the process. The AQL focuses on producer's risk. The selection of a

---

sampling plan can also be made on the basis of the lot tolerance percent defective (LTPD). The LTPD is the highest proportion defective that is considered acceptable for a given lot. The LTPD focuses on consumer's risk.

## THE MISUNDERSTANDING

The manufacturing division (MD) of a major corporation produced consumer goods for sale in the company's retail stores. The retail division (RD) required that the MD provide evidence of the quality of the product they produced. The MD utilized ANSI/ASQ Z1.4 sampling inspection by attributes to verify the quality of each lot shipped to the RD. They provide a certificate for each lot indicating that the lot meets the 1 percent AQL.

The RD had a quality control department that periodically sampled the quality of goods in the company's warehouses awaiting shipment to the retail stores. An RD quality inspector notified the MD that she had found a lot of their product in the warehouse that was defective. The MD dispatched the quality assurance manager to the warehouse to meet with the inspector.

"I selected 200 samples at random from this lot and found 4 defective units. That's a defect rate of 2 percent. We had agreed on a defect rate of 1%, so I have rejected this lot."

Clearly there had been a misunderstanding when the specification was set. An AQL of 1 percent is the long-run average defect percentage of the process not the maximum defective level of the process. The MD understood the 1 percent specification to be an AQL while the RD understood it to be a lot tolerance percent defective (LTPD)—the highest defective rate that can be considered to be acceptable.

This is a frequently encountered problem that results from lack of knowledge of the Z1.4 sampling plans and OC curves in general. Many users of Z1.4 ignore the OC curves entirely. The keys to preventing misunderstandings illustrated here are to fully understand the sampling plan to be used and to specify fully the particular plan to be used in purchasing contracts.

When used for inspecting outgoing lots, acceptance sampling plans are often used in conjunction with 100 percent screening of rejected lots where defective items are replaced with acceptable ones. This is known as rectifying inspection. The average outgoing quality (AOQ) is defined as "the expected average quality level of outgoing product for a given value of incoming product quality" (Quality Glossary, 2002, 44). For a process with an incoming long-run average fraction defective, $p$, the AOQ for an acceptance sampling plan with rectifying inspection can be computed as:

$$AOQ = P_{ac}xp\left(\frac{N-n}{N}\right) \tag{11.1}$$

where $P_{ac}$ is the probability of accepting the lot, $p$ is the true fraction defective in the lot, $N$ is the lot size, and $n$ is the sample size.

If $N$ is large relative to $n$, Equation 11.2 provides a reasonable approximation to Equation 11.1.

$$AOQ = P_a p \qquad (11.2)$$

The AOQ changes as the incoming average fraction defective changes. As Figure 11.5 indicates, when lots contain a very low average fraction defective, p, the average fraction defective of outgoing lots is low. Most lots pass without the need for rectifying inspection. As p increases for incoming lots, those lots that pass contain a higher fraction defective, resulting in a higher p for outgoing lots. As p increases further, more lots are rejected and are subject to 100 percent rectifying inspection. The p for lots after rectifying inspection is theoretically 0 (assuming there are no errors in the 100 percent inspection process).

The highest point on the AOQ curve represents the average outgoing quality limit (AOQL). The AOQL represents the highest possible average fraction defective in the outgoing lots resulting from the acceptance sampling plan with rectifying inspection.

All sampling plans require that the specific units for testing be selected randomly. By random we mean that each unit has an equal opportunity to be selected as a test unit. Without random selection, the probability of making a Type I or a Type II error cannot be estimated. One way of thinking about what is meant by the term "statistically valid" is that for a sampling plan to be statistically valid one must be able to estimate the probability of error. Therefore a sampling plan that does not use random sampling cannot be statistically valid.

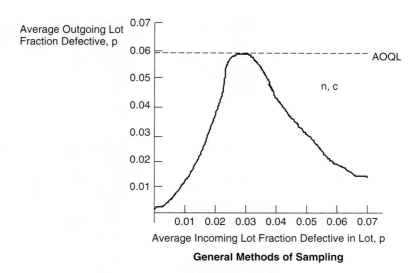

**General Methods of Sampling**

**Figure 11.5.** Average Outgoing Quality (AOQ) Curve

## Methods of Sampling

There are several methods of sampling that are applicable to acceptance sampling plans. These include:

Simple random sampling

Stratified random sampling

Systematic sampling

Cluster sampling

There are advantages and disadvantages to each method.

*Simple random sampling* is the most common method of sampling. This method is defined as "the process of selecting sample units so all units under consideration have the same probability of being selected" (Quality Glossary, 2002, 58). Random sampling frequently utilizes a list of random numbers to determine which units are selected as part of the sample. Figure 11.6 demonstrates one approach to simple random sampling. A pallet load of boxes that comprises a lot is to be evaluated using acceptance sampling. For a sampling plan that calls for the random selection of eight boxes for inspection, each box is assigned a sequential number. Using the table of two-digit random numbers in the figure and starting in column 1, eight boxes (numbers 9, 15, 4, 12, 29, 11, 24, 7) would be selected for inspection. (Note: the numbers 67, 56, 89, 91, 59, 83, 69 are ignored because they are outside the range of the sequence of box numbers.)

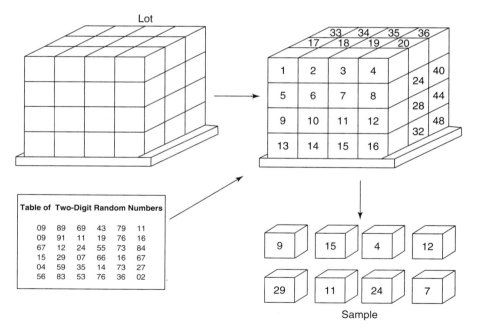

**Figure 11.6.** Simple Random Sampling

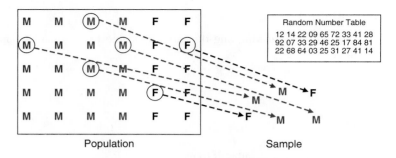

**Figure 11.7.** Stratified Random Sampling

*Stratified random sampling* is used when simple random sampling might produce a sample that would not be representative of the lot. Such a case exists when lots are comprised of the output of several processes. In order to properly represent the lot, the sample should consist of random samples from each process in the proportion that each comprises in the lot. Figure 11.7 shows a population consisting of 20 (67%) males (**m**) and 10 (33%) females (**f**). Stratified random sampling results in a sample containing 4 (67%) males and 2 (33%) females.

Consider a lot comprised of 1000 parts produced on two machines, A and B. Machine A produces twice as many parts per hour as Machine B. Therefore the lot to be sampled consists of approximately 67 percent Machine A parts and 33 percent Machine B parts. The sampling plan calls for 80 parts to be selected for inspection. Using stratified random sampling, 53 parts (80 × 0.67) should be taken at random from the portion of the lot produced by Machine A, and 27 parts (80 × 0.33) should be taken at random from the portion of the lot produced by Machine B.

*Systematic sampling* involves selecting parts for inspection according to a set schedule or plan. An example of systematic sampling would be selecting every *n*th part for inspection from a continuous process. An advantage of systematic sampling is its simplicity. A disadvantage of systematic sampling is that it is not random and it may mask some types of periodic variation in the process. For example, consider the case of the candy kisses shown in Figure 11.8. If they are produced on a machine with three extruders, and one extruder is producing defective candy, systematically sampling every third unit would result in a sample that is 100 percent defective or 100 percent acceptable. In neither case would the sample accurately represent the process.

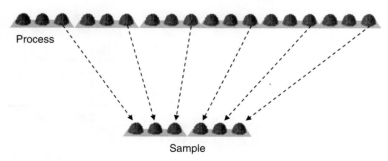

**Figure 11.8.** Systematic Sampling

*Cluster sampling* involves identifying a typical subgroup (cluster) in the population and taking a random sample from the subgroup to represent the population (*ANSI/ASQ Z1.4–2003*, 4). Consider the example used in Figure 11.6. If each box on the pallet contained 100 parts, and a sample of 80 was to be selected for inspection, the eight randomly selected boxes could be considered clusters and 10 parts could be randomly selected from each box.

## SAMPLING TYPES

There are four main sampling types used with acceptance sampling plans:

Single sampling
Double sampling
Multiple sampling
Sequential sampling

Under *single sampling*, one sample is taken at random from the lot under consideration, and the decision to accept or reject the lot is based upon the results of the inspection of the single sample.

Under *double sampling*, a sample smaller than that used for single sampling is taken from the lot for inspection. The results of the inspection may result in one of three decisions:

Accept the lot
Reject the lot
Resample the lot

Figure 11.9 compares single and double sampling procedures.

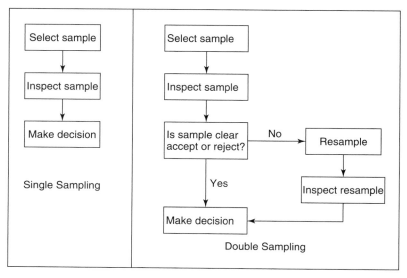

**Figure 11.9.**   Single versus Double Sampling

If the inspection results do not result in a clear-cut accept-or-reject decision, a second sample is taken at random from the lot for inspection. The decision to accept or reject the lot is based upon the result of the inspection of the cumulative sample (i.e., the first and second samples combined).

Under *multiple sampling*, the procedure is the same as for double sampling "except that the number of successive samples required to reach a decision might be more than two" (*ANSI/ASQ Z1.4–2003*, 6).

*Sequential sampling* is a version of multiple sampling whereby units are selected from the lot one at a time. After each unit is inspected a decision is made to accept the lot, reject the lot, or select another unit for inspection.

## SAMPLING PLANS

Three types of sampling plans will be discussed in this section:

Sampling inspection by attributes (*ANSI/ASQ Z1.4-2003*)

Sampling inspection by variables (*ANSI/ASQ Z1.9-2003*)

Dodge-Romig sampling

The sampling inspection by attributes and variables plans focuses on the acceptable quality level (AQL) and the producer's risk. Dodge-Romig sampling plans focus on the lot tolerance percent defective (LTPD) and the consumer's risk.

### Sampling Inspection by Attributes

The most widely accepted plan for sampling inspection by attributes is *ANSI/ASQ Z1.4–2003*. This plan evolved from the now obsolete *MIL-STD 105*. There are seven inspection levels in the Z1.4 system, four special inspection levels (S-1, S-2, S-3, S-4) for use when small sample sizes are required, and three general inspection levels (I, II, III). Usually the general inspection levels are used. General inspection level II is referred to as normal. General inspection level III requires a larger sample size and thus provides more discrimination. General inspection level I requires a smaller sample size and provides less discrimination.

The combination of inspection level and lot size is used to determine the specific sampling plan to use (see Figure 11.10). For example, referring to Figure 11.10, if the lot size is 200 and general inspection level II is to be used, sampling plan code letter G (Figure 11.12) is selected.

The sampling type (single, double, or multiple) must be selected and the AQL used. For example, using Figure 11.12 single sampling and a 1.5 percent AQL, a sample

Table I—Sample Size Code Letters

(See 9.2 and 9.3)

| Lot or Batch Size | Special Inspection Levels | | | | General Inspection Levels | | |
|---|---|---|---|---|---|---|---|
| | S-1 | S-2 | S-3 | S-4 | I | II | III |
| 2 to 8 | A | A | A | A | A | A | B |
| 9 to 15 | A | A | A | A | A | B | C |
| 16 to 25 | A | A | B | B | B | C | D |
| 26 to 50 | A | B | B | C | C | D | E |
| 51 to 90 | B | B | C | C | C | E | F |
| 91 to 150 | B | B | C | D | D | F | G |
| 151 to 280 | B | C | D | E | E | G | H |
| 281 to 500 | B | C | D | E | F | H | J |
| 501 to 1200 | C | C | E | F | G | J | K |
| 1201 to 3200 | C | D | E | G | H | K | L |
| 3201 to 10000 | C | D | F | G | J | L | M |
| 10001 to 35000 | C | D | F | H | K | M | N |
| 35001 to 150000 | D | E | G | J | L | N | P |
| 150001 to 500000 | D | E | G | J | M | P | Q |
| 500001 and over | D | E | H | K | N | Q | R |

**Figure 11.10.** Table I of ANSI/ASQ Z1.4. (*Source*: ANSI/ASQ Z1.4, 10. © 2003, American Society for Quality. Used with permission.)

of size 32 must be taken from the lot. If one or zero nonconformities are found, the lot is accepted. If two or more nonconformities are found, the lot is rejected.

The OC curve for this sampling plan may be found in Chart G at the top of Figure 11.11. Find the curve labeled 1.5, and read the probability of accepting a lot ($P_{ac}$) on the vertical axis for a given true quality (percent defective) for a submitted lot (horizontal axis). For a true percent defective of 10 percent, the probability of accepting a given lot using this sampling plan would be approximately 0.15 or 15 percent. Selected tabulated values of the OC curves are found at the bottom of Figure 11.11 in Table X-G-1. The probability of accepting a lot with 11.6 percent nonconforming units would be 0.10 or 10.0 percent according to the table.

---

### EXAMPLE 11.1

A manufacturer receives a lot containing 250 small electric motors from a new supplier. The purchase order agreement specifies the use of ANSI/ASQ Z1.4, single sampling, general inspection level II, and an AQL of 1.5%.

The incoming inspector uses Table I of Z1.4 (Figure 11.10) to determine that Sampling Plan Code Letter G should be used. Table X-G-2 of Z1.4 (Figure 11.12) specifies a sample size of 32 units. The configuration of the lot facilitates simple random sampling. The inspector uses the random number table in Appendix A to select 32 units from the lot. Inspection of the 32 units finds that 31 units are acceptable and one unit is defective. Table X-G-2 of Z1.4 (Figure 11.12) indicates the lot should be accepted if one or zero units are defective and rejected if two or more units are defective. Therefore the inspector accepts the lot. Note: the one defective unit should be segregated from the lot and held for appropriate disposition.

---

Integral to the effectiveness of this sampling plan is the employment of the switching rules. These are summarized in Figure 11.13 taken from the standard. Sampling starts with normal inspection (Figure 11.14). When two out of five consecutive lots are not accepted, a switch is made to tightened inspection (Figure 11.15). Tightened inspection requires a larger sample size and uses a smaller acceptance number. This brings the OC curve closer to the ideal shape (Figure 11.4). Normal inspection may resume when five consecutive lots are accepted under tightened inspection. Should five lots not be accepted while on tightened inspection, sampling under Z1.4 should be discontinued.

A switch is often made from normal to reduced inspection (Figure 11.16) when 10 consecutive lots are accepted under normal inspection, production is steady, and the switch is approved by the responsible authority. This enables the lot sentence to be determined using a smaller sample size. Figures 11.14–11.16 contain the master tables for normal, tightened, and reduced inspection for single sampling plans. Z1.4 also contains similar master tables for double and multiple sampling plans.

Table X-G—Tables For Sample Size Code Letter: G
Individual Plans

Chart G—Operating Characteristic Curves for Single Sampling Plans
(Curves for Double and Multiple Sampling are Matched as Closely as Practicable)

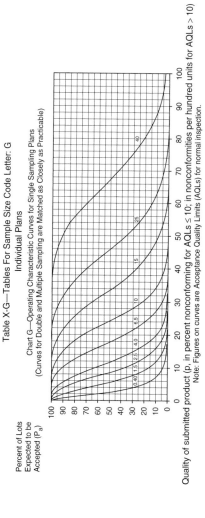

Percent of Lots
Expected to be
Accepted ($P_a$)

Quality of submitted product (p, in percent nonconforming for AQLs ≤ 10; in nonconformities per hundred units for AQLs > 10)

Note: Figures on curves are Acceptance Quality Limits (AQLs) for normal inspection.

Table X-G-1—Tabulated Values for Operation Characteristic Curves for Single Sampling Plans

| $P_a$ | 0.40 | 1.5 | 2.5 | 4.0 | 6.5 | 10 |
|---|---|---|---|---|---|---|
| | p (in percent nonconforming) | | | | | |
| 99.0 | 0.0314 | 0.471 | 1.40 | 2.67 | 5.88 | 9.73 |
| 95.0 | 0.160 | 1.12 | 2.60 | 4.38 | 8.50 | 13.1 |
| 90.0 | 0.329 | 1.67 | 3.49 | 5.56 | 10.2 | 15.1 |
| 75.0 | 0.895 | 3.01 | 5.42 | 7.98 | 13.4 | 19.0 |
| 50.0 | 2.14 | 5.19 | 8.27 | 11.4 | 17.5 | 23.7 |
| 25.0 | 4.24 | 8.19 | 11.9 | 15.4 | 22.3 | 29.0 |
| 10.0 | 6.94 | 11.6 | 15.8 | 19.7 | 27.1 | 34.1 |
| 5.0 | 8.94 | 14.0 | 18.4 | 22.5 | 30.1 | 37.2 |
| 1.0 | 13.4 | 19.0 | 23.8 | 28.1 | 36.0 | 43.2 |
| | 0.65 | 2.5 | 4.0 | 6.5 | 10 | X |
| | Acceptance Quality Limits (Tightened Inspection) | | | | | |

| Acceptance Quality Limits (Normal Inspection) | | | | | | | | | | | |
|---|---|---|---|---|---|---|---|---|---|---|---|
| 0.40 | 1.5 | 2.5 | 4.0 | 6.5 | 10 | X | 15 | X | 25 | X | 40 |
| p ( in nonconformities per hundred units) | | | | | | | | | | | |
| 0.0314 | 0.464 | 1.36 | 2.57 | 5.58 | 9.08 | 11.0 | 14.9 | 19.1 | 23.4 | 32.3 | 39.3 |
| 0.160 | 1.11 | 2.56 | 4.26 | 8.17 | 12.4 | 14.7 | 19.3 | 24.0 | 28.9 | 38.9 | 46.5 |
| 0.329 | 1.66 | 3.44 | 5.45 | 9.85 | 14.6 | 17.0 | 21.9 | 27.0 | 32.2 | 42.7 | 50.8 |
| 0.899 | 3.00 | 5.40 | 7.92 | 13.2 | 18.6 | 21.4 | 26.9 | 32.6 | 38.2 | 49.7 | 58.4 |
| 2.17 | 5.24 | 8.36 | 11.5 | 17.7 | 24.0 | 27.1 | 33.3 | 39.6 | 45.8 | 58.3 | 67.7 |
| 4.33 | 8.41 | 12.3 | 16.0 | 23.2 | 30.3 | 33.8 | 40.7 | 47.6 | 54.4 | 67.9 | 78.0 |
| 7.20 | 12.2 | 16.6 | 20.9 | 29.0 | 36.8 | 40.6 | 48.1 | 55.6 | 62.9 | 77.4 | 88.1 |
| 9.36 | 14.8 | 19.7 | 24.2 | 32.9 | 41.1 | 45.1 | 53.0 | 60.8 | 68.4 | 83.4 | 94.5 |
| 14.4 | 20.7 | 26.3 | 31.4 | 41.0 | 50.0 | 54.4 | 63.0 | 71.3 | 79.5 | 95.6 | 107.0 |
| 2.5 | 4.0 | 6.5 | 10 | X | 15 | X | 25 | X | 40 | X | |

Note: Binomial distribution used for percent nonconforming computations; Poisson for nonconformities per hundred units.

**G**
**PLANS**

**Figure 11.11.** Code Letter G Plan. (*Source:* ANSI/ASQ Z1.4, 43. © 2003 American Society for Quality. Used with permission.)

# G PLANS

Table X-G-2—Sampling Plans for Sample Size Code Letter: G

All data cells show **Ac Re** (Acceptance number, Rejection number).

| Type of Sampling Plan | Cumulative Sample Size | \<Less than 0.40\> | 0.40 | 0.65 | X | 1.0 | 1.5 | 2.5 | 4.0 | 6.5 | 10 | X | 15 | X | 25 | X | 40 | \<Higher than 40\> | Cumulative Sample Size |
|---|---|---|---|---|---|---|---|---|---|---|---|---|---|---|---|---|---|---|---|
| | | *Acceptance Quality Limits (Normal Inspection)* | | | | | | | | | | | | | | | | | |
| Single | 32 | ▽ | 0 1 | Use Code Letter F | Use Code Letter J | Use Code Letter H | 1 2 | 2 3 | 3 4 | 5 6 | 7 8 | X | 10 11 | X | 14 15 | X | 21 22 | △ | 32 |
| Double | 20 | ▽ | * | | | | 0 2 | 0 3 | 1 4 | 2 5 | 3 7 | | 5 9 | | 7 11 | | 11 16 | △ | 20 |
| | 40 | | | | | | 1 2 | 3 4 | 4 5 | 6 7 | 8 9 | | 12 13 | | 18 19 | | 26 27 | | 40 |
| Multiple | 8 | ▽ | * | | | | # 2 | # 2 | # 3 | # 4 | 0 4 | | 0 5 | | 1 7 | | 2 9 | △ | 8 |
| | 16 | | | | | | # 2 | 0 3 | 0 3 | 1 5 | 1 6 | | 3 8 | | 4 10 | | 7 14 | | 16 |
| | 24 | | | | | | 0 2 | 0 3 | 1 4 | 2 6 | 3 8 | | 6 10 | | 8 13 | | 13 19 | | 24 |
| | 32 | | | | | | 0 3 | 1 4 | 2 5 | 3 7 | 5 10 | | 8 13 | | 12 17 | | 19 25 | | 32 |
| | 40 | | | | | | 1 3 | 2 4 | 3 6 | 5 8 | 7 11 | | 11 15 | | 17 20 | | 25 29 | | 40 |
| | 48 | | | | | | 1 3 | 3 5 | 4 6 | 7 9 | 10 12 | | 14 17 | | 21 23 | | 31 33 | | 48 |
| | 56 | | | | | | 2 3 | 4 5 | 6 7 | 9 10 | 13 14 | | 18 19 | | 25 26 | | 37 38 | | 56 |
| *Acceptance Quality Limits (Tightened Inspection)* | | Less than 0.65 | 0.65 | 1.0 | X | 1.5 | 2.5 | 4.0 | 6.5 | 10 | X | 15 | X | 25 | X | 40 | X | Higher than 40 | |

△ = Use next preceding sample size code letter for which acceptance and rejection numbers are available.

▽ = Use next subsequent sample size code letter for which acceptance and rejection numbers are available.

Ac = Acceptance number.

Re = Rejection number.

\* = Use single sampling plan above (or alternatively use code letter K).

\# = Acceptance not permitted at this sample size.

**Figure 11.12.** Code Letter G Plan (*Source:* ANSI/ASQ Z1.4, 44. © 2003, American Society for Quality, used with permission.)

**Switching Rules of ANSI Z1.4 System**

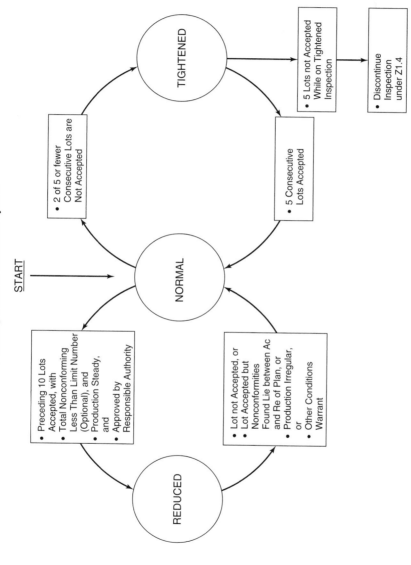

**Figure 11.13.** Figure 1 from ANSI/ASQ Z1.4. (*Source:* ANSI/ASQ Z1.4, 9. © 2003 American Society for Quality. Used with permission.)

Table II-A—Single Sampling Plans for Normal Inspection (Master Table)

(See 9.4 and 9.5)

Acceptance Quality Limits, AQLs, in Percent Nonconforming Items and Nonconformities per 100 Items (Normal Inspection)

*Each cell gives "Ac Re" (Ac = Acceptance number, Re = Rejection number). ↓ = use first sampling plan below the arrow; ↑ = use first sampling plan above the arrow.*

| Sample Size Code Letter | Sample Size | 0.010 | 0.015 | 0.025 | 0.040 | 0.065 | 0.10 | 0.15 | 0.25 | 0.40 | 0.65 | 1.0 | 1.5 | 2.5 | 4.0 | 6.5 | 10 | 15 | 25 | 40 | 65 | 100 | 150 | 250 | 400 | 650 | 1000 |
|---|---|---|---|---|---|---|---|---|---|---|---|---|---|---|---|---|---|---|---|---|---|---|---|---|---|---|---|
| A | 2 | ↓ | ↓ | ↓ | ↓ | ↓ | ↓ | ↓ | ↓ | ↓ | ↓ | ↓ | ↓ | ↓ | ↓ | ↓ | ↓ | 0 1 | 1 2 | 2 3 | 3 4 | 5 6 | 7 8 | 10 11 | 14 15 | 21 22 | 30 31 |
| B | 3 | ↓ | ↓ | ↓ | ↓ | ↓ | ↓ | ↓ | ↓ | ↓ | ↓ | ↓ | ↓ | ↓ | ↓ | ↓ | 0 1 | 1 2 | 2 3 | 3 4 | 5 6 | 7 8 | 10 11 | 14 15 | 21 22 | 30 31 | 44 45 |
| C | 5 | ↓ | ↓ | ↓ | ↓ | ↓ | ↓ | ↓ | ↓ | ↓ | ↓ | ↓ | ↓ | ↓ | ↓ | 0 1 | 1 2 | 2 3 | 3 4 | 5 6 | 7 8 | 10 11 | 14 15 | 21 22 | 30 31 | 44 45 | ↑ |
| D | 8 | ↓ | ↓ | ↓ | ↓ | ↓ | ↓ | ↓ | ↓ | ↓ | ↓ | ↓ | ↓ | ↓ | 0 1 | 1 2 | 2 3 | 3 4 | 5 6 | 7 8 | 10 11 | 14 15 | 21 22 | 30 31 | 44 45 | ↑ | ↑ |
| E | 13 | ↓ | ↓ | ↓ | ↓ | ↓ | ↓ | ↓ | ↓ | ↓ | ↓ | ↓ | ↓ | 0 1 | 1 2 | 2 3 | 3 4 | 5 6 | 7 8 | 10 11 | 14 15 | 21 22 | 30 31 | 44 45 | ↑ | ↑ | ↑ |
| F | 20 | ↓ | ↓ | ↓ | ↓ | ↓ | ↓ | ↓ | ↓ | ↓ | ↓ | ↓ | 0 1 | 1 2 | 2 3 | 3 4 | 5 6 | 7 8 | 10 11 | 14 15 | 21 22 | 30 31 | 44 45 | ↑ | ↑ | ↑ | ↑ |
| G | 32 | ↓ | ↓ | ↓ | ↓ | ↓ | ↓ | ↓ | ↓ | ↓ | ↓ | 0 1 | 1 2 | 2 3 | 3 4 | 5 6 | 7 8 | 10 11 | 14 15 | 21 22 | 30 31 | 44 45 | ↑ | ↑ | ↑ | ↑ | ↑ |
| H | 50 | ↓ | ↓ | ↓ | ↓ | ↓ | ↓ | ↓ | ↓ | ↓ | 0 1 | 1 2 | 2 3 | 3 4 | 5 6 | 7 8 | 10 11 | 14 15 | 21 22 | 30 31 | 44 45 | ↑ | ↑ | ↑ | ↑ | ↑ | ↑ |
| J | 80 | ↓ | ↓ | ↓ | ↓ | ↓ | ↓ | ↓ | ↓ | 0 1 | 1 2 | 2 3 | 3 4 | 5 6 | 7 8 | 10 11 | 14 15 | 21 22 | 30 31 | 44 45 | ↑ | ↑ | ↑ | ↑ | ↑ | ↑ | ↑ |
| K | 125 | ↓ | ↓ | ↓ | ↓ | ↓ | ↓ | ↓ | 0 1 | 1 2 | 2 3 | 3 4 | 5 6 | 7 8 | 10 11 | 14 15 | 21 22 | 30 31 | 44 45 | ↑ | ↑ | ↑ | ↑ | ↑ | ↑ | ↑ | ↑ |
| L | 200 | ↓ | ↓ | ↓ | ↓ | ↓ | ↓ | 0 1 | 1 2 | 2 3 | 3 4 | 5 6 | 7 8 | 10 11 | 14 15 | 21 22 | 30 31 | 44 45 | ↑ | ↑ | ↑ | ↑ | ↑ | ↑ | ↑ | ↑ | ↑ |
| M | 315 | ↓ | ↓ | ↓ | ↓ | ↓ | 0 1 | 1 2 | 2 3 | 3 4 | 5 6 | 7 8 | 10 11 | 14 15 | 21 22 | 30 31 | 44 45 | ↑ | ↑ | ↑ | ↑ | ↑ | ↑ | ↑ | ↑ | ↑ | ↑ |
| N | 500 | ↓ | ↓ | ↓ | ↓ | 0 1 | 1 2 | 2 3 | 3 4 | 5 6 | 7 8 | 10 11 | 14 15 | 21 22 | 30 31 | 44 45 | ↑ | ↑ | ↑ | ↑ | ↑ | ↑ | ↑ | ↑ | ↑ | ↑ | ↑ |
| P | 800 | ↓ | ↓ | ↓ | 0 1 | 1 2 | 2 3 | 3 4 | 5 6 | 7 8 | 10 11 | 14 15 | 21 22 | 30 31 | 44 45 | ↑ | ↑ | ↑ | ↑ | ↑ | ↑ | ↑ | ↑ | ↑ | ↑ | ↑ | ↑ |
| Q | 1250 | ↓ | ↓ | 0 1 | 1 2 | 2 3 | 3 4 | 5 6 | 7 8 | 10 11 | 14 15 | 21 22 | 30 31 | 44 45 | ↑ | ↑ | ↑ | ↑ | ↑ | ↑ | ↑ | ↑ | ↑ | ↑ | ↑ | ↑ | ↑ |
| R | 2000 | ↓ | 0 1 | 1 2 | 2 3 | 3 4 | 5 6 | 7 8 | 10 11 | 14 15 | 21 22 | 30 31 | 44 45 | ↑ | ↑ | ↑ | ↑ | ↑ | ↑ | ↑ | ↑ | ↑ | ↑ | ↑ | ↑ | ↑ | ↑ |

↓ = Use the first sampling plan below the arrow. If sample size equals or exceeds lot size, carry out 100 percent inspection.

↑ = Use the first sampling plan above the arrow.

Ac = Acceptance number.

Re = Rejection number.

**Figure 11.14.** Table II-A from ANSI/ASQ Z1.4. (*Source:* ANSI/ASQ Z1.4, 11. © 2003 American Society for Quality. Used with permission.)

Table II-B—Single Sampling Plans for Tightened Inspection (Master Table)

(See 9.4 and 9.5)

Acceptance Quality Limits (Tightened Inspection)

In each cell below, values are given as "Ac Re" (Acceptance number / Rejection number). ↓ = use first sampling plan below arrow (if sample size equals or exceeds lot or batch size, do 100 percent inspection). ↑ = use first sampling plan above arrow.

| Sample Size Code Letter | Sample Size | 0.010 | 0.015 | 0.025 | 0.040 | 0.065 | 0.10 | 0.15 | 0.25 | 0.40 | 0.65 | 1.0 | 1.5 | 2.5 | 4.0 | 6.5 | 10 | 15 | 25 | 40 | 65 | 100 | 150 | 250 | 400 | 650 | 1000 |
|---|---|---|---|---|---|---|---|---|---|---|---|---|---|---|---|---|---|---|---|---|---|---|---|---|---|---|---|
| A | 2 | ↓ | ↓ | ↓ | ↓ | ↓ | ↓ | ↓ | ↓ | ↓ | ↓ | ↓ | ↓ | ↓ | ↓ | ↓ | ↓ | 0 1 | ↓ | 1 2 | 2 3 | 3 4 | 5 6 | 8 9 | 12 13 | 18 19 | 27 28 |
| B | 3 | ↓ | ↓ | ↓ | ↓ | ↓ | ↓ | ↓ | ↓ | ↓ | ↓ | ↓ | ↓ | ↓ | ↓ | ↓ | 0 1 | ↓ | 1 2 | 2 3 | 3 4 | 5 6 | 8 9 | 12 13 | 18 19 | 27 28 | 41 42 |
| C | 5 | ↓ | ↓ | ↓ | ↓ | ↓ | ↓ | ↓ | ↓ | ↓ | ↓ | ↓ | ↓ | ↓ | ↓ | 0 1 | ↓ | 1 2 | 2 3 | 3 4 | 5 6 | 8 9 | 12 13 | 18 19 | 27 28 | 41 42 | ↑ |
| D | 8 | ↓ | ↓ | ↓ | ↓ | ↓ | ↓ | ↓ | ↓ | ↓ | ↓ | ↓ | ↓ | ↓ | 0 1 | ↓ | 1 2 | 2 3 | 3 4 | 5 6 | 8 9 | 12 13 | 18 19 | 27 28 | 41 42 | ↑ | ↑ |
| E | 13 | ↓ | ↓ | ↓ | ↓ | ↓ | ↓ | ↓ | ↓ | ↓ | ↓ | ↓ | ↓ | 0 1 | ↓ | 1 2 | 2 3 | 3 4 | 5 6 | 8 9 | 12 13 | 18 19 | 27 28 | 41 42 | ↑ | ↑ | ↑ |
| F | 20 | ↓ | ↓ | ↓ | ↓ | ↓ | ↓ | ↓ | ↓ | ↓ | ↓ | ↓ | 0 1 | ↓ | 1 2 | 2 3 | 3 4 | 5 6 | 8 9 | 12 13 | 18 19 | 27 28 | 41 42 | ↑ | ↑ | ↑ | ↑ |
| G | 32 | ↓ | ↓ | ↓ | ↓ | ↓ | ↓ | ↓ | ↓ | ↓ | ↓ | 0 1 | ↓ | 1 2 | 2 3 | 3 4 | 5 6 | 8 9 | 12 13 | 18 19 | 27 28 | 41 42 | ↑ | ↑ | ↑ | ↑ | ↑ |
| H | 50 | ↓ | ↓ | ↓ | ↓ | ↓ | ↓ | ↓ | ↓ | ↓ | 0 1 | ↓ | 1 2 | 2 3 | 3 4 | 5 6 | 8 9 | 12 13 | 18 19 | 27 28 | 41 42 | ↑ | ↑ | ↑ | ↑ | ↑ | ↑ |
| J | 80 | ↓ | ↓ | ↓ | ↓ | ↓ | ↓ | ↓ | ↓ | 0 1 | ↓ | 1 2 | 2 3 | 3 4 | 5 6 | 8 9 | 12 13 | 18 19 | 27 28 | 41 42 | ↑ | ↑ | ↑ | ↑ | ↑ | ↑ | ↑ |
| K | 125 | ↓ | ↓ | ↓ | ↓ | ↓ | ↓ | ↓ | 0 1 | ↓ | 1 2 | 2 3 | 3 4 | 5 6 | 8 9 | 12 13 | 18 19 | 27 28 | 41 42 | ↑ | ↑ | ↑ | ↑ | ↑ | ↑ | ↑ | ↑ |
| L | 200 | ↓ | ↓ | ↓ | ↓ | ↓ | ↓ | 0 1 | ↓ | 1 2 | 2 3 | 3 4 | 5 6 | 8 9 | 12 13 | 18 19 | 27 28 | 41 42 | ↑ | ↑ | ↑ | ↑ | ↑ | ↑ | ↑ | ↑ | ↑ |
| M | 315 | ↓ | ↓ | ↓ | ↓ | ↓ | 0 1 | ↓ | 1 2 | 2 3 | 3 4 | 5 6 | 8 9 | 12 13 | 18 19 | 27 28 | 41 42 | ↑ | ↑ | ↑ | ↑ | ↑ | ↑ | ↑ | ↑ | ↑ | ↑ |
| N | 500 | ↓ | ↓ | ↓ | ↓ | 0 1 | ↓ | 1 2 | 2 3 | 3 4 | 5 6 | 8 9 | 12 13 | 18 19 | 27 28 | 41 42 | ↑ | ↑ | ↑ | ↑ | ↑ | ↑ | ↑ | ↑ | ↑ | ↑ | ↑ |
| P | 800 | ↓ | ↓ | ↓ | 0 1 | ↓ | 1 2 | 2 3 | 3 4 | 5 6 | 8 9 | 12 13 | 18 19 | 27 28 | 41 42 | ↑ | ↑ | ↑ | ↑ | ↑ | ↑ | ↑ | ↑ | ↑ | ↑ | ↑ | ↑ |
| Q | 1250 | ↓ | ↓ | 0 1 | ↓ | 1 2 | 2 3 | 3 4 | 5 6 | 8 9 | 12 13 | 18 19 | 27 28 | 41 42 | ↑ | ↑ | ↑ | ↑ | ↑ | ↑ | ↑ | ↑ | ↑ | ↑ | ↑ | ↑ | ↑ |
| R | 2000 | ↓ | 0 1 | ↓ | 1 2 | 2 3 | 3 4 | 5 6 | 8 9 | 12 13 | 18 19 | 27 28 | 41 42 | ↑ | ↑ | ↑ | ↑ | ↑ | ↑ | ↑ | ↑ | ↑ | ↑ | ↑ | ↑ | ↑ | ↑ |
| S | 3150 | 0 1 | ↑ | 1 2 | 2 3 | 3 4 | 5 6 | 8 9 | 12 13 | 18 19 | 27 28 | 41 42 | ↑ | ↑ | ↑ | ↑ | ↑ | ↑ | ↑ | ↑ | ↑ | ↑ | ↑ | ↑ | ↑ | ↑ | ↑ |

↓ = Use first sampling plan below arrow. If sample size equals or exceeds lot or batch size, do 100 percent inspection.
↑ = Use first sampling plan above arrow.
Ac = Acceptance number.
Re = Rejection number.

**Figure 11.15.** Table II-B from ANSI/ASQ Z1.4. (*Source:* ANSI/ASQ Z1.4, 12. © 2003 American Society for Quality. Used with permission.)

Table II-C—Single Sampling Plans for Reduced Inspection (Master Table)

*(See 9.4 and 9.5)*

Acceptance Quality Limits (Reduced Inspection)†

*Each cell below gives the pair "Ac Re" (Acceptance number / Rejection number). ↓ = use first sampling plan below arrow; ↑ = use first sampling plan above arrow.*

| Sample Size Code Letter | Sample Size | 0.010 | 0.015 | 0.025 | 0.040 | 0.065 | 0.10 | 0.15 | 0.25 | 0.40 | 0.65 | 1.0 | 1.5 | 2.5 | 4.0 | 6.5 | 10 | 15 | 25 | 40 | 65 | 100 | 150 | 250 | 400 | 650 | 1000 |
|---|---|---|---|---|---|---|---|---|---|---|---|---|---|---|---|---|---|---|---|---|---|---|---|---|---|---|---|
| A | 2 | ↓ | ↓ | ↓ | ↓ | ↓ | ↓ | ↓ | ↓ | ↓ | ↓ | ↓ | ↓ | ↓ | ↓ | ↓ | ↓ | 0 1 | 1 2 | 2 3 | 3 4 | 5 6 | 7 8 | 10 11 | 14 15 | 21 22 | 30 31 |
| B | 2 | ↓ | ↓ | ↓ | ↓ | ↓ | ↓ | ↓ | ↓ | ↓ | ↓ | ↓ | ↓ | ↓ | ↓ | ↓ | ↓ | 0 1 | 1 2 | 2 3 | 3 4 | 5 6 | 7 8 | 10 11 | 14 15 | 21 22 | 30 31 |
| C | 2 | ↓ | ↓ | ↓ | ↓ | ↓ | ↓ | ↓ | ↓ | ↓ | ↓ | ↓ | ↓ | ↓ | 0 1 | 0 2 | 1 3 | 1 4 | 2 5 | 3 6 | 5 8 | 7 10 | 10 13 | 14 17 | 21 24 | ↑ | ↑ |
| D | 3 | ↓ | ↓ | ↓ | ↓ | ↓ | ↓ | ↓ | ↓ | ↓ | ↓ | ↓ | ↓ | 0 1 | 0 2 | 1 3 | 1 4 | 2 5 | 3 6 | 5 8 | 7 10 | 10 13 | 14 17 | 21 24 | ↑ | ↑ | ↑ |
| E | 5 | ↓ | ↓ | ↓ | ↓ | ↓ | ↓ | ↓ | ↓ | ↓ | ↓ | ↓ | 0 1 | 0 2 | 1 3 | 1 4 | 2 5 | 3 6 | 5 8 | 7 10 | 10 13 | 14 17 | 21 24 | ↑ | ↑ | ↑ | ↑ |
| F | 8 | ↓ | ↓ | ↓ | ↓ | ↓ | ↓ | ↓ | ↓ | ↓ | ↓ | 0 1 | 0 2 | 1 3 | 1 4 | 2 5 | 3 6 | 5 8 | 7 10 | 10 13 | 14 17 | 21 24 | ↑ | ↑ | ↑ | ↑ | ↑ |
| G | 13 | ↓ | ↓ | ↓ | ↓ | ↓ | ↓ | ↓ | ↓ | ↓ | 0 1 | 0 2 | 1 3 | 1 4 | 2 5 | 3 6 | 5 8 | 7 10 | 10 13 | 14 17 | 21 24 | ↑ | ↑ | ↑ | ↑ | ↑ | ↑ |
| H | 20 | ↓ | ↓ | ↓ | ↓ | ↓ | ↓ | ↓ | ↓ | 0 1 | 0 2 | 1 3 | 1 4 | 2 5 | 3 6 | 5 8 | 7 10 | 10 13 | 14 17 | 21 24 | ↑ | ↑ | ↑ | ↑ | ↑ | ↑ | ↑ |
| J | 32 | ↓ | ↓ | ↓ | ↓ | ↓ | ↓ | ↓ | 0 1 | 0 2 | 1 3 | 1 4 | 2 5 | 3 6 | 5 8 | 7 10 | 10 13 | 14 17 | 21 24 | ↑ | ↑ | ↑ | ↑ | ↑ | ↑ | ↑ | ↑ |
| K | 50 | ↓ | ↓ | ↓ | ↓ | ↓ | ↓ | 0 1 | 0 2 | 1 3 | 1 4 | 2 5 | 3 6 | 5 8 | 7 10 | 10 13 | 14 17 | 21 24 | ↑ | ↑ | ↑ | ↑ | ↑ | ↑ | ↑ | ↑ | ↑ |
| L | 80 | ↓ | ↓ | ↓ | ↓ | ↓ | 0 1 | 0 2 | 1 3 | 1 4 | 2 5 | 3 6 | 5 8 | 7 10 | 10 13 | 14 17 | 21 24 | ↑ | ↑ | ↑ | ↑ | ↑ | ↑ | ↑ | ↑ | ↑ | ↑ |
| M | 125 | ↓ | ↓ | ↓ | ↓ | 0 1 | 0 2 | 1 3 | 1 4 | 2 5 | 3 6 | 5 8 | 7 10 | 10 13 | 14 17 | 21 24 | ↑ | ↑ | ↑ | ↑ | ↑ | ↑ | ↑ | ↑ | ↑ | ↑ | ↑ |
| N | 200 | ↓ | ↓ | ↓ | 0 1 | 0 2 | 1 3 | 1 4 | 2 5 | 3 6 | 5 8 | 7 10 | 10 13 | 14 17 | 21 24 | ↑ | ↑ | ↑ | ↑ | ↑ | ↑ | ↑ | ↑ | ↑ | ↑ | ↑ | ↑ |
| P | 315 | ↓ | ↓ | 0 1 | 0 2 | 1 3 | 1 4 | 2 5 | 3 6 | 5 8 | 7 10 | 10 13 | 14 17 | 21 24 | ↑ | ↑ | ↑ | ↑ | ↑ | ↑ | ↑ | ↑ | ↑ | ↑ | ↑ | ↑ | ↑ |
| Q | 500 | ↓ | 0 1 | 0 2 | 1 3 | 1 4 | 2 5 | 3 6 | 5 8 | 7 10 | 10 13 | 14 17 | 21 24 | ↑ | ↑ | ↑ | ↑ | ↑ | ↑ | ↑ | ↑ | ↑ | ↑ | ↑ | ↑ | ↑ | ↑ |
| R | 800 | 0 1 | 0 2 | 1 3 | 1 4 | 2 5 | 3 6 | 5 8 | 7 10 | 10 13 | 14 17 | 21 24 | ↑ | ↑ | ↑ | ↑ | ↑ | ↑ | ↑ | ↑ | ↑ | ↑ | ↑ | ↑ | ↑ | ↑ | ↑ |

▼ = Use first sampling plan below arrow. If sample size equals or exceeds lot or batch size, do 100 percent inspection.
▲ = Use first sampling plan above arrow.
Ac = Acceptance number.
Re = Rejection number.
† = If the acceptance number has been exceeded, but the rejection number has not been reached, accept the lot, but reinstate normal inspection (see 10.1.4).

**Figure 11.16.** Table II-C from ANSI/ASQ Z1.4. (*Source*: ANSI/ASQ Z1.4, 13. © 2003, American Society for Quality. Used with permission.)

## EXAMPLE 11.2

A manufacturer receives a lot containing 250 small electric motors from an existing supplier. The purchase order agreement specifies the use of ANSI/ASQ Z1.4, single sampling, general inspection level II, and an AQL of 1.5%. Quality Control records indicate the last 12 lots from this supplier have been accepted and that Reduced Inspection (Figure 11.13) has been approved.

The incoming inspector uses Table 1 of Z1.4 (Figure 11.10) to determine that Sampling Plan Code Letter G should be used. Table II-C of Z1.4 (Figure 11.16) specifies a sample size of 13 units. The configuration of the lot facilitates simple random sampling. The inspector uses the random number table in Appendix A to select 13 units from the lot. Inspection of the 13 units finds that 12 units are acceptable and one unit is defective. Table II-C of Z1.4 (Figure 11.16) indicates that the lot should be accepted if zero units are defective and rejected if two or more units are defective. If one unit is defective the footnote specifies that the lot should be accepted, but that normal inspection should be reinstated for the next lot. Therefore the inspector accepts the lot and notes in the Quality Control record that the next lot must be inspected using Normal Inspection. Note: the one defective unit should be segregated from the lot and held for appropriate disposition.

## Sampling Inspection by Variables

*ANSI/ASQ Z1.9-2003* comprises standards for sampling inspection by variables. Z1.9 evolved from the now obsolete *MIL-STD 414*. These plans "apply to a single quality characteristic which can be measured on a continuous scale, and for which the quality is expressed in terms of percent nonconforming" (*ANSI/ASQ Z1.9–2003*, vii). The plans "assume that measurements of the quality characteristic are independent, identically distributed normal random variables" (*ANSI/ASQ Z1.9–2003*, vii).

Variables data provide more information than do attributes data. Attributes data simply define the units under test as *conforming* (acceptable) or *nonconforming* (not acceptable). Variables data provide actual measurement data for the quality characteristic under consideration, thus providing information such as how close the observations are to the specification limit—information that is not available using attributes data. The Z1.9 procedures generally follow the plan for using *ANSI/ASQ Z1.4–2003*. The switching rules (for switching to/from normal, tightened, and reduced inspection) are essentially identical to those for *ANSI/ASQ Z1.4–2003*.

There are five inspection levels in the Z1.9 system: two special inspection levels (S3 and S4,) and three general inspection levels (I, II, and III). Usually the general inspection levels are used. As with sampling inspection by attributes, the combination of inspection level and lot size is used to determine the specific sampling plan to use (see Figure 11.17). For example, using Figure 11.17, if the lot size is 200, the specification is one-sided (single specification limit), and general inspection level II is used and sample size code letter G (Figure 11.18) is selected.

Table A-1
AQL Conversion Table

| For Specified AQL Values Falling within These Ranges | | | Use this AQL Value |
|---|---|---|---|
| – | to | 0.109 | 0.10 |
| 0.110 | to | 0.164 | 0.15 |
| 0.165 | to | 0.279 | 0.25 |
| 0.280 | to | 0.439 | 0.40 |
| 0.440 | to | 0.669 | 0.65 |
| 0.700 | to | 1.09 | 1.0 |
| 1.10 | to | 1.64 | 1.5 |
| 1.65 | to | 2.79 | 2.5 |
| 2.80 | to | 4.39 | 4.0 |
| 4.40 | to | 6.99 | 6.5 |
| 7.00 | to | 10.9 | 10.0 |

Table A-2[1]
Sample Size Code Letters[2]

| Lot Size | | | Special S3 | Special S4 | General I | General II | General III |
|---|---|---|---|---|---|---|---|
| 2 | to | 8 | B | B | B | B | C |
| 9 | to | 15 | B | B | B | B | D |
| 16 | to | 25 | B | B | B | C | E |
| 26 | to | 50 | B | B | C | D | F |
| 51 | to | 90 | B | B | D | E | G |
| 91 | to | 150 | B | C | E | F | H |
| 151 | to | 280 | B | D | F | G | I |
| 281 | to | 400 | C | E | G | H | J |
| 401 | to | 500 | C | E | G | I | J |
| 501 | to | 1,200 | D | F | H | J | K |
| 1,201 | to | 3,200 | E | G | I | K | L |
| 3,201 | to | 10,000 | F | H | J | L | M |
| 10,001 | to | 35,000 | G | I | K | M | N |
| 35,001 | to | 150,000 | H | J | L | N | P |
| 150,001 | to | 500,000 | H | K | M | P | P |
| 500,001 | and | over | H | K | N | P | P |

[1]The theory governing inspection by variables depends on the properties of the normal distribution and, therefore, this method of inspection is only applicable when there is reason to believe that the frequency distribution is normal.

[2]Sample size code letters given in body of table are applicable when the indicated inspection levels are to be used.

**Figure 11.17.** Tables A-1 and A-2 of ANSI/ASQ Z1.9. (*Source*: ANSI/ASQ Z1.9, 5–6. © 2003 American Society for Quality. Used with permission.)

Table B-1                                           Standard Deviation Method
Master Table for Normal and Tightened Inspection for Plans Based on Variability Unknown
(Single Specification Limit—Form 1)

| Sample Size Code Letter | Sample Size | Acceptance Quality Limits (Normal Inspection) | | | | | | | | | | | |
|---|---|---|---|---|---|---|---|---|---|---|---|---|---|
| | | T | 0.10 | 0.15 | 0.25 | 0.40 | 0.65 | 1.00 | 1.50 | 2.50 | 4.00 | 6.50 | 10.00 |
| | | k | k | k | k | k | k | k | k | k | k | k | k |
| B | 3 | | | | | | | | | 1.12 | 0.958 | 0.765 | 0.566 |
| C | 4 | | | | | | | 1.46 | 1.34 | 1.17 | 1.01 | 0.815 | 0.617 |
| D | 5 | | | | | 1.77 | 1.65 | 1.52 | 1.40 | 1.24 | 1.07 | 0.874 | 0.675 |
| E | 7 | | 2.22 | 2.13 | 2.00 | 1.88 | 1.75 | 1.62 | 1.50 | 1.33 | 1.15 | 0.955 | 0.755 |
| F | 10 | 2.44 | 2.34 | 2.24 | 2.11 | 1.98 | 1.84 | 1.71 | 1.59 | 1.41 | 1.23 | 1.03 | 0.828 |
| G | 15 | 2.53 | 2.42 | 2.32 | 2.19 | 2.06 | 1.92 | 1.79 | 1.65 | 1.48 | 1.30 | 1.09 | 0.885 |
| H | 20 | 2.58 | 2.47 | 2.37 | 2.23 | 2.10 | 1.96 | 1.83 | 1.69 | 1.51 | 1.33 | 1.12 | 0.916 |
| I | 25 | 2.61 | 2.50 | 2.40 | 2.26 | 2.13 | 1.98 | 1.71 | 1.72 | 1.53 | 1.35 | 1.14 | 0.935 |
| J | 35 | 2.66 | 2.55 | 2.45 | 2.31 | 2.18 | 2.03 | 1.89 | 1.76 | 1.57 | 1.39 | 1.18 | 0.968 |
| K | 50 | 2.72 | 2.61 | 2.50 | 2.36 | 2.22 | 2.07 | 1.94 | 1.80 | 1.61 | 1.42 | 1.21 | 1.00 |
| L | 75 | 2.77 | 2.66 | 2.55 | 2.41 | 2.27 | 2.12 | 1.98 | 1.84 | 1.65 | 1.46 | 1.25 | 1.03 |
| M | 100 | 2.80 | 2.69 | 2.58 | 2.43 | 2.29 | 2.14 | 2.00 | 1.86 | 1.67 | 1.48 | 1.26 | 1.05 |
| N | 100 | 2.84 | 2.73 | 2.62 | 2.47 | 2.33 | 2.18 | 2.03 | 1.89 | 1.70 | 1.51 | 1.29 | 1.07 |
| P | 200 | 2.85 | 2.73 | 2.62 | 2.47 | 2.33 | 2.18 | 2.04 | 1.89 | 1.70 | 1.51 | 1.29 | 1.08 |
| | | 0.10 | 0.15 | 0.25 | 0.40 | 0.65 | 1.00 | 1.50 | 2.50 | 4.00 | 6.50 | 10.00 | |

Acceptance Quality Limits (Tightened Inspection)

All AQL values are in percent nonconforming. T denotes plan used exclusively on tightened inspection and provides symbol for identification of appropriate OF curve.

Use first sampling plan below arrow; that is, both sample size as well as k value. When sample size equals or exceeds lot size, every item in the lot must be inspected.

**Figure 11.18.** Table B-1 of ANSI/ASQ Z1.9. (*Source*: ANSI/ASQ Z1.9, 36. © 2003 American Society for Quality. Used with permission.)

---

## EXAMPLE 11.3:   EXAMPLE OF SAMPLING INSPECTION BY VARIABLES CALCULATIONS

A lot containing 50 bottles of a pressurized solution is presented for inspection. The specification for this product requires that the pressure in each bottle not exceed 50 psi (single specification limit). [Normal inspection level II is used with an AQL of 2.5%]. Using Figures 11.17 and 11.18, a sample of size 5 is required and the k value (acceptability constant) to be used is 1.24. The calculations, using Form 1, are:

Sample Size (n) = 5
AQL = 2.5%
Acceptability Constant (k) = 1.24

The samples are randomly selected and tested with the following results obtained:

| Sample | Pressure, psi | Pressure Squared |
|--------|--------------|------------------|
| 1 | 49.5 | 2,450.25 |
| 2 | 49.2 | 2,420.64 |
| 3 | 49.2 | 2,420.64 |
| 4 | 49.4 | 2,440.36 |
| 5 | 49.1 | 2,410.81 |
| Sum of measurements = | 246.4 | |
| Sum of squared measurements = | | 12,142.70 |

Correction Factor $[CF = (\Sigma x)^2/n] = 12,142.59$
Corrected Sum of Squares $[SS = \Sigma x^2 - CF] = 12,142.70 - 12,142.59 = 0.11$
Variance $[V = SS/(n-1)] = 0.11/4 = 0.028$
Estimated Lot Standard Deviation $[s = \sqrt{V}] = \sqrt{0.028} = 0.167$
Sample Mean $[\overline{X} = \Sigma x/n] = 49.28$
Specification Limit $[U] = 50.00$
$(U - \overline{X})/s = 4.31$
Compare $(U - \overline{X})/s$ with k: $4.31 > 1.24$
Accept the lot since $(U - \overline{X})/s$ is greater than k.

Sample size code letter G specifies a sample of size 15 be randomly selected from the lot. Note that this is less than half the size of the sample required for the same lot size under sampling inspection by attributes. Sampling inspection by variables provides roughly the same discriminating ability (OC curve) using a smaller sample size than sampling inspection by attributes. If the AQL selected is 2.5 percent, the k value (acceptability constant) to be used is 1.48. Example 11.3 illustrates the calculations required to determine the disposition of a lot using this sampling plan.

## Dodge-Romig Sampling Plans

Dodge-Romig sampling plans are designed for use with rectifying inspection where rejected lots are subjected to 100 percent inspection. There are Dodge-Romig tables for desired AOQL levels. These tables show the sample size, n, (based upon the lot size) and acceptance number, c, for the specified AOQL. The tables also show the resulting LTPD where the probability of acceptance, $P_{ac}$, on the OC curve is equal to 0.10 (see Figure 11.19).

Using the partial table in Figure 11.19, the sample size for a lot of size 300 taken from a process whose process average proportion defective is 0.75 percent would be 26. The acceptance number would be 1 (accept with zero or one nonconforming units, reject with two or more). The probability of accepting a lot with 14.6 percent nonconforming would be 0.10. This means that the probability of rejecting incoming lots as bad as 14.6 percent defective is 0.90 (1.00–0.10).

Single-Sampling Plans for AOQL = 3.0%

| Lot Size | Process Average | | | | | | | | | | | | | |
|---|---|---|---|---|---|---|---|---|---|---|---|---|---|---|
| | 0–0.06% | | | 0.07–0.60% | | | 0.61–1.20% | | | 1.21–1.80% | | | 1.81–2.40% | | |
| | LTPD | | | LTPD | | | LTPD | | | LTPD | | | LTPD | | |
| | n | c | % | n | c | % | n | c | % | n | c | % | n | c | % |
| | | | | | | | | | | | | | | | |
| 11–50 | 10 | 0 | 19.0 | 10 | 0 | 19.0 | 10 | 0 | 19.0 | 10 | 0 | 19.0 | 10 | 0 | 19.0 |
| 51–100 | 11 | 0 | 18.0 | 11 | 0 | 18.0 | 11 | 0 | 18.0 | 11 | 0 | 18.0 | 11 | 0 | 18.0 |
| 101–200 | 12 | 0 | 17.0 | 12 | 0 | 17.0 | 12 | 0 | 17.0 | 25 | 1 | 15.1 | 24 | 1 | 15.1 |
| 201–300 | 12 | 0 | 17.0 | 12 | 0 | 17.0 | 26 | 1 | 14.6 | 26 | 1 | 14.6 | 26 | 1 | 14.6 |
| 301–400 | 12 | 0 | 17.0 | 12 | 0 | 17.0 | 26 | 1 | 14.7 | 26 | 1 | 14.7 | 41 | 2 | 12.7 |
| | | | | | | | | | | | | | | | |

**Figure 11.19.** Extract from Dodge-Romig AOQL Table (Dodge & Romig, 1959).

There also are Dodge-Romig tables for desired LTPD levels. These tables show the sample size, n (based upon the lot size), and acceptance number, c, for the specified LTPD. The tables also show the resulting AOQL for each plan (see Figure 11.20).

Using the partial table in Figure 11.20, the sample size for a lot of size 300 taken from a process whose process average proportion defective is 0.45 percent would be 165. The acceptance number would be 0 (accept with zero nonconforming units, reject with one or more). The AOQL associated with this sampling plan (assuming rectifying inspection) would be 0.10 percent.

Single-Sampling Plans for LTPD = 1.0%

| Lot Size | Process Average | | | | | | | | | | | | | |
|---|---|---|---|---|---|---|---|---|---|---|---|---|---|---|
| | 0 | | | 0.01–0.10% | | | 0.11–0.20% | | | 0.31–0.40% | | | 0.41–0.50% | | |
| | AOQL | | | AOQL | | | AOQL | | | AOQL | | | AOQL | | |
| | n | c | % | n | c | % | n | c | % | n | c | % | n | c | % |
| 1–120 | All | 0 | 0 | All | 0 | 0 | All | 0 | 0 | All | 0 | 0 | All | 0 | 0 |
| 121–150 | 120 | 0 | 0.06 | 120 | 0 | 0.06 | 120 | 0 | 0.06 | 120 | 0 | 0.06 | 120 | 0 | 0.06 |
| 151–200 | 140 | 0 | 0.08 | 140 | 0 | 0.08 | 140 | 0 | 0.08 | 140 | 0 | 0.08 | 140 | 0 | 0.08 |
| 201–300 | 165 | 0 | 0.10 | 165 | 0 | 0.10 | 165 | 0 | 0.10 | 165 | 0 | 0.10 | 165 | 0 | 0.10 |
| 301–400 | 175 | 0 | 0.12 | 175 | 0 | 0.12 | 175 | 0 | 0.12 | 175 | 0 | 0.12 | 175 | 0 | 0.12 |
| | | | | | | | | | | | | | | | |

**Figure 11.20.** Extract from Dodge-Romig LTPD Table (Dodge & Romig, 1959).

## SUMMARY

Inspection of 100 percent of the units comprising lots is often not practical. Acceptance sampling provides a means for making the decision to either accept or reject the lot based upon the inspection of a sample taken from that lot. There is an appropriate place for acceptance sampling even within a statistical process control environment. It is important to understand the theory of sampling in order to properly utilize sampling plans. There are sampling plans that focus on the AQL (producer's risk) and others that focus on the LTPD (consumer's risk). Each type of sampling plan has its appropriate place within the quality system. Understanding the bases for each type of sampling plan can enable users to select the correct type for their situation.

All of the sampling plans rely on random sampling in order to ensure validity of the result. Samples may be selected using simple, stratified, systematic, and cluster sampling. Each has advantages and disadvantages. Each sampling plan has an associated operating characteristics (OC) curve that enable estimation of the Type I and Type II errors associated with the plan.

## DISCUSSION QUESTIONS

1. Discuss the integration of acceptance sampling with statistical process control in a quality system.
2. Why is it important that a sample taken from a lot be random?
3. What is meant by the term "statistically valid"?
4. Discuss the information to be obtained from the OC curve for a particular sampling plan.
5. How can a quality engineer make the OC curve closer to the ideal shape?
6. Discuss the significance of the difference between AQL and LTPD.
7. What method of sampling would be most appropriate when the population consists of two categories of members in unequal numbers?
8. Discuss the circumstances where cluster sampling would be appropriate.
9. What are "switching rules" and why are they important?
10. What are some of the risks associated with using systematic sampling?
11. What is the difference between simple random sampling and stratified random sampling? When might stratified random sampling be appropriate?
12. Why might 100 percent inspection not result in zero defective products in a lot?
13. What are the conditions that would make 100 percent inspection infeasible?
14. Why do quality experts say that statistical process control (SPC) is preferable to acceptance sampling?
15. Explain the differences between ANSI/ASQ Z1.4 and ANSI/ASQ Z1.9.
16. Explain the difference between Type I and Type II errors.

# PROBLEMS

1. Supplier A ships materials to your company in lots of 200 units. Your company uses an ANSI/ASQ Z1.4 acceptance sampling plan (general inspection level II) to inspect incoming lots of material. Supplier A has been on tightened inspection, but the last five consecutive lots have been accepted. What sample size code letter should be used for the next lot?

2. Using the OC curve in Figure 11.3 of the text, what is the probability of accepting a lot whose true fraction defective is 0.04?

3. Using the OC curve in Figure 11.3 of the text, what is the probability of rejecting a lot whose true fraction defective is 0.03?

4. Use the first two digits in the first column of the random number table in Appendix A to select five sample boxes from the lot depicted in Figure 11.6. Which five boxes would be selected?

5. There are 600 female and 400 male students enrolled in basic mathematics courses at State University. The chair of the Mathematics Department wants to select a stratified random sample of 50 students to participate in a survey. How many male and how many female students should be in the sample of 50?

6. A company is using sampling plan code letter G of ANSI/ASQ Z1.4 to inspect an incoming lot of material. They are using normal inspection, single sampling, and an AQL of 2.5 percent. Using Figure 11.12 in the text, how many units from the lot should be inspected? What disposition should be made of the lot if one defective unit is found in the sample? If one defective units are found in the sample?

7. The Ace Manufacturing Company just received a lot of 3000 units from Ron's Metal Extrusions, Inc., a new supplier. Ace uses ANSI/ASQ Z1.4. What sampling plan code letter should they use for this lot?

8. The Ace Manufacturing Company just received a lot of 3000 units from Ron's Metal Extrusions, Inc. This is the eleventh lot received since Ron's became a supplier to Ace. The previous 10 lots were accepted under ANSI/ASQ Z1.4. What sampling plan code letter should they use for the sixth lot?

9. The Ace Manufacturing Company just received a lot of 3000 units from Ron's Metal Extrusions, Inc. Ron's is a long-time supplier to Ace. Ace has been using reduced inspection under ANSI/ASQ Z1.4. The most recent lot from Ron's, received last week, was rejected. What sampling plan code letter should they use for this lot received this week?

10. A company is using Sampling Plan Code Letter G of ANSI/ASQ Z1.4 to inspect an incoming lot of material. They are using normal inspection, double sampling, and an AQL of 4.0 percent. The inspector found two defective units in the sample of 20. What action should the inspector take? What

action is appropriate if only one defective unit is found in the first 20 units inspected? What action is appropriate if five defective units are found in the first 20 units inspected?

11. A company is using the Dodge-Romig Single-Sampling Plans for AOQL = 3.0 percent to inspect an incoming lot of material containing 350 units. Based on past experience, the average proportion defective for this supplier's process is 0.10 percent. Using Figure 11.19 in the text, how many units from the lot should be inspected? What disposition of the lot should be made if two units in the sample are found to be defective?

12. A company is using the Dodge-Romig Single-Sampling Plans for LTPD = 1.0 percent to inspect an incoming lot of material containing 350 units. Based on past experience, the average proportion defective for this supplier's process is 0.10 percent. Using Figure 11.20 in the text, how many units from the lot should be inspected? What disposition of the lot should be made if one unit in the sample is found to be defective?

13. A company is using General Inspection Level II of ANSI/ASQ Z1.9 to inspect an incoming lot of material. What sample size code letter should they use for a lot containing 300 units?

## CASE STUDY 11.1: *The Turkell Stud Mill*

© 1996 Victor E. Sower, Ph.D., C.Q.E.

The Turkell Stud Mill is part of an international wood products corporation headquartered in the United States. The Turkell Mill produces dimensional lumber used in the construction industry. Your quality consulting firm has been engaged to assist Turkell in improving their incoming log inspection process. The general manager estimates that the mill incurs losses in excess of $100,000 per year due to overpayment for logs.

Turkell purchases its logs primarily from independent loggers. These loggers transport logs they cut to Turkell on trucks which contain from 20 to 50 logs. Because all of Turkell's products have a nominal length of 8 feet, they cut the logs into 8'9'' blocks before milling. Logs whose length is not a multiple of 8''9'' contain unusable wood that must be chipped and sold to one of the company's paper mills. The value of the chips is a small fraction of the value of the studs produced from useable lengths.

The problem is that the company has found that it is not feasible to inspect every log as received. Incoming logs may contain up to four blocks (35'). Trucks may contain up to 50 logs. With the current inspection procedure, only the logs on the outside of the shipment (face logs) can be accurately measured for length. The only way to accurately measure the length of all logs in a shipment is to "spread them"—that is, to unload the truck in the inspection area. This process is expensive and too time consuming to be feasible.

Currently, when a truckload of logs arrives at the mill, all of the logs receive an end inspection for cracks, decay, and similar defects, and the end diameter is measured. Four outside (face) logs are measured for length using a tape measure. An adjustment is made for any of the four measured logs that is not a block multiple. A block shorter than 8'9" is value adjusted. If all of the four logs measured require adjustment, the load is spread and all the logs are measured. Using the lengths obtained from the sample of four logs, the end diameters, and a "taper factor," the number of board feet in the shipment is determined. The payment to the logger is determined from the number of board feet in the load.

Based upon information obtained from the six previous months' milling operation, it is believed that 4.23 percent of the incoming logs are shorter than block length. Incoming inspection records from the same period indicate that about 10 percent of the short blocks are found and the appropriate adjustment made. The value lost by failing to adjust for a short block is about $9.00. The mill purchases between 250,000 and 300,000 logs per year.

There are other lumber mills in the area to which the loggers can sell their logs. The Turkell Mill general manager is concerned that if the inspection time per load is significantly increased, or if a new inspection process is perceived by the loggers to be unfair, he will lose many of his suppliers to other mills. He has asked that you evaluate the situation and make recommendations for reducing their losses due to short blocks that are missed at incoming inspection.

## EXERCISES AND ACTIVITIES

1. Last week your incoming quality inspector accepted a lot of 200 units of motor housings from Lexco Co. using ANSI/ASQ Z1.4, normal inspection, and an AQL of 1.5 percent. This morning the production manager came into

your office with a box containing eight defective motor housings. "You guys in Quality Control are not doing your jobs," he said, more than a little irritated. I collected these defective housings from the lot you accepted last week. "I thought we were using a sampling plan that guaranteed we would not accept lots with greater than 1.5 percent defective units. This lot had 4 percent defective units in it. What's going on here?" How should you respond to the production manager?

2. Purchase a bag of jelly beans. How would you ensure that a sample taken of a bulk item like jelly beans would be random?

3. Purchase 20 small bags of Plain M&Ms™. Consider this to be a lot. Devise a random sampling plan to select a sample of 30 individual M&Ms™ from the lot for inspection. If the inspection involves tasting, explain why 100 percent inspection would be inappropriate.

## SUPPLEMENTARY READINGS

*ANSI/ASQC S2-1995. Introduction to Attribute Sampling.*

*ANSI/ASQ Z1.4-2003. Sampling Procedures and Tables for Inspection by Attributes.*

*ANSI/ASQ Z1.9-2003. Sampling Procedures and Tables for Inspection by Variables for Percent Nonconforming.*

Dodge, H. F., & H. G. Romig. (1959). *Sampling Inspection Tables, Single and Double Sampling,* 2nd edition. New York: Wiley.

Duncan, A. J. (1986). *Quality Control and Industrial Statistics,* 5th edition. Homewood, NJ: Irwin.

*MIL-STD-1235C. Continuous Sampling Plan 1 (CSP-1).* (1988).

*MIL-STD-1916. DOD Preferred Methods for Acceptance of Product.* (1996).

## REFERENCES

*ANSI/ASQ Z1.4-2003. Sampling Procedures and Tables for Inspection by Attributes.*

*ANSI/ASQ Z1.9-2003. Sampling Procedures and Tables for Inspection by Variables for Percent Nonconforming.*

Deming, W. E. (1986). *Out of the Crisis.* Cambridge, MA: MIT Press.

Dodge, H., & H. Romig. (1959). *Sampling Inspection Tables, Single and Double Sampling,* 2d edition. New York: Wiley.

Gitlow, H., A. Oppenheim, & R. Oppenheim. (1995). *Quality Management,* 2nd edition. Burr Ridge, IL: Irwin.

Montgomery, D. C. (1996). *Introduction to Statistical Quality Control,* 3rd edition. New York: John Wiley & sons.

"Quality Glossary." (2002). *Quality Progress* 35(7), 43–61.

Sower, V. E., J. Motwani, & M.J. Savoie. (1993). "Are Acceptance Sampling and Statistical Process Control Complementary or Incompatible?" *Quality Progress* 26(9), 85–89.

# CHAPTER TWELVE

# *Quality Costs*

## CHAPTER OBJECTIVES

After completing this chapter, the reader should be able to:

- list and define the four categories of quality costs;
- assign specific costs to each cost of quality (COQ) category;
- discuss the goal of a quality cost system;
- discuss quality cost data collection, interpretation, and reporting; and
- discuss the importance of integrating COQ with continuous quality improvement.

Allusions to quality costs first appeared in the 1930s in the work of Shewhart (1931) and, to a lesser extent, Miner (1933) and Crocket (1935). Formalization of the concept of cost of quality developed in the 1950s from the work of Joseph Juran (1951), Armand Feigenbaum (1957), and Harold Freeman (1960). Armand Feigenbaum, in his 1956 article that launched the terminology of total quality control, discussed three categories of quality costs: prevention costs, appraisal costs, and failure costs. He argued that "the ultimate end result is that total quality control brings about a sizable reduction in overall quality costs, and a major alteration in the proportions of the three cost segments" (Feigenbaum, 1956). ASQ's Quality Cost Committee, established in 1961, worked to formalize the concept and to promote its use (Bottorff, 1997). Philip Crosby's publication of *Quality is Free* in 1979 provided probably the biggest boost to popularizing the COQ concept beyond the quality profession (Beecroft, 2001). In that work, Crosby (1979, 15) wrote that "quality is measured by the cost of quality which . . . is the expense of nonconformance—the cost of doing things wrong." The term "cost of quality" was coined by Crosby. The term "cost of poor quality" (COPQ) is becoming more popular. For the purpose of the discussion in this chapter, these terms are considered synonymous.

Some companies estimate their total cost of (poor) quality (COQ) to be as much as 30–40 percent of a product's sales price (Harrington, 2004). Imagine the value that would be created if that could be eliminated. Where does each dollar saved on COQ go?

**COQ Savings**

Gross Profit

Cost of quality (COQ is a "term coined by Philip Crosby referring to the cost of poor quality."

Cost of poor quality (COPQ) is the "costs associated with providing poor quality products or services."

(Quality Glossary, 2002, 47)

Cost of quality can be used to evaluate a quality system and facilitate efforts directed toward improving the performance of that system. A routine and systematic approach to collecting and classifying quality costs is considered to be an important part of a modern quality system.

## THE CATEGORIES OF QUALITY COSTS

Historically, quality costs have been divided into three main categories: *prevention* costs, *appraisal* costs, and *failure* costs. ASQ subdivides failure costs into *internal* and *external failure* costs, yielding four categories (Campanella, 1999, 5) (see Figure 12.1).

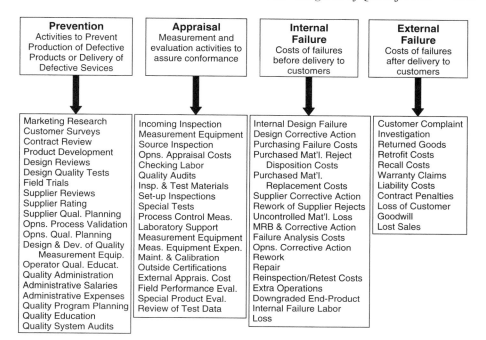

| **Prevention**<br>Activities to Prevent<br>Production of Defective<br>Products or Delivery of<br>Defective Sevices | **Appraisal**<br>Measurement and<br>evaluation activities to<br>assure conformance | **Internal Failure**<br>Costs of failures<br>before delivery to<br>customers | **External Failure**<br>Costs of failures<br>after delivery to<br>customers |
|---|---|---|---|
| Marketing Research<br>Customer Surveys<br>Contract Review<br>Product Development<br>Design Reviews<br>Design Quality Tests<br>Field Trials<br>Supplier Reviews<br>Supplier Rating<br>Supplier Qual. Planning<br>Opns. Process Validation<br>Opns. Qual. Planning<br>Design & Dev. of Quality<br>    Measurement Equip.<br>Operator Qual. Educat.<br>Quality Administration<br>Administrative Salaries<br>Administrative Expenses<br>Quality Program Planning<br>Quality Education<br>Quality System Audits | Incoming Inspection<br>Measurement Equipment<br>Source Inspection<br>Opns. Appraisal Costs<br>Checking Labor<br>Quality Audits<br>Insp. & Test Materials<br>Set-up Inspections<br>Special Tests<br>Process Control Meas.<br>Laboratory Support<br>Measurement Equipment<br>Meas. Equipment Expen.<br>Maint. & Calibration<br>Outside Certifications<br>External Apprais. Cost<br>Field Performance Eval.<br>Special Product Eval.<br>Review of Test Data | Internal Design Failure<br>Design Corrective Action<br>Purchasing Failure Costs<br>Purchased Mat'l. Reject<br>    Disposition Costs<br>Purchased Mat'l.<br>    Replacement Costs<br>Supplier Corrective Action<br>Rework of Supplier Rejects<br>Uncontrolled Mat'l. Loss<br>MRB & Corrective Action<br>Failure Analysis Costs<br>Opns. Corrective Action<br>Rework<br>Repair<br>Reinspection/Retest Costs<br>Extra Operations<br>Downgraded End-Product<br>Internal Failure Labor<br>Loss | Customer Complaint<br>Investigation<br>Returned Goods<br>Retrofit Costs<br>Recall Costs<br>Warranty Claims<br>Liability Costs<br>Contract Penalties<br>Loss of Customer<br>Goodwill<br>Lost Sales |

**Figure 12.1.** Examples of Quality Cost Elements (*Source*: Adapted from Campanella, 1999, 188–189)

*Prevention costs* are "the costs of all activities specifically designed to prevent poor quality in products and services" (Campanella, 1999, 5). ASQ defines prevention costs as "costs incurred by actions taken to prevent a nonconformance from occurring" (Quality Glossary, 2002, 55), and the ASQ Quality Cost Committee (Campanella, 1999, 5, 202–204) lists 31 specific elements of prevention costs (see Figure 12.1). These include the following: (1.1.1) marketing research, (1.1.2) customer/user perception surveys/clinics, (1.2) product/service design development, (1.2.5) field trials, (1.3) purchasing prevention costs, (1.3.1) supplier reviews, (1.3.2) supplier rating, (1.4) operations (manufacturing or service) prevention costs, (1.4.5) operator quality education, (1.4.6) operator SPC/process control, (1.5) quality administration, (1.5.1) administrative salaries, (1.5.3) quality program planning, (1.5.7) quality system audits, (1.6) other prevention costs. A principle associated with quality cost systems is that dollars spent in prevention are worth more than those spent in the other categories because these are the only dollars spent to prevent the production of poor-quality products and services. For this reason, prevention costs are often viewed as investments rather than costs.

*Appraisal costs* are defined as "the costs associated with measuring, evaluating, or auditing products or services to ensure conformance to quality standards and performance requirements" (Campanella, 1999, 23). The ASQ Quality Cost Committee (Campanella, 5, 202–204) lists 25 specific elements of appraisal costs. These include purchasing appraisal costs, receiving or incoming inspections and tests, measurement equipment, operations (manufacturing or service) appraisal costs, planned operations inspections, tests, audits, checking labor, set-up inspections and tests, maintenance and calibration labor, external appraisal costs, field-performance evaluation, review of test and inspection data, and miscellaneous quality evaluations.

*Internal failure costs* are defined as "the costs resulting from products or services not conforming to requirements or customer/user needs" that "occur prior to delivery or shipment . . . to the customer" (Campanella, 1999, 23). Included in the 26 internal failure cost elements (Campanella, 1999, 5, 202–204) are product/service design failure costs (internal), rework due to design changes, scrap due to design changes, purchasing failure costs, purchased material reject disposition costs, supplier corrective action, operations (product or service) failure costs, material review and corrective action costs, troubleshooting or failure analysis costs (operations), operations rework and repair costs, scrap costs (operations), internal failure labor losses, and other internal failure costs.

*External failure costs* are defined as "the costs resulting from products or services not conforming to requirements or customer/user needs" that "occur after delivery or shipment of the product, and during or after furnishing of a service, to the customer" (Campanella, 1999, 23). The ASQ Quality Cost Committee (Campanella, 1999, 5, 202–204) provides the following list of specific external failure cost elements: complaint investigations/customer or user service; returned goods; retrofit costs; recall costs; warranty claims; liability costs; penalties; customer/user goodwill; lost sales; other external failure costs.

Deming referred to these external failure costs as "costs of warranty." According to Deming (1982, 121–123), costs of warranty are "unknown and unknowable." He illustrates this point by citing a 1983 survey that showed a satisfied car owner is likely to buy four more cars of the same make over the following 12 years. A dissatisfied owner will share his or her complaints with an average of 16 other people. The lost profit (cost effect) resulting from these potential customers who now might not consider this make of automobile is extremely difficult to determine.

Crosby does not share the same despair that these costs are unknowable. According to Crosby (1979, 16), "those who assume that some tasks are just plain unmeasureable" are wrong. "Anything can be measured if you have to do it." Most organizations have some means in place to track costs of returned goods. Many also systematically track retrofit and recall costs, and the cost of warranty claims, and may also provide information about penalty costs. Often tracking complaint investigations is simply a matter of adding an extra category to a time-reporting system or reclassifying an indirect time cost category. Information about liability costs will be time-offset from the incident that created the cost, depending upon when the liability is recognized by the accounting system. It is the other elements of external failure cost that prove to be so elusive.

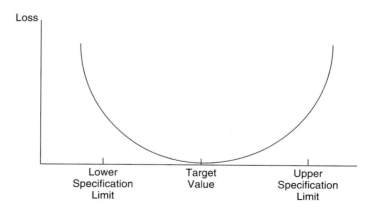

**Figure 12.2.** Taguchi Loss Function

G. Taguchi's (1986, 1) work suggests that failure costs are traditionally understated. He developed a loss function that shows that there is a cost (loss) incurred when products conform to specifications but do not fall exactly on the target value. The loss increases the further away the actual value is from the target value (see Figure 12.2). An illustration of this concept involves the production of gold-plated contacts for use in automobile air bags. Contacts where the gold plating is applied to the high side of the specification create extra material costs for the manufacturer and may result in a tolerance build-up problem for the customer. Contacts plated on the low side of the specification may suffer from reduced reliability under certain field conditions. In both cases, the plating thickness is within the specification limits but not on the target value. Quality cost systems that only track the costs of nonconforming products and services miss the extra costs associated with failing to produce products on the target value.

## THE GOAL OF A COQ SYSTEM

According to Crosby (1979, 103), the goal of a quality cost system is to provide a means of showing management "that reducing the cost of quality is in fact an opportunity to increase profits without raising sales, buying equipment, or hiring new people." In addition to getting management's attention, a cost of quality system also "provides a measurement base for seeing how quality improvement is doing" (Crosby, 1979, 104). Campanella (1999, 9) echoes this idea by defining the "goal of any quality cost system . . . is to facilitate quality improvement efforts that will lead to operating cost reduction opportunities . . . The strategy for using quality costs is quite simple: (1) take direct attack on failure costs in an attempt to drive them to zero; (2) invest in the 'right' prevention activities to bring about improvement; (3) reduce appraisal costs according to results achieved; and (4) continuously evaluate and redirect prevention efforts to gain further improvement."

Many companies do a poor job of tracking their costs of quality. A recent study (Sower, Quarles, & Broussard, 2007) found that about 66 percent of the 393 firms surveyed did not systematically track COQ. Among the reasons cited are:

- lack of management support or absence of management interest in tracking such costs. Specific explanations concerning this lack of support included lack of concern for how much and in what way quality does pay; management philosophy and company culture not supportive of quality costing; quality costing being "paperwork" that management does not perceive to have enough value; and management belief that there is no value in any efforts to fully measure costs of quality.

- company economic conditions or status contribute to the lack of cost of quality tracking. These include the company being a start-up company; a growing company with business practice behind the times; a lean company with little overhead; company is too small; and downsizing.

- lack of knowledge of "how" to track the cost of quality and of the benefits of a COQ program was a common reason cited for not tracking. This category includes not knowing what elements to include in the cost of quality; lack of knowledge of quality principles from management on down; and lack of experienced manpower to accomplish the task.

- lack of adequate accounting and computer systems necessary to track cost of quality. Specific explanations in this regard deal with a lack of tools to collect, organize, filter, and report quality costs; no accounting mechanism provided in financial reporting system to track quality costs; and the accounting system and resources being inadequate to perform standard COQ calculations common in the industry.

- organizations do not see the benefit of COQ or that they need to focus on areas that they perceive to be more important. Table 12.1 is an example of COQ report that enumerates the time costs. This type of report can support better decisions.

Often, only customer returns [cost of warranty in Deming's (1982, 123) terms] are tracked and recorded as quality costs. The costs of providing test and inspection facilities and personnel are lumped into overhead. Scrap costs are booked as a material cost variance. Rework costs are recorded as a labor variance or sometimes even included as part of the standard labor cost. Such an accounting system provides "visible figures" that understate the true cost of quality. These flawed data produce flawed decisions.

"Cost of Finding Lost Bags Put at $1.6 Billion a Year." This headline in the February 22, 2005, *Houston Chronicle* documents one example of the cost of poor quality in an industry that is in financial crisis. The industry is investigating replacing bar code labels with radio frequency identification (RFID) tags to allow remote tracking of baggage in an effort to minimize this cost.

**TABLE 12.1. Example of Cost of Quality Report**

| Cost | This Month Amount | % of Total | % of Sales | % of Costs | Last Month Amount | % of Total | % of Sales | % of Costs |
|---|---|---|---|---|---|---|---|---|
| **Prevention Costs** | | | | | | | | |
| Quality Planning Seminar | 11,000 | | | | 500 | | | |
| QA Manager's Salary | 6,000 | | | | 6,000 | | | |
| QA Engineering | 28,000 | | | | 27,000 | | | |
| Process Capability Studies | 4,000 | | | | 7,000 | | | |
| QIS Costs | 4,500 | | | | 5,500 | | | |
| SPC Training | 3,500 | | | | 8,500 | | | |
| TOTAL | $ 57,000 | 36.8% | 2.59% | 4.75% | $ 54,500 | 33.9% | 2.10% | 4.12% |
| **Appraisal Costs** | | | | | | | | |
| Test Laboratory | 24,000 | | | | 26,000 | | | |
| Gage Calibration & R&R | 2,000 | | | | 1,000 | | | |
| Receiving Inspection | 6,000 | | | | 6,500 | | | |
| Process Inspection | 18,000 | | | | 19,500 | | | |
| TOTAL | $ 50,000 | 32.3% | 2.27% | 4.17% | $ 53,000 | 33.0% | 2.04% | 4.42% |
| **Internal Failure Costs** | | | | | | | | |
| Scrap | 19,500 | | | | 21,500 | | | |
| Rework | 14,000 | | | | 13,300 | | | |
| Downgrade Costs | 6,500 | | | | 7,400 | | | |
| TOTAL | $ 40,000 | 25.8% | 1.82% | 3.33% | $ 42,200 | 26.4% | 1.62% | 3.25% |
| **External Failure Costs** | | | | | | | | |
| Returned goods | 4,400 | | | | 6,300 | | | |
| Warranty repair costs | 3,700 | | | | 4,800 | | | |
| TOTAL | $ 8,100 | 5.2% | 0.37% | 0.68% | $ 11,100 | 6.9% | 0.43% | 0.85% |
| **TOTAL QUALITY COSTS** | $ 155,000 | 100% | 7.05% | 12.92% | 160,800 | 100% | 6.18% | 12.34% |
| **SALES** | $ 2,200,000 | | | | $ 2,600,000 | | | |
| **TOTAL COSTS** | $1,200,000 | | | | $1,300,000 | | | |

## COQ DATA COLLECTION, INTERPRETATION, AND REPORTING

Collection of quality cost data usually begins with an analysis of data already being collected by cost accounting. Much of the cost of quality data is probably already being collected, but is classified into budget categories instead of quality cost categories. With the assistance of the cost accountant, the quality engineer can identify a substantial portion of the quality cost information. For example, salaries for inspectors, quality control technicians and others whose primary function involves sampling, inspection and testing of incoming materials, work in progress, and finished goods can be broken out of the indirect salaries budget category and identified as appraisal costs. Indirect time reported by direct labor personnel to accomplish rework can be identified in the labor variance accounts and be classified as internal failure costs. Scrap costs listed in a material usage variance account can be identified as internal failure costs. Customer returns listed in a returns and allowances budget account can be identified as external failure costs. Money spent for employee training in quality principles and methods can be extracted from indirect cost categories and identified as prevention costs (see Table 12.1).

The collaboration with the cost accounting function cannot end with the identification of certain quality costs. A system must be developed to routinely track and report cost of quality data. These cost of quality systems are most effective (as are budget systems) when they report actual dollars and also when those dollars are related to an appropriate base. An increase or decrease in total cost of quality does not tell the whole story unless, for example, sales are constant. If sales are rising and all other things are equal, quality costs would be expected to rise proportionally. Reporting quality costs as a percentage of sales provides a better (if still incomplete) picture of real trends in quality costs. In a dynamic product-pricing environment, a sales base might not be the most appropriate. Fluctuations in price will affect sales and in turn affect quality costs as a percentage of sales. In this case a production unit base might make more sense. An even better approach might be to report quality costs as a percentage of total manufacturing costs. This ratio of cost dollars to cost dollars avoids some of the distortions due to price changes that can result from reporting the ratio of cost dollars to sales dollars (all other factors remain constant).

A company tracks COQ both as a percentage of sales and total cost. A price change can distort the information in COQ if calculated as a percentage of sales. COQ as a percentage of cost is unaffected by a price change. Consider the effect of a 5% increase in sales prices at the beginning of Month 2.

|                    | Month 1    | Month 2    |
|--------------------|------------|------------|
| Sales, $           | 1,000,000  | 1,050,000  |
| COQ, $             | 200,000    | 200,000    |
| Total Cost, $      | 700,000    | 700,000    |
| COQ/Sales, %       | 20.0       | 19.0       |
| COQ/Total Cost, %  | 28.6       | 28.6       |

COQ/Sales have improved but the only real change is the price increase.

An increase in production costs can distort the information in COQ if calculated as a percentage of total costs. Consider the effect of a 5 percent increase in total cost at the beginning of Month 2.

|                    | Month 1    | Month 2    |
|--------------------|------------|------------|
| Sales, $           | 1,000,000  | 1,000,000  |
| COQ, $             | 200,000    | 200,000    |
| Total Cost, $      | 700,000    | 735,000    |
| COQ/Sales, %       | 20.0       | 20.0       |
| COQ/Total Cost, %  | 28.6       | 27.2       |

COQ/Total Cost has improved but the only real change is the cost increase.

Some quality costs do not show up immediately. When product delivery pipelines are long, customer returns resulting from a production problem might not begin to show up for months after the problem has been identified and corrected. The quality cost system must provide sufficient detail to be able to account for this lag.

Collection of COQ data is facilitated in companies already using activity-based costing (ABC) and/or enterprise resource planning (ERP) systems. ABC "can be considered the mathematics used to reassign costs accurately to cost objects, that is, outputs, products, services, customers. Its primary purpose is for profitability analysis" (Cokins, 1946, 40). ABC systems flow resource costs into final cost objects. These can be further differentiated into user-defined categories called activity metrics or attributes. Among the most commonly used activity metrics are quality costs as shown in Figure 12.3. Use of activity metrics in an ABC system can be a relatively simple way to collect, analyze, and report COQ data.

While activity-based costing provides the conceptual underpinning for capturing and managing the cost of quality, ERP systems provide the recordkeeping and reporting processes that can be used to apply those concepts. ERP systems (such

| Prevention | Appraisal | Internal Failure | External Failure |
|---|---|---|---|
| • Training<br>• Advanced quality planning<br>• SPC implementation<br>• Error proofing | • Receiving inspection<br>• On-line inspection<br>• End-of-line inspection | • Scrap<br>• Rework<br>• Unplanned downtime | • Response to complaints<br>• Warranty charges<br>• Expediting late shipments<br>• Product liability lawsuits |

**Figure 12.3.** Examples of ABC Cost of Quality Activity Metrics (*Source*: Adapted from Cokins, 1996.)

as SAP R/3) can be used to record and report the cost of quality in either simple or complex applications. For example, in the R/3 system, this can be accomplished either through the controlling (CO) module that is a basic element of the system or through the more sophisticated quality management (QM) module that functions in addition to the basic system.

In using the CO module, the process can range from including inspection activities as an element of the routing of a manufactured product to creating "internal orders" to capture and report the costs of the various quality activities that occur in operations. Routing element activities could be used to determine appraisal costs. Internal orders could be used to capture prevention and failure costs.

In the more sophisticated QM application, quality-related costs can be collected and evaluated as well as settled (charged) to overhead cost centers, production orders, WBS elements, sales orders, projects, or processes. In the QM module, these costs are recorded when processing quality inspections (appraisal) or when processing quality notifications for rework (internal or external failure costs). The QM module also provides the capabilities to establish sample-drawing instructions, produce inspection instructions, accumulate and settle appraisal costs for several materials or inspection lots, accumulate appraisal costs for single inspection lots, and accumulate nonconformity costs (internal and external). In conjunction with the controlling module, the QM module produces reports for use in managing quality related costs.

*Activity-based costing* (ABC) is a cost accounting system that accumulates costs based on activities performed and then uses cost drivers to allocate these costs to products or other bases, such as customers, markets, or projects. It is an attempt to allocate overhead costs on a more realistic basis than direct labor or machine hours.

*Enterprise resources planning* (ERP) is a framework for organizing, defining, and standardizing the business processes necessary to effectively plan and control an organization so the organization can use its internal knowledge to seek external advantage.

(Blackstone & Cox, 2005, 2, 38)

# INTEGRATING QUALITY COSTS INTO THE QUALITY IMPROVEMENT SYSTEM

ANSI/ISO/ASQ Q9004-2000 suggests financial measurement as an appropriate way to assess "the organization's performance in order to determine whether planned objectives have been achieved." Reporting quality system activities and effectiveness in financial terms is an increasingly important approach to linking continual improvement of the quality system to performance improvement of the organization. The state of a firm's quality system is reflected in the way in which costs are distributed among the cost of quality categories. This cost distribution is also helpful in identifying ways in which quality dollars might be spent more effectively. Figure 12.4a illustrates

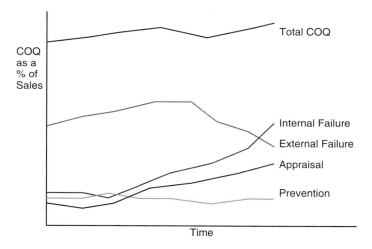

**Figure 12.4a.** Cost of Quality Distribution Over Time

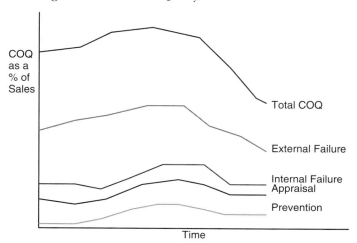

**Figure 12.4b.** Cost of Quality Distribution Over Time

changes in one firm's cost of quality (COQ) distribution over time. In this illustration, the firm reacted to increasing external failure costs simply by increasing the number of inspectors (appraisal cost). Increased inspection detected more nonconforming parts that increased the internal failure cost. Although external failure costs were decreased, the total cost of quality was not reduced.

Figure 12.4b shows a different reaction to the same situation. In this case the firm responded to increasing external failure costs by spending time and money to discover the root cause of the problem and to improve its quality system to correct the problem and prevent its recurrence. While internal failure costs and appraisal costs increased initially, they declined over time as the quality system was improved. And over time, the total cost of quality declined.

Prevention costs can be viewed as a form of investment rather than as a cost because dollars allocated here work to prevent the production of nonconforming products or services. Appraisal costs detect nonconforming products after they are produced, and failure costs account for the nonconforming products produced. As it is cheaper to do things right the first time, it is logical to seek to increase prevention costs as a proportion of total quality costs. The question of what proportions are appropriate for each category is best addressed in relative terms. How does this period's distribution compare to last period's? How does our distribution compare with best-of-class companies? Over time, increasing prevention costs coupled with decreasing costs in the other three categories, and decreasing total cost of quality can be an indication of an improving quality system. And each dollar saved in total COQ reduction translates into an additional dollar of earnings.

The quality-improvement tools discussed in Chapter 8 can be employed to analyze cost of quality data and to provide direction for improvement efforts based upon that analysis. In a situation where total COQ are increasing due primarily to an increase in external failure costs (Figure 12.4a, close to origin), Pareto analysis of the returned goods and warranty service data would reveal the most frequent reasons for failure. Figure 12.5 clearly shows that most of the customer returns are associated with the switch—with "broken switch" being the single most frequently occurring problem. Cause-and-effect analysis (Figure 12.6) is undertaken to determine possible

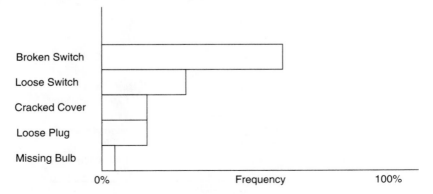

**Figure 12.5.**  Pareto Analysis of Returned Product Data

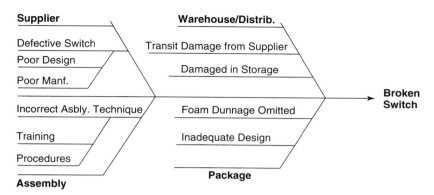

**Figure 12.6.** Cause-and-Effect Analysis—Broken Switch

causes for broken switches. Each cause is investigated, and the principle root cause of the increasing external failure costs can be identified. Effective corrective action can now be directed toward the specific root cause of the problem.

In this example, the root cause was determined to be supplier related—a high proportion of nonconforming switches was being received from the supplier. Investigation showed that the problem resulted from poor manufacturing practices in the supplier's facility. Initially, total COQ increased as the firm worked with the supplier to correct the problem. After the problem was corrected, both internal and external failure costs decreased substantially while prevention costs increased as the firm adopted a supplier-certification program to improve the quality system to prevent recurrence of this type of problem. The total COQ was substantially decreased.

It should be remembered that quality systems, not COQ systems, create improvement. But without some systematic approach to tracking COQ, it is more difficult to identify potential areas for improvement and to track improvement results (see Figure 12.7). A COQ system did not generate the $53 million first year savings at Xerox (Carr, 1955) or the cumulative $1.5 billion savings at Dow Chemical (1999). It was the quality systems in these companies that were responsible for these savings. The COQ identified the problem areas and documented the costs and savings over time.

Cost of quality information can provide input to broader measures of organizational performance such as the balanced scorecard (Kaplan & Norton, 1992). The balanced scorecard looks at a business organization from four perspectives: financial (how do we look to shareholders?); internal (what must we excel at?); customer (how do customers see us?); and innovation and learning (can we continue to improve and create value?). Cost of quality information can be used to operationalize some of the measures used to assess these perspectives. For example, reductions in total quality costs manifest as increased profits (financial). Reductions in internal failure costs reflect greater manufacturing efficiency (internal). Lower external failure costs may reflect improved customer satisfaction (customer). Sustained reduction in total COQ may reflect improved manufacturing learning (innovation and learning).

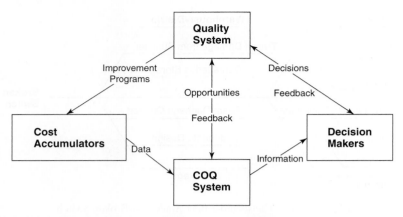

**Figure 12.7.** COQ System as Translator or Overlay (*Source*: Sower & Quarles, 2003, 626)

## SUMMARY

Cost of quality systems do not of themselves improve quality. But they can provide valuable information and feedback to the quality-improvement process. This chapter discussed the quality cost system and its component categories of quality costs—prevention, appraisal, internal failure, and external failure—and how a COQ system can be integrated into an organization's quality management and improvement system. The purpose of a quality cost system is to guide continuous improvement efforts and to provide a measurement base to evaluate the effectiveness of those efforts. Close to real time feedback about improvement efforts provided in business terms (dollars) can result in the conversion of the outputs of the continuous improvement process from intangible to tangible. An effective continuous improvement program guided by the cost of quality system will result in reduced total quality costs and increased profit.

*Acknowledgement:* Thanks to Dr. N. Ross Quarles for his contributions to this chapter.

## DISCUSSION QUESTIONS

1. Of what value is a cost of quality system to an organization?
2. Why might there be some initial conflict between an organization's cost accounting and quality engineering departments in starting a cost of quality program?
3. Why might prevention costs be referred to as an investment while failure costs might be referred to as true costs?
4. Why does Deming refer to external failure costs as "unknown and unknowable"?
5. Contrast Deming's and Crosby's views about the ability to quantify external failure costs.
6. How do Taguchi's ideas about quality costs differ from the traditional view?

7. Why would you expect that incorporating a COQ system with a system of continuous quality improvement would result in a short-term increase in the overall cost of quality?

8. As an organization's cost of quality program matures, how would you expect the ratios among the four COQ categories to change?

9. How does activity-based costing facilitate the determination of quality costs?

10. Discuss how the tools of quality can be used in conjunction with a cost of quality system for continuous improvement.

11. How would you classify the cost of conducting inspection of manufactured products as part of the implementation phase of a statistical process control system? Should they be classified as prevention costs or appraisal costs? Present arguments for both classifications and then take a position and defend it.

12. Does a COQ system create improvement? Discuss.

13. What would you expect the short-term effects on total quality costs to be for a company that is in the initial stages of implementing a new system of continuous quality improvement?

14. How would you suggest estimating the cost associated with the loss of customer good will due to a product recall?

## PROBLEMS

1. Classify the following quality costs:

| Cost | Amount |
|------|--------|
| Product Recall Cost | $10,500 |
| Rework Rejected Outgoing Lot | 2,500 |
| Freight for Rejected Goods from Customer | 450 |
| TQM Training Class for Operators | 3,000 |
| Quality Engineers' Salary | 12,000 |
| In-process Inspection | 5,600 |
| Down-time Due to Rejected Parts | 4,500 |
| Quality Audit of Supplier | 1,500 |

Report the total quality costs by category.

2. If sales for the period are $1,400,000, calculate the quality costs in Problem 1 as a percentage of sales. What conclusions can be drawn? What are the advantages and disadvantages of reporting quality costs as a percentage of sales?

3. If total costs of production are $1,000,000, calculate the quality costs in Problem 1 as a percentage of total costs. What conclusions can be drawn? What are the advantages and disadvantages of reporting quality costs as a percentage of total costs?

**4.** Classify the following quality costs:

| Cost | Amount |
|---|---|
| Defective Product Returned by Customers | $10,500 |
| Rework Rejected Outgoing Lot | 2,500 |
| Freight for Defective Goods from Customer | 450 |
| TQM Training Class for Operators | 3,000 |
| Quality Engineers' Salary | 12,000 |
| In-process Inspection | 5,600 |
| Down-time Due to Rejected Parts | 4,500 |
| Quality Audit of Supplier | 1,500 |

The company has reason to believe that for every customer that returns a defective product, five others do not. Estimate the true external failure cost for the company.

**5.** Classify the following quality costs:

| Cost | Amount |
|---|---|
| Special Inspection for Implementing SPC | $4,000 |
| ISO 9001 Audit | 20,000 |
| Cost of Parts Made Obsolete by New Design | 8,000 |
| Return Goods Technician's Salary | 30,000 |
| Warranty Repair Costs | 12,000 |
| Cost to Conduct MRB | 1,100 |
| Audit of Key Supplier | 4,500 |

Report the total quality costs by category.

**6.** The Ace Manufacturing Company has been tracking COQ for the past two years. The following data are available:

| | Last Year, $000 | This Year, $000 |
|---|---|---|
| Sales | 1,352 | 1,529 |
| Cost of Goods Sold | 1,105 | 1,200 |
| Prevention Cost | 10 | 50 |
| Appraisal Cost | 100 | 100 |
| Internal Failure Cost | 150 | 150 |
| External Failure Cost | 80 | 80 |
| Total COQ | 340 | 380 |

Compare the two years. What conclusions can you draw?

7. The Ace Manufacturing Company has been tracking COQ for the past three years. The following data are available:

| | Two Years Ago ($000) | Last Year ($000) | This Year ($000) |
|---|---|---|---|
| Sales | 1,352 | 1,529 | 1,688 |
| Cost of Goods Sold | 1,105 | 1,200 | 1,360 |
| Prevention Cost | 10 | 50 | 40 |
| Appraisal Cost | 100 | 100 | 50 |
| Internal Failure Cost | 150 | 150 | 45 |
| External Failure Cost | 80 | 80 | 20 |
| Total COQ | 340 | 380 | 155 |

Compare the three years. What conclusions can you draw?

8. Second National Bank has recently begun trying to track COQ. Categorize these costs into the appropriate COQ categories and make a recommendation to the manager.

| Cost | Amount |
|---|---|
| Overtime Due to Out-of-Balance Accounts | $5,000 |
| Entry Posted to Wrong Customer Account | 1,000 |
| Time Spent Resolving Customer Complaints | 7,000 |
| Misprinted Personalized Checks | 1,500 |
| Incorrect Data Entered for New Customer | 2,000 |
| Misrouted Loan Applications | 1,000 |
| Missed Deadlines for Loan Closings | 2,500 |

## CASE STUDY 12.1: *HI-HO YO-YO, Inc.*

©2005 Victor E. Sower, Ph.D.,C.Q.E.

Hi-Ho Yo-Yo, Inc. (HHYY) was founded in 1993 by two business school graduates who thought there ought to be alternatives to the video game craze. Searching for a toy that could have mass market appeal they settled on yo-yos. Yo-yos have a nostalgic appeal to the baby boomer generation and are a novelty plaything for generation X. So, the main marketing thrust of HHYY is directed toward parents and grandparents rather than to the children who will actually play with the yo-yos. The latest advertising campaigns show 50-ish men competing in 1950's era yo-yo competitions, grandmothers showing their grandsons how to do yo-yo tricks, and pre-teen girls trying to get their yo-yos away from their dads who are monopolizing them. This advertising campaign has been highly effective. After a couple of rough start-up years, HHYY achieved profitability in 1996 and has seen sales and profits increase each year since then.

## PAST YEAR'S PROFIT & LOSS (P&L) STATEMENT

Sales for FY Last Year are about 5 percent higher than for FY Previous Year. Profits for FY Last Year are up by about 4 percent over FY Previous Year. Product prices were generally flat in FY Last Year and FY Previous Year and are projected to stay flat through FY This Year.

Your boss, Sarah Chen, QA manager at Hi-Ho Yo-Yo, has asked you to meet with her to discuss a new system she has read about. "We're under pressure to increase profits in the face of flat sales. I just attended a meeting of the local section of ASQ and heard a presentation about a system called cost of quality. If we apply that approach to Hi-Ho Yo-Yo, we might be able to identify some areas where we can reduce quality costs and improve profits. Here's a copy of last year's P&L. I'd like you to use it to identify and classify our cost of quality. In the presentation they said that prevention costs should be viewed as an investment. After you have classified the quality costs, determine how much we would add to profits if we could reduce all quality costs except prevention costs by 50 percent. That will provide me with the information I need to see how much we could budget for increased prevention activities in order to effect the 50 percent reduction in the other three categories. I need your report as soon as possible."

You take the P&L and head back to your office wishing you had paid closer attention in accounting class. "A few hours with the books and a fresh pot of coffee and I should be ready to write my report," you say to yourself.

Hi-Ho Yo-Yo Statement of Profit & Loss for Last Year

| | | FY Last Year | Percent of Sales |
|---|---|---|---|
| **SALES** | | | |
| Gross Revenues | | $32,356,128 | |
| *Less* Sales Returns | | 1,633,534 | 5.32 |
| Net Revenues | | 30,722,594 | 100.00 |
| *Less* Cost of Goods Sold (COGS) | | 22,895,818 | 74.52 |
| Gross Profit | | 7,826,776 | 25.48 |
| *Less* S, G, & A | | 3,636,218 | 11.84 |
| *Less* R&D Exp. | | 545,821 | 1.78 |
| **NET PROFIT OR LOSS** | | 3,644,737 | 11.86 |
| | | | |
| **COGS** | | | |
| Direct Materials | | | |
| | Freight In | 663,263 | 2.16 |
| | Material Price Variance | −5,398 | −0.02 |
| | Material Usage Variance | 1,489,533 | 4.85 |
| | Standard Material Cost | 6,675,111 | 21.73 |
| | Purchase Discounts | −12,806 | −0.04 |
| | Inventory Adjustment | 196,020 | 0.64 |
| Total Materials | | 9,005,723 | 29.31 |
| Direct Labor | | | |
| | Labor Rate Variance | 291,631 | 0.95 |
| | Labor Efficiency Variance | 423,876 | 1.38 |
| | Standard Labor Cost | 2,288,258 | 7.45 |
| | Downtime | 1,137,588 | 3.70 |
| Total Labor | | 4,141,353 | 13.48 |
| | | | |
| Indirect Mfg. Costs | | | |
| | Depreciation | 2,856,017 | 9.30 |
| | Safety & Insurance | 446,501 | 1.45 |
| | MRO Supplies | 502,765 | 1.64 |
| | Occupancy Cost | 557,652 | 1.82 |
| | Salary Supervisor | 368,519 | 1.20 |
| | Salary Indirect | 1,232,139 | 4.01 |
| | Salary Engineer | 352,040 | 1.15 |
| | Salary QA | 408,366 | 1.33 |
| | Rework Labor | 604,327 | 1.97 |
| | Repairs | 305,817 | 1.00 |
| | Property Taxes | 789,512 | 2.57 |
| | Utilities | 1,255,437 | 4.09 |
| | Overhead Variance | 69,650 | 0.23 |
| Total Indirect Mfg. Costs | | 9,748,742 | 31.73 |
| **Total COGS** | | 22,895,818 | 74.52 |

## CASE STUDY 12.2: *Acme, Ltd.*

©2005 Victor E. Sower, Ph.D., C.Q.E.

The general manager of the Manufacturing Division of Acme, Ltd. is preparing for an upcoming P&L meeting with her boss and representatives from Corporate Accounting. She begins by reviewing the data she has collected.

| Category | Last Year | This Year |
|----------|-----------|-----------|
| Sales | $25,000,000 | $30,000,000 |
| COGS | 21,250,000 | 25,500,000 |
| S,G, & A | 2,000,000 | 2,400,000 |
| Net Profit | 1,750,000 | 2,100,000 |

Prices for the company's products and costs have remained relatively constant for the past year.

As she digs a little deeper, she becomes concerned about rising quality costs. Total COQ last year was $3,187,500. This year it has gone up to $3,825,000—a $637,500 increase. She is certain that the accountants will see this as an unreasonable increase in quality costs. She is concerned about the best way to present the COQ figures at the meeting to show the true picture. How do you interpret this increase and what advice would you offer her about the best way to present the information?

## EXERCISES AND ACTIVITIES

1. Obtain an income statement from a company's annual report or 10K statement. Classify as many of the costs listed there as possible into COQ categories. What does the COQ distribution tell you about the company? What suggestions would you make to the company based on your analysis?

2. Locate an article or case study that documents the use of a balanced scorecard by a business organization. Based on the article you find, identify ways in which COQ and balanced scorecard can work together to document and improve the performance of the firm.

## SUPPLEMENTARY READINGS

ANSI/ASQC Q9004-1-1994. *Quality Management and Quality Systems Elements-Guidelines.*
ANSI/ISO/ASQ Q9004-2000. *Quality Management Systems: Guidelines for Performance Requirements,* 6.8

Campanella, J. (ed.). (1999). *Principles of Quality Costs: Principles, Implementation, and Use*, 3rd edition. Milwaukee, WI: ASQ Quality Press.

Crosby, P. B. (1979). *Quality is Free*. New York: McGraw-Hill.

Deming, W. E. (1982). *Out of the Crisis*. Cambridge, MA: MIT Center for Advanced Engineering Study.

Feigenbaum, A. V. (1956). "Total Quality Control." *Harvard Business Review* 34(6), 93–101. Reprinted in Sower, V. E., J. Motwani, & M. J. Savoie. (1995). *Classic Readings in Operations Management*. Ft. Worth: Dryden, 307–321.

Giakatis, G., T. Enkawa, & K. Washitani. (2001). "Hidden Quality Costs and the Distinction Between Quality Cost and Quality Loss." *Total Quality Management* 12(2), 179–190.

Kaplin, R., & D. Norton. (1992). "The Balanced Scorecard—Measures that Drive Performance." *Harvard Business Review* 70(1), 71–79.

*MIL-STD-1520C*. (1986) *Corrective Action and Disposition System for Nonconforming Material*.

Sower, V., R. Quarles, & S. Cooper. (2002). "Cost of Quality Distribution and Quality System Maturity: An Exploratory Study." *ASQ's 56th Annual Quality Congress Proceedings*, 343–354.

Sower, V. E., & R. Quarles. (2003). "Cost of Quality: Why More Organizations Do Not Use If Effectively." ASQ's 57th Annual Quality Congress Proceedings, 625–637.

Sower, V. E. (2004). "Estimating External Failure Costs: A Key Difficulty in COQ Systems." *ASQ's 58th Annual Quality Congress Proceedings*, 547–551.

Sower, V. E., R. Quarles, & E. Broussard. (2007). "Cost of Quality Usage and Its Relationship to Quality System Maturity." *International Journal of Quality and Reliability Management* 24(2), 121–140.

Taguchi, G. (1986). *Introduction to Quality Engineering*. Tokyo: Asian Productivity Organization.

# REFERENCES

*ANSI/ISO/ASQ Q9004-2000. Quality Management Systems: Guidelines for Performance Requirements*.

Beecroft, G. (2001). "Cost of Quality and Quality Planning Affect the Bottom Line." *The Quality Management Forum* 27(1), 1–7.

Blackstone, J. & J. Cox (eds.). (2005). *APICS Dictionary*, 11th edition. Alexandria, VA: APICS.

Bottorff, D. (1997). "COQ Systems: The Right Stuff." *Quality Progress* 30(3), 33–35.

Campanella, J. (ed.). (1999). *Principles of Quality Costs*, 3rd edition. Milwaukee, WI: ASQ Quality Press.

Carr, L. (1995). "How Xerox Sustains the Cost of Quality." *Management Accounting* 76(2), 26–32.

Cokins, G. (1996). *Activity-Based Cost Management: Making It Work*. Boston: McGraw-Hill.

Crocket, H. (1935). "Quality, but Just Enough." *Factory Management and Maintenance* 93(June), 245–246.

Crosby, P. (1979). *Quality is Free*. New York: McGraw-Hill.

Deming, W. E. (1982). *Out of the Crisis*. Cambridge, MA: MIT Center for Advanced Engineering Study.

Dow Chemical. *1999 Annual Report to Shareholders*.

Feigenbaum, A. V. (1956). "Total Quality Control." *Harvard Business Review* 34(6), 93–101.

Reprinted in Sower, V., J. Motwani, & M. Savoie. (1995). *Classic Readings in Operations Management*. Ft. Worth: Dryden, 307–321.

Feigenbaum, A. V. (1957). "The Challenge of Total Quality Control." *Industrial Quality Control* (May), 17–23.

Freeman, H. (1960). "How to Put Quality Costs to Use." *Transactions of the Metropolitan Conference, ASQC*.

Harrington, H. (2004). "Measuring Money and Quality." *Quality Digest* 24(2), 18.

Juran, J. M. (1951). *Quality Control Handbook*, 1st edition. New York: McGraw-Hill.

Kaplan, R., & D. Norton. (1992). "The Balanced Scorecard—Measures that Drive Performance." *Harvard Business Review* 70(1), 71–79.

Miner, D. (1933). "What Price Quality?" *Product Engineering*, 300–302.

"Quality Glossary." (2002). *Quality Progress* 35(7), 43–61.

Shewhart, W. (1931). *Economic Control of Manufactured Product*. New York: D. Van Nostrand Co., Inc.

Sower, V. E., R. Quarles, & E. Broussard. (2007). "Cost of Quality Usage and Its Relationship to Quality System Maturity." *International Journal of Quality and Reliability Management* 24(2), 121–140.

Taguchi, G. (1986). *Introduction to Quality Engineering*. Tokyo: Asian Productivity Organization.

# SECTION V

# QUALITY MANAGEMENT

## CHAPTER THIRTEEN

# Human Factors in Quality

## CHAPTER OBJECTIVES

After completing this chapter, the reader should be able to:

- understand the importance of human factors in quality;
- discuss leading theories of motivation;
- understand the team process;
- discuss the various roles necessary within a team;
- understand the basics of group dynamics and approaches to conflict resolution;
- discuss the stages of group development and ways to move from one stage to the next;
- understand the importance of developing consensus in a team; and
- discuss professional and ethical standards in the quality field.

Continuous quality improvement is continuous change. Many who have tried to institute change in any type of organization believe that the natural tendency of humans is to resist change. But there is evidence that change can be managed in ways that encourage people to buy in to the change process. Efforts to manage the quality-improvement process should begin with an understanding of some of the barriers to that process and approaches to dealing with those barriers.

From the Hawthorne Studies, Maslow's Hierarchy of Needs, and Hertzberg's two-factor theory to Stephen Covey's (1986) maturity continuum, there have been many motivational theories and principles developed and applied to individual workers. Employees (human resources) are integral parts of the quality system of any organization. However, they are often treated as *just* the "hands" of the organization—that is, the part of the organization where actual work is accomplished. The modern view is that employees are more than just "hands." Human resource management is directed toward making employees true partners with management in the effective operation of the enterprise.

Teams introduce a new dimension to the management process. In order to fulfill their charter, team leaders and team members must be educated in the rudiments of team dynamics. When team members realize that some conflict is normal and they and their leaders understand how to productively manage that conflict, the team's performance will be enhanced.

Quality professionals are part of the human resources of the enterprise. All employees must adhere to the rules, regulations, and policies of the organization that employs them. But certified quality professionals are also subject to the professional and ethical standards of the quality discipline.

## BARRIERS TO QUALITY IMPROVEMENT EFFORTS

Barriers to effective quality-improvement efforts take many forms. Examples of common barriers are a failure to correctly understand customers' requirements, failure to understand the capability of the production system, failure to track defects, failure to repair suboptimized processes, and failure to track quality costs. Deming (1981–1982) assigns most of the blame for these barriers to management. His 14 Points are written for management: "... no one else in the company can work effectively on quality and productivity unless it is obvious that the top people (management) are working on their obligations." In Deming's view, most of these barriers are the results of ineffective management.

Even when top management is committed and involved, there can be significant barriers to quality-improvement efforts. These can often be traced to a lack of communication.

Communication of quality begins at the very top of the organization. Top management must set a course and make a commitment to a defined level of quality today, and commit to continuous improvement for tomorrow. This commitment and direction must be clearly communicated throughout the organization. By "clearly communicated," we mean that each employee must recognize the quality goals of the organization and clearly understand how the job they do impacts the quality of the organization's goods and services.

Once the quality goals have been communicated, employees must receive training on the tools and techniques used to measure and ensure the quality of the good/service. This training may take a number of different forms—from self-paced on-line learning to formal classroom instruction.

Once trained, employees must integrate the training into the day-to-day operations of the organization. Management must be present in each of these steps to ensure the employees have the support and resources needed to fully achieve and maintain the targeted quality levels.

## HUMAN RESOURCE MANAGEMENT

"Human resource management refers to the practices and policies you need to carry out the people or personnel aspects of your management job" (Dessler, 1997, 2). This section will examine two facets of human resource management: motivation theories and group dynamics.

## Motivation Theories

Managers are charged with motivating their employees (human resources) to work to achieve the goals of the organization as efficiently and effectively as possible. Managers then by definition accomplish their objectives through the work of others. For this reason it is incumbent upon managers to understand how to effectively motivate their employees.

Early insight into the motivation of workers resulted from studies conducted in the 1920s at the Hawthorne Plant of Western Electric. The initial studies were guided by the principles of scientific management—that there is "one best way" of doing a job—and focused on determining the effect of illumination on worker productivity. During the course of the experiments, it was found that productivity increased for both the variable and control groups regardless of the level of illumination. When these experiments were abandoned, the report concluded that the most important variable in the study was "the psychology of the individual" (Snow, 1927).

Further studies at Hawthorne examined factors other than illumination levels. For example, the relay assembly experiments at Hawthorne found that supervisor's style and the formation of small groups to build esprit de corps were more important than pay in increasing worker productivity.

There were no theories to explain the results of the Hawthorne Studies. Subsequently, theories that attempted to explain motivation and how it contributes to performance were developed. Four of these, often referred to as *classic theories of motivation*, are Maslow's Hierarchy of Needs, McGregor's theory X and theory Y, McClelland's acquired needs theory, and Herzberg's two factor theory. These classic theories provide insight into what motivates people. The influence of these theories on Deming is evident in his 14 Points.

According to Maslow (1964) there are five levels of motivators arranged in a hierarchy as shown in Figure 13.1. Higher-level needs are motivators only after lower-level needs have been satisfied. According to this theory, attempting to appeal to employees' ego needs while the employees are still striving to meet their physiological needs will be unsuccessful. For example, attempting to motivate minimum-wage employees with promises of inflated job titles would not be expected to be the most effective strategy according to Maslow's theory.

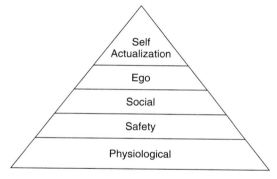

**Figure 13.1.** Maslow's Hierarchy of Needs

McGregor (1960) defines two approaches to management. The *classic* approach arises from Taylor's scientific management and is called theory X. According to theory X, workers inherently dislike work and must be coerced, controlled, and threatened in order to motivate them to work to achieve organizational objectives. Theory X suggests that workers actively avoid responsibility and that the worker's desire for security is the primary motivator. At the other extreme is theory Y, which is derived from participatory approaches to management. Theory Y suggests that work is a natural activity for humans, that workers will actively work to achieve goals to which they are committed, and that workers possess considerable ingenuity and imagination that is waiting to be tapped. McGregor suggests that theory Y is the best approach for managers.

McClelland (1961) suggested that workers have distinct motivational profiles. These profiles consist of the relative strengths of their needs for achievement (n-ACH), affiliation (n-AFF), and power (n-POW). The implications of McClelland's theory are that understanding a particular employee's profile is the first step to designing motivational incentives for the employee. According to McClelland's theory, it is unlikely that the same incentive system will have the same effect on Employee A in Figure 13.2 as on Employee B. Employee A has high power, moderate achievement, and low affiliation needs, while Employee B has low power, moderate achievement, and high affiliation needs.

Herzberg's (1966) theory proposes that job satisfaction and job dissatisfaction are *not* two extremes of a single continuum. Rather there are two separate continuums. One has job satisfaction and no job satisfaction at the extremes; the other has job dissatisfaction and no job dissatisfaction at the extremes. Needs that when satisfied can lead to job satisfaction are called *motivators*. The other category of needs, called *hygiene* needs, can only lead to no job dissatisfaction. According to this theory, increasing pay or improving supervision can only decrease the level of worker job dissatisfaction. These actions will not result in increased worker job satisfaction. Table 13.1 contains examples of motivators and hygiene factors.

Managers often find that these classic theories are oversimplified and sometimes contradictory. Today's manager faces a complex and dynamic environment.

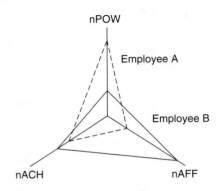

**Figure 13.2.** Example of Employee Profiles

**TABLE 13.1.   Examples of Herzberg's Two Factors**

| Motivators | Hygiene Factors |
| --- | --- |
| Recognition | Pay |
| Responsibility | Security |
| Achievement | Supervisors |
| Personal growth | Working Conditions |

Employees are not all the same. No one theory can possibly deal with all the environmental factors. No *single* theory can provide the *prescription* for motivating *all* employees in *every* situation. But taken together, they can be useful to today's manager.

### Integration of the Classic Motivational Theories

Wilkinson, Orth, and Benfari (1986) provide a motivational model that integrates the classic theories in a way that enables the manager to adjust to changing social and organizational environments and differences among people. The integrated theory results in eight conclusions:

1. Herzberg's dissatisfiers are similar to Maslow's first two levels of need plus some small increment in each of the top three needs in his hierarchy.
2. These dissatisfiers tend to be related to the autocratic structured management style of Taylor or McGregor's theory X.
3. Morse and Lorsch have identified this autocratic style as more effective for routine tasks.
4. Herzberg's satisfiers are similar to Maslow's top three levels of need.
5. McClelland's achievement, power, and affiliation needs are a different mix of Maslow's top three levels of need.
6. Herzberg's satisfiers are related to the participative management style described by McGregor as theory Y.
7. McGregor's theory Y style, according to Morse and Lorsch, appears more effective for tasks with high levels of complexity.
8. The nature of the people and of the tasks being performed causes higher and higher levels of dependency, diversity, uncertainty, complexity, education, and professionalism. Therefore, the greater the observed difference between reactive and proactive behavior, the greater the applicability of Multiple Influences.

The integrated Multiple Influences Model can assist managers in adjusting managerial style to "the realities of human motivation in the workplace" and provide guidance for "how to proceed in developing work systems, given the social and organizational environment and the nature of people."

### Process Theories of Motivation

The classic motivational theories do not provide much information about how motivation actually occurs. The process theories of motivation attempt to explain how behavior is influenced.

Vroom's expectancy theory (1964) defines the four primary variables of motivation as choice, expectancy, instrumentality, and valance. People are motivated to make choices about how they are to behave. That choice is influenced by their expectation of achieving rewards that satisfy given needs. Low expectations of reward are unlikely to greatly influence choice. Instrumentality is the probability assigned by the individual that a particular performance will lead to a specific reward. Valence is the value that the individual places on the specific reward. Vroom theorized that expectancy, instrumentality, and valance were related to motivation as follows:

$$\text{Motivation} = f(\text{expectancy} \times \text{instrumentality} \times \text{valance})$$

Porter and Lawler (1968) extended expectancy theory by distinguishing between the effects of intrinsic rewards (e.g., recognition, achievement) and extrinsic rewards (e.g., advancement, salary increases). Porter and Lawler found that satisfaction was related to actual performance and the real outcomes resulting from that performance.

Managers must be careful when setting up reward systems to motivate specific behavior. Careful consideration must be given to the ramifications of motivating certain behaviors. For example, a bonus promised to a purchasing manager based on expenditures on raw materials as a percentage of sales might motivate the purchase of low-cost, low-quality materials. A better approach, although much harder to measure, might be to base the bonus on total cost of ownership of the materials (purchase price + inspection cost + failure cost due to materials + effect of materials on production efficiency + . . . ).

## EMPLOYEE INVOLVEMENT AND TEAMS

Employee involvement (EI) develops naturally from the classic motivation theories and is a key tenet of total quality management. Employee involvement varies among organizations from information sharing, where management makes the decisions and then communicates the decisions to the employees, to total self-direction, where managers facilitate total self-management in an all-team organization (Orsburn, et al., 1990). The use of formal groups or teams is a frequent manifestation of EI in organizations.

Many different types of groups or teams are utilized in organizations. Temporary teams form for a particular, limited purpose and disband when that purpose is achieved. Examples of temporary teams include problem-solving teams, product-design teams, and systems-integration teams. Permanent groups include quality circles, management teams, and self-managed work teams.

One recent study identified the importance of time and training in team development (Banker, et al., 1996). Other studies have identified four factors as being important influences on group effectiveness (Bedeian, 1993). These factors are group size, spatial constraints, group cohesiveness, and group norms. Group effectiveness tends to decrease when groups become too large. Ishikawa (1984, 4) explicitly recognized this in his definition of a quality circle as "a *small* group which voluntarily performs quality control activities within a single workshop." The American Society for Quality (ASQ) is more specific in its definition, specifying "small" as "10 or fewer" (Bemowski, 1992, 26).

As the physical distance between workers increases, group effectiveness tends to decrease. This means that work station layouts that place workers in close proximity to each other can increase work group effectiveness. For example, a U-shaped layout will likely result in better communication and group effectiveness than a straight-line layout.

Group cohesiveness is the "degree to which group members form a strong collective unit reflecting a feeling of oneness" (Bedeian, 1993, 507). This factor interacts with group size in that smaller groups tend to be more cohesive. The more threatening the external environment in which the group is working, the greater the tendency toward cohesiveness. This can be seen in military basic training units where unit cohesiveness is rapidly developed because all of the unit members are immersed in a very hostile environment (everyone fears the drill instructor). High group status and similarity among members are other important factors in developing cohesiveness.

Group norms, the standards for group behavior, develop over time. Greater commitment to group norms is a reflection of greater group cohesiveness. The more congruent group norms are with the personal norms of the members, the more cohesive the group.

## The Care and Feeding of Teams

Research has shown that the behavior of employees changes when they are formed into teams. One study by Marks, et al. (1986) reported that productivity and absenteeism improved when employees participated in quality circles. Griffin (1988) documented improvements in job satisfaction, organizational commitment, and job performance when employees participated in quality circles. However, his study determined that these improvements tend to be short term, and they tend to disappear after about 18 months.

After an initial burst of enthusiasm, quality circles often tend to "wind down" as the most obvious problems have been addressed. Among the keys to sustained success are continuous and visible management involvement, legitimate recognition, and effective communication. Token efforts will not achieve long-term results.

# ORGANIZATION AND IMPLEMENTATION OF QUALITY TEAMS

Quality teams are designed to exploit the synergy created when multiple people focus their attention on a single problem. Optimal team size is five to ten (Ishikawa, 1984, 4; Bemowski, 1992, 26), with the effort usually focused on a single problem or effort.

Quality teams may be implemented within a department or functional area or cover a broad spectrum of the organization (often referred to as cross-functional teams). Some examples of the types of teams that are used are (Brocka & Brocka, 1992, 147):

| Example | Scope |
|---|---|
| Corrective Action Team | Short-term, single purpose |
| Quality Circle | Long-term, multiple-task focus |
| Focus Group | Short-term, single-task |
| Self-Managing | Daily operations |
| Process Action Team | Short-term, but regularly formed |

Regardless of the makeup, these teams share certain characteristics that help to ensure their success (see Table 13.2).

**TABLE 13.2. Characteristics of Quality Teams**

- Number of members is five to eight
- Work from a Team Charter that clearly defines the problem, mission, and evaluation criteria
- Have a specific focus as identified in the Team Charter
- May be self-directed or have a team leader

## Principles of Team Leadership and Facilitation

Wearing the same shirts doesn't make you a team.

Vince Lombardi

### What is a Team?

A team is a group of people assembled to focus their knowledge, experience, and skills on a specific task.

### Who Makes up a Team?

A team is made up of a team leader, team members, and a facilitator. Each plays a unique role in helping the team achieve its goals.

## Roles and Responsibilities of the Team Leader

Roles of a team leader include coach, mentor, and active participant. The ways in which these roles are operationalized will vary according to the nature of the group—its readiness for empowerment, and its stage of development (Johnson, 1993, 92). For example, a more directive leadership style might be more appropriate in the early stages of team development while a more supportive leadership style would be appropriate as the team matures.

*Coach:* The team leader is a coach. The team leader is not there to direct, but to guide. Just as an athletic coach trains her charges, the team leader must make sure that the team members are capable of performing the duties requested of them. Team members with all the necessary tools to solve a problem are a rare find. Therefore, the team leader must be ready to solicit the training necessary to provide the team members with the tools needed to accomplish the task.

*Mentor:* The team leader is the first-level source of information for the team members. Even though in many cases, the team leader knows little more than the team members about the problem, the team members will look to him/her for guidance and direction. The team leader must provide as much input as possible to the team members—not in the form of "giving away answers" but in the form of questions and focus.

*Active Participant:* In addition to all of the other roles and responsibilities associated with being a team leader, he/she must remain an active participant in the team. The team leader is the head of the team and must be ready to support the members as they tackle difficult problems. The most important thing to remember is to lead by example, not with words. In other words, walk the talk.

Responsibilities of a team leader include effective communication, team building, win-win negotiations, and conflict resolution.

With regard to effective communication, it is the role of the team leader to ensure that all team members have an equal opportunity to voice their views. No one person should be allowed to dominate the meeting. The environment should be conducive to open, timely, and honest communication without fear of retribution from other members of the team.

With regard to team building, it is the role of the team leader to take the group of individuals assembled at the first meeting and turn them into a successful team. Attributes of a high performance team, as outlined in Table 13.3, include:

1. Mission Alignment
2. Participative Leadership
3. Shared Responsibility
4. Open Communications
5. Focus on Problem Elimination
6. Dedication to Change
7. Welcome Diversity

## TABLE 13.3. Attributes of a High Performance Team

1. Mission Alignment:
   - Clear Statement of Team:
     - purpose
     - functions served
     - values
     - vision
   - Buy in by members
   - Constantly communicated internally and externally
   - Can be improved by
     - developing a vision
     - setting goals
2. Participative Leadership
   - Set the example
   - Eliminate artificial barriers
   - Free up and empower creativity
   - Coach, counsel and encourage
   - Provide rapid feedback
   - Can be improved by:
     - understanding leadership style
     - improving supervision skills
3. Shared Responsibility
   - Top performance is responsibility of all
   - Members are interdependent
   - Clear responsibilities and authorities
   - Recognition and rewards shared by all
   - Can be improved by:
     - clarifying roles
     - improving decision making
     - involving workers in problem solving
4. Open Communications
   - Begin at the top
   - Driven up, down, and sideways
   - Require learning to listen
   - Build climate of trust
   - Can be improved by:
     - resolving conflict
     - listening
     - giving feedback

(*continued*)

**TABLE 13.3.** *(continued)*

5. Focus on Problem Elimination
   - Eliminate—don't compromise
   - Establish specific goals
   - Attack the process
   - Tap job knowledge/creativity
   - Target root causes
   - Measure progress
   - Celebrate success
   - Can be improved by:
     - identifying issues
     - forming focus groups
     - using a problem solving process
     - finding solutions
6. Dedication to Change
   - Change is the continuum
   - Anticipate it
   - Plan for it
   - Thrive on it
   - Two types:
     - change due to inspiration
     - change due to desperation
   - Can be improved by:
     - understanding the technology of change
     - using the proper tools to manage it
7. Welcome Diversity
   - Recognize and complement each other's strengths and weaknesses
   - Develop SYNERGY: The simultaneous actions of separate entities which together have greater total effect than the sum of their individual effects
   - Can be improved by:
     - learning about each other
     - learning about yourself
     - sharing of information, ideas, and experiences

With regard to win/win negotiations, the team leader must use collaborative efforts to reach consensus and win/win decisions with the team. Failure to achieve consensus is most often manifested by voting and compromising. It is the role of the team leader to ensure that all team members are in agreement as to the problem to be solved and the solution method to be utilized.

When conflict occurs (and it will), the team leader must be prepared to mediate the dispute. *It is not the job of the team leader to assume the role of judge and jury.*

**TABLE 13.4.   Team Member Selection Criteria**

- People Skills:
  - Open communicator
  - Good listener
  - Self motivated
- Personal Characteristics
  - Participative
  - Enthusiastic
  - Cooperative
  - Sense of humor
  - Meets commitments
  - Team player
  - Experienced in subject area
  - Constructively challenges the status quo
- Readiness
  - Available to attend meetings
  - Available to do research/collect data
  - Willing to make a contribution

Rather, the team leader should facilitate discussion between all members of the team (not just the conflicting members) regarding the best way to proceed.

It would be a mistake, however, to assume that no conflict within a team is a strength. "Teams that lack open conflict are dying entities.... groups that have any vitality at all, any ideas, any instincts for growth will have conflicts" (Harvey & Drolet, 1994, 20–21). It is the proper management of that conflict that can make it a strength instead of a weakness for the team.

## Selecting Team Members

It is preferable that team members be volunteers. However, it is the job of the team leader to select the members for the team. With the help of the team's facilitator, the team leader should look for members who meet all or most of the criteria listed in Table 13.4.

## Roles and Responsibilities of the Team Members

Team members are responsible for developing the team's work plan, including establishing action items and follow-up responsibilities. Team members are also responsible for establishing the meeting schedule based on the magnitude of the assignment and the time limit, and assigning a recorder. Recording is not the responsibility of the facilitator!

Finally, team members must execute the work plan. Execution includes conducting the necessary research and analyses, developing conclusions, identifying solutions and alternatives, making recommendations, producing the deliverable, presenting the deliverable to the client, and celebrating the achievement.

### Roles and Responsibilities of the Facilitator

The facilitator is there to aid the team leader. Team facilitators are *not* there to run the meetings, identify the problem, or develop the solution. The team facilitator will keep the team focused on the assignment as defined in the charter by the customer.

Some of the roles and responsibilities associated with the facilitator include:

- Availability to answer questions and provide guidance
- Attending the kick-off meeting for the team
- Attending meetings of first-time team leaders
- Helping the team leader to develop the agenda for the first meeting including develop the work plan
- Developing the meeting schedule, identifying the target date for presenting the deliverable
- Keeping the team focused on the assignment, discouraging digression
- Serving as a liaison between the team and the client
- Aiding in the technical review of reports
- Helping in assembling and distributing the report to management
- Helping the team prepare to do its briefing
- Preparing management to receive the report from the team
- Providing help in politically sensitive situations (e.g., dealing with a team member's boss who reneges on the time commitment agreed to with the team member)

## CRITICAL ACTION ITEMS IN THE TEAM LIFE CYCLE

There are critical actions that must be taken by any team wishing to be successful. These can be broken down into items done before the project is undertaken (preliminary), items done while the project is underway (ongoing), and items done when the project is completed (final). Each of these areas is listed in Table 13.5.

## WHAT IS A TEAM CHARTER?

- Source of charter
- The team's charter will narrowly define a problem or function to be studied, analyzed, or assessed
- The charter identifies the deliverable and its time frame
- The charter defines the "what and why," not the "how to"
- The charter includes:
  - the name of the team
  - the statement of the problem

      – the scope of the assignment
      – the deliverable to be produced
      – the time limit for the assignment

**TABLE 13.5. Critical Action Items in the Team Life Cycle**

Preliminary Action Items
- Identify the problem or area to be addressed
- Select team members with the facilitator's assistance
  - Look for volunteers
- Obtain the support and commitment from the team member's manager and the team members
- Schedule the first meeting
  - Make introductions and brainstorm the team's guidelines
  - Work with the team to prepare a charter

On-Going Action Items
- Handle meeting room logistics
- Prepare and distribute the meeting minutes and agenda for the next meeting
- Provide the customer with periodic status reports

Final Action Items
- Present initial briefing to management on possible solutions
  - Include lessons learned by the team
- Get feedback from management on which solution to implement
  - Written response to the team leader
- Implement solution
- Provide management with a final briefing on performance of solution
- Incorporate management comments into final briefing
- Distribute final draft to all upper management

Example 13.1 is a real team charter developed in a business organization in Texas.

---

## EXAMPLE 13.1

XYZ Associates
Supporting Services
The Woodlands, Texas

## TEAM CHARTER

### What are Our Principles?

Our work together will be grounded in trust, honesty, empathy, support, and commitment to one another and our common purpose. Seeking to read, know, listen to, and understand one another will deepen our personal trust and foster appreciation of differing perspectives. Expanded communication will contribute to clearer expectations, enhance participation in decision making, and result in greater alignment with team goals.

## Whom do we Serve?

Together, we have been employed to provide our **external clients** better, faster and less expensive services that grow the businesses of XYZ. We recognize that to accomplish quality delivery, we must also serve our **internal clients** by providing business consulting, a secure and comfortable work environment, on-time deliverables with zero defects and costs below market, immediate responses to their requests and concerns, and tools that offer easy access to Supporting Services. We also serve our **Supporting Services** clients—the associates we are responsible to manage and those in other markets—by seeking to eliminate the roadblocks that stifle business success and growth in their careers.

## How will we Know we are Successful?

We will know that we are successful when we have attained a business reputation that results in a waiting list of client teams that want to work with us, and other associates wanting to work in our Supporting Services group.

In order to attain this business reputation, our common purpose will be to achieve the following: (1) *Serving Our Clients Well* as reflected in a Customer Engagement Score of 90+ on Overall Experience, (2) Developing committed associates who are engaged and recognized for their contributions, and who are willing to strive for an *Associate Engagement* score of 94+, and (3) *Strengthening Our Business* by continually accomplishing both productivity and quality gains resulting in a positive *impact* on XYZ's business.

## How will we Work Together?

Communication

The way we communicate as a team is critical to our success. We will communicate with honest intentions, therefore, what we need to say will be thought out and planned. We will say what we mean. Our communication will be timely and inclusive as everyone's input and participation is important. Clarification will be sought if the communication is not clear. We are all responsible for taking the initiative to communicate. We will listen and respond with empathy by coming to understand the other person's point of view. The breaking of a confidence is serious matter; the consequence is loss of trust, and this has serious negative impact on the quality of communication.

Building Trust

Every team member recognizes that trust is nurtured by the honoring of commitments. We will do what we say and will always follow through. Our day-to-day interactions will be conducted with integrity. When uncertain, we will grant one another the benefit of the doubt. We are committed to one another's success. Therefore, no team member will be left behind. Due to this commitment, presenting honest, open and necessary feedback will be a team norm.

Problem Solving and Decision Making

When solving problems, we commit to work the issue until we reach consensus. We will define the root cause and focus on the desired outcome. There are no bad ideas—all input is welcome and will help us challenge assumptions and reach creative solutions. Decision-makers will be identified up front; most often, strategic decisions will be pushed up and tactical decisions will be pushed down. We recognize that not all decisions will be unanimous. We will collaborate and compromise when necessary, but we will all support and "own" the decision, once made.

Conflict Resolution

Conflict is inevitable and within bounds, productive. We will resolve disagreements by truly listening to and valuing the opinions of each member, questioning each other respectfully, and empathizing with the values of each member. In moments of intense conflict, a single mediator will be enlisted to listen impartially and provide assistance that hopefully leads to agreement between the two parties. If individual mediation is not successful, the team will be called upon to render a decision. We recognize that in many cases, conflict can be minimized by strong working relationships. We will take time out to laugh together while working or enjoying outside team activities.

## How will we Hold One Another Accountable?

We recognize that the effectiveness of our team is dependent on the actions of all. Interactions will be respectful, and mutual trust will enable us to freely confront one another even when it is uncomfortable. Trust also will provide the assurance that alone we do not have to "watch our back." Supporting other team members when they are not present to represent themselves will be the norm. Collective decisions will be owned and supported by the team. Each of us will follow through and close the loop on what we say we are going to do.

We will answer to our team for performance on operational and personal goals. We recognize that these commitments are essential to the long-term survival and growth of our company. We will share pertinent information effectively and timely, and to the right parties. We understand the importance of utilizing the strength of our team, and will consult with others. When mistakes are made the assurance is there that we will be forgiven and we will move on.

We are pledged to meet periodically to review our processes and commitments.

### What should we Expect of the Team's Leadership?

In our team, "leadership" is an action, not a noun. It is the responsibility of each member to be proactive in identifying issues and seeking the active involvement of those affected in creating solutions. Having the courage to step up to a problem and solve it is critical behavior to team success.

### How will we Appreciate One Another, and Recognize, Reward, and Celebrate Team Successes?

Each member of the team is important and is to be appreciated for the contributions made to team success. We will periodically celebrate our victories, and support one another in our losses. Individually and as a team we will actively seek ways to recognize laudable performance by any member of Supporting Services. We realize that personal appreciation is a valuable motivator and we will seek to recognize often the contributions of others.

### Together, we have Learned . . .

that it is easier to solve problems if we listen to one another and focus on end results, and that the freedom to share thoughts, ideas, and solutions enables the team to "do the impossible." We can count on one another!

*Source:* Dr. Joseph Kavanaugh, Sam Houston State University.
Used with permission.

## GENERAL INFORMATION AND GUIDELINES FOR TEAMS

- The more clearly the problem is stated, the better the problem can be understood.
- The more specific the scope of the assignment, the narrower the focus with fewer deviations from the assignment.
- The charter should spell out "what needs to be done." The team's work plan will spell out "how it will be done."
- Select people with the most knowledge, experience, and skill in the topic or subject that you can find.
- Select only experienced facilitators; weak facilitators are detrimental to the team's performance.
- Limit the number of team members from five to ten.

- Get a commitment of time and availability for potential team members from the team member's manager; otherwise, find someone else.
- Establish a time limit for the assignment.
- The team should meet regularly for a minimum of 1.5 hours. The specific meeting schedule and duration is driven by the work plan activities and the time frame established by the customer.
- The team should call upon "topical" or "subject matter" experts for consultation and clarification when necessary.
- Trust, mutual respect, and recognition of each team member's contributions are the guiding principles of the team

## TEAM DYNAMICS MANAGEMENT AND CONFLICT RESOLUTION

Calling a group or work unit a team implies that it has a particular process of working together, one in which members identify and fully use one another's resources and facilitate their mutual interdependence toward more effective problem solving and task accomplishment. Therefore, team building is an effort in which a team:

- studies its own process of working together
- acts to create a climate in which members' energies are directed toward problem solving
- maximizes the use of all members' resources for this process

Team building components include:

1. Mission: define the overall mission or objective for which the team has been formed.
2. Organization
   - Select the right people
   - Establish external interfaces
   - Clearly define responsibility and authority
   - Clarify individual roles
3. Leadership
   - Designate a leader
   - Establish and follow ground rules
   - Give rewards and recognition for contributions
   - Ensure appropriate control for maturity and motivation of workers
4. Commitment
   - Gladly accept responsibility
   - Take pride in quality work
5. Goals: Define long- and short-range goals necessary to accomplish the mission. Ensure that each goal is:

- clear and specific
- measurable
- achievable
- prioritized
- communicated to team members
- trackable
- periodically revised, as necessary

6. Communication
   - Balanced participation
   - Listen to ideas
   - Ensure that mutual trust exists
   - Limit interruptions

7. Delegation
   - To the lowest level possible
   - Focus on methods that lead to results
   - Implement using specific guidelines or standard procedures
   - Identify available resources (human, financial, technical, and organizational)
   - Identify accountability and standards to be used in evaluating results
   - Identify consequences of performance/nonperformance

8. Meetings
   - Set up a meeting schedule with defined durations
   - Hold additional meetings only when clearly necessary
   - Define specific outcomes for the meeting
   - Invite those who can make a specific contribution
   - Prepare and follow a specific agenda which is distributed ahead of the meeting start time
   - Monitor and facilitate discussion to achieve the desired outcome
   - Summarize and record decisions, actions, responsible parties, and due dates
   - Review meeting process with an eye toward improvement
   - Follow up to ensure meeting outcomes are executed

9. Problem solving and decision making
   - Identify problems
   - Identify and evaluate alternatives
   - Encourage participation from all members
   - Seek consensus on decisions
   - Ensure timely decisions
   - Assign action items to specific team members

10. Conflict Resolution
    - Identify disagreements before they escalate
    - Challenge ideas and processes, not individuals
    - Address conflict, don't avoid it

11. Evaluation
    - Achieve goals

- Evaluate the process
- Be open to feedback
- Be willing to change the process and content as necessary

# STAGES OF GROUP DEVELOPMENT

As a team forms, adds, or subtracts members, it goes through four stages of group development (Tuckman, 1965; Plovnick, et al., 1975):

1. Forming
2. Storming
3. Norming
4. Performing

## Forming

This stage is the transition from individual to member status. It's also a period of testing behavior and dependence on formal or informal leadership. Members discover what behaviors are acceptable to the group.

Characteristics of the Team

- Reluctant participation (quiet group)
- Suspicion and fear
- Anxiety about the new situation
- Testing of leader and members
- Minimal work accomplished

Team Members Behaviors

- Almost all comments directed to the leader
- Direction and clarification sought
- Status accorded to group members based on their roles outside the group
- Members fail to listen, resulting in non-sequitur statements
- Issues are discussed superficially, with much ambiguity

Team Members Concerns

- Who am I in this group?
- Who are the others?
- Will I be accepted?
- Will he or she value me?
- Is the leader competent?

- Will I be capable?
- Who is the leader?
- What is my role?
- What tasks will I have?

EffectiveTeam Leader Behaviors

- Provide structure by holding regular meetings and assisting in task and role clarification
- Encourage participation by all, domination by none
- Facilitate learning about one another's areas of expertise and preferred working modes
- Share all relevant information
- Encourage members to ask questions of you and one another

Helpful Methods for Leading a Team in this Stage

- Use icebreakers
- Agree upon a set of meeting guidelines
- Plan agendas
- Set-up for shared responsibilities
- Follow-up

## Storming

Members recognize the extent of the task demand and respond emotionally to the perceived requirements. As a way of expressing their individuality, they often become hostile or overbearing as they jostle for positions within the group.

Characteristics of the Team

- Resistance to the task
- Increased tension
- Concern about individual roles and status (i.e., what's in it for me?)
- Minimal work accomplished
- Conflict over control among the group's members and with the leader

Team Members Behaviors

- Attempts made to gain influence, suggestions, proposals
- Subgroups and coalitions form, with possible conflict among them
- The leader is tested and challenged (possibly covertly)
- Members judge and evaluate one another and the leader, resulting in ideas being shot down
- Task avoidance

Team Members Concerns

- How much autonomy will I have?
- Will I have influence over others?

- What is my place in the pecking order?
- Personal level: Who do I like? Who likes me?
- Issues level: Do I have some support in here?

Team Leader Behaviors

- Engage in joint problem solving; have members give reasons why idea is useful and how to improve it
- Establish a norm supporting the expression of different viewpoints
- Discuss the group's decision-making responsibility appropriately
- Encourage members to state how they feel as well as what they think when they obviously have feelings about an issue
- Provide group members with the resources needed to do their jobs, to the extent possible (when this is not possible, explain why)

Helpful Methods

- Refer to agreed-upon meeting guidelines
- Use consensus exercises
- Explain the stages of group development
- Conduct review of meeting, including critique

## Norming

Members accept the team, its idiosyncrasies, and their own roles within that group. Emotional conflict lessens, and the task is accepted.

Characteristics of the Team

- Group formation and solidarity
- Sense of team cohesiveness
- Sharing among the group (open discussion)
- Attempt to achieve maximum harmony
- Constructively expressed emotions
- Moderate work accomplished

Team Members Behaviors

- Members, with one another's support, can disagree with the leader
- The group laughs together; members have fun; some jokes made at the leader's expense
- A sense of "we-ness" and attention to group norms is present
- The group feels superior to other groups in the organization
- Members do not challenge one another as much as the leader would like

Team Members Concerns

- How close should I be to the group members?
- Can we accomplish our tasks successfully?
- How do we compare to other groups?
- What is my relationship to the leader?

Team Leader Behaviors

- Talk openly about your own issues and concerns.
- Have group members manage agenda items, particularly those in which you have a high stake.
- Give a request for both positive and constructive negative feedback in the group.
- Assign challenging problems for consensus decisions (e.g., budget allocations).
- Delegate as much as the members are capable of handling; help them as necessary.

Helpful Methods

- Adhere to agenda
- Reinforce team behaviors

## Performing

Because the team has established its interpersonal norms, it is now capable of diagnosing problems and making decisions using consensus.

Characteristics of the Team

- Constructive self-change occurs
- Team tends to check its own behavior
- Maximum work is accomplished
- Differentiation and productivity

Team Members Behaviors

- Roles are clear and each person's contribution is distinct
- Members take the initiative and accept one another's initiatives
- Open discussion and acceptance of differences among members in their backgrounds and modes of operation
- Challenging one another leads to creative problem solving
- Members seek feedback from one another and from the leader to improve their performances

Team Members Concerns

- Concerns of earlier stages have been resolved

Team Leader Behaviors:

- Jointly set goals that are challenging
- Look for new opportunities to increase the group's scope
- Question assumptions and traditional ways of behaving
- Develop mechanisms for ongoing self-assessment by the group
- Appreciate each member's contribution
- Develop members to their fullest potential through task assignments and feedback.

Helpful Methods

- Include critique in agenda
- Encourage questioning of decisions
- Promote motivational activities
- Watch for group resistance to completing the process

## CREATING A WIN-WIN SITUATION

Teams make many decisions as they progress through the process; the key is to make them *effectively*. The two components involved in reaching an effective decision are quality and acceptance.

*Quality* refers to how good the decision is or how well it meets the needs of the problem. Here the team looks at different alternatives to determine how well they correct the situation. Using a problem-solving process will help to determine the best "quality" decision.

*Acceptance* refers to how well the decision is accepted by the affected group. It is necessary to know that the decision will be actively supported by all involved. After all, there are many ways to do the same thing. The optimum choice should be an alternative on which the team can reach consensus. Teams reach an effective decision by balancing how well each alternative corrects the situation (quality) with how well it will be accepted and supported by the group (acceptance).

$$Effectiveness = Quality + Acceptance$$

### Consensus

A team reaches consensus through a collaborative effort. Consensus implies the voluntary giving of consent. Therefore, a team reaches consensus when each member decides to actively support the decision. This does not mean that everyone totally agrees that the final decision is the best, but that everyone will support the decision that has been made by the group.

Consensus is a *win/win method*. As opposed to voting, consensus guarantees that no one will lose because the final decision is not made until everyone can live with it. This ensures buy-in from each individual, which gives everyone ownership in the decision and commitment to implementation.

Consensus is achieved through the team members' active discussion of the issues surrounding the decision. Each person must bring his or her knowledge and experience into the discussion. Of course, this process takes time, and consensus can sometimes be difficult to attain.

The following guidelines can help the team achieve consensus. Each team member should:

- consider his/her position on the subject prior to the meeting
- obtain any data possible to support that position
- recognize the obligation to share his/her opinion with the group
- be willing to listen to the opinions and thoughts of every other team member
- be open to changing his/her personal position
- encourage differences of opinion in order to clarify issues
- avoid conflict-inducing techniques (i.e., voting, compromising, etc.)

## CREATIVE VIRTUAL TEAMS AT AMERICAN GENERAL LIFE COMPANIES

Organizing creative work teams is a bit of an art and a science, usually requiring collaboration and a clear process. Much is known about teamwork and process design. However, because creativity and insight are unpredictable components of great ideas, reliably producing successful innovations has remained elusive for most companies. Many companies have searched for ways to generate more quality ideas to enter their innovation pipelines, and to date, most market solutions rely upon computer-based collaboration.

In 2007, American General Life Companies introduced a different concept, the Brain Trooper program, which, through virtual work teams, continually generates creative concepts with real potential. These ideas often require more work to become implementation-ready, but the first and most unpredictable component of innovation, creativity, flourishes in the Brain Trooper team design.

The ingredients to the Brain Trooper program's success are the teams' diversity, size, creativity training, strong facilitation, process design, and trust among members. Brain Trooper teams are formed of mixtures of 6–8 employees from various business lines, geographies, functional areas, experience levels, hierarchical levels, and backgrounds. Each member brings a wealth of knowledge from his or her professional and personal experiences. However, a team is most successful when its membership includes a mixture of both subject matter experts (SMEs) and novices relative to the subject matter at hand. Guided by a strong facilitator, the teams employ creative tools to generate high quality concepts. The importance of strong facilitation cannot be overstated. During training, team members develop trust in one another, and this trust has been consistently rated among Brain Trooper program participants as the most important component of their success.

Because the team members are geographically dispersed and travel funds are limited, most team meetings are virtual rather than face-to-face. Most creativity tools are designed to be used face-to-face; however, the Brain Trooper teams at American General Life Companies have shown that, with trust among team members, strong facilitation, and some adaptations, traditional tools can be used very effectively for virtual team meetings.

When working virtually on creative assignments (i.e., by teleconference or video conference), it is necessary to make a few adaptations to traditional creative techniques. Brainstorming by telephone requires more pausing and listening than is required in face-to-face brainstorming, because it is not known who will be the next person to speak and, when using the telephone, there are few, if any, nonverbal clues about who may have something to say. Video conferences do not solve this issue, and actually may be a hindrance to the free-flow necessary for creativity, because team members tend to focus attention on the screen and away from the informal discussion that would normally be happening among the participants who are gathered in a single room. For this reason, Brain Troopers actually prefer working by telephone, once strong relationships have been established through training. The Nominal Group Technique is particularly effective in a virtual format, because it helps ensure that no one person or group will dominate over other people or groups in other locations.

Meeting protocols also must be adapted to work for virtual creative teams. An agenda is useful, but the agenda should not drive the meeting. It should simply serve to remind participants that the meeting's goals are to create concepts, hear updates from research, resume a prior discussion, listen to a guest speaker, etc. Each visual aid must be prepared in advance, and either modified while the whole team is viewing the document through desktop sharing or collaboration software or modified by one person after the meeting and circulated among the meeting's participants for confirmation of the document's accuracy. If desktop sharing or collaboration software is not being used, the speaking team member must use very descriptive language to help others on the phone know what he or she is drawing or referencing so that they can follow the conversation. Ironically, electronic white board technology has not been overly helpful to our Brain Troopers in virtual team meetings, because of its complexity and unsuitability to the types of documents being created. Note taking is more challenging in creative teams, because the conversation wanders; however, written summaries have proven very useful, perhaps necessary, to those who attended a meeting when resuming conversations in later meetings. Unlike notes from project meetings, written summaries have not proven very useful in helping absent members of creative teams become informed, because creative concepts often require having been present to fully understand them. In any case, Brain Troopers have found it very important to begin each meeting with a summary of what transpired at the last team meeting, using such notes, so that all who are present may make meaningful contributions.

(*Source:* Lisa Shumway, Manager of the Center of Innovation, American General Life Companies. Used with permission.)

# PROFESSIONAL AND ETHICAL STANDARDS

Professionals are expected to hold themselves to a high ethical standard. Employees must observe the organization's code of ethics. Certified quality professionals are required to subscribe to the American Society for Quality's Code of Ethics.

## ASQ CODE OF ETHICS

### Fundamental Principles

ASQ requires its members and certification holders to conduct themselves ethically by:

**I.** Being honest and impartial in serving the public, their employers, customers, and clients.

**II.** Striving to increase the competence and prestige of the quality profession, and

**III.** Using their knowledge and skill for the enhancement of human welfare.

Members and certification holders are required to observe the tenets set forth below:

### Relations with the Public

Article 1—Hold paramount the safety, health, and welfare of the public in the performance of their professional duties.

### Relations with Employers and Clients

Article 2—Perform services only in their areas of competence.

Article 3—Continue their professional development throughout their careers and provide opportunities for the professional and ethical development of others.

Article 4—Act in a professional manner in dealings with ASQ staff and each employer, customer or client.

Article 5—Act as faithful agents or trustees and avoid conflict of interest and the appearance of conflicts of interest.

**Relations with Peers**

Article 6—Build their professional reputation on the merit of their services and not compete unfairly with others.

Article 7—Assure that credit for the work of others is given to those to whom it is due.

(Reprinted with permission from http://www.asq.org/about-asq/who-we-are/ethics.html © 2009 ASQ. No further distribution allowed without permission.)

But good ethical performance goes beyond mere adherence to an organization's code of ethics. A professional should avoid even the appearance of impropriety. Some organizations have made this part of their code of ethics. For example, at IBM, employees are not allowed to accept anything from suppliers. An IBM employee's having even an inexpensive gift pen with a supplier's name on it might cause other suppliers to suspect that the employee favors that supplier over others—an appearance of impropriety. A professional's reputation is an enormous asset and once lost, cannot easily be recovered.

## SUMMARY

Barriers that inhibit quality improvement efforts exist. Often these barriers share a common cause—poor communication. The responsibility for removing the barriers rests with management.

The classic theories of motivation and the process theories of motivation provide insight into why some things motivate some people but not others. Maslow proposes these differences may be due to the individual's place in a hierarchy of needs. McGregor suggests that the differences may be due to the manager's approach. McClelland suggests it relates to the needs of the employee, while Hertzberg differentiates between those things that can increase satisfaction and those things that can merely create no dissatisfaction. The process theories of motivation provide insight into how behavior is influenced. These theories help managers develop a motivation system that is more likely to be effective.

Simply gathering several people together does not create a team. There are roles and responsibilities that must be fulfilled in order to turn a group of people into a team. Groups move through stages from forming to performing. This is a natural process, but each stage requires its own type of leadership. The ultimate objective is to create a team that produces high-quality decisions that are accepted by the affected groups.

Ethical behavior is expected of quality professionals. This means, at a minimum, that the quality professional abides by his or her employer's code of ethics and that of the American Society for Quality.

# DISCUSSION QUESTIONS

1. Discuss what Deming means when he says that most of the barriers to quality-improvement efforts are management's responsibility.
2. What are some actions that could be taken to improve communication of quality within an organization?
3. What are the key roles and responsibilities of a team leader?
4. What does the word *synergy* mean as it applies to teams?
5. Is conflict within a team always bad? Discuss.
6. Compare the roles and responsibilities of team leader and team facilitator.
7. What are some ways to move a team out of the storming stage to the norming stage?
8. Is developing consensus better than voting on a decision in a team? Discuss.
9. What are some ways to achieve consensus?
10. Does consensus mean that everyone on the team must agree completely with all decisions made by the team? Discuss.
11. What are the essential elements of a team charter? What potential difficulties might a good team charter help prevent?
12. Discuss the meaning of the term "appearance of impropriety." Discuss some examples of actions that could create an appearance of impropriety.

## CASE STUDY 13.1:   *Tom's Team*

©2008 Victor E. Sower, Ph.D., C.Q.E.

"Tom, put together a team to correct the increasing proportion of defective XRO products being produced on Line 2." This was the last thing Bob Wilson, general manager, said before the staff meeting adjourned; it was directed to Tom Tubb, quality assurance manager.

Immediately upon his return to his office, Tom called his supervisors together. "Bob is concerned about the high proportion of rejected XRO units on Line 2. Consider yourselves a team. Find out what the problem is and get back to me before the staff meeting next week."

1. What do you think of Tom's approach to forming a team to address the problem?
2. What kinds of problems could you foresee with his approach that might inhibit the team's ability to solve the problem?
3. Suggest approaches that Tom should have used to carry out the directive from Bob.

## CASE STUDY 13.2: *Self Directed Work Teams at BHI*

The Kick-Off Meeting for the Self Directed Work Team—February 1997

"Are you ready?" George, the machine shop manager at BHI, asked, looking at Shane. Shane was an internal consultant at BHI assigned to George. It was February 1997 and, after eight months of planning, the production machine shop unit of BHI was about to launch an initiative to introduce self-directed work teams to the machine shop floor.

"Let's make this happen," Shane responded, as he walked with George to the front of the break room in the manufacturing building at BHI's Houston, Texas, facility.

George began the meeting by greeting the machinists. "I'd like to welcome you all to the beginning of a journey. What we begin today will have a dramatic impact on how we conduct our business in the future. Recently, we conducted a market survey with our customers regarding our performance and their upcoming needs. The results of the customer survey told us that on-time delivery, quality, and the right quantity of our tools would be the difference for the future. We can't work any harder than we are now. We will have to be efficient and work smarter."

"We are going to split up certain departments and be process-oriented. This starts with the machine shop and its support areas. Effective today, all 34 of you have been assigned to self-directed work teams (SDWTs), numbered 1 through 9. Each team has a certain product or process they will be responsible for. In the past, these units have focused primarily on their own functions within a hierarchical structure. Now, they will be directly focused on providing support either to clients or to manufacturing groups. They will begin to function much more as client-focused teams. This will improve communication, ownership, and give the machine shop the support we need."

There were some general murmurs from the crowd as George continued by detailing the responsibilities for each of the teams. There were some snickers of skepticism from the crowd. After all, management had talked about major changes before, but little happened.

"Are we really going to be allowed to make decisions pertaining to our area?" a machinist asked, glaring at Bob, the foreman.

"Yes," George responded. "It will be simple decisions in the beginning, and then as the teams mature, so will the responsibilities and rewards."

"What if this doesn't work?" someone shouted from the back of the room.

George raised his voice and very clearly said, "There is no going back—we must make this work—and failure is not an option. If you don't want to be a part of the team concept, then I suggest you find somewhere else to work. Meeting dismissed!"

There was a lot of grumbling and discussion from the machinists as they left the room. Some were excited about the changes; others thought things were just fine as they were; still others mulled over the question of "what's in it for me?" while the skeptics grumbled about "why are we doing this anyway?"

Two weeks after the initial meeting, the machine shop was slowly getting the message that George was really serious about the changes. Every time he was questioned about the SDWT initiative and whether management was really committed to the changes, his response was always the same, "There is no going back."

## THE QUANTITY DEBATE—JUNE 1997

Prior to May 1997 the machine shop had no formal responsibility to inspect their own parts before sending them to quality control. Subsequently, under the new SDWT process, they did assume these inspection responsibilities.

After the radial-bearing team had its big re-election fight, Shane started checking in at least once every two weeks with the three teams for which he had responsibility. He hoped that with more frequent monitoring, some of these problems could be headed off early before they exploded.

Three weeks after the second election, Shane had a message to deliver. George wanted the teams to know that if any of the SDWTs found all their errors for three straight months, he would reward that team with some special team shirts and hats. As Shane walked through the radial bearing team area during break-time, he noticed Barry at Arthur's Mazak M-5 machine. Barry explained that the bearing team had decided to rotate their breaks; that way the work could continue and the machines wouldn't stop running.

"George told us the demand for radial bearings was still increasing, and if we hit 42 parts per day, he would serve us a customer breakfast," Barry reported to Shane.

A customer breakfast was a company tradition. Usually, when a customer came in for the whole day, they were served a catered meal with all the finery of a first-class restaurant—white linens, candles, and china. This format had also been used for other special occasions, but was perceived by the shop floor as a "management-only" ritual.

Later that week, Shane was summoned to George's office. George was irate. "When they make major changes like that, you have to let me know," he shouted.

"What change in particular are you talking about?" Shane asked calmly.

"The work order quantity of the radial-bearing team. I had that set at five pieces per order for the last year. We are behind. By keeping the quantity around five, each customer gets some of what they need. In addition, we earn a 10 percent profit for each radial bearing and they sell for $2,800 each. If we don't maintain $40,000 profit each month, we'll all lose our jobs!"

On its own decision, the team had changed the work-order quantity from five to fifteen to increase production efficiencies. Shane remembered that the bearing team had discussed the quantity issue in some detail at a previous team meeting. The issue was that the team was spending more time setting up the machine to run the parts than actually running them. Often, it would take three to four hours to fully set up a machine to handle a parts production run that might only take an hour. By changing the work order quantity, the team was able to make longer production runs and recover some of the machine set up time.

George continued, "I want you to go out there and have them change that back, today!"

Shane picked his words carefully, "George, I can't do that."

"Then I will," yelled George.

Shane matched the tone so George was certain to understand this was serious. "Look, you go out there and change that quantity back and you'll have destroyed everything that we've done in the last six months. You wanted improvements, and they're doing what you requested of them. Do you really want to stop what you have started?"

George countered, "They weren't supposed to go this far; that wasn't in their job descriptions."

"True," Shane replied, "but we never highlighted work-order quantity as a boundary. Let them try this for two weeks, and if it doesn't work, then I'll talk to them about changing the quantity back."

George grumbled, "We'll see where this goes. Two weeks."

As a result of the change in the work order quantity, over the next six months the team was able to move from being several hundred parts behind to being six weeks ahead in its production schedule. This resulted in customer orders being filled completely, rather than shipping partially filled orders, as had been the case under they previous work-order quantity. George never commented about the team's decision again.

## THE TEAM SUCCEEDS—DECEMBER 1997

"Prior to forming the radial-bearing team, the machine shop produced an average of 5 parts per day in January and received 13 discrepant material reports (DMRs) from the plant's Quality Control Department," stated George, as he handed out Figure 1. "In November the team produced an average of 31 parts per day and received 16 DMRs."

"Congratulations. It looks like significant cost savings and efficiency have been gained as you have identified problems and resolved them. I have also noticed that you have increased your daily production of bearings," responded Shane.

"Yes, this is true. We met on our own and made some more tooling changes to reduce the setup time. We are able to produce at least five parts more per day using the new process," the team leader said, beaming.

George thanked the team for their increased production, and handed out tan shirts and hats to recognize their accomplishment in finding all of their errors for three straight months. They read "The Bearing Bears" and displayed the company logo. The hats even had military-style gold trim on their brims.

| | DEC '96 | JAN '97 | FEB '97 | MAR '97 | APR '97 | MAY '97 | JUN '97 | JUL '97 | AUG '97 | SPT '97 | OCT '97 | NOV '97 |
|---|---|---|---|---|---|---|---|---|---|---|---|---|
| SDWT | 0 | 0 | 0 | 0 | 0 | 4 | 5 | 5 | 9 | 12 | 16 | 16 |
| QC | 3 | 13 | 13 | 20 | 17 | 4 | 4 | 1 | 3 | 0 | 0 | 0 |
| CC | 0 | 0 | 0 | 0 | 0 | 1 | 0 | 0 | 0 | 0 | 0 | 0 |
| TOTAL | 3 | 13 | 13 | 20 | 17 | 9 | 9 | 6 | 12 | 12 | 16 | 16 |

| | DEC '96 | JAN '97 | FEB '97 | MAR '97 | APR '97 | MAY '97 | JUN '97 | JUL '97 | AUG '97 | SPT '97 | OCT '97 | NOV '97 |
|---|---|---|---|---|---|---|---|---|---|---|---|---|
| Parts Made per Day | 9 | 5 | 19 | 20 | 16 | 23 | 30 | 24 | 31 | 29 | 30 | 31 |
| No. of Days Worked | 22 | 23 | 20 | 21 | 22 | 22 | 21 | 23 | 21 | 22 | 23 | 20 |

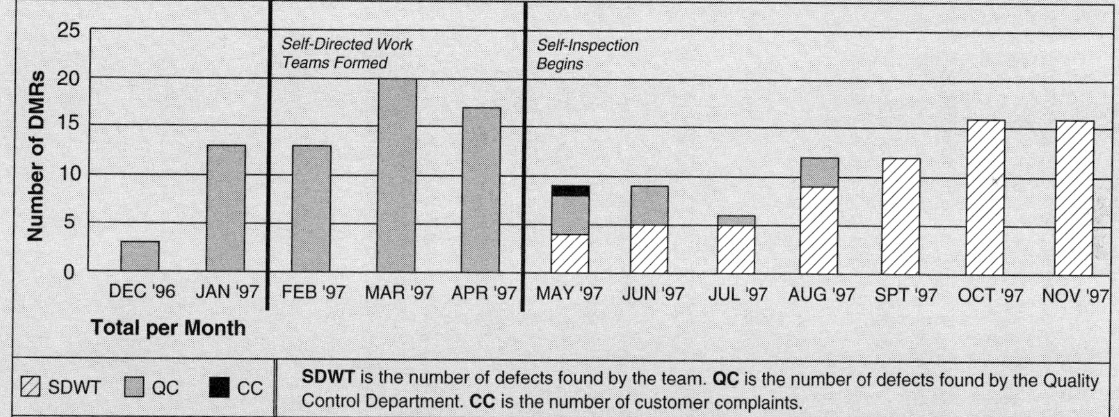

Total per Month

Legend: SDWT | QC | CC

**SDWT** is the number of defects found by the team. **QC** is the number of defects found by the Quality Control Department. **CC** is the number of customer complaints.

**DMR** (Discrepant Material Report) is a report that highlights the dimension(s) of a machined part that is not per print and, consequently, will not perform to specification. One **DMR** is written for each discrepant part.

**Figure 1.** Number of DMRs/Parts per Day—Bearing

"These will be the envy of the machine shop," one of the machinists predicted.

"Wear them proudly," George encouraged.

1. What objectives did BHI seek to accomplish through the introduction of SDWTs? Were these objectives accomplished?
2. Analyze the data in Figure 1 and present it in a way that best demonstrates the impact of the SDWT initiative.
3. Discuss George and Shane's approach to launching the SDWT initiative. How did they try to motivate the employees to accept the change?
4. Discuss Shane's approach to dealing with George's demand that he change the work order quantity back to five. What would be the impact on the team if Shane had lost the argument and had to change the work-order quantity back?

## EXERCISES AND ACTIVITIES

1. Assign a case study as a group project. Have the group create a team charter and assign team roles prior to addressing the case. Have the group plan the project and prepare a network diagram for the project. Make these assignments due early in the project cycle and well before the due date for the final case study report.
2. Collect published codes of ethics from as many business organizations and professional associations as possible. Compare these documents—what are their good and bad points? What is omitted that should be included? Use your comparisons to develop a model code of ethics for a business or professional organization.

## SUPPLEMENTARY READINGS

Deming, W. E. (1981–1982). "Improvement of Quality and Productivity through Action by Management." *National Productivity Review* 1(1), 12–22. Reprinted in Sower, V. E., J. Motwani, & M. J. Savoie. (1995). *Classic Readings in Operations Management*. Ft. Worth, TX: Dryden, 231–247.

Deming, W. E. (1986). *Out of the Crisis*. Cambridge, MA: MIT Press.

Dessler, G. (2005). *Human Resource Management*, 10th edition. Upper Saddle River, NJ: Prentice Hall.

Ishikawa, K. (1984). *Quality Control Circles at Work*. Tokyo: Asian Productivity Organization.

Johnson, R. S. (1993). *TQM: Leadership for the Quality Transformation*. Milwaukee, WI: ASQC Quality Press.

Lindsay, W. M., & J. A. Petrick. (1997). *Total Quality and Organization Development*. Boca Raton, FL: St. Lucia Press.

Wilkinson, H. E., C. D. Orth, & R. C. Benfari. (1986). "Motivation Theories: An Integrated Operational Model." *SAM Advanced Management Journal* 51(4), 24–31.

# REFERENCES

Banker, R. D., J. M. Field, R. G. Schroeder, & K. K. Sinha. (1996). "Impact of Work Teams on Manufacturing Performance: A Longitudinal Study." *Academy of Management Journal* 39(4), 867–890.

Bedeian, A. G. (1993). *Management*, 3rd edition. Ft. Worth, TX: Dryden.

Bemowski, K. (1992). "The Quality Glossary." *Quality Progress* 25(2), 26.

Brocka, B., & M. S. Brocka. (1992). *Quality Management, Implementing the Best Ideas of the Masters*. Burr Ridge, IL: Irwin.

Covey, S. R. (1986). *The Seven Habits of Highly Successful People*. New York: Simon & Schuster.

Deming, W. E. (1981–1982). "Improvement of Quality and Productivity through Action by Management." *National Productivity Review* 1(1), 12–22. Reprinted in Sower, V. E., J. Motwani, & M. J. Savoie. (1995). *Classic Readings in Operations Management*. Ft. Worth, TX: Dryden, 237.

Dessler, G. (1997). *Human Resource Management*. Upper Saddle River, NJ: Prentice Hall.

Griffin, R. (1988). "Consequences of Quality Circles in an Industrial Setting: A Longitudinal Assessment." *Academy of Management Journal* 31(2), 338–358.

Harvey, T. R., & B. Drolet. (1994). *Building Teams, Building People*. Lancaster, PA: Technomic Publishing Co.

Herzberg, F. (1966). *Work and the Nature of Man*. New York: World Publishing.

Ishikawa, K. (1984). *Quality Control Circles at Work*. Tokyo: Asian Productivity Organization.

Johnson, R. S. (1993). *TQM: Leadership for the Quality Transformation*. Milwaukee, WI: ASQC Quality Press.

Marks, M., P. Mirvis, E. Hackett, & J. Grady. (1986). "Employee Participation in a Quality Circle Program: Impact on Quality of Work Life, Productivity, and Absenteeism." *Journal of Applied Psychology* 71(1), 61–69.

Maslow, A. H. (1964). *Motivation and Personality*. New York: McGraw-Hill.

McClelland, D. C. (1961). *The Achieving Society*. New York: Van Nostrand.

McGregor, D. (1960). *The Human Side of Enterprise*. New York: McGraw-Hill.

Orsburn, J. D., L. Moran, E. Musselwhite, & J. H. Zenger. (1990). *Self-Directed Work Teams*. Omewood, IL: Business One Irwin.

Plovnick, M., R. Fry, & I. Rubin. (1975). "New Developments in O.D. Technology: Programmed Team Development." *Training and Development Journal* 29(4), 19–26.

Porter, L., & E. Lawler. (1968). *Managerial Attitudes and Performance*. Homewood, IL: Irwin.

Snow, C. E. (1927). *Tech Engineering News* (November).

Tuckman. (1965). "Developmental Sequence in Small Groups." *Psychological Bulletin* 63(6), 384–399.

Vroom, V. (1964). *Work and Motivation*. New York: Wiley.

Wilkinson, H. E., C. D. Orth, & R. C. Benfari. (1986). "Motivation Theories: An Integrated Operational Model." *SAM Advanced Management Journal* 51(4), 24–31.

## Table of Four-Digit Random Numbers

| | | | | |
|------|------|------|------|------|
| 9301 | 9230 | 4867 | 0187 | 0816 |
| 5940 | 0570 | 0928 | 5713 | 8673 |
| 1946 | 7308 | 6931 | 2841 | 1919 |
| 0537 | 9197 | 0743 | 4714 | 6096 |
| 1816 | 4086 | 0715 | 6195 | 8700 |
| 6202 | 7127 | 5954 | 9829 | 4855 |
| 0244 | 6758 | 6637 | 6566 | 6365 |
| 0891 | 5979 | 9763 | 7810 | 6287 |
| 7515 | 0854 | 1741 | 6595 | 0046 |
| 1325 | 7991 | 1112 | 2058 | 7569 |
| 0721 | 3172 | 8962 | 2091 | 0473 |
| 4433 | 2218 | 1901 | 7107 | 9716 |
| 4468 | 8196 | 0488 | 3589 | 4992 |
| 0223 | 0292 | 1896 | 8921 | 9520 |
| 7252 | 5788 | 8036 | 0469 | 6751 |
| 7663 | 8327 | 2893 | 7572 | 6988 |
| 8802 | 0494 | 5366 | 7901 | 7360 |
| 7643 | 4017 | 6199 | 1368 | 2370 |
| 6223 | 5258 | 0812 | 9480 | 0843 |
| 9552 | 0478 | 0011 | 3984 | 9297 |

Generated using NWA Quality Analyst™

Table of Four-Digit Random Numbers

(continued using A 5 Quality Analyzer)

# APPENDIX B

| Areas under the Standard Normal Distribution Curve from $-\infty$ to z | 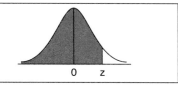 |
|---|---|

Standard Normal Distribution Table

| z | 0.00 | 0.01 | 0.02 | 0.03 | 0.04 | 0.05 | 0.06 | 0.07 | 0.08 | 0.09 |
|---|---|---|---|---|---|---|---|---|---|---|
| 0.0 | .5000 | .5040 | .5080 | .5120 | .5160 | .5199 | .5239 | .5279 | .5319 | .5359 |
| 0.1 | .5398 | .5438 | .5478 | .5517 | .5557 | .5596 | .5636 | .5675 | .5714 | .5753 |
| 0.2 | .5793 | .5832 | .5871 | .5910 | .5948 | .5987 | .6036 | .6064 | .6103 | .6141 |
| 0.3 | .6179 | .6217 | .6255 | .6293 | .6331 | .6368 | .6406 | .6443 | .6480 | .6517 |
| 0.4 | .6554 | .6591 | .6628 | .6664 | .6700 | .6736 | .6772 | .6808 | .6844 | .6879 |
| 0.5 | .6915 | .6950 | .6985 | .7019 | .7054 | .7088 | .7123 | .7157 | .7190 | .7224 |
| 0.6 | .7257 | .7291 | .7324 | .7357 | .7389 | .7422 | .7454 | .7486 | .7517 | .7549 |
| 0.7 | .7580 | .7611 | .7642 | .7673 | .7703 | .7734 | .7764 | .7794 | .7823 | .7852 |
| 0.8 | .7881 | .7910 | .7939 | .7967 | .7995 | .8023 | .8051 | .8078 | .8106 | .8133 |
| 0.9 | .8159 | .8186 | .8212 | .8238 | .8264 | .8289 | .8315 | .8340 | .8365 | .8389 |
| 1.0 | .8413 | .8438 | .8461 | .8485 | .8508 | .8531 | .8554 | .8577 | .8599 | .8621 |
| 1.1 | .8643 | .8665 | .8686 | .8708 | .8729 | .8749 | .8770 | .8790 | .8810 | .8830 |
| 1.2 | .8849 | .8869 | .8888 | .8907 | .8925 | .8944 | .8962 | .8980 | .8997 | .9015 |
| 1.3 | .9032 | .9049 | .9066 | .9082 | .9099 | .9115 | .9131 | .9147 | .9162 | .9177 |
| 1.4 | .9192 | .9207 | .9222 | .9236 | .9251 | .9265 | .9279 | .9292 | .9306 | .9319 |
| 1.5 | .9332 | .9345 | .9357 | .9370 | .9382 | .9394 | .9406 | .9418 | .9429 | .9441 |
| 1.6 | .9452 | .9463 | .9474 | .9484 | .9495 | .9505 | .9515 | .9525 | .9535 | .9545 |
| 1.7 | .9554 | .9564 | .9573 | .9582 | .9591 | .9599 | .9608 | .9616 | .9625 | .9633 |
| 1.8 | .9641 | .9649 | .9656 | .9664 | .9671 | .9678 | .9686 | .9693 | .9699 | .9706 |
| 1.9 | .9713 | .9719 | .9726 | .9732 | .9738 | .9744 | .9750 | .9756 | .9761 | .9767 |
| 2.0 | .9772 | .9778 | .9783 | .9788 | .9793 | .9798 | .9803 | .9808 | .9812 | .9817 |
| 2.1 | .9821 | .9826 | .9830 | .9834 | .9838 | .9842 | .9846 | .9850 | .9854 | .9857 |
| 2.2 | .9861 | .9864 | .9868 | .9871 | .9875 | .9878 | .9881 | .9884 | .9887 | .9890 |
| 2.3 | .9893 | .9896 | .9898 | .9901 | .9904 | .9906 | .9909 | .9911 | .9913 | .9916 |
| 2.4 | .9918 | .9920 | .9922 | .9925 | .9927 | .9929 | .9931 | .9932 | .9934 | .9936 |
| 2.5 | .9938 | .9940 | .9941 | .9943 | .9945 | .9946 | .9948 | .9949 | .9951 | .9952 |
| 2.6 | .9953 | .9955 | .9956 | .9957 | .9959 | .9960 | .9961 | .9962 | .9963 | .9964 |
| 2.7 | .9965 | .9966 | .9967 | .9968 | .9969 | .9970 | .9971 | .9972 | .9973 | .9974 |
| 2.8 | .9974 | .9975 | .9976 | .9977 | .9977 | .9978 | .9979 | .9979 | .9980 | .9981 |
| 2.9 | .9981 | .9982 | .9982 | .9983 | .9984 | .9984 | .9985 | .9985 | .9986 | .9986 |
| 3.0 | .9987 | .9987 | .9987 | .9988 | .9988 | .9989 | .9989 | .9989 | .9990 | .9990 |
| 3.1 | .9990 | .9991 | .9991 | .9991 | .9991 | .9992 | .9992 | .9992 | .9993 | .9993 |
| 3.2 | .9993 | .9993 | .9994 | .9994 | .9994 | .9994 | .9994 | .9995 | .9995 | .9995 |
| 3.3 | .9995 | .9995 | .9995 | .9996 | .9996 | .9996 | .9996 | .9996 | .9996 | .9997 |
| 3.4 | .9997 | .9997 | .9997 | .9997 | .9997 | .9997 | .9997 | .9997 | .9997 | .9998 |

Akao, Y. (1990). *Quality Function Deployment: Integrating Customer Requirements into Produc Design*. Cambridge, MA: Productivity Press.

American Society for Quality Control Statistics Division. (1983). *Glossary & Tables for Statistical Quality Control*. Milwaukee, WI: ASQC Quality Press.

American Society for Quality Statistics Division. (2005). *Glossary & Tables for Statistical Quality Control*, 4th edition. Milwaukee, WI: ASQ Quality Press.

Amrine, H., J. Ritchey, C. Moodie, & J. Kmec. (1993). *Manufacturing Organization and Management*, 6th edition. Englewood Cliffs, NJ: Prentice Hall.

*ANSI/ASQC M1-1996. American National Standard for Calibration Systems.*

*ANSI/ASQC Q1-1986. American National Standard Generic Guidelines for Auditing of Quality Systems.*

*ANSI/ASQC Q10011-1, 2, 3-1994. Guidelines for Auditing Quality Systems.*

*ANSI/ASQC S2-1995. Introduction to Attribute Sampling.*

*ANSI/ASQ Z1.4-2003. Sampling Procedures and Tables for Inspection by Attributes.*

*ANSI/ASQ Z1.9-2003. Sampling Procedures and Tables for Inspection by Variables for Percent Nonconforming.*

*ANSI/ISO/ASQ QE 19011S-2004. Guidelines for Quality and/or Environmental Management Systems Auditing—U.S. Version with Supplemental Guidance Added.*

*ANSI/ASQC Q9000-1-1994. American National Standard Quality Management and Quality Assurance Standards—Guidelines for Selection and Use.*

*ANSI/ISO/ASQ Q9000-2000. Quality Management Systems—Fundamentals and Vocabulary.*

*ANSI/ISO/ASQ Q9000-2008. American National Standard Quality Management Systems—Fundamentals and Vocabulary.*

*ANSI/ISO/ASQ Q9001-2000. Quality Management Systems—Requirements.*

*ANSI/ISO/ASQ Q9001-2008. Quality Management Systems—Requirements.*

*ANSI/ISO/ASQ Q9004-2000. Quality Management Systems—Guidelines for Performance Improvements.*

*ANSI/ISO/ASQ Q9004-2008. Quality Management Systems—Guidelines for Performance Improvements.*

Arter, D. R. (2003). *Quality Audits for Improved Performance*, 3rd edition. Milwaukee, WI: ASQ Quality Press.

*ASQC Automotive Division Statistical Process Control Manual.* (1986). Milwaukee, WI: ASQC Quality Press.

ASQ Statistics Division. (2005). *Glossary & Tables for Statistical Quality Control*, 4th edition. Milwaukee, WI: ASQ Quality Press.

ASQC Statistics Division. (1983). *Glossary & Tables for Statistical Quality Control*. Milwaukee, WI: ASQC Quality Press.

*ASTM, ASTM STP 15D. ASTM Manual on Presentation of Data and Control Chart Analysis.* (1976). Philadelphia: American Society for Testing and Materials.

Babacus, E., & G. Boller. (1992). "An Empirical Assessment of the SERVQUAL Scale." *Journal of Business Research* 24, 253–268.

Babakus, E., C. Bienstock, & J. Van Scotter. (2004). "Linking perceived Quality and Customer Satisfaction to Store Traffic and Revenue Growth." *Decision Sciences* 35(4), 713–737.

*Baldrige Award Application Forms.* (2009–2001). Gaithersburg, MD: NIST.

Banker, R. D., J. M. Field, R. G. Schroeder, & K. K. Sinha. (1996). "Impact of Work Teams on Manufacturing Performance: A Longitudinal Study." *Academy of Management Journal* 39, 867–890.

Barfield, O. (1988). *History in English Words*. Great Barrington, MA: Inner Traditions/Lindisfarne Press. Reprint of original 1953 edition. London: Faber & Faber.

Barker, J. (1990). *The Business of Paradigms*. Burnsville, MN: Charthouse International Learning Corp.

Barrentine, L. (1999). *An Introduction to Design of Experiments—A Simplified Approach*. Milwaukee, WI: ASQ Quality Press.

Barrentine, L. B. (2003). *Concepts for R&R Studies*, 3rd edition, Milwaukee, WI: ASQC Quality Press.

Bedeian, A. G. (1993). *Management*, 3rd edition. Ft. Worth, TX: Dryden.

Beecroft, G. (2001). "Cost of Quality and Quality Planning Affect the Bottom Line." *The Quality Management Forum* 27(1), 1–7.

Bemowski, K. (1992). "The Quality Glossary," *Quality Progress* 25(2), 18–29.

Bishara, R., & M. Wyrick. (1994). "A Systematic Approach to Quality Assurance Auditing." *Quality Progress* 27(12), 67–70.

Boggs, W. (2004). "TQM and Organizational Culture: A Case Study." *Quality Management Journal* 11(2), 42–52.

Bothe, D. R. (1988). "SPC for Short Production Runs." *Quality* 27(12), 58–59.

Bottorff, D. (1997). "COQ Systems: The Right Stuff." *Quality Progress* 30(3), 33–35.

Bowersox, D. J., & D. J. Closs. (1996). *Logistical Management: The Integrated Supply Chain Process*. New York: McGraw-Hill.

Bradshaw, G., & S. Wright. (ND). http://www.wam.umd.edu/~stwright/WrBr/taleplane.html.

Breyfogle, F., J. Cupello, & B. Meadows. (2001). *Managing Six Sigma*. New York: John Wiley & Sons.

Brocka, B., & M. S. Brocka. (1992). *Quality Management: Implementing the Best Ideas of the Masters*. Burr Ridge, IL: Irwin.

Bronson Methodist Hospital. (2005). *2005 Malcolm Baldrige National Quality Award Application Summary*.

Burns, Robert. (1785). *To a Mouse*

Burr, I. (1967). "The Effect of Non-Normality on Constants for X-bar and R Charts." *Industrial Quality Control* 23(9), 563–568.

Camp, R. (1995). *Business Process Benchmarking: Finding and Implementing Best Practices*. Milwaukee, WI: ASQC Quality Press.

Campanella, J. (ed.) (1999). *Principles of Quality Costs: Principles, Implementation, and Use*, 3rd edition. Milwaukee: ASQ Quality Press.

Carr, L. (1995). "How Xerox Sustains the Cost of Quality." *Management Accounting* 76(2), 26–32.

Chambers, J. (1969). "Beginning a Multidimensional Theory of Creativity." *Psychological Reports* 25(3), 779–799.

Chen, C., & H. Roth. (2005). *The Big Book of Six Sigma Training Games*. New York: McGraw-Hill.

Clarke, T. (1996). "Organizational Climate, Productivity and Creativity". Paper prepared for the Canadian Government Working Group on Rewards, Recognition and incentives (November) http://www.stargate-consultants.ca/artcexec.htm.

Cokins, G. (1996). *Activity-Based Cost Management: Making it Work*. Boston: McGraw-Hill.

Cooper, J. (ed.). (1997). *Plato: Complete Works*. Indianapolis, IN: Hackett Publishing Co., Inc., 898–921.

Covey, S. R. (1986). *The Seven Habits of Highly Successful People*. New York: Simon & Schuster.

Crocket, H. (1935). "Quality, but Just Enough." *Factory Management and Maintenance* 93(June), 245–246.

Cronin, J., & S. Taylor. (1992). "Measuring Service Quality: A Reexamination and Extension." *Journal of Marketing* 56(3), 55–68.

Crosby, P. (1979). *Quality is Free*. New York: McGraw-Hill.

Deane, R., & R. Burgess. (1998). "Experiential Teaching Techniques in Quality Management: The Roman Catapult." *Quality Management Journal* 5(2), 58–66.

Deming, W. (1982). *Out of the Crisis*. Cambridge, MA: MIT Center for Advanced Engineering Study.

Deming, W. (1981–1982). "Improvement of Quality and Productivity through Action by Management." *National Productivity Review* 1(1), 12–22. Reprinted in Sower, V. E., J. Motwani, & M. J. Savoie. (1995). *Classic Readings in Operations Management*, Ft. Worth, TX: Dryden, 231–247.

Deming, W. (1993). *The New Economics for Industry, Government, Education*. Cambridge, MA: MIT Center for Advanced Engineering Study.

Dessler, G. (2005). *Human Resource Management*, 10th edition. Upper Saddle River, NJ: Prentice Hall.

Dewar, D. (2005). *Timely Tips for Teams* (April). E-newsletter of CQI International.

Dodge, H. F. (1928). "A Method of Rating Manufactured Product." *The Bell System Technical Journal* 7(April), 350–368.

Dodge, H. F., & H. G. Romig. (1959). *Sampling Inspection Tables, Single and Double Sampling*, 2nd edition. New York: Wiley.

Dow Chemical. *1999 Annual Report to Shareholders*.

Duncan, A. J. (1986). *Quality Control and Industrial Statistics*, 5th edition. Homewood, IL: Irwin.

Evans, J. (1990). *Creative Thinking in the Decision and Management Sciences*. Cincinnati, OH: Southwestern.

Evans, J., & W. Lindsay. (2005). *The Management and Control of Quality*, 6th edition. Mason, OH: Thomson South-Western, 694.

Farago, F. T. (1994). *Handbook of Dimensional Measurement*, 3rd edition. New York: Industrial Press.

Farnum, N. R. (1992). "Control Charts for Short Runs: Nonconstant Process and Measurement Error." *Journal of Quality Technology* 24(July), 138–144.

Feigenbaum, A. V. (1993). *Total Quality Control*, 3rd edition. New York: McGraw-Hill.

Feigenbaum, A. V. (1957). "The Challenge of Total Quality Control." *Industrial Quality Control* (May), 17–23.

Feigenbaum, A. V. (1956). "Total Quality Control." *Harvard Business Review* 34(6), 93–101. Reprinted in Sower, V., J. Motwani, & M. Savoie. (1995). *Classic Readings in Operations Management*. Ft. Worth, TX: Dryden, 307–321.

Feigenbaum, A. V. (1951). *Quality Control—Principles, Practice, and Administration*. New York: McGraw-Hill. Reprinted in Sower, V. E., J. Motwani, & M. J. Savoie. (1995). *Classic Readings in Operations Management*. Ft. Worth, Texas: Dryden, 289–306.

Fiorentino, R., & M. Perigord. (1994). "Going From an Investigative to a Formative Auditor." *Quality Progress* 27(10), 61–65.

Fisher, R. A. (1958). *Statistical Methods for Research Workers*, 13th edition. Edinburgh: Oliver & Boyd.

Franco, V. (2001). "Adopting Six Sigma." *Quality Digest* 21(6), 28–32.

Freeman, H. (1960). "How to Put Quality Costs to Use." *Transactions of the Metropolitan Conference, ASQC*.

Giakatis, G., T. Enkawa, & K. Washitani. (2001). "Hidden Quality Costs and the Distinction between Quality Cost and Quality Loss." *Total Quality Management* 12(2), 179–190.

Galloway, D. (1994). *Mapping Work Processes*. Milwaukee, WI: ASQ Quality Press.

Garvin, D. (1984). "What Does Product Quality Really Mean?" *Sloan Management Review* 26(1), 25–43.

Garvin, D. G. (1987). "Competing on the Eight Dimensions of Quality." *Harvard Business Review* 65(6), 101–109. Reprinted in Sower, V. E., J. Motwani, & M. J. Savoie. (1995). *Classic Readings in Operations Management*, Ft. Worth, TX: Dryden, 323–339.

Garvin, D. (1988). *Managing Quality:The Strategic and Competitive Edge*. New York: The Free Press.

George, M. (2002). *Lean Six Sigma*. New York: McGraw-Hill.

Gitlow, H., A. Oppenheim, & R. Oppenheim. (1995). *Quality Management*, 2nd edition. Burr Ridge, IL: Irwin.

"Give Employees the Freedom to Fail." (2006). *Inside Supply Management*, September 9.

Gotlow, H., D. Levine, & E. Popovich. (2006). *Design for Six Sigma for Green Belts and Champions*. Upper Saddle River, NJ: Prentice Hall.

Griffin, R. (1988). "Consequences of Quality Circles in an Industrial Setting: A Longitudinal Assessment." *Academy of Management Journal* 31(2), 338–358.

Griffith, G. (2003). *The Quality Technician's Handbook*. Englewood Cliffs, NJ: Prentice Hall.

Griffith, G. (1986). *Quality Technician's Handbook*. New York: John Wiley & Sons.

Hamel, G. (2001). "The Why, What, and How of Management Innovation." *Harvard Business Review* 84(2), 72–84.

Harrington, H. (2004). "Measuring Money and Quality." *Quality Digest* 24(2), 18.

Harry, M., & R. Schroeder. (2000). *Six Sigma: The Breakthrough Management Strategy Revolutionising the World's Top Corporations*. New York: Currency/Doubleday.

Harvey, T. R., & B. Drolet. (1994). *Building Teams, Building People*. Lancaster, PA: Technomic Publishing Co.

Hauser, J., & D. Clausing. (1988). "Quality Function Deployment: Integrating Customer Requirements into Product Design." *Harvard Business Review* 66(3), 63–73.

Herzberg, F. (1966). *Work and the Nature of Man*. New York: World Publishing.

Hickman, T. K., & W. M. Hickman. (1992). *Global Purchasing*. Homewood, IL: Business One Irwin.

Hill, T. (2000). *Manufacturing Strategy: Text and Cases*. Burr Ridge, IL: Irwin/McGraw-Hill.

Hoffer, J., J. George, & J. Valacich. (1996). *Modern Systems Analysis and Design*. Reading, MA: The Benjamin/Cummings Publishing Company, Inc.

Huberman, A., & M. Miles. (1994). "Data Management and Analysis Methods." In *Handbook of Qualitative Research*, edited by N. Denizin & Y. Lincoln. Thousand Oaks, CA: Sage.

Hutchins, G. (1992). *Purchasing Strategies for Total Quality*. Homewood, IL: Business One Irwin.

Ishikawa, K. (1984). *Quality Control Circles at Work*. Tokyo: Asian Productivity Organization.

ISO 8402. (1990). *International Standard ISO/CD 8402-1, Quality Concepts and Terminology—Part 1: Generic Terms and Definitions*. Geneva, Switzerland: International Organization for Standardization.

ISO 10012:2003. *Measurement Management Systems—Requirements for Measurement Processes and Measuring Equipment*.

ISO 5725-1,2,3-1994. *Accuracy (trueness and precision) of Measurement Methods and Results*.

Jain, C. (2003). "Benchmarking New Product Forecasting." *The Journal of Business Forecasting* (Fall), 27–28.

Johnson, R. S. (1993). *TQM: Leadership for the Quality Transformation*. Milwaukee, WI: ASQC Quality Press.

Juran, J. (1970). "Consumerism and Product Quality." *Quality Progress* 3(7), 18. Reprinted in Sower, V. E., J. Motwani, & M. J. Savoie. (1995). *Classic Readings in Operations Management*. Ft. Worth, Texas: Dryden, 249–275.

Juran, J. M. (1951). *Quality Control Handbook*, 1st edition. New York: McGraw-Hill.

Juran, J. M. (1986). "The Quality Trilogy." *Quality Progress* 19(8), 19–24. Reprinted in Sower V., J. Motwani, & M. Savoie (1995). *Classic Readings in Operations Management*. Ft. Worth: Dryden, 277–287.

Juran, J. M., & F. Gryna. (1980). *Quality Planning and Analysis*, 2nd edition. New York: McGraw-Hill Book Company.

Juran, J. M. (1988). *Juran on Planning for Quality*. New York: The Free Press.

Juran, J. M., & F. M. Gryna. (1988). *Quality Control Handbook*, 4th edition. New York: McGraw-Hill.

Juran, J. M. (1992). *Juran on Quality by Design: The New Steps for Planning Quality into Goods and Services*. Milwaukee, WI: ASQ Quality Press.

Juran, J. M., F. Gryna, & J. DeFeo. (2007). *Quality Planning and Analysis*, 5th edition. New York: McGraw-Hill.

Kaplan, R., & D. Norton. (1992). "The Balanced Scorecard: Measures that Drive Performance." *Harvard Business Review* 74(1), 71–79.

Kaplan, R., & D. Norton. (2001). *The Strategy-Focused Organization*. Boston: Harvard Business School Press.

Keley, E., J. Ashton, & T. Bornstein. (ND). "Applying Benchmarking in Health." *Quality Assurance Project*, Bethesda, MD: Center for Human Services. http://www.qaproject.org/pubs/PDFs/Benchfinal.pdf.

Kepner, C., & B. Tregoe. (1965). *The Rational Manager: A Systematic Approach to Problem Solving and Decision Making*. New York: McGraw-Hill.

Khalil, T. (2000). *Management of Technology*. Boston: McGraw-Hill.

Krippendorff, K. (2004). *Content Analysis: An Introduction to Its Methodology*. Thousand Oaks, CA: Sage.

Krishnamoorthi, K. (1992). *Reliability Methods for Engineers*. Milwaukee, WI: ASQ Quality Press.

Leenders, M. R., & H. E. Fearon. (1997) *Purchasing and Supply Management*, 11th edition. Chicago: Irwin.

Levin, M. (2003). *Improving Product Reliability: Strategies and Implementation*. Milwaukee, WI: ASQ Quality.

Lindsay, W. M., & J. A. Petrick. (1997). *Total Quality and Organization Development*. Boca Raton, FL: St. Lucia Press.

Mader, D. (2003). "DFSS and Your Current Design Process." *Quality Progress* 36(7), 88–89.

Madu, C., & C. Kuei. (1993). "Introducing Strategic Quality Management." *Long Range Planning* 26(6), 121–131.

*Malcolm Baldrige National Quality Award 2009-2010 Education Criteria for Performance Excellence*. Milwaukee, WI: ASQ Quality Press.

Malhortra, N. (1993). *Marketing Research*. Englewood Cliffs, CA: Prentice Hall.

Mallozzi, J. (2003). "Harnessing THz for Medical Applications." *R&D* 45(10), 28.

Marks, M., P. Mirvis, E. Hackett, & J. Grady. (1986). "Employee Participation in a Quality Circle Program: Impact on Quality of Work Life, Productivity, and Absenteeism." *Journal of Applied Psychology* 71(1), 61–69.

Maslow, A. H. (1964). *Motivation and Personality*. New York: McGraw-Hill.

Mayer, M. (2006). "Turning Limitations into Innovation." *Business Week Online* (February 1, 2006), 1–2.

McClelland, D. C. (1961). *The Achieving Society*. New York: Van Nostrand.

McCoy, M. (1999). "Six Sigma Gaining as Improvement Method." *Chemical & Engineering News* 77(45), 11–12.

McCoy, M. (2001). "Dow Chemical." *Chemical & Engineering News* 79(25), 21–26.

McGregor, D. (1960). *The Human Side of Enterprise*. New York: McGraw-Hill.

McIngvale, J. (2002). *Always Think Big*. Chicago, IL: Dearborn Trade Publishing.

Measurement Quality Division. (2004). *The Metrology Handbook*. Milwaukee, WI: ASQ Quality Press.

Melnyk, S., & R. Christensen. (2002). "Deconstructing the Metric." *APICS—The Performance Advantage* 12(9), 20.

Miles, M., & A. Huberman. (1998). *Qualitative Data Analysis: An Expanded Sourcebook*, 2nd edition. Newbury Park, CA: Sage.

Mills, C. (1989). *The Quality Audit: A Management Evaluation Tool*. Milwaukee, WI: ASQC Quality Press.

MIL STD 105E. (1989). *Sampling Procedures and Tables for Inspection by Attributes*. Washington, DC: U.S. Government Printing Office.

MIL-STD-1235C. (1988). *Single and Multilevel Continuous Sampling Procedures and Tables for Inspection by Attributes*.

MIL-STD-1520C. (1986). *Corrective Action and Disposition System for Nonconforming Material*.

MIL-STD-1916. (1996). *DOD Prefered Methods for Acceptance of Product*.

Miner, D. (1933). "What Price Quality?" *Product Engineering* (August): 300–302.

Mintzberg, H., J. Lampel, J. Quinn, & S. Ghoshal. (2003). *The Strategy Process*. Upper Saddle River, NJ: Prentice Hall.

Montgomery, D. C. (2005). *Design and Analysis of Experiments*, 3rd edition. Hoboken, NJ: John Wiley & Sons.

Montgomery, D. (2005). *Introduction to Statistical Quality Control*, 5th edition. New York: John Wiley & Sons.

Morris, A. S. (1991). *Measurement and Calibration for Quality Assurance*. Englewood Cliffs, NJ: Prentice Hall.

Morrow, C., & L. McNeese. (2002). "A Simple Way to Digest SPC." 2002 *Proceedings of the ASQ Annual Quality Congress*.

Oakes, D., & R. Westcott (eds.). (2001). *The Certified Quality Manager Handbook*, 2nd edition. Milwaukee, WI: ASQ Quality Press.

Osborn, A. (1963). *Applied Imagination*, 3rd edition. New York: Scribner's.

Orsburn, J. D., L. Moran, E. Musselwhite, & J. H. Zenger. (1990). *Self-Directed Work Teams*. Homewood, IL: Business One Irwin.

*Oxford English Dictionary*, 2nd edition. (1989). http://www.askoxford.com

Pennella, C. R. (2004). *Managing the Metrology System*, 3rd edition. Milwaukee, WI: ASQ Quality Press.

Parasuraman, A., V. Zeithaml, & L. Berry. (1988). "SERVQUAL: A Multiple-Item Scale for Measuring Consumer Perceptions of Service Quality." *Journal of Retailing* 61(1), 12–40.

Parnes, S., R. Noller, & A. Biondi (eds.). (1977). *Guide to Creative Action*. New York: Scribner's.

Peace, G. S. (1993). *Taguchi Methods: A Hands On Approach*. Reading, MA: Addison-Wesley.

Plato. (1992). (Original circa 390 BC). *Republic*. Translated by G. M. A. Grube, revised by C. D. C. Reeve. Indianapolis: Hackett.

Plovnick, M., R. Fry, & I. Rubin. (1975). "New Developments in O.D. Technology: Programmed Team Development." *Training and Development Journal* 29(4), 19–25.

Plsek, P. (1998). "Incorporating the Tools of Creativity into Quality Management." *Quality Progress* 31(3), 21–28.

Porter, M. (1980). *Corporate Strategy*. Boston: The Free Press.

Porter, L., & E. Lawler. (1968). *Managerial Attitudes and Performance*. Homewood, IL: Irwin.

Provost, L., & R. Sproul. (1996). "Creativity and Improvement: A Vital Link." *Quality Progress* 29(8), 101–107.

Pryor, M., J. White, & L. Toombs. (1998). *Strategic Quality Management*. Houston, TX: Dame.

Pyzdek, T. (2003). *The Six Sigma Handbook*. New York: McGraw-Hill.

Pyzdek, T. (2003). "DMAIC and DMADV." http://www.pyzdek.com.

Pyzdek, T. (1999). "Why Six Sigma is Not Enough." *Quality Digest* 19(2), 26.

Pyzdek, T. (1993). "Process Control for Short and Small Runs." *Quality Progress* 26(4), 51–60.

"QS 9000 Trivia." (1997). *Quality Digest* 17(8), 10.

"Quality Glossary." (2002). *Quality Progress* 35(7), 43–61.

*Quality System Requirements QS-9000*, 2nd edition, February 1995 (fourth printing July 1996).

Quigley, P. (2000). *Readers' Digest*.

Rakich, J. (2000). "Strategic Quality Planning." *Hospital Topics: Research and Perspectives on Healthcare* 78(2), 5–11.

Advisory Group on Reliability of Electronic Equipment. (1957). "Reliability of Military Electronic Equipment". Report by Advisory Group on Reliability of Electronic Equipment, Office of the Secretary of Defense (R&D) (June). Washington, DC: U.S. Government Printing Office.

Rice, C. (1994). "How to Conduct an Internal Quality Audit and Still Have Friends." *Quality Progress* 27(6), 39–41.

Robinson, A., & S. Stern. (1997). *Corporate Creativity*. San Francisco: Berrett-Koehler.

Rodriguez, R. N. (1992). "Recent Developments in Process Capability Analysis." *Journal of Quality Technology* 24(4), 176–187.

Roy, R. (1990). *A Primer on the Taguchi Method*. New York: Van Nostrand Reinhold.

Russell, J. (2001). *ISO 9001 Conspectus*. Milwaukee, WI: ASQ Quality Press.

Russell, J. (2003). *Process Auditing Techniques Guide*. Milwaukee, WI: ASQ Quality Press.

Shewhart, W. (1939). *Statistical Method from the Standpoint of Quality Control*. Washington, DC: Graduate School of the Department of Agriculture. Republished in 1980 by General Publishing Company, Toronto, Canada.

Shewhart, W. (1931). *Economic Control of Manufactured Product*. New York: D. Van Nostrand Co., Inc. Republished in 1980 as a 50th Anniversary Commemorative Reissue by ASQ Quality Press, Milwaukee, WI.

Shewhart, W. "Excerpts from Economic Control of Manufactured Product." (1931). "Excerpts from Statistical Method from the Viewpoint of Quality Control." (1939). Reprinted in Sower V. E., J. Motwani, & M. Savoie. (1995). *Classic Readings in Operations Management*. Ft. Worth: Dryden, 191–230.

Shingo, Shigeo. (1986). *Zero Quality Control: Source Inspection and the Poka-yoke System.* Cambridge, MA: Productivity Press.

Sidawi, D. (2003). "Nanocrystals Enable Diverse Applications." *R&D* 45(10), 24–25.

Sinha, M., & W. Willborn. (1985). *The Management of Quality Assurance.* New York: John Wiley & Sons.

Snee, R., & R. Hoerl. (2003). *Leading Six Sigma.* Upper Saddle River, NJ: Prentice Hall.

Snow, C. E. (1927). "Research on Industrial Illumination: A Discussion of the Relation of Illumination Intensity to Productivity Efficiency." *Tech Engineering News* 8(6), 257, 272–274, 283

Solin, S. (2004). "Magnetic Field Nanosensors." *Scientific American* (June), 71–77.

Sower, V. E., J. Motwani, & M. Savoie. (1993). "Are Acceptance Sampling and Statistical Process Control Complementary or Incompatible?" *Quality Progress* 26(9), 85–89.

Sower, V. E., J. Motwani, & M. Savoie. (1994). "Delta Charts for Short Run Statistical Process Control." *International Journal of Quality & Reliability Management* 11(6), 50–56.

Sower, V. E., J. Motwani, & M. J. Savoie. (1995). *Classic Readings in Operations Management,* Ft. Worth, TX: Dryden.

Sower, V. E., J. Duffy, W. Kilbourne, G. Kohers, & P. Jones. (2001). "The Dimensions of Service Quality for Hospitals: Development and Use of the KQCAH Scale." *Health Care Management Review* 26(2), 47–59.

Sower, V. E., R. Quarles, & S. Cooper. (2002). "Cost of Quality Distribution and Quality System Maturity: An Exploratory Study." *ASQ's 56th Annual Quality Congress Proceedings,* 343–354.

Sower, V. E., & R. Quarles. (2003). "Cost of Quality: Why More Organizations Do Not Use if Effectively." *ASQ's 57th Annual Quality Congress Proceedings,* 625–637.

Sower, V. E. (2004). "Estimating External Failure Costs: A Key Difficulty in COQ Systems." *ASQ's 58th Annual Quality Congress Proceedings,* 547–551.

Sower, V. E., & F. Fair. (2005). "There is More to Quality than Continuous Improvement: Listening to Plato." *Quality Management Journal* 12(1), 8–20.

Sower, V. E., R. Quarles, & E. Broussard. (2007). "Cost of Quality Usage and Its Relationship to Quality System Maturity." *International Journal of Quality and Reliability Management* 24(2), 121–140.

Sower, V. E. (2007). "Benchmarking in Hospitals: When You Need More than a Scorecard." *Quality Progress* 40(8), 58–60.

Sower, V. E., J. Duffy, & G. Kohers. (2008). *Benchmarking for Hospitals: Achieving Best-in-Class Performance Without Having to Reinvent the Wheel.* Milwaukee, WI: ASQ Quality Press.

Stamatis, D. (2003). *Failure Mode and Effect Analysis: FMEA from Theory to Execution,* 2nd edition. Milwaukee, WI: ASQ Quality Press.

Stevenson, W. (2009). *Operations Management,* 8th edition. Boston: McGraw-Hill/Irwin.

Stix, G. (2004). "A Confederacy of Smarts." *Scientific American* 290(6), 40–45.

Sullivan, L. (1986). "Quality Function Deployment." *Quality Progress* 19(6), 39–50.

Suntag, C. (1993). *Inspection and Inspection Management.* Milwaukee, WI: ASQC Quality Press.

Tadikamalla, P. (1994). "The Confusion over Six-Sigma Quality." *Quality Progress* 27(11), 83–85.

Taguchi, G., & Y. Wu. (1980). *Introduction to Off-Line Quality Control.* Nagoya: Central Japan Quality Control Association.

Taguchi, G., E. Elsayed, & T. Hsiang. (1989). *Quality Engineering in Production Systems.* New York: McGraw-Hill.

Taguchi, G., (1986). *Introduction to Quality Engineering*. White Plains, NY: Asian Productivity Organization UNIPUB.

Taguchi, G. (1986). *Introduction to Quality Engineering*. Tokyo: Asian Productivity Organization.

Taguchi, G., & S. Konishi, (1987). *Orthogonal Arrays and Linear Graphs*. Dearborn, MI: American Supplier Institute.

Taguchi, G., S. Chowdhury, & Y. Wu. (2005). *Taguchi's Quality Engineering Handbook*. Hoboken, NJ: John Wiley & Sons.

Tennant, C., & P. Roberts. (2000) "Hoshin Kanri: A Technique for Strategic Quality Management." *Quality Assurance* 8(2), 77–90.

Terninko, J. (2003). "Reliability/Mistake Proofing Using Failure Mode and Effects Analysis (FMEA)." *ASQ's 57th Annual Quality Congress Proceedings*, 515–526.

Traver, R. W. (1962). "Measuring Equipment Repeatability—The Rubber Ruler." *1962 ASQC Annual Convention Transactions*. Milwaukee, WI: ASQC Quality Press.

Tuckman. (1965). "Developmental Sequence in Small Groups." *Psychological Bulletin* 63(6), 384–399.

Tunner, J. R. (1990). *A Quality Technology Primer for Managers*. Milwaukee, WI: ASQC Quality Press.

Vaisnys, V. (2000). "Retaining Creative Employees." *Innovative Leader* 9(10), Article No. 494.

Vroom, V. (1964). *Work and Motivation*. New York: John Wiley & Sons.

Walton, M. (1986). *The Deming Management Method*. New York: Perigee Books.

Western Electric. (1956). *Statistical Quality Control Handbook*. Indianapolis: Western Electric Co.

Wilkinson, H. E., C. D. Orth, & R. C. Benfari. (1986). "Motivation Theories: An Integrated Operational Model." *SAM Advanced Management Journal* 51(4), 24–31.

# Index